Innovative Consumer Co-operatives

Consumer co-operatives provide a different approach to organizing business through their ideals of member ownership and democratic practice. Every co-operative member has an equal vote regardless of his or her own personal capital investment. The co-operative movement can also be an important force in promoting development and self-sufficiency in poorer areas, particularly in non-industrialised countries.

This book explores in depth the fortunes of the Consumers Co-operative of Berkeley, which became the largest consumer co-operative in the United States with 116,000 members in 1984 and viewed nationally as a leader in innovative retail practices and a champion of consumer rights. The Consumers Co-operative of Berkeley is promoted by both supporters and opponents of the co-operative business model as a significant example of what can go wrong with the co-operatives.

This book will provide the first in-depth analysis of the history of the Berkeley Co-operative using its substantial but little used archives and oral histories to explore what the Berkeley experience means for the co-operative business model. The specific chapters relating to Berkeley will be organised around particular themes to highlight the issues relating to the co-operative business model and the local context of Berkeley. The themes relate to developments in Berkeley and the Bay Area in terms of the economy, politics and the retail environment; the management of the Berkeley co-operative, looking at governance, financial management and strategic decisions; relationship of management with members, employees and the community; and finally, the relationship of the Berkeley Co-operative with the broader co-operative movement.

The core message of the book is that it is not inevitable that consumer co-operatives fail, but that the story of Berkeley story can provide insights that can strengthen the co-operative business model and minimise failures on the scale of Berkeley occurring in the future.

Greg Patmore is Emeritus Professor of Business and Labour History at the University of Sydney Business School, Australia.

Routledge International Studies in Business History

Series editors: Jeffrey Fear and Christina Lubinski

Making Managers in Canada, 1945–1995
Companies, Community Colleges, and Universities
Jason Russell

The Evolution of Business
Interpretative Theory, History and Firm growth
Ellen Mølgaard Korsager

Multinational Enterprise, Political Risk and Organisational Change
From Total War to Cold War
Edited by Neil Forbes, Takafumi Kurosawa and Ben Wubs

Co-operation and Globalisation
The British Co-operative Wholesales, the Co-operative Group and the World since 1863
Anthony Webster

The Age of Entrepreneurship
Business Proprietors, Self-employment and Corporations Since 1851
Robert J. Bennett, Harry Smith, Cary van Lieshout, Piero Montebruno and Gill Newton

Business, Ethics and Institutions
The Evolution of Turkish Capitalism in Global Perspectives
Edited by Asli M. Colpan and Geoffrey Jones

Innovative Consumer Co-operatives
The Rise and Fall of Berkeley
Greg Patmore

For more information about this series, please visit: www.routledge.com/Routledge-International-Studies-in-Business-History/book-series/SE0471

For a full list of titles in this series, please visit www.routledge.com

Innovative Consumer Co-operatives

The Rise and Fall of Berkeley

Greg Patmore

LONDON AND NEW YORK

First published 2020 by Routledge

2 Park Square, Milton Park, Abingdon, Oxon OX14 4RN
605 Third Avenue, New York, NY 10017

Routledge is an imprint of the Taylor & Francis Group, an informa business

First issued in paperback 2022

Publisher's Note

The publisher has gone to great lengths to ensure the quality of this reprint but points out that some imperfections in the original copies may be apparent.

Library of Congress Cataloging-in-Publication Data
Names: Patmore, Greg, author.
Title: Innovative consumer co-operatives : the rise and fall of Berkeley Greg Patmore.
Description: New York, NY : Routledge, 2020. |
Series: Routledge international studies in business history |
Includes bibliographical references and index.
Identifiers: LCCN 2019059197 (print) |
LCCN 2019059198 (ebook) | ISBN 9781138614109 (hardback) |
ISBN 9780429464201 (ebook)
Subjects: LCSH: Consumers Cooperative of Berkeley—History. |
Consumer cooperatives—California—Berkeley—History.
Classification: LCC HD3286.B47 P38 2020 (print) |
LCC HD3286.B47 (ebook) | DDC 334/.50979467—dc23
LC record available at https://lccn.loc.gov/2019059197
LC ebook record available at https://lccn.loc.gov/2019059198

ISBN: 978-1-138-61410-9 (hbk)
ISBN: 978-1-03-233633-6 (pbk)
DOI: 10.4324/9780429464201

Typeset in Sabon
by codeMantra

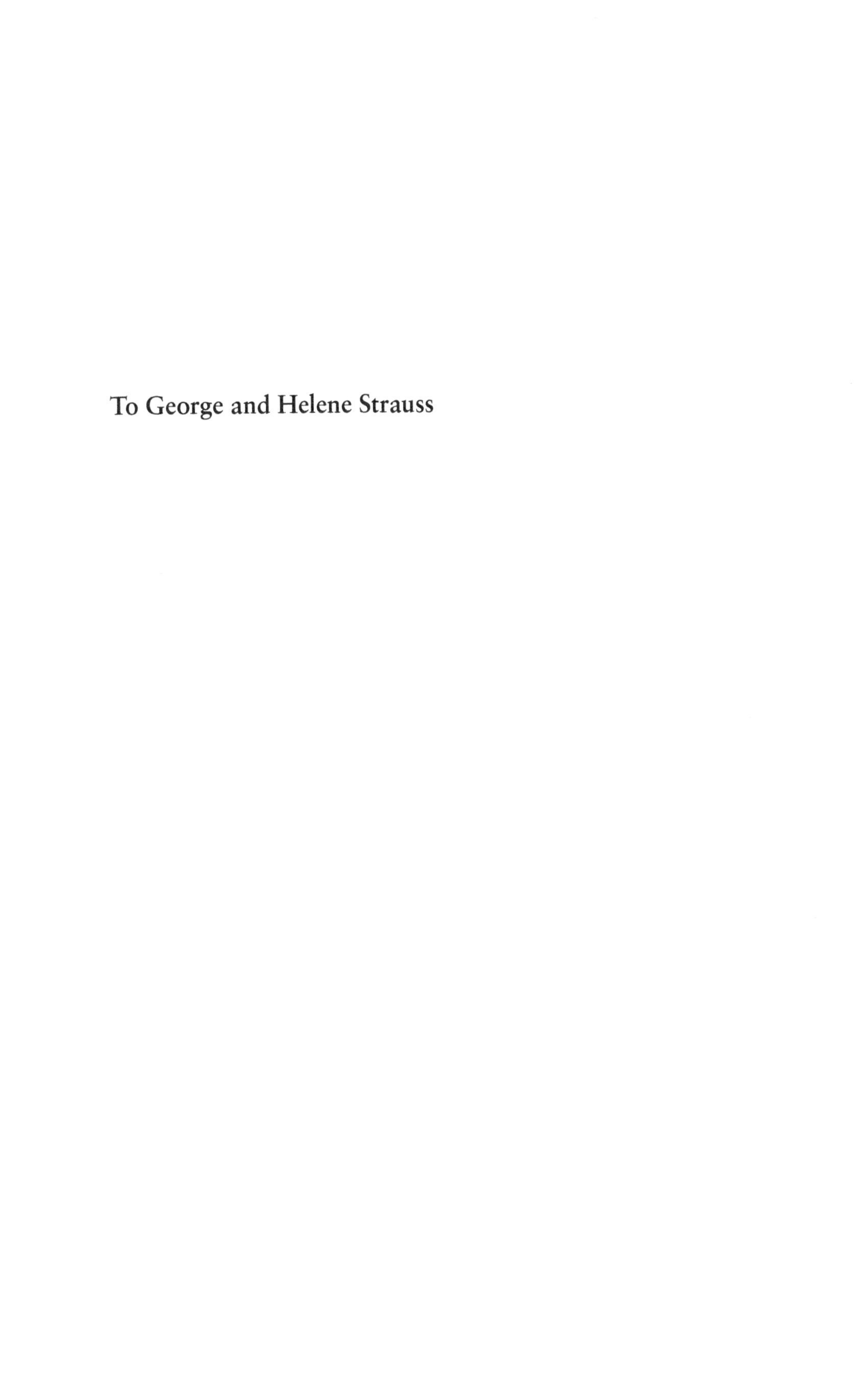

To George and Helene Strauss

Contents

List of Illustrations ix
List of Tables xi
Acknowledgments xiii
List of Abbreviations xv

1 Consumer Co-operatives: Theory and Practice 1

2 International Consumer Co-operative Movement Before 1993 25

3 Consumer Co-operatives in the US before 1993 56

4 The Origins and Early Years of the Berkeley Co-operative until 1947 76

5 Gaining a Foothold: 1947–1961 105

6 Politics and Expansion: 1962–1971 137

7 Instability and Final Expansion: 1972–1980 171

8 Chaos and Collapse: 1981–1993 200

9 Conclusion 226

Index 233

Illustrations

1.1 CCB CO-OP Labels, 1972. Courtesy of Berkeley Historical Society (BHS) #10464 6
2.1 Rochdale Toad Lane Store as a Museum. Courtesy of the Berkeley Historical Society 30
2.2 Holyoake House in Manchester. Photographer Greg Patmore 36
4.1 Berkeley Rose Garden, September 2019. Courtesy of Helen Warner, Photographer 80
4.2 Robert Neptune and Early Berkeley Store. Courtesy of Berkeley Historical Society 84
4.3 CCB Delivery Truck. Courtesy of Berkeley Historical Society #2566 89
4.4 Camp Sierra Lecture. Courtesy of Berkeley Historical Society 98
5.1 Arvid Nelson, Member #2 breaking ground for remodeling of University Avenue Store, April 1953. Courtesy of Berkeley Historical Society #2216 111
5.2 Shattuck Avenue Site, 1959. Courtesy of Berkeley Historical Society 113
5.3 CCB UN Day, 21 October 1961. Courtesy of Berkeley Historical Society 117
5.4 Books Unlimited, University Avenue Store, 1960. Courtesy of Berkeley Historical Society 130
6.1 CCB Board, 1964. Seated from left: Jessie Coles, Maudelle Miller, George Little, Clinton White, Margedant Hayakawa. Standing from the Left: Edward Barankin, Robert Treuhaft, Robert Arnold, Hans Lescke, Tom Farris, Earle Fuller. Courtesy of Berkeley Historical Society #10455 143
6.2 Home Economist Nancy Bratt at Marin Center, 1967. Courtesy of Berkeley Historical Society #10460 146
6.3 The Art of Kiddie Korral Children, February 1965. Courtesy of Berkeley Historical Society 148

6.4 Recycling at CCB. Courtesy of Berkeley Historical Society #10472 155
7.1 CCB Education Staff, 1975. Courtesy of Berkeley Historical Society 182
7.2 Nutrition Labels, 1972. Courtesy of Berkeley Historical Society 185
7.3 White House Meeting, 1978. Courtesy of Berkeley Historical Society 193
9.1 The Former CCB Store in Shattuck Avenue, Berkeley, a Safeway Store in September 2019. Courtesy of Helen Warner, photographer 229

Tables

4.1 CCB Finances 1939–1946 (Neptune, 1977, p. 191) 90
4.2 Number of Members 1939–1946 (Neptune, 1977, p. 191) 92
5.1 CCB Finances 1947–1961 (Neptune, 1977, p. 191) 114
5.2 CCB Interest on Shares and Patronage Refunds 1951–1961 (BHS, 1995, p. 50) 114
5.3 CCB Number of Members 1947–1961 (Neptune, 1977, p. 191) 116
5.4 AC Membership and Financial Performance 1947–1961 (Neptune, 1977, p. 190) 126
6.1 CCB Finances 1962–1971 (Neptune, 1977, p. 191) 145
6.2 Number of Members 1962–1971 and Member Per Capita Equity, Interest on Capital and Patronage Refund (BHS, 1995, pp. 50, 67; Neptune, 1977, p. 191) 150
6.3 AC Membership and Financial Performance 1962–1971 (Neptune, 1977, p. 190) 161
7.1 CCB Finances 1972–1980 (Neptune, 1977, p. 191; Neptune, 1982, p. 21) 173
7.2 Number of Members from 1972 to 1980 and Member Per Capita Equity, Interest on Capital and Patronage Refund (BHS, 1995, pp. 52, 56, 67; Neptune, 1977, p. 191, 1982, p. 21) 181
7.3 AC Membership and Financial Performance 1972–1980 (Neptune, 1977, p. 190; Neptune, 1982, p. 21) 190
8.1 CCB Assets, Volume, Financial Performance 1981–1987 (Neptune, 1997, p. 20; Patmore, 2017, p. 523) 202
8.2 CCB Membership 1981–1987 (Neptune, 1997, p. 20; Patmore, 2017, p. 523) 207

Tables

[illegible]

Acknowledgments

I wish to acknowledge the support of many people and institutions that made the completion of this book possible. I would like to thank George and the late Helene Strauss, to whom the book is dedicated, for their kindness and friendship during my many visits to Berkeley, which began as a Visiting Scholar in 1987. George took me on a tour of the CCB Shattuck Avenue Store in 1987, which sparked my interest in the co-operative. I would also like to thank David Brody, Susan Brody, Emilie Strauss and John Logan for their role in making me feel welcome in Berkeley. The Berkeley Historical Society played a key role in the research for the book by giving me access to their manuscripts, oral histories and photograph collection, a number of which are published in the book. Therese Pipe, Bill Roberts, John Aronovici and their colleagues from the Society were of great assistance, with a special acknowledgment of Therese for her role in capturing the oral histories of former CCB staff and activists. Barbara Bogue gave me access to the papers of her father, Bob March, while Michael Fullerton, Adolph Kamil, Bruce Miller, Bob Schildgen and Betsy Wood chatted to me about their experiences in the CCB. I thank the staffs of the Bancroft Library at the University of California, Berkeley, which holds the major CCB manuscript collection, the Department of Labor Library in Washington DC, the Berkeley Public Library, Harry S. Truman Presidential Library, Ronald Reagan Presidential Library and the National Co-operative Archive in Manchester, UK, for their assistance. I would also like to thank Mary Del Plato from Routledge for her support and encouragement. The research was funded from the University of Sydney School of Business. The book also includes an early finding from an Australian Research Council Discovery Grant (DP170100573). The Institute for Research on Labor & Employment at University of California, Berkeley provided a base for the research when I was a Visiting Scholar there during 2015. Finally, I would like to thank my wonderful wife Helen Warner, who accompanied me on my trips to Berkeley and provided me with photographs for the book.

Abbreviations

AC	Associated Co-operatives
ACCI	Arts and Crafts Co-operative Inc.
ACDC	AC Development Department
ACNC	Associated Co-operatives of Northern California
ACSC	Associated Co-operatives of Southern California
AFL	American Federation of Labor
AGM	Annual General Meeting
AR	Annual Report
BAHA	Berkeley Architectural Heritage Association
BAND	Bay Area Neighborhood Development Foundation
BART	Bay Area Rapid Transit
BCA	Berkeley Citizens' Action
BCC	Berkeley City Council
BCEA	Berkeley Co-operative Employees' Association
BCU	Berkeley Co-operative Union
BDC	Berkeley Democratic Club
BHS	Berkeley Historical Society
BL	Bancroft Library (University of California, Berkeley)
BOD	Board of Directors
BWP	Berkeley Women for Peace
CACW	Californian Co-operative Wholesale
CANG	Californian Army National Guard
CARE	Co-operative for American Remittances to Europe (subsequently the E stood for Everywhere)
CCA	Consumers Co-operative Association
CCB	Consumers Co-operative of Berkeley
CCC	Congress of Center Councils (CCB)
CCCC	Center Council Chairperson's Committee
CCE	Co-operative Central Exchange
CCFCU	Co-op Center Federal Credit Union
CCM	Consumers Co-operative of Monterey
CCW	Central Co-operative Wholesale
CEC	Consumer Employee Co-operative (Berkeley)
CFA	Consumer Federation of America

CIA	Central Intelligence Agency
CIL	Center for Independent Living
CIO	Congress of Industrial Organizations
CLUSA	Co-operative League of the USA
CMP	Community Memory Project
CN	Co-op News (CCB)
CO	Cooperativa Obrera Limitada (Argentina)
COD	Cash on Delivery
CORE	Congress of Racial Equality
CPC	Consumer Protection Committee (CCB)
CPIC	Consumer and Information Protection Committee (CCB)
CPRR	Central Pacific Railroad
CU	Co-operative Union (UK)
CWS	Co-operative Wholesale Society (England)
EDP	Electronic Data Processing
EHO	*El Hogar Obrero* (Argentina)
EPIC	End Poverty in California
ESOP	Employee Stock Ownership Plan
fc	front cover
FCL	Federated Co-operatives Limited (Canada)
FICD	Fund for International Co-operative Development
FSM	Free Speech Movement
HRRC	Harlem River Consumer Co-operative
IAPSA	Industrial and Provident Societies Act (UK)
ICA	International Co-operative Alliance
ICCS	Ithaca Consumer Co-operative Society
IIR	Institute of Industrial Relations (UCB)
ILO	International Labour Organization
ILWU	International Longshore and Warehouse Union
IOB	Investor Owned Business
IRFC	Ithaca Real Food Co-operative
IWW	Industrial Workers of the World
JCCU	Japanese Consumers' Co-operative Union
KF	Kooperativa Förbundet (Sweden)
MSI	Mutual Service Insurance Companies of St. Paul
MOB	Member Owned Business
NAF	*Nordisk Andelsforbund*
NC	National Co-operatives Inc. (US)
NCBA	National Co-operative Business Association
NCCB	National Consumer Co-operative Bank
NCC	North Coast Co-operative (Arcata)
NCCC	Northern California Co-operative Council
NCGA	National Co-operative Grocers Association
NCOG	New Co-op Organizing Group (Berkeley)
NCS	Northern California Supermarkets

NSW	New South Wales (Australia)
NSWCWS	NSW Co-operative Wholesale Society (Australia)
NOCC	North Oakland Center Council (CCB)
NYT	New York Times
NTEA	National Tax Equality Association
NIRA	National Industrial Recovery Act
NZ	New Zealand
OFC	Organic Foods Co-op (Berkeley)
OPEU	Office and Professional Employees Union
PAC	Palo Alto Co-operative
PACT	Promoters of Active Co-operatism (CCB)
PCL	Pacific Co-operative League
PCS	Pacific Co-operative Services
PLCS	Pacific League Co-operative Stores
PO	*Parti Ouvrier* (Belgium, France)
RCIA	Retail Clerks International Association
RNLP	Richard Neil Lerner Papers (BL, UCB)
RRGPRRL	Ronald Reagan Governor's Papers, Ronald Reagan Library
RRL	Right Relationship League
SAAC	Shattuck Avenue Center Council (CCB)
SCWS	Scottish Co-operative Wholesale Society (UK)
SDS	Students for a Democratic Society
SOTF	Strategic Options Task Force (CCB, July 1986)
TASC	Toward an Active Student Community
TACC	Telegraph Avenue Center Council (CCB)
TPLA	Truman Presidential Library and Archives
UC	University of California
UCB	University of California, Berkeley
UFCWU	United Food and Commercial Workers Union
UFW	United Farm Workers
UK	United Kingdom
UN	United Nations
US	United States
USCA	University Students' Co-operative Association (UCB)
USFDA	US Food and Drug Administration
USSR	Union of Soviet Socialist Republics
WCG	Women's Co-operative Guild (UK)
WFCUA	Workers' and Farmers' Co-operative Unity Alliance

1 Consumer Co-operatives
Theory and Practice

This chapter provides a framework for understanding the rise and fall of the Consumers Co-operative of Berkeley (CCB). It initially explores the concept of a co-operative as a Member Owned Business (MOB) and then focuses on the idea of a consumer co-operative. The chapter then looks at issues facing the governance and management of consumer co-operatives such as formation, finance, marketing and labor relations. Finally, this chapter concludes by exploring historical factors that account for the fluctuating fortunes of the co-operative movement, both at the local and societal level.

Defining a Co-operative

The co-operative is an MOB as opposed to an IOB (Investor Owned Business). Members either work for the co-operative, as in the case of a worker co-operative, or consume goods and services such as groceries, as in the case of a consumer co-operative, or grain storage facilities, as in the case of an agricultural co-operative. Johnston Birchall (2011b, p. 4) has defined MOB as a:

> business organization that is owned and controlled by members who are drawn from one (or more) of three types of stakeholder – consumers, producers and employees – and whose benefits go mainly to these members.

MOBs are not charities in that they provide goods and services to members, and while they are sometimes considered to be 'nonprofit', they must make a surplus to cover costs and provide for future capital investments. MOBs are contrasted to IOBs, with the focus of the former being on people and the latter money. Investors can appropriate profits and increases in share value, whereas members can take the surpluses and give priority to other objectives such as quality of service, community assistance and better conditions for employees. More generally, the existence of a member-owned sector provides more choice for members who may value the benefits of membership over the goods and services (Birchall, 2011b, pp. 8–9).

Co-operatives as MOBs have been defined by a set of principles. The origins of these principles lie in the formation of the Rochdale consumer co-operative model in 1844, in the wake of an unsuccessful weavers' strike over wages. A group of 'pioneers', dominated by skilled and supervisory trades, in Rochdale, England, started the movement to combat low wages, high prices and poor quality food (Patmore and Balnave, 2018, p. 2). As Wilson, Webster and Vorberg-Rugh note (2013, p. 37), the "principles of this model both spread across the world and survived to the present as the 'ideal.'"

Birchall (1994, pp. 54–64) notes that there were nine fundamental principles set out in the early rules and publications of the Rochdale co-operative. The first principle is related to *democracy*, and the Rochdale consumer co-operatives differ from other businesses in that the management is based on democratic principles with 'one member one vote' rather than 'one vote one share'. This meant that someone holding 100 shares had the same number of votes as someone holding 1 share. These rights also extended to women before women had the right to vote in the political sphere. The second principle was *open membership*, whereby individuals had an opportunity to join on their own free will (Birchall, 2011a, p. 7). The third principle was *fixed and limited interest on capital*. This principle recognized the need to attract capital through members' shares by rewarding shareholders with interest on their shares and limiting the interest payment on shares so that it did not undermine the need to reinvest capital in the co-operative to ensure maintaining and upgrading facilities. This principle was also linked with limitations on the size of shareholdings to ensure that wealthy individuals did not use their economic influence to distort the democratic process (Wilson, Webster and Vorberg-Rugh, 2013, pp. 38–39). The fourth principle was *the distribution of the surplus as a dividend on purchases*. This is the 'divi', associated traditionally with consumer co-operatives, and the dividend encouraged forced saving by members and gave the co-operative a short-term capital boost as dividends tended to be paid quarterly, for example, at a rate of 6 percent on their purchases. In worker co-operatives, the dividend could be distributed from the surplus based on member's wages (Holyoake, 1893, p. 156; Webb and Webb, 1930, pp. 12–15).

The fifth principle was *cash trading*. There was strong hostility to giving credit to poorer people because of the growth of debt; many earlier co-operatives had failed due to the provision of unsecured excessive credit. There was a hope that this principle would encourage thrift among members, who would not live beyond their means (Cole, 1944, pp. 69–70; Wilson, Webster and Vorberg-Rugh, 2013, pp. 40–42).

The sixth was to sell *only pure and unadulterated food*. This reflected a widespread mid-nineteenth-century practice of substituting cheaper and even dangerous ingredients, such as water in milk and sawdust in bread, to reduce the costs of production (Cole, 1944, pp. 70–71). The seventh principle was *education*. Education related not only to learning co-operative principles, but also to technical education and the 'intellectual improvement' of members, highlighting a belief that education could improve moral character. There would be a levy on funds to finance educational programs (Birchall, 1994, pp. 61–62; Cole, 1944, pp. 71–72). The eighth principle was *political and religious neutrality*. This was to avoid conflict in the early co-operative movement, and there is no evidence that early members were denied membership on political and religious grounds. The final principle was the *disposal of net assets without profit to members*. If the co-operative was wound up, then members would receive what they held in their share accounts and any remaining assets would be distributed to other co-operatives and charities. This would stop individuals from trying to take over the co-operative to gain control over its assets (Birchall, 1994, pp. 62–63).

Despite the significance of Rochdale principles, they were not necessarily strictly followed by co-operatives. For example, there were consumer co-operatives that breached the principle of cash-only transactions in favor of credit for reasons such as the provision of credit facilities by competitors, seasonal variations of rural income and the impact of unfavorable economic and industrial events such as strikes on household income (Balnave and Patmore, 2015, p. 1134). Co-operatives have taken loans from nonmembers, even other storekeepers, and allowed outside investors to purchase shares to raise capital, which can undermine democratic control by members (Atherton, Birchall, Mayo and Simon, 2012, p. 13; Carr-Saunders, Sargent Florence and Peers, 1940, p. 131).

The International Co-operative Alliance (ICA), the international co-operative organization, from 1930 became a forum to redefine the Rochdale principles considering the wide variation of practice by co-operatives (Patmore and Balnave, 2018, p. 4). Two principles that fell out of favor over time were cash trading and political and religious neutrality. The former was viewed as a business practice rather than a key principle, while the latter clashed with the political culture of some co-operative movements which had organized on political or religious lines. The Rochdale Society became associated with the radical liberal politics in England, and eventually the Rochdale consumer co-operatives in the UK formed the Co-operative Party in 1917 and entered an electoral alliance with the Labour Party in 1927. Beyond the UK, there are examples of co-operative movements such as in Belgium, Finland and Italy, where co-operatives have been established along the lines of political ideology and religion (Birchall, 1994, pp. 114–116; Birchall, 1997, p. 58; Hilson, 2002, pp. 11–18). Despite this, the idea of political neutrality became a source of contention in some consumer retail co-operatives. One view interpreted the issue of political neutrality as the co-operative movement not supporting political parties during elections. Another view was that co-operatives should not involve themselves in any contentious political issue (including sympathetic action in support of strikes), beyond political lobbying relating to specific consumer issues in the case of consumer retail co-operative, such as state-regulated minimum pricing of staples such as milk (Balnave and Patmore, 2017, p. 19).

The Consumer Co-operative

While there are a variety of different types of co-operatives, including worker, agricultural and financial co-operatives, the retail consumer co-operative was the focus of the early co-operative movement. Consumer retail co-operatives arise from a failure of private retailers to supply goods at a sufficient price, quantity or quality. Consumers purchase shares in the co-operative and elect a board of management to govern the co-operative. The board of management appoints managers to run the co-operative and purchase goods for the co-operative. The traditional Rochdale model involves consumers receiving dividends on their purchases and interest on their shares and other investments in the co-operative such as member bonds. The shares of co-operatives are not publically traded but remain in the co-operative if a member leaves or dies. To survive and prosper, the co-operative must have a sufficient surplus after paying a dividend and interest to invest in improvements, particularly in a competitive retailing environment. There are variations with members paying an annual fee and receiving member discount prices rather than dividends (Birchall, 2011b, ch. 3).

There can be difficulties, clearly defining a consumer co-operative. Agricultural co-operatives, which are primarily concerned with supplying agricultural goods and services to farmers, may widen their scope to supply household goods and broaden their membership to include the public (Hilson, Neunsinger and Patmore, 2017, p. 5). There can be retailing enterprises run as worker co-operatives such as the Cheese Board Collective in Berkeley, a worker co-operative since 1971 and currently operating a bakery and a café (The Cheese Board Collective, 2018). The co-operative provision of financial services, housing or insurance may arise as an adjunct to the activities of consumer co-operatives (Hilson, Neunsinger and Patmore, 2017, p. 5). There can also be hybrid or multi-stakeholder co-operatives that bring together workers, consumers and other parties such as suppliers. These co-operatives raise questions of how those interests are going to be represented in the governance of the co-operative, with workers and consumers, for example, having equal representation on the Board of Directors (BD) even though consumer members may outnumber worker owners. An example of this is Eroski, which is a co-operative supermarket chain that commenced in the Basque Region in 1969 and now operates in Spain and France. There are approximately 12,000 workers who are 'worker partners' and over seven million customer members or 'client partners', with the worker partners and the client partners having equal representation at the Annual General Meeting (AGM) and the governing board (Birchall and Sacchetti, 2017). There also are transformational co-operatives where the form of the co-operative shifts over time to match changes in local economic conditions. The Macleay Co-operative on the mid-North coast of New South Wales (NSW) in Australia, founded in 1905, began as a dairy co-operative with a butter factory and transformed into a retail co-operative as the dairy industry went into decline (Patmore, 2012, p. 10).

One important extension of retail co-operatives are wholesale co-operatives. While many retail consumer co-operatives developed relationships with non-cooperatives' wholesalers to survive, there were early examples of opposition from traditional wholesalers and manufacturers to supplying co-operatives. There were also concerns about consumer co-operatives bidding against each other in a competitive market. In the early years of the movement in Great Britain, the purchasing of stock was a major concern to co-operative management committees and managers were subject to greater scrutiny than in non-cooperative retailers (Purvis, 1998, pp. 57–61). As Gurney (1996, p. 94) notes, "wholesaling was vital to co-operative success as it reduced costs and helped solve the problem of boycotting; with a strong wholesale organization, co-operators could buy their supplies directly from the manufacturer, thereby cutting out the capitalistic middleman." To meet these issues in Great Britain, the English Co-operative Wholesale Society (CWS) and the Scottish Co-operative Wholesale Society (SCWS) began trading in 1864 and 1868, respectively (Birchall, 1994, pp. 81–87). The survival of consumer co-operatives since the Second World War has rested partially on their ability to develop integrated systems of wholesaling to match the economies of the larger non-cooperative retail chains (Ekberg, 2012, pp. 1007, 1115).

One of the important developments associated with the rise of these wholesale bodies was the creation of a common co-operative label. The CWS in the UK initiated branding its own name for its own produce and some of its suppliers. A notable example occurred in July 1884 when the CWS made a deal with Armour and Company, a leading US meat processer, to produce tinned meat with the CWS label (Webster, Wilson and Vorberg-Rugh, 2017, p. 579; Illustration 1.1).

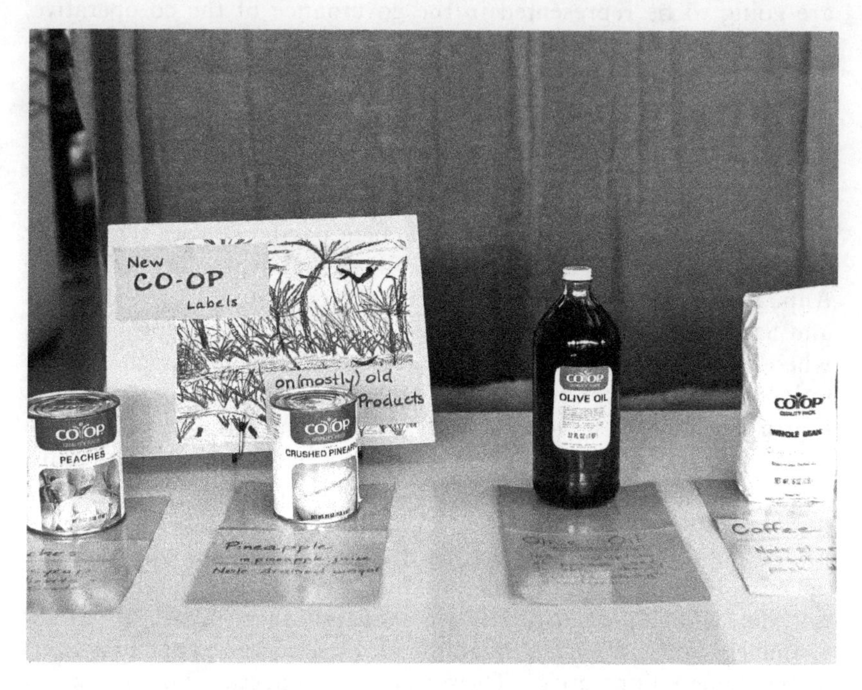

Illustration 1.1 CCB CO-OP Labels, 1972. Courtesy of Berkeley Historical Society (BHS) #10464.

Forming and Managing a Consumer Co-operative

The traditional way through which consumer co-operatives are formed is by individuals voluntarily getting together and forming a co-operative. They generally must raise their own capital and initially provide their own labor on a voluntary basis to get the co-operative started. They can start on a small scale with a buyer club, whereby members contribute collectively to the purchase of items and then distribute according to their contribution to the club. There may be no store under this arrangement, but there may be some money set aside to provide the capital for the purchase of an existing store or the building of a new store (Neptune, 1977, pp. 9–11).

A less common way in which consumer co-operatives have been formed is where an existing owner of a retail business offers to mutualize. One example of this is the Nuriootpa Co-operative in the Barossa Valley of South Australia where a local retailer decided, following the death of his male heir during the Second World War, to allow the community to take over his store. The town had a long history of community projects, including a community hotel run by a trust. There was a small group of individuals who had a sufficiently large amount of capital to make the project viable, and co-operative membership was open to all members of the community. The existing goodwill, inventories, store staff and management were transferred over to the store, removing many of the issues involved with starting up a new retailing business (Balnave and Patmore, 2015, p. 1148). A larger scale example occurred with Migros in Switzerland in 1940, when the founder Gottlieb Duttweiler converted a large retail chain into 12 regional co-operatives grouped into a federation (Birchall, 2011b, p. 57).

Once established, co-operative stores may expand through the recruitment of new members and opening branches in new locations or through the purchase of existing stores. The Rochdale co-operative in the UK expanded by opening branches from 1856; the first branch in Oldham Road was a result of members wanting to have a store located in their Rochdale neighborhood. There were concerns that the opening of branches could lead to competition with other nearby co-operatives, but in the case of the Castleton co-operative this was overcome by an agreement to absorb the co-operative and become another branch in 1857. Further pressure by local members in 1859 led to the opening of a co-operative at Bamford in direct competition with the Hooley Bridge Co-operative, despite its protests. After this, the number of branches multiplied and independent co-operatives were absorbed; there were nine branches by 1863 (Cole, 1944, p. 91; Holyoake, 1893, pp. 36, 129, 143–145). Consumer co-operatives should be careful about expanding into areas where there is insufficient support for co-operativism or where there are established retailers. There are also problems with maintaining the democratic ethos as there are more members in a greater number of locations with different interests. A governmental structure must be developed that maintains effective member participation and democratic control, but ensures efficient administration. As Jerry Voorhis (1961, p. 176), a leading US co-operator, noted, "there is also the problem of maintaining informed interest, loyalty, concern and a sense of responsibility among... members ..."

One issue for consumer co-operatives growth is expansion into areas where populations are poor and socially disadvantaged. They may not have sufficient finances to raise the capital necessary to establish a co-operative or ensure sufficient earnings for the consumer co-operative to survive. Margaret Llewellyn Davies, the daughter of a Christian Socialist minister of religion and secretary of the Women's Co-operative Guild (WCG) in the UK from 1889 to 1921, believed that co-operative stores should be for all and not just for those who could afford it. The WCG's initial aim was to promote loyalty to the co-operative store, but it expanded into a mass movement for working-class women that promoted progressive issues. Davies, to assist the access of the poor, supported membership fees paid by installment, voting based on purchasing activity rather than share capital and minimization of dividends to reduce prices. Following the WCG's argument, the Sunderland Co-operative Society in 1902 opened a 'People's Store' that not only had a grocery store, butchers' shop, flour store and the provision for the sale of cheap hot soup, but also had two resident social workers to promote self-help among the poor. While the Store proved to be financially viable, disputes between the social workers and the Society's directors led to the workers' resignations and the store being wound up. The experiment was against the background of attitudes that blamed the poor for their poverty and sympathetic calls for legislative intervention rather than self-help (Cole, 1944, pp. 221–233; Hilson, 2017, p. 74; Jeffs, 1996, p. 79). As Cole (1944, p. 223) noted in the UK, "co-operation remained a movement of the better-off workers."

While there may be sufficient members to form the consumer co-operative, they may not provide sufficient capital through membership fees to expand the co-operative and there may not be sufficient members to keep down costs through a high level of sales turnover. Consumer co-operatives must recruit members through a broad range of strategies that include word of mouth and advertising the benefits of co-operative membership through a variety of forms of media. One issue that arises in historical literature is whether the best message for recruiting is based on the quality and value of the products or the broader ideological appeal of co-operatives (Balnave and Patmore, 2010). Voorhis (1961, p. 176) again noted that the appeal of the co-operatives was:

> often a conventional one – straight product advertising – and not often an exposition of how and why co-operatives are a different kind of business, one that *should* listen to consumers' needs and wishes because those same consumers own it.

The dividend was initially viewed as a major attraction for members of consumer co-operatives. 'Dividend days' were looked forward to by members because they provided additional cash for a range of goods and services, including the payment of medical bills, school fees for children, the purchase of backyard poultry and even seaside holidays. There were problems for co-operatives in managing dividends, as they had to develop a system to record them. As co-operatives grew, these could be difficult to manage. There were a variety of systems used to record purchases for the distribution of dividends. Some systems relied on members to keep records of purchases by retaining their receipts. Under this system those members who did not keep accurate records would find themselves missing out on the full extent of their dividend. Employees had to calculate the dividends after the member provided receipts in a very short period prior to issuing the dividend. More recent methods require the member to do little as the co-operative keeps records of the member's purchases and calculates the dividend automatically. This has been an area where consumer co-operatives have benefitted from computer technology with members being able to swipe a membership card, which records their transactions and calculates their dividends. An unexplained and considerable drop in the dividend also caused issues for co-operatives, as this could be viewed by members as the first sign of financial difficulties and lead to a withdrawal of capital. Historically, management has tried to maintain a dividend at a constant level to maintain confidence and provide clear explanations for any dramatic shifts in dividend policy (Patmore and Balnave, 2018, pp. 5–6).

While the cash gains made through regular dividends were important initially in attracting and maintaining members, they lost their appeal particularly in the postwar period when large capitalist retail supermarkets could offer immediate specials or discounts at the point of sale. There were also major problems providing high dividends based on members' purchases for co-operatives running supermarkets, which relied on high turnover of sales with very low profit margins to remain competitive. In the UK, there was recognition that the political principles of co-operation were not sufficient to maintain interest in the co-operative, with a 1950 internal survey finding that only 3 percent of customers gave political principles as the main reason for shopping at co-operatives. The UK co-operatives by the early 1950s combined high dividends with the savings arising from the adoption of self-service to maintain a competitive edge. However, as other retail stores adopted self-service, there were downward pressures on the level of dividends due to competition. Co-operative stores also found it necessary to offer gimmicks to attract members and patronage such as a free quarter pound of tea to each customer (Shaw and Alexander, 2008, pp. 74–5).

Consumer co-operatives initially drew their capital primarily from the shares of members. Some early co-operatives based their capital on one-off subscriptions when members joined to finance expansion, but this was insufficient for capital needs and they failed. Many early English consumer co-operatives collapsed because they refused to pay interest on share capital and discouraged members from purchasing a larger number of shares. Another issue that arose was the minimum cost of shares, which, if they were too high, could act as a deterrent for new members. To overcome the problem of a high minimum share cost, some consumer co-operatives permitted new members to pay a smaller amount and then allowed their dividends on purchases to accumulate to the full amount. There were also concerns that share capital could be withdrawn, which could arise on a large scale if there was a crisis of confidence in the co-operative, and further threaten solvency. Co-operatives have required shareholders to give reasonable notice if large amounts of shares are to be withdrawn and, in extreme cases, freeze withdrawal (Patmore and Balnave, 2017, p. 420).

Consumer co-operatives therefore found it necessary to attract individuals to purchase large amounts of shares, even though it meant these individuals still had the same vote as shareholders with limited amounts of capital. As a result, consumer co-operatives had to provide competitive returns on capital compared to other financial institutions such as banks or members would withdraw capital or not invest new capital if returns were higher elsewhere. There were limits on the number of shares that an individual could have due to concerns that large shareholders could exercise undue influence over the co-operative because of the possibility of the withdrawal of their capital and abrogation of democratic principles (Birchall, 1994, p. 57).

From the earliest days, it was recognized that shares were not enough to provide capital for the co-operative. The UK Industrial and Provident Societies Act (IAPSA) of 1852 allowed for individuals with then maximum shareholding of £100 to invest up to a further £400 in loan capital. Even regarding loan capital, there was a limited liability in British co-operatives; the principle followed that it was better to have many small investors rather than a small number of large investors to ensure that no one could dominate the co-operative society. For these loan capital investors, the consumer co-operatives provided internal bonds, debentures and certificates of indebtedness at attractive interest rates. Some of these investors, which could even include private sector shopkeepers, could invest in the co-operative even if they were not members as they considered it a convenient institution into which to place their money (Patmore and Balnave, 2017, p. 421).

Consumer co-operatives could generate their own capital through their business activities. Again, the retention of capital had to be balanced against the level of dividends and the payment of interest on shares and other member investments. This could be a controversial issue at members' general meetings and required the co-operative management to convince members of the need to invest in the upgrading and expansion of co-operative services. Co-operatives could also encourage members to invest their dividend based on patronage back into the co-operative in the form of additional shares and interest-bearing securities. This surplus capital becomes collective capital, which individual members have no claim on and reduces the co-operatives' exposure to fluctuations in share capital (Patmore and Balnave, 2017, p. 421).

Consumer co-operatives then face the issue of where to invest these surpluses. They could be with other sections of the co-operative movement, such as co-operative banks and credit unions, or with other financial institutions. Some co-operatives invested their money with wholesale co-operatives to assist the development of the wholesale co-operative and provide a return on their investment. In Sweden, Kooperativa Förbundet (KF), the co-operative union and wholesale society, established a fund system to help it expand and overcome supply boycotts. Co-operative societies deposited their savings with interest in the special funds, which in the short term created stability for the KF and allowed the KF from the 1920s onwards to build or buy industries to supply co-operative members with goods. It was estimated in the 1930s that 70 percent of the outside investments of British co-operative retail societies were placed in co-operative societies, mainly wholesalers. The investment of co-operative funds in wholesale societies or co-operative central bodies was not without risk. The Australian Association of Co-operatives collapsed in 1993 due to problems associated with its internal banking services to members, including bad loans. (Patmore and Balnave, 2017, p. 421).

Another approach is for the smaller co-operatives to merge into larger co-operatives to have sufficient capital to manage the modern supermarkets and hypermarkets. Patrizia Battilani (2003, pp. 110–112) argues that this process transformed the Italian consumer co-operatives during the 1950s and 1960s and explains the greater success of consumer co-operatives in Italy compared to other European countries. There were, however, problems with these mergers, as the larger size of the co-operatives distanced members from the general management and reduced the importance of members and the boards of directors who represented them.

The co-operatives continually must generate sales and market the co-operative to survive. While co-operatives may on paper have a large membership, there is no guarantee that members will shop there. The growth of large-scale retail chains, with economies of scale in warehousing, purchasing and marketing, has posed a major problem for co-operatives. In the case of small co-operatives in specific localities, advertising is generally restricted to store pamphlets and great reliance is placed on word of mouth. By the 1930s, the UK propaganda meetings, particularly successful in rural villages, brought together co-operative education and sales to promote the consumer co-operative through talks by co-operative officials, variety performances, fashion shows, advertising films and social evenings. Where consumer co-operatives are in highly competitive situations such as large cities, they may produce their own newsletters as well as advertise in local newspapers. At a national level, wholesalers such as in England have run newspaper, radio and television campaigns (Carr-Saunders, Sargent Florence and Peers, 1940, pp. 123–126).

In addition to advertising, there have been a number of strategies to ensure that co-operative members continue to trade at the co-operative. Many co-operatives returned dividends in the form of a token, which could only be used at the co-operative for purchases such as milk and bread. Tokens could also be purchased in advance to minimize the need for credit later. Where dividends have fallen out of fashion, concessions have been given to members in the form of price cuts, member-only specials and competitions offering prizes (Carr-Saunders, Sargent Florence and Peers, 1940, p. 121).

While price competition may have become more important than the ideological message of obtaining members and sales, co-operatives in many countries saw an advantage in marketing themselves in terms of consumer health protection and the environment. An early Rochdale principle from 1860 related to the sale of pure and unadulterated food, which was concerned with wholesome and untainted food that sold according to full weight and measure so that members would not be short changed (Birchall, 1994, pp. 59–61). The KF in Sweden, for example, as early as 1911 published articles in its newspaper *Kooperatören* on nutrition and broadened the discussion in the 1920s to include product information and taste. There was a greater emphasis on labeling, organic food, recyclable packaging and local produce in the 1960s and the 1970s. In Italy, the 1979 Congress of Association of Consumer Co-operatives came out in support of a focus on consumer health and the environment with co-operative label products focusing on nutritional health, controlling the use of additives and the elimination of food colorants (Aléx, 2003, pp. 258–9; Battilani, 2003, p. 121).

There have been claims that consumer co-operatives are more sympathetic to their workforce than their competitors. The labor and co-operative movements have similar roots in industrialization and the idea of collectivism, and share a strong emphasis on member control through democratic practices and ensuring the best for their members and the community (Wetzel and Gallagher, 1987, p. 517). Some co-operators have viewed the labor movement as the "natural ally of the co-operative movement."[1]

However, co-operatives are also businesses that need to ensure a surplus to survive and compete in a capitalist economy with businesses that are not organized on co-operative principles. This has the potential to place co-operatives in conflict with organized labor, particularly regarding labor costs, and ensuring that recognized wage standards, whether through statutory regulation or collective bargaining, are observed. There may also be a stronger commitment to the consumer co-operative by employees if they possess shares in their capacity as consumers and are part owners. A notable if dated study is the work of Kurt Wetzel and Daniel Gallagher examining the intensity and frequency of strikes in Saskatchewan co-operatives in Canada, where they concluded that with the centralization and professionalization of labor relations, co-operatives may become indistinguishable in their labor practices from IOBs (Wetzel and Gallagher, 1987).

There have been continued concerns that employees as members would use their voting power at members' meetings to override traditional managerial prerogatives, such as disciplinary decisions, as well as increase wages and place further competitive pressures on the co-operative. These fears led some consumer retail co-operatives to place limits on the employees' rights as shareholders by not allowing them to stand for election to the management committee or BD, vote in board elections or even in some cases preventing employees from joining the co-operative. Some consumer retail co-operatives, however, have allowed for direct employee representation, whereby employees directly elect their own members of the committee or board (Carr-Saunders, Sargent Florence and Peers, 1940, pp. 88–91; Ostergaard and Hasley, 1965, p. 142).

There have also been strong arguments within the consumer co-operative movement over the relative interests of consumers and workers – consumption versus production and the development of the idea of 'consumer sovereignty' in consumer co-operatives. This was heightened in the UK by the movement of consumer retail co-operative into the production of goods for their stores during the second half of the nineteenth century, with some arguing for the supremacy of consumers' interests over workers' interests and the primacy of consumption over production. While there was recognition of the need to pay fair wages, strikes by workers challenged consumers' interests by raising prices (Wetzel and Gallagher, 1987, pp. 519–521). There was also a view put forward by Beatrice Potter (later Webb, 1891, p. 239) that workers' interests in consumer retail co-operatives would be looked after by their union membership and that consumer retail co-operatives and trade unions combined "would make the workers practically paramount in the State."

While there has been a debate about the status of workers in consumer retail co-operatives, there have been claims made over the years that consumer retail co-operative were better employers than their capitalist competitors and enjoyed good relationships with the trade union movement. Co-operatives generally encouraged workers to join unions, with the English CWS insisting from 1919 that employees become trade unionists. It was estimated that 94 percent of the members of the National Union of Distributive and Allied Workers in the UK in 1931 were co-operative employees. The consumer retail co-operatives also led the way on industrial issues such as shop employee working hours in the UK. Consumer retail co-operatives, such as the Plymouth Co-operative in the UK, supported union-made goods as part of their appeal to consumers for selling quality products.

In addition to being sympathetic employers, consumer retail co-operatives provided support for unions in industrial disputes through financial assistance to strikers and consumer boycotts. Co-operatives in Australian, Canadian and UK coalfields provided credit to miners during industrial disputes (Balnave and Patmore, 2017, p. 11).

While the relationship between consumer retail co-operative and unions brought advantages for both movements, there were also tensions. In the 1920s, there were complaints that unions in the US did not provide reciprocal support by enthusiastically encouraging members to shop at the co-operative. There were concerns in the UK that unions unfairly put pressure on the co-operatives, which were viewed as sympathetic, to leverage increases in wages and conditions from their capitalist retail competitors. Co-operative workers expressed their discontent with working conditions by going on strike and forming their own unions (Balnave and Patmore, 2017, pp. 11–13).

One issue of concern for unions about the operations of consumer retail co-operatives was the widespread use of voluntary labor, particularly during the start-up of co-operatives, or periods of economic difficulty, where there are insufficient funds to pay staff. The Royal Arsenal Co-operative in the UK from its formation in 1868 until 1878 relied on the voluntary efforts of its management committee to run the store, assisted by a Mrs. McLeod, who voluntarily cleaned the store after each day. Her death and the growth of the society led to the appointment of its first full-time member of staff (Rhodes, 1998, p. 6). Some contemporary Australian and US consumer retail co-operatives obtain volunteer labor from members by offering discounts on purchases (Balnave and Patmore, 2017, p. 14).

Despite the general view that co-operatives are favorable to unions, there are examples of unorganized co-operatives. In rural areas of Australia, despite union coverage, consumer retail co-operatives have often had limited or no union presence in the workplace. Some of these co-operatives offered extensive welfare provisions and emphasized the ability for worker voice in the organization through their membership of the co-operative (Balnave and Patmore, 2017, p. 14).

One crucial issue, particularly for co-operatives, is the quality and commitment of management. There are long-standing concerns within the co-operative movement about the training of co-operative managers and the commitment of managers to the co-operative ideology, particularly if they were recruited from the private sector. The report of the Co-operative Independent Commission in the UK in 1958 found a major problem with the management of co-operatives, which it rated as varying from deplorable to excellent. UK co-operatives recruited their staff almost exclusively from school-leavers, who were expected to work their way up the ranks of the local society and learn the business without any specialized training. Co-operative managers earned less than their private sector counterparts. There were also divergent practices regarding the relationship between the BD and the co-operative managers. At one extreme, there were boards of directors, who interfered in the micromanagement of the stores. They failed to engage in long-term planning and demoralized store managers. At the other extreme, boards acted as "consumer's vigilance committees," giving the managers a great deal of autonomy and only blaming them when things went wrong. Management training became a major priority for the UK co-operative movement in the postwar period to remain solvent and competitive with the growing retail chains (Birchall, 1994, pp. 146–150; Cole, 1951, pp. 150–4).

Why Do Consumer Co-operatives Grow and Decline?

Historians have suggested a number of economic, political and social factors that assist the formation and growth of co-operatives. Market failures are an important explanation for the rise of co-operatives. Price inflation and its impact on real wages and purchasing power is one key factor for consumer co-operatives. As prices rise, consumers look for ways to reduce their grocery bills. By cutting out the 'middle man' and redistributing the surplus back to consumers, co-operatives can have a downward effect on prices (Birchall, 2011b, pp. 27–28).

Periods of unrest, when disenchantment with the prevailing economic and social order leads to an interest in alternative ways of controlling both consumption and production, is another important factor in explaining the development of co-operatives. Such periods include the industrial revolution in the UK, the Great Depression of the 1930s and the counterculture movements of the 1960s and 1970s (Patmore and Balnave, 2018, p. 14). One notable response to these periods of unrest from the earliest days was to build utopian communities based on co-operative ideals. Two nineteenth-century examples of this are Robert Owen's New Harmony in the USA during the 1820s[2] and the 'New Australia' settlement in Paraguay during the 1890s (Kellet, 1997).

Once a favorable political and legal environment is established for co-operatives, this may further enhance the growth and development of co-operatives. A good example of the state encouraging co-operatives can be seen in Italy (Sarina and Fici, 2015). After the Second World War, the Italian co-operative movement developed in a context of general recognition for the role it could play in the economic and social development of the country. Article 45 of the 1946 Italian Constitution recognizes the social role of co-operatives as based on mutuality and nonprofit goals and encourages the law to promote co-operative development. Favorable laws followed that assisted the growth of co-operatives, such as the 1977 legislation that allowed undistributed profits to be set aside in indivisible reserves and not be liable for corporate tax, a measure that increased co-operative self-finance considerably (Battilani, Balnave and Patmore, 2015, pp. 65–67).

Immigration and religion played an important role in spreading co-operative ideas internationally. British immigrants in Australia and New Zealand (NZ), particularly in the coalmining areas, and Finns notably in Michigan, Minnesota and Wisconsin in the US established consumer co-operatives in those countries. Jewish emigration to Palestine encouraged co-operation there in the interwar period, and by the end of 1937 over 1,000 Arab and Jewish co-operatives had been established, including credit unions, agricultural marketing societies, irrigation co-operatives, consumer co-operatives and housing co-operatives (Patmore and Balnave, 2018, p. 15).

A variety of religious groups through their beliefs and clergy have promoted co-operatives. Catholic interest in co-operatives grew with Giuseppe Toniolo's foundation of the Catholic Union for Social Studies in 1889 in Italy and Pope Leo XIII's Rerum Novarum in 1891, which highlighted the Church's need to address the concerns of the poor and labor. In Italy, the focus was on financial co-operatives, agricultural co-operatives and consumer co-operatives (Zamagni and Zamagni, 2010, p. 48). An important Catholic movement in promoting co-operatives can be seen in the example of the Antigonish movement. It started at the St Francis Xavier University in Nova Scotia, Canada, in 1930 and approached co-operative development with study circles that identified local problems and proposed co-operative solutions, particularly credit unions. The Antigonish movement had a wide international impact, including the Caribbean in the 1950s, South Korea and Zimbabwe. While the Catholic Church played an important role in the international spread of co-operatives, Protestant clergy were also important. Toyohiko Kagawa, a Japanese Christian evangelist, promoted co-operatives in Japan and overseas and published an influential book *Brotherhood Economics* (1936) that emphasized financial co-operation as a means of achieving international peace (Patmore and Balnave, 2018, pp. 15–16).

Support for cooperatives has historically come from farmer groups and the labor movement. Farmers have established not only agricultural co-operatives but also the Rochdale consumer co-operatives in rural areas to buy in bulk, ensure continuity of supply and keep prices down. Where farmers are well organized, farmers' political parties and lobby groups have provided legislative support for co-operatives. Labor movements may also support consumer cooperatives to protect real wages by keeping prices down and preventing profiteering. Union organizers have promoted the formation of cooperatives as a counter to the influence of company stores or expensive general stores. This link between the movements is strong in the UK with the Co-operative Party affiliation with the Labour Party (Balnave and Patmore, 2008, p. 98; Curl, 2012, p. 347; Keillor, 2000, pp. 310–311).

One factor that several scholars have recently explored is the link between the formation and survival of co-operatives and their local community and region, particularly in rural areas. The social and economic networks built in a locality or region, whether it be in the Mondragon region of Spain or a village in India or rural communities in Australia, promote a sense of 'localism' and encourage a 'propensity to co-operate' (Balnave and Patmore, 2006, pp. 51–52, Birchall, 2011b, pp. 24–25). As Nicole Robertson (2010, p. 213) has noted for consumer co-operatives: "for some of its members, the role of a co-operative society within a community extended beyond the realms of grocery shopping." They become enmeshed in the cultural and social environment of the community by sponsoring local sporting groups, for example, through financial sponsorship and forms of assistance. Co-operatives become a core institution in the local community promoting employment and retaining profits with the community. Consumer co-operatives promote 'buy local' campaigns to ensure that residents of particular communities purchase from local businesses and they do not spend money elsewhere. These campaigns are designed to preserve local job opportunities and maintain viable communities. There are examples of consumer co-operatives ensuring the maintenance of the retail profile of the community by stocking goods formerly sold by businesses that have closed and even purchasing failed businesses to ensure that the goods and services continue to be provided to the community (Balnave and Patmore, 2006, pp. 63–65; Robertson, 2012, p. 935). Localism could also have a downside for the broader co-operative movement with local co-operative societies preferring their local autonomy in buying and being reluctant to purchase from centralized co-operative wholesalers (Webster, 2012, pp. 886–890).

The sense of community underlying consumer co-operatives was reinforced by a cultural dimension. While the growth of co-operative movement provided a means of consumption and economic reward through the dividend, the consumption practices of the co-operative were highly specific, as they were not privately owned stores run for profit, and "the practice, ritual and symbolism of co-operative trading constituted co-operative culture in a fundamental sense" (Gurney, 1996, p. 61). Despite the Rochdale principles, the co-operative societies provided credit during times of stress such as unemployment and industrial strife. It was a center of community life, owned by working people, where members and their families shopped and interacted. Co-operative culture in England included tours of CWS factories and recreational activities such as reading rooms, marches, tea parties, festivals, plays and choirs (Patmore and Balnave, 2018, p. 85). All these various activities "strengthened understanding of and support for co-operative ideology, and strongly embedded societies within their localities" (Wilson, Webster and Vorberg-Rugh, 2013, p. 40).

Retail co-operatives have also faced challenges that have led to their decline and disappearance. There are many reasons for the decline of consumer co-operatives, including economic prosperity, demographic changes and competition from the non-cooperative sector. The decline of working-class communities in mining areas and the waning population in rural areas due to mechanization in agriculture and economies of scale brought about by the consolidation of rural properties have had a negative impact on consumer co-operatives. Increasing car ownership in rural areas in developed economies created further difficulties for consumer co-operatives reliant on their remoteness for success (Patmore and Balnave, 2018, p. 18).

Poor management and even corruption can aid the decline and collapse of consumer co-operatives, as with other types of businesses. The Griffith consumer co-operative, which was in the Riverina region of Australia and had 7,063 members in 1980, was poorly managed in its final decade of operations. The general manager of the co-operative was forced to relinquish his post due to health reasons in 1981 after 25 years of service. The BD overlooked suitable possible successors in the co-operative's management and appointed several subsequent managers, one with limited retailing experience and all with no co-operative management experience. The co-operative operated for six months in 1983 without a general manager and one secretary of the co-operative was charged by police with falsifying accounts, which deepened the co-operative's financial problems. The co-operative also entered a new venture, the Driver Superstore, in 1980, which ended in financial disaster and the closure of the Superstore. The co-operative never recovered and an angry meeting of shareholders decided to sell the business and premises in May 1989 (Balnave and Patmore, 2010, pp. 67, 74).

There can also be ideological challenges to the principles that underlay co-operatives that weaken them. Antidemocratic movements and ideas that promote individual over collective behavior do not favor co-operatives. Communist and Fascist states have attacked co-operatives and incorporated them into the state. The Nazi's, after gaining government in Germany in 1933, dissolved the German Central Union, which was the German organization affiliated to the ICA, and forced the amalgamation of the four main co-operative organizations into a state controlled body with directors appointed by the government, which the ICA refused to recognize as it breached co-operative principles (ICA, 1934, pp. 82–86). In the Union of Soviet Socialist Republics (USSR), Stalin in 1935 abolished all urban consumer co-operatives and replaced them with state agencies. All assets were seized and there was no compensation for members (Birchall, 2011b, p. 37). The recent rise of the Chicago School of Economics and the push toward privatization and deregulation during the 1980s and the following two decades created a climate that favored the IOB and co-operative demutualization (Battilani and Schröter, 2012).

While there are a range of factors that can explain the growth and decline of consumer co-operatives, there is a view that co-operative failures may arise from systemic problems inherent in all co-operative structures. These ideas are drawn from agricultural economics in specific relationship to agricultural co-operatives. Co-operatives arise from market failures and a revolt against the present economic and political system, especially during economic downturns, and when times improve either fail or are demutualized. They tend to be less flexible in shifting their economic focus than IOBs, as markets change, due to their democratic governance and their attachment to the original objectives that underlay their formation. As they get bigger, there tend to be more competing interest groups, which leads to conflict and a tendency for those with goals relating to organizational gain rather than co-operative ideals to take over. The co-operative increasingly behaves like an IOB with corporate-orientated aspirations such as profitability and financial stability taking priority over member-centered goals such as the level of service and economic democracy (Cook, 1995; Helmberger, 1966; Hind, 1999). Cook and Buress (2009) have noted five phases: economic justification; organizational design; growth, glory and heterogeneity; recognition and introspection; and choice, whether to 'tinker, reinvent, spawn' or set up a 'separate entrepreneurial venture' or 'exit'. The 'life cycle' theory has been used to explain the survival and demise of agricultural co-operatives (Mazzarol, T., Mamouni Limnios, E. and Simmons, R., 2014, p. 137).

While this 'life cycle' approach can be criticized for determinism, the long life span of some co-operatives indicates that co-operative demise is not inevitable, as co-operative members and managers have a choice and can adapt their organizations and objectives without compromising the essential democratic nature of co-operative enterprises, even shifting forms as is the case of transformational co-operatives (Cook and Buress, 2009, pp. 14–15). Two examples of agricultural co-operatives that have survived the fluctuations of the business cycle are Land O' Lakes in the US, founded in 1921, and NORCO in Australia, founded in 1895 (Keillor, 2000, pp. 2000–296; Ryan, 1995, p. 129). While the life cycle approach may be questioned for agricultural co-operatives, there has been a least one attempt to apply to consumer co-operatives – the CCB, described as a "classic example of co-operative organizational failure" (Terfloth, 2018).

Conclusion

This introductory chapter has highlighted significant issues about consumer co-operatives and provided a framework for the understanding the history of the CCB. Consumer co-operatives are MOBs and not charities that deliver benefits and services to members. They are defined by an evolving set of principles that flow from the development of the Rochdale consumer co-operatives through the ICA to the present day. Despite these principles, there are variations in practice and between differing legal jurisdictions. Consumer co-operatives are distinguished from other types of businesses for their principle that one member has one vote irrespective of their number of shares and their focus on members and the communities rather than external investors, as in the case of an IOB. There can be sometimes difficulties in distinguishing consumer co-operatives from other types of co-operatives that engage in the retailing of household goods such as agricultural co-operatives. There can also be hybrid co-operatives that bring together workers and consumers as owners and transformational co-operatives which can change their type. Finally, co-operatives may move into wholesaling to ensure the supply and quality of goods by forming wholesale co-operatives.

While the management of consumer co-operatives shares many of the same problems with the managers of capitalist retailers, they do face unique challenges. Consumer co-operatives not only have to attract customers to the store, but also establish a commitment by consumers to joining the co-operative and investing in it. Over time, the appeal of the dividend and the promise of democracy have not been enough to sustain interest and patronage, as capitalist competitors provide on-the-spot specials and discounts. While there has been a focus on pure and unadulterated food since the earliest days of the consumer co-operative movement, a growing dimension of the consumer co-operatives' appeal in recent years has been a focus on organic, local and environmentally friendly products.

Capitalization, labor relations and the quality of management have remained ongoing issues for consumer co-operatives. Shareholdings are not sufficient for investment and can be a volatile form of capital if members lose confidence. Co-operatives have looked at other ways to raise capital such as debentures, but are generally wary of allowing a small group to control a large amount of the co-operative's capital. The preference is to expand collective capital through investments, which have been targeted toward other sections of the co-operative movement, but still have risk. Many consumer co-operatives have merged into larger co-operatives to increase the level of capitalization and benefit from economies of scale. While consumer co-operatives have generally had good relationships with employees and the labor movement, there are tensions. There are ongoing fears about employees using their membership rights to influence the labor policies of consumer co-operatives and the notion of 'consumer sovereignty', whereby consumer rights of representation in consumer co-operatives are paramount over those of workers. There are also concerns about inadequately trained managers coming up through the ranks, who may not be able to adjust to rapid changes in the business environment.

There are factors that have favored the development of consumer co-operatives, including market failures, periods of political and social unrest, immigration, favorable clergy and community. There also factors that weaken them, including competition from the non-cooperative sector, antidemocratic governments and unfavorable ideologies such as neoclassical economics. While there is a notion of a life cycle for co-operatives, the fate of co-operatives is not predetermined and shaped by the choices of managers and members. Overall, however, individual consumer co-operatives can fail like all other businesses if they are poorly managed.

Against the background of this introduction, Chapters 2 and 3 provide the general context for the development of the CCB by examining the history of consumer co-operatives internationally and specifically in the US. The remainder of the book is organized along chronological lines, with an examination of the community context, and the exploration of themes relating to the CCB: management, members, employees, community and the relationship of the broader co-operative movement.

The next three chapters examine a general period of prosperity for the CCB. Chapter 4 explores the specific context of the formation of the CCB and its early years, until its merger with the Berkeley Co-operative Union (BCU) in 1947. Chapter 5 examines the period from 1947 to 1962, when the CCB took a cautious approach to expansion linking any expansion to the level of membership in any locality outside Berkeley, with the first major expansion being to the nearby growing center of Walnut Creek in 1957. Chapter 6 examines the rapid growth of the co-operative during the 1960s, which arose from expansion into new areas such as Marin County and purchasing a chain store. Against the background of political upheaval in Berkeley and beyond, the CCB was divided between Moderates who believed in the Rochdale principle of political neutrality and Progressives who argued that the CCB had to take a stance on the political controversies of the 1960s.

The remaining chapters focus on the decline of the CCB and conclude the book. Chapter 7 explores the beginning period of instability for the CCB with the departure of Eugene Mannila, who had been general manager since 1947, in December 1971. While there followed a series of managers, which exacerbated poor decision-making and planning, the CCB continued to expand with the opening of the San Francisco North Point Shopping Centre and the purchase of the three Mayfair chain stores in Oakland in 1974, as part of a plan to expand the co-operative's activities to less affluent areas of the Bay Area. Chapter 8 explores the final years of the CCB, whose finances further deteriorated in the 1980s and began shutting stores to save costs from 1981, with a brief unsuccessful attempt to revive its fortunes by reopening a store in Marin County. From 1989 to 1991, the CCB board sold off the remaining assets and the California Supreme Court approved the dissolution of the CCB in May 1993. Chapter 9 reexamines the various ideas that explain the fluctuating fortunes of the CCB and how the co-operative's history provides a deeper understanding of consumer co-operatives.

Notes

1 *Swamp Monster Speaks*, July 1979, p. 1, Box 1 File 16. BANC MSS 94/220c. Richard Neil Lerner Papers (hereafter RNLP), UCB Bancroft Library (hereafter BL). Courtesy of BL, UCB.
2 *The Co-operative Magazine and Monthly Herald*, January 1826, pp. 11–17.

References

Aléx, P., 2003, "From Alternative to Trademark: The Consumer Co-operative Movement in Sweden," In Amsab-Institute of Social History, ed., *Consumerism versus Capitalism? Co-operatives seen from an International Comparative Perspective*, Ghent, Amsab-Institute of Social History, pp. 95–107.

Atherton, J., Birchall, J., Mayo, E. and Simon, G., 2012, *Practical Tools for Defining Co-operative and Mutual Enterprise*, Manchester, Co-operatives UK.

Balnave, N. and Patmore, G., 2006, "Localism and Rochdale Co-operation: The Junee District Co-operative," *Labour History*, 91, pp. 47–68.

Balnave, N. and Patmore, G., 2008, "'Practical Utopians'. Rochdale Consumer co-operatives in Australia and New Zealand," *Labour History*, 95, pp. 97–110.

Balnave, N. and Patmore, G., 2010, "Marketing Community and Democracy: Rural Rochdale Co-operatives in Australia," *Consumption Markets & Culture*, 13 (1), pp. 61–77.

Balnave, N. and Patmore, G., 2015, "The Outsider Consumer Co-operative: Lessons from the Community Co-operative Store (Nuriootpa), 1944–2010," *Business History*, 57 (8), pp. 1133–54.

Balnave, N. and Patmore, G. (2017), "Rochdale Consumer Co-operatives in Australia and New Zealand," In Hilson, M., Neunsinger, S., and Patmore, G., eds., *A Global History of Consumer Co-operation since 1850: Movements and Businesses*, Leiden and Boston, CA, Brill, pp. 456–480.

Battilani, P., 2003, "How to the Beat Competition with Losing the Co-operative Identity: The Case of the Italian Consumer Co-operatives," In Amsab-Institute of Social History, ed., *Consumerism vs. Capitalism? Co-operatives Seen from an International Comparative Perspective*, Ghent, Amsab-Institute of Social History, pp. 109–126.

Battilani, P., Balnave, N. and Patmore, G., 2015, "Consumer Co-operatives in Australia and Italy," In Jensen, A., Patmore, G. and Tortia E., eds., *Cooperative Enterprises in Australia and Italy. Comparative analysis and theoretical insights*, Florence, Firenze University Press, pp. 57–73.

Battilani, P. and Schröter, H., 2012, "Demutualization and Its Problems," In Battilani, P. and Schröter, H., eds., *The Co-operative Business Movement, 1950 to the Present*, Cambridge, Cambridge University Press, pp. 263–275.

Birchall, J., 1994, *Co-op: The People's Business*, Manchester, The University of Manchester Press.

Birchall, J., 1997, *The International Co-operative Movement*, Manchester, The University of Manchester Press.

Birchall, J., 2011a, "A Member-Owned Business Approach to the Classification of Co-operatives and Mutuals," *Journal of Co-operative Studies*, 44 (2), pp. 4–15.

Birchall, J., 2011b, *People-Centered Businesses. Co-operatives, Mutuals and the Idea of Membership*, Houndsmills, Palgrave Macmillan.

Carr-Saunders, A.M., Sargent Florence, P. and Peers, R., 1940, *Consumers' Co-operation in Great Britain. An Examination of the British Co-operative Movement*, 3rd ed., London, George Allen and Unwin.

Cole, G.D.H., 1944, *A Century of Co-operation*, Manchester, Co-operative Union.

Cole, G.D.H., 1951, *The British Co-operative Movement in a Socialist Society*, London, George Allen & Unwin.

Cook, M.L., 1995, "The Future of US Agricultural Co-operatives: A Neo-Institutional Approach," *American Journal of Agricultural Economics*, 77 (5), pp. 1153–1159.

Cook, M.L. and Burress, M.J., 2009, "A Co-operative Life Cycle Framework," available at http://departments.agri.huji.ac.il/economics/en/events/p-cook.pdf (accessed 29 January 2018).

Curl, J., 2012, *For All the People: Uncovering the Hidden History of Co-operation, Co-operative Movements, and Communalism in America*, 2nd ed., Oakland, CA, PM Press.
Ekberg, E., 2012, "Confronting Three Revolutions: Western European Consumer Co-operatives and Their Divergent Development," *Business History*, 54 (6), pp. 1004–1021.
Gurney, P., 1996, *Co-operative Culture and the Politics of Consumption in England, 1870–1930*, Manchester, Manchester University Press.
Helmberger, P.G., 1966, "Future Roles for Agricultural Co-operatives," *Journal of Farm Economics*, 48 (5), pp. 1427–1435.
Hilson, M., 2002, "Consumers and Politics: The Cooperative Movement in Plymouth 1890–1920," *Labour History Review*, 67 (1), pp. 7–27.
Hilson, M., 2017, "Rochdale and Beyond: Consumer Co-operation in Britain," In Hilson, M., Neunsinger, S. and Patmore, G., eds., *A Global History of Consumer Co-operation since 1850: Movements and Businesses*, Leiden, Brill, pp. 59–77.
Hilson, M., Neunsinger, S. and Patmore, G., 2017, "A Global History of Consumer Co-operation since 1850," In Hilson, M., Neunsinger, S. and Patmore, G., eds., *A Global History of Consumer Co-operation since 1850: Movements and Businesses*, Leiden, Brill, pp. 3–16.
Hind, A.M., 1999, "Co-operative Life Cycles and Goals," *Journal of Agricultural Economics*, 50 (3), pp. 536–548.
Holyoake, G.J., 1893, *The History of the Rochdale Pioneers*, London, Swan, Sonnenschein & Co.
ICA, 1934, *Report of Proceedings of the Fourteenth Congress of the International Co-operative Alliance at London, 4th to 7th September, 1934*, London, ICA.
Jeffs, M., 1996, "Margaret Llewelyn Jones and the Women's Co-operative Guild," In Lancaster B. and Maguire P., eds., *Towards the Co-operative Movement. Essays in the History of Co-operation*, Loughborough, The Co-operative College, pp. 74–82.
Kagawa, T., 1936, *Brotherhood Economics*, New York, Harper & Bros.
Kellet, J., 1997, "William Lane and 'New Australia': A Reassessment," *Labour History*, 72, pp. 1–18.
Mazzarol, T., Mamouni Limnios, E. and Simmons, R., 2014, "To Be or Not to Be a Co-op? The Case of Australia's Grain Co-operatives CBH and ABB Grain," In Mazzarol, T., Reboud, S., Mamouni Limnios, E., and Clark, D., eds., *Research Handbook on Sustainable Co-operative Enterprise: Case Studies of Organisational Resilience in the Co-operative Business Model*, Cheltenham, Northampton, MA, Edward Elgar Publishing, pp. 151–184.
Neptune, R., 1977, *California's Uncommon Markets. The Story of Consumers Co-operatives 1935–1976*, 2nd ed., Richmond, CA, Associated Co-operatives.
Ostergaard, G.N. and Halsey, A.H., 1965, *Power in Co-operatives. A Study of the Internal Politics of British Retail Societies*, Oxford, Basil Blackwell.
Patmore, G., 2012, "Introduction. A Short History of Co-operatives in Australia," In Derby, M., ed., *Building a Better Australia. 50+ Stories of Co-operation*, Victoria Park, Western Australia, IYC 2012 Secretariat, pp. 8–10.
Patmore, G. and Balnave, N., 2017, "Managing Consumer Co-operatives: A Historical Perspective," In Hilson, M., Neunsinger S., and Patmore, G., eds.,

A Global History of Consumer Co-operation since 1850: Movements and Businesses, Leiden and Boston, CA, Brill, pp. 413–430.

Patmore, G. and Balnave, N., 2018, *A Global History of Co-operative Business*, London, Routledge.

Potter, B., 1891, *The Co-operative Movement in Great Britain*, London, Swan Sonnenschein.

Purvis, M., 1998, "Stocking the Store: Co-operative Retailers in North-East England and Systems of Wholesale Supply circa 1860–77," *Business History*, 40 (4), pp. 55–78.

Rhodes, R., 1998, *An Arsenal for Labour. The Royal Arsenal Co-operative Society and Politics 1896–1996*, Manchester, Holyoake Books.

Robertson, N., 2010, *The Co-operative Movement and Communities in Britain, 1914–1960*, Farnham, Ashgate.

Robertson, N., 2012, "Collective strength and mutual aid: Financial provisions for members of co-operative societies in Britain," *Business History*, 54 (6), pp. 925–944.

Ryan, M., 1995 *A Centenary History of Norco 1895–1995*, Lismore, Norco.

Sarina, T. and Fici, A., 2015, "A Comparison between Australian and Italian Co-operative Law," In Jensen, A., Patmore, G. and Tortia E., eds., *Cooperative Enterprises in Australia and Italy. Comparative Analysis and Theoretical Insights*, Florence, Firenze University Press, pp. 21–36.

Shaw, G. and Alexander, A., 2008, "British Co-operative Societies as Retail Innovators: Interpreting the Early Stages of the Self-service Revolution," *Business History*, 50 (1), pp. 62–78.

Terfloth, K., 2018, "Co-operative Life Cycle Theory," available at http://usaskstudies.coop/documents/pdfs/Co-op%20Life%20Cycle%20Theory.pdf (accessed 29 January 2018).

The Cheese Board Collective, 2018, "The Cheese Board Collective," available at http://cheeseboardcollective.coop/ (accessed 29 January 2018).

Voorhis, J., 1961, *American Co-operatives. Where They Come From. What They Do. Where Are They Going*? New York, Harper & Row.

Webb, S. and Webb, B., 1930, *The Consumers' Co-operative Movement*, London, Longmans, Green & Co.

Webster, A., 2012, "Building the Wholesale: The development of the English CWS and British co-operative Business 1863–90," *Business History*, 54 (6), pp. 883–904.

Wetzel, K.W. and Gallagher, D.G., 1987, "A Conceptual Analysis of Labour Relations in Cooperatives," *Economic and Industrial Democracy*, 8 (4), pp. 517–540.

Wilson J., Webster A. and Vorberg-Rugh R., 2013, *Building Co-operation. A Business History of the Co-operative Group*, 1863–2013, Oxford, Oxford University Press.

Zamagni, S. and Zamagni, V., 2010, *Cooperative Enterprise: Facing the Challenge of Globalization*, Cheltenham, Edward Elgar.

2 International Consumer Co-operative Movement Before 1993

This chapter places the CCB in its international context. It explores the history of the international consumer co-operative movement from its origins in the industrial revolution of the UK and the ideas of Robert Owen and William King to the early 1990s. It explores the early forms of consumer co-operatives and the events that led to the establishment in 1844 of the Rochdale consumer co-operative, which is viewed as the model of consumer co-operation. The chapter then traces the expansion of the Rochdale consumer co-operative movement in the UK and beyond, with the establishment of co-operative wholesaling and the formation of the ICA in 1895. It then examines the challenges of the twentieth century with the rise of totalitarian ideas, world wars, the Great Depression and the post-Second World War period, when consumer co-operatives faced the rise of large chain stores and rise of neo-liberalism in the 1980s. This chapter does not examine the US experience, which will be the focus of the next chapter.

Industrialization and the Early Consumer Co-operative Movement in the UK: 1759–1820

While there may have been earlier forms of mutualism and co-operation, the rise of the consumer co-operative movement is associated with the onset of industrial revolution and the beginnings of modern capitalism in the 1760s in England. The development of new steam technology and the breakdown of agricultural life due to the enclosure of land to increase farm production brought larger numbers of workers to the growing, overcrowded and insanitary industrial towns to work in factories where large-scale production was needed to match the growing demand. Workers faced long hours, received meager wages and worked at a pace that was at odds with preindustrial life. Workers also had to deal with the 'truck system', which was eventually outlawed, where unscrupulous employers forced workers to obtain low-quality and highly priced goods at stores owned and operated by them by paying them with script that was only redeemable at those stores. Workers could also be tied by debt to a shopkeeper due to fluctuating incomes, as they could no longer grow their food in the fast-growing urban areas. These issues underlay the early worker interest in retail co-operatives (Birchall, 1994, pp. 1–6, 10–13; Wilson, 1995, p. 33).

Against the background of the Napoleonic Wars, there were outbreaks of unrest in England such as food riots over prices and the scarcity of food. More organized forms of opposition were trade unions and the Chartist movement. The latter, before its demise in 1860, called for parliamentary reform and the enfranchisement of the working-class (Patmore and Balnave, 2018, pp. 28–29).

Another response was the formation of early co-operatives. From 1759 to 1820, at least 46 flour and bread societies were established in parts of England and Scotland to retail bread and flour at below the prevailing local 'market price'. They challenged the high prices and poor quality of bread arising from 'adulterating' flour through mixing in substances such as china clay. These societies were directly owned by consumers or operated indirectly through a local friendly society. They represented vertical integration into retail distribution and beyond that into bakeries and flour milling and highlight a market failure in terms of the rapid increase in the price of grain. The earliest known of these societies were formed in 1759 associated with government dockyard workers at Chatham (Middlesex) and Woolwich (Kent). They spread into England and Scotland with the Hull Anti-Mill recruiting 1,435 members in 1795 and opening a mill in June 1797. The average life of these companies was 48 years, with the Hull Anti-Mill surviving for 100 years. A small number of these societies were to link themselves later with the growing Rochdale consumer co-operative movement (Bamfield, 1998, pp. 16–21, 31).

There are early examples of broader retail co-operatives, which did not specifically focus on milling and baking. A Weaver's Society in Fenwick in Scotland began as early as 1769 to purchase necessities. While friendly societies such as the Blue Ball Club in Blidworth in 1771 did buy goods such as cheese for resale to members, the earliest known English retailing co-operative was the Oldham Co-operative Supply Company established in 1795. At least one English baking society, the Sheerness Economical Society, extended into co-operative retailing in 1816 (Patmore and Balnave, 2018, p. 30).

Robert Owen, Dr. William King and Early Co-operatives 1820–1844

Two significant individuals arose in the UK that had a major impact on the development of co-operatives – Robert Owen and Dr. William King. Robert Owen, born in Wales, began work as a shop assistant at a drapers' shop at the age of nine. He eventually became a manager of a spinning mill. He married the daughter of David Dale, one of the largest cotton mill owners in Britain, and took over the management of the

New Lanark mills in Scotland from his father-in-law after he and several associates purchased it. He established a reputation for creating humane conditions at New Lanark where workers received high wages and good working conditions (Patmore and Balnave, 2018, p. 31).

Owen, however, was not satisfied with his achievements at New Lanark despite popular acclaim. He first popularized his ideas in *A New View of Society*, published in 1813, and coined the term 'co-operative and economical society' in January 1821 in the first issue of his magazine *The Economist*. Owen was concerned with the impact of industrialization upon the living standards of workers. Owen called for the creation of villages of mutual co-operation, which would have a population of between 500 and 1,500 people and would transform capitalism, as workers would produce for themselves and exchange surplus goods with other co-operative villages. He relied for capital on wealthy subscribers, who would either form joint stock companies or become trustees, with the common property as security (Patmore and Balnave, 2018, pp. 31–32).

King was a medical practitioner who was born in Ipswich, England, in 1786, and in 1821 moved to the small coastal town of Brighton, which had about 25,000 inhabitants. Like Owen, King was concerned about declining living standards of workers. King believed that industrialization by 1828 had led to the decline of wages to one-third of what they were 100 years previously and workers were on the verge of starvation.[1] King advocated through his magazine *The Co-operator* (which began publication on 1 May 1828) that Owen's supporters should open stores and use the surpluses to emancipate themselves. He, like Owen, believed that workers would establish self-sufficient communities that would buy land for the unemployed to work and provide sickness benefits. Unlike Owen, Kings' motivation was partly religious and he believed that these co-operative communities could operate in the current society without any need for a radical transformation (Patmore and Balnave, 2018, pp. 32–33).

A movement developed that combined elements of both King and Owen's ideas. While London provided an initial base for the discussion of Owenite ideas, the broader movement began in 1826 in Brighton, which was a fast-growing town where the older skilled trades faced rising unemployment as industrialization hit. While some co-operators saw themselves as saving to set up communities such as Orbiston in Scotland and Exeter in England,[2] others established 'union shops' to sell their own products like workers' co-operatives and build up capital to form a co-operative community like Orbiston. King used the Brighton Co-operative Trading Association, later the Brighton Co-operative Society formed in 1827, as a model for his propaganda. There were about 70 contributing members who bought £5 shares in small payments. They sold goods to subscribers and their families such as candles, mutton, bread and tea, and the co-operative appointed by February 1828 their first full-time employee, William Bryan, a trade unionist, as agent or storekeeper. A surplus from the sale of these groceries was invested in a lease of 28 acres, where members were paid to cultivate the lease as a garden and nursery at higher than the prevailing rate of wages. Except for Wales, stores could be found in every industrial area of Britain and Ireland. The strength of the movement is highlighted by eight Co-operative Congresses, the first of which was held in Manchester in May 1831 and the last in Halifax in April 1835 (Cole, 1944, pp. 25–27; Durr, 1988, pp. 18–20).

The co-operative movement, however, virtually collapsed by 1834. The Brighton Co-operative disappeared in 1832 with a few of its members taking out their capital and buying a fishing boat. There was an economic depression that reduced the earnings of co-operators and a collapse of the rising trade union movement due to employer lockouts, such as in the London building trades, and government repression. The legal status of co-operatives was uncertain, which made them vulnerable to mismanagement and fraud, and there were management issues in the co-operatives as they did not know how to distribute profits unless they dissolved their co-operatives to make a payout (Patmore and Balnave, 2018, p. 35).

A small number of co-operatives survived and new ones were established after 1834. While the Owenite movement was in decline, Chartists saw co-operative stores as supplementing their drive for political reform as a form of economic power and a way of raising funds for their cause. There were amendments in July 1834 to the friendly societies legislation that extended the scope of the legislation to include all societies established for any legal purpose. This allowed co-operatives to register and gain some legal recognition and financial security. These societies generally divided profits per their share capital, with most societies dividing the profits equally as each member held only one share. An exception to this rule was a small number of societies that paid dividends per the amount purchased by individual members at the society's store. The co-operative society at Paddock in West Yorkshire went even further toward the Rochdale model, with its 1839 rules providing for the first payment from profits of 5 percent interest on all loans, subscriptions and donations and the remaining profits, if any, distributed individually per the amount of money paid for goods. While there may have been a continued interest in using the surplus from these stores to found Owenite communities, the co-operatives seemed primarily concerned with supplying unadulterated food at reasonable prices. Overall it is estimated that between 1835 and 1844 there were at least 120 retail societies and 25 more specialized trading societies in England, selling everything from bread to shoes manufactured by their members, in operation at various times (Purvis, 1986; Thornes, 1988, pp. 39–42).

The Establishment of the Rochdale Co-operative 1844

Rochdale, an East Lancashire mill town 16 kilometers north-east of Manchester, by 1844 had a population of 25,000 inhabitants with another 40,000 living in nearby villages. Its major industries were woolen manufacture, especially flannel, and the spinning and weaving of cotton goods. The handloom was still in wide use for woolen goods, including flannels, but the handloom weavers were facing increasing competition from steam-powered machinery. Wages were in decline for the handloom weavers and work was irregular. Both the cotton and woolen industries faced wild fluctuations in demand with the flannel trade being hit hard by US tariff developments in 1828 and 1841, which led to a sudden and severe fall in exports. By the early 1840s, economic depression had led to large-scale unemployment and hunger (Cole, 1944, pp. 39–42, 54).

The Rochdale workers tried to address these issues in a variety of ways, including the involvement in nonconformist religious sects such as Wesleyanism and trade union activity, with a major strike in 1844, despite the Weavers' Union negotiating an agreement with more liberal employers, leading to a major defeat and the weavers looking for alternative solutions to their grievances, including emigration. The Rochdale co-operative pioneers were influenced by the emerging co-operative movement. James Smithies, for example, had a bound copy of King's *The Co-operator*, which he circulated among the other pioneers such as Samuel Ashworth. During the earlier wave of co-operatives, a Rochdale Friendly Co-operative Society had been formed in 1830 following a strike by flannel weavers, but folded in 1835 due to the provision of excessive credit (Birchall, 1994, pp. 39–41; Thompson, 2012, p. 14).

Weavers and others at a meeting on 15 August 1844 formed a co-operative in Rochdale. The Rochdale Society of Equitable Pioneers was registered under the Friendly Societies legislation on 24 October 1844, with 40 subscribers paying three pence a week to raise capital to open a store, and its store commenced business on the evening of Saturday 21 December 1844 on the ground floor of a warehouse at 31 Toad Lane, Rochdale, with opening hours from 8pm to 10pm. There were some immediate issues such as the small amount of capital to purchase stock, which affected the price and quality of the early goods for sale, which were sugar, butter, flour, oatmeal and tallow candles. Shares were one pound each and the Society's rules provided for a range of activities beyond running the store, including the construction of houses for members, the manufacture of goods, the purchase or rent of land for cultivation to allow the employment of the unemployed and the opening of a Temperance Hotel. Owenism was still an influence, with the objective being to establish a "self-supporting-home colony" (Patmore and Balnave, 2018, pp. 41–42; Illustration 2.1).

Illustration 2.1 Rochdale Toad Lane Store as a Museum. Courtesy of the Berkeley Historical Society.

While the formation of the Rochdale co-operative and its principles has influenced the development of the international co-operative movement, it brought together ideas from other co-operatives and organizations that predated it. They based their first rules on the Rational Sick and Burial Society, which had been formed in Manchester in February 1842. The Society arose from an Owenite critique of friendly societies, which were viewed as having too high surpluses and wasting money on processions and feasts. The democratic principles of one member and one vote also underlay Chartism, trade unions, friendly societies, the nonconformist chapels and other co-operatives. The rules of the Ripponden Co-operative, which was approximately 16 kilometers from Rochdale and flourishing, provided for democratic government and admitted women as members as early as 1833, with 19 female members by 1842. The idea of fixed and limited interest on invested capital was one of Owen's principles, while the concept of a dividend on purchases was found in earlier co-operatives since the mid-1820s. Alexander Campbell, the Scottish socialist and co-operator, had advocated the dividend on purchases since 1822 and had lectured in Rochdale in 1840. He claims also to have been consulted by the Rochdale Pioneers in 1843 and 1844. There was a long-standing concern about the provision of credit to workers and a preference for cash payment dating back to the flour mill and baking co-operatives. The April 1832 Co-operative Congress in London adopted a report rejecting credit, and the earlier Rochdale co-operative failed for providing excessive credit for members (Patmore and Balnave, 2018, p. 42).

Beyond Rochdale: The UK 1844–1914

From 1844 to 1914, there was a major growth of consumer co-operatives in the UK, with an expansion of consumer co-operatives into wholesaling, agriculture, manufacturing and financial services. Co-operative membership grew steadily in Britain from 350,000 in 1873, when accurate data begins, to 3,054,000 in 1914, with an average annual growth of 5.3 percent. While the number of retail consumer co-operatives peaked in 1903 at 1,455, the average number of members of a society grew from 564 in 1881 to 2,205 in 1914 (Cole 1944, p. 371). By 1914, retail co-operatives supplied between 7 and 9 percent of Britain's total retail trade and 17–19 per cent of Britain's total trade in groceries and provisions (Wilson, Webster and Vorberg-Rugh, 2013, p. 99).

There are several explanations for the growth of consumer retail co-operatives in the UK. While there were fluctuating economic conditions, such as the slide into depression in 1875 for instance, this did not reverse growth but generally slowed it during periods of economic downturn. The only exception to this is 1881, which may be explained by a poor economic climate but also could be accounted for by changes in the statistical definition of co-operatives. While the economic conditions fluctuated, this did not undermine a long-term growth in working-class living standards, which gave workers greater disposable income to purchase from and invest in retail co-operatives. The growth of consumer co-operatives was linked to the spread of trade unionism to unskilled workers and the rise of the WCG, particularly from 1885 to 1890. Trade unionism grew to four million by 1914 and socialist and labor organizations became a significant force. Compared to consumer co-operatives, trade unions were more favorably affected by booms and more unfavorably affected by slumps. While consumer co-operatives lost sales in downturns, their membership remained relatively stable compared to trade unions, as workers still depended on them for the necessities of life (Cole, 1944, pp. 179–188, 370–372; Wilson, Webster and Vorberg-Rugh, 2013, pp. 56, 100).

The consumer co-operatives did not have any major rivals, as chain stores did not begin to emerge until the 1870s and department stores did not take off until the end of the century. The co-operatives were attractive to workers with dividends and a safe place to put their additional savings in shares or the provision of loans to the co-operative. They were also democratically run and committed to unadulterated food at fair prices (Birchall, 1994, pp. 66–72).

The early co-operative movement also played an active role in promoting the Rochdale principles and engaging in political lobbying to obtain favorable legislation. The Rochdale Co-operative did not keep its success to itself and promoted its business model to others. Using the cheap and quick 'penny postage' system that was invented in 1840, William Cooper, the Auditor and later Secretary of the Rochdale Co-operative, wrote many letters to others highlighting the development of the Rochdale Co-operative. George Jacob Holyoake, a former Owenite missionary, wrote a history of the Rochdale Pioneers, which was published 1857, and had wider effect not only in Britain but also internationally with translations into many languages, including French, Spanish and Italian. It was reprinted 13 times between 1858 and 1907. Holyoake went on lecture tours explaining the Rochdale system. Lobbying and influential parliamentary allies secured the passage of the IAPSA of 1852, which gave the co-operatives recognized legal status, and further amendments in 1862 gave co-operatives limited liability and income tax exemptions (Patmore and Balnave, 2018, pp. 53–55).

The early consumer co-operatives saw a need to set up a co-operative wholesaler. Private retailers saw co-operatives as unwelcome competition and threatened boycotts of wholesalers who supplied co-operative stores. At Cramlington near Newcastle, the co-operative store in 1864 could not obtain flour despite obtaining quotes, with supplies eventually being obtained from a Newcastle merchant on the condition that his identity was kept secret. In the early years of the movement in Great Britain, the purchasing of goods for sale was a major concern to co-operative management committees, with the newer co-operatives having little knowledge about where and when to buy (Purvis, 1998b, pp. 57–61; Redfern, 1913, p. 41).

After several attempts, the final push to enter co-operative wholesaling came in 1863 with the formation of the CWS. The 1862 amendments to the IAPSA provided the legal basis for the CWS by authorizing co-operatives to hold shares in another co-operative and allowing them to advance capital to them. A special conference in Manchester in April

1863 established the CWS. The CWS provided goods to co-operatives on a cost price basis, with a commission to cover its costs and minimize stock to reduce the risk of price fluctuations undermining capital. The CWS was a federation of retail co-operatives or a 'co-operative of co-operatives'. The new wholesaler was registered under the IAPSA in August 1863 and by October 1863 48 retail co-operatives joined. It appointed a temporary buyer in December 1863 and commenced trading in a small warehouse in Manchester on 14 March 1864 with butter, coffee, tea, sugar and soap being among its first goods. While the CWS sold only to co-operative stores, the co-operatives were free to buy elsewhere; this undermined the CWS and strengthened private competitors. In Scotland, consumer co-operatives formed their own SCWS in August 1868 to trade only with registered consumer retail societies, with the CWS allowing their Scottish members to transfer their shares to the SCWS (Patmore and Balnave, 2018, pp. 58–59, 79).

The development of the co-operative wholesaling underlay the growth of the co-operative movement in Britain. The CWS grew dramatically from its humble beginnings in 1864 to a global enterprise by 1914 with capital of almost £10 million and net sales of almost £35 million (Redfern, 1913 p. 418–419; Redfern, 1938, p. 532). The headquarters of the CWS remained in Manchester with several blocks of imposing offices and warehouses. The CWS established branches in Newcastle-on-Tyne in 1871 and London in 1874 and depots, warehouses and salesrooms throughout England to serve regional needs. At the branches the CWS built conference halls for business meetings and co-operative gatherings. There was also stability in CWS management with John Mitchell from Rochdale serving as chair from 1874 until his death in 1895. The CWS was highly centralized, with the General Committee or BD following a set of consistent policies and strategies. By 1905, the CWS was the 16th largest company in Britain, with £4.4 million in capital (Patmore and Balnave, 2018, p. 74).

One source of CWS growth was that it became a direct importer of cheap foods from abroad, which were either processed in Britain such as corn or flour or the country of origin such as bacon. For the year ending December 1909, the CWS imported £7,077,968 from outside the UK, with Denmark being the largest supplier with £3,530,904 for butter, bacon and eggs and the US with £1,311,355 for cheese, bacon, lard, flour and canned goods. Other significant suppliers in order were Sweden, Austria, Canada and Germany. The CWS established depots outside Britain, the first being for butter in Tipperary in Ireland in 1868, and locations such as New York in 1876, Hamburg in 1874 and Sydney, Australia, in 1897. The depots had resident buyers who purchased local supplies and shipped them back to England. The CWS purchased a bacon factory in Denmark in 1900, a tea estate in Ceylon in 1902 and three further tea estates in Ceylon in 1913, while constructing a new bacon factory at Tralee in Ireland in 1901. The CWS, concerned about shipping rates, furthered vertical integration by entering the steamship business through purchasing its first steamship, the SS *Plover* in May 1876 and launching the SS *Pioneer* in 1879. It sent buyers overseas, to Greece in autumn for example, to visit large growers who provided supplies for dried fruit and to pay cash on delivery (Patmore and Balnave, 2018, pp. 75–76).

The CWS, to ensure supplies for its stores, also moved into production of basic products such as shoes, soap, clothing, furniture, biscuits, pickles and jams. The expansion into production was because of growing demand by the co-operative retailers, concerns about quality and reliability and manufacturers boycotts of the co-operative sector. There was also a need to enter competition with private manufacturers, who the retail co-operatives preferred to buy from. There was an estimate in 1885 that 176 co-operative societies in Southern England only purchased 25 percent of their goods from the CWS. CWS production diverted the profits made otherwise by private manufacturers and retailers back into the co-operative movement through dividends, which amounted to £652,818 in 1914. The CWS set up new factories that used the latest mass production techniques and ensured competitiveness, with one manager visiting the US in 1889 to inspect the latest shoe-making machinery. The first CWS factories were started in 1873, when the CWS opened a confectionery and biscuit factory at Crumpsall near Manchester and opened a boot factory in Leicester. Other factories included chocolate and cocoa production in Luton that opened in 1887. The CWS also expanded into agriculture in England and tourism (Patmore and Balnave, 2018, pp. 76–77).

There was controversy about the CWS moving to set up factories, with critics arguing that production should be done by producer co-operatives, where workers would share both management and profits. There was skepticism about these ventures, which included co-operative coal mines, as a number had failed in the 1860s and 1870s. The CWS twice experimented unsuccessfully with paying a bonus on any surplus made to its own workers. Aware of these failures, Mitchell, the CWS chair, was a strong supporter of the 'federalist principle' that consumer, rather than producer, control underpinned the co-operative movement. His personal support for the 'federal principle' helped embed it as the main doctrine of the English co-operative movement (Patmore and Balnave, 2018, pp. 77–78). Mitchell won the support of the influential Beatrice Potter (1891, pp. 117–169), later Webb, who as noted previously was an advocate of 'consumer sovereignty' over workers in the consumer co-operative movement.

The CWS also moved into banking and insurance. The growing consumer co-operatives faced the issue of where to invest their growing surpluses. The CWS in 1871 had opened a banking department, later known as the Loan and Deposit Department, which received deposits from co-operative societies with surplus funds and made advances to co-operative societies who needed short-term capital for expansion. By 1912 the CWS Bank's annual turnover was £158 million. The British co-operative movement also expanded its activities into insurance. Some co-operatives were uninsured, while others were paying premiums to insurance companies, funds that could be retained by the co-operative movement. It established in 1899 the Co-operative Insurance Society, which was absorbed into the CWS and the SCWS in 1913 (Patmore and Balnave, 2018, pp. 82–84).

The British consumer co-operatives developed into a national movement. The *Co-operative News*, which was founded in 1871, became recognized as the official publication of the co-operative movement and had a circulation approaching 50,000 copies per week by 1898 (Cole, 1944, pp. 202–203). There was a revival of co-operative conferences, with the first being held in London in 1869, which led to the formation of the Co-operative Union (CU). The CU was open to co-operatives of all kinds, including producer co-operatives and building societies in Britain and Ireland. It became a debating forum by organizing the Annual Congresses and engaged in political lobbying on behalf of the movement. The CU provided business services such as accounting and co-operative education, opening its Manchester headquarters, Holyoake House, in 1911. By 1913 the CU membership represented 1,272 co-operative societies with a membership of 2,874,574. Co-operative women organized through the WCG, which was formed in 1883, and encouraged the formation of women's guilds at each consumer co-operative. The movement was reinforced by co-operative culture and ideology with its own practices, symbols and rituals such as reading rooms, marches and choirs (Patmore and Balnave, 2018, pp. 82–85; Illustration 2.2).

Beyond the UK before 1914

There was an expansion of consumer co-operatives internationally beyond the UK. Three major developments underpin this growth – the growth of international trade, immigration and colonialization. The development of railways and steam ships allowed cheaper foreign foods into Europe, with American wheat and later Canadian and Indian wheat arriving in Britain at half the local price (Birchall, 1994, p. 70). Communication also became faster with the expansion of the telegraph, alongside railways and underneath oceans, and the invention of the telephone, with the first transcontinental telephone connection in the US occurring in 1914 (Birchall, 2011, p. 158). Immigration reached unprecedented levels in the second half of the nineteenth century, with millions coming from across Europe, initially from North-Western Europe and spreading to Southern Europe and Eastern Europe. There were 3.4 million Europeans who emigrated between 1821 and 1850, 8.1 million from

Illustration 2.2 Holyoake House in Manchester. Photographer Greg Patmore.

1851 to 1880 and 32.1 million from 1881 to 1915 (Graff, Kenwood and Loughheed, 2013, pp. 54–55). Some immigrants, for instance, from Britain, Germany, Italy and Finland, brought with them ideas about co-operation. Colonization by European powers, the US and the newly industrializing power of Japan spread to all corners of the globe with a 'scramble' to secure territories in Africa and Asia. European settlers in these colonies drew from Rochdale traditions to establish their own consumer co-operatives (Patmore and Balnave, 2018, p. 71).

While consumer co-operation became dominant in the UK by 1914, it also developed in other European countries. Although the UK had the largest number of members and turnover among countries with available data or estimates, some countries such as Russia had more co-operatives, while others such as Denmark and Switzerland had a greater proportion of co-operative members relative to the total population. There were also wholesale societies in countries, including Germany, Russia, Denmark and France (Gide, 1922, pp. 49, 165).

The Rochdale model had an influence on the development of these consumer co-operatives as it provided a concrete example of success, but this does not imply a simple translation of the model (Eklund, 2007, pp. 129–130). There were delays, as the Rochdale model had its greatest impact, for example, on France during the final quarter of the nineteenth century, where it was a major source of ideas such as the dividend. Many of those promoting the Rochdale model in Europe had a middle-class background and supported it as a way of ensuring social harmony, which clashed with working-class interest in consumer co-operatives as part of a socialist movement. There were local influences underlying the development of mainland European consumer co-operatives in the mid-nineteenth century as well as the Rochdale example in Britain. Giuseppe Mazzini, who was a significant figure in Italian unification and an acquaintance of Holyoake, believed in the coexistence of capital and labor and not in class war. He saw co-operatives as a valuable way of bringing Italians together in the struggle for Italian independence and unification. The British influence persisted, with Holyoake being a guest at a conference of Italian co-operatives in October 1886, which decided to set up an Italian federation of co-operatives, renamed the *Lega Nazionale* in 1893 (Earle, 1986, pp. 11, 16–17). Hans Christian Sonne, a local pastor, who founded a Danish consumer co-operative at Thisted in 1866 that set the pattern for the Danish movement, was inspired by both the Rochdale pioneers and the German financial co-operatives (Christiansen, 2012, p. 25).

Within each country there were geographical concentrations. The level of industrialization is important, with the industrial north-east of France and Saxony and neighboring districts in Germany being the focus of consumer co-operatives. The rise of the Belgian co-operative movement was linked to the failure of private retailers to meet the needs of workers in growing industrial centers. Consumer co-operation by contrast was weaker in agricultural areas, except for Denmark. Large cities with their diversity of trades, social anonymity and retail competition made it difficult to organize consumer co-operatives. Many of the largest French consumer co-operatives were found in medium-sized industrial towns such as Lille and Amiens, while the larger Lyon, despite a co-operative tradition, produced many smaller and weaker societies (Purvis, 1998a, pp. 150–155, 160; Strikwerda, 1999, pp. 70–71).

The European consumer co-operative movements differed in their practices and politics. While the British and the Swiss consumer co-operatives were politically neutral concerning party politics, the consumer co-operatives of Belgium and Northern France overtly associated with socialist politics. The *Parti Ouvrier* (PO) in France and Belgium received financial support from the consumer co-operatives, and co-operative premises provided accommodation for trade unions and the socialist party. The Belgian PO Congress in 1910 called for the international extension of the link between co-operatives and socialism to fight capitalism. Independent working-class consumer co-operatives developed in Russia and its territories, Finland and the Ukraine during the early decades of the twentieth century. While British consumer co-operatives only gave a limited amount of their funds to education and social activities, there was a greater funding of these activities by the socialist consumer co-operatives of Belgium and Northern France (Purvis, 1998a, pp. 156–157, 161–162; Strikwerda, 1999, pp. 71–73, 77).

The strong identification of some European co-operative movements with socialist parties splintered the co-operative movement with anti-socialists such as the Catholic Church forming their own conservative co-operatives. While Catholic co-operatives were slow to develop in Belgium due to the opposition of Catholic shopkeepers, by 1914 there were almost 30,000 Catholic consumer co-operators. There were also those who saw the co-operative movement as the third way between capitalism and socialism such as the French economist, Charles Gide, who was concerned that workers would turn to Marxism. He wanted to win them back to co-operation and pioneer a new economic system – the Co-operative Commonwealth (Patmore and Balnave, 2018, p. 92; Strikwerda, 1999, p. 75).

A more favorable political climate assisted the spread of co-operatives in Europe. French governments, to gain the support of the growing working-class and avoid social unrest, took a more liberal approach to co-operatives. There was opposition with small private traders, who protested from the 1880s in many European countries against state concessions to consumer co-operatives, particularly taxation. Consumer co-operatives were granted exemptions from commercial taxation on the condition that they only traded with their own members and did not compete with private traders for the general trade, with these measures reinforced in Germany by legislation in 1889 and 1896 with significant financial penalties (Purvis, 1998a, pp. 159–160).

In the Americas, there was an interest in consumer co-operatives in Canada from the 1830s as industrialization occurred. The Canadian consumer co-operatives were linked to co-operative developments in the US. They also spread in mining communities by British immigrants from the 1860s in areas such as Nova Scotia, where they provided competition to company stores. The continued British influence on the development of Canadian consumer co-operatives is highlighted by George Keen, the first General Secretary of the Co-operative Union of Canada from its formation in 1909 until 1944. He was an English immigrant and great admirer of Holyoake and the Rochdale model (Macpherson, 1999, pp. 332–339).

A significant co-operative movement developed in Argentina, with British, German and French immigrants bringing their co-operative experiences with them. While there was a consumer co-operative in 1885, it was short-lived. Juan B. Justo, a doctor, became a major promoter of co-operatives, writing an influential pamphlet on co-operatives and founding *El Hogar Obrero* (EHO) in 1905. EHO initially focused on providing economical housing for its members, but expanded to consumer co-operatives (Delom, 1943, p. 41).

From the 1860s there were waves of interest in Rochdale consumer co-operatives in both Australia and NZ. Settlers established the first consumer co-operative at Riwaka in the Nelson area of NZ in 1844. Holyoake's *Self-Help by the People* was reviewed in *The Empire* newspaper in Sydney in August 1858.[3] An Australian Rochdale consumer co-operative was formed in Brisbane barely 15 years after the establishment of the Rochdale movement in England. Rochdale co-operatives could be found in mining districts and metropolitan areas of Australia and NZ. British immigrant miners played an important role in bringing the Rochdale principles to coalmining districts, in which retail co-operatives became a common feature. Four consumer co-operatives in the Hunter Valley of New South Wales (NSW) in 1912 founded the NSW Co-operative Wholesale Society (NSWCWS). Overall the Australian consumer co-operatives remained relatively small compared to European countries, with approximately 51 societies in 1913 (Patmore and Balnave, 2018, pp. 64–65, 100–101).

Colonialization and European settlement played a significant role in the expansion of co-operatives in Africa and Asia. In both the French and British territories of Africa and Asia there was interest in co-operatives. French settlers in Algeria were interested in co-operatives. A co-operative in Algiers was founded in 1864 after a visit by Alfred Cobden, the Member for Rochdale in the British House of Commons, which exchanged products in return for manufactured Parisian goods. While the focus in South Africa was on agricultural co-operatives, there was some interest in consumer co-operatives, with a co-operative founded at Pietermaritzburg in Natal in 1892. By 1904 there were at least six operating in South Africa, with two at Cape Town, one at Durban, one at Kimberley, one at Uitenhage and one in Johannesburg, with four federated with the English CWS to import supplies (Patmore and Balnave, 2018, pp. 103–104).

While the development of co-operatives in Asia and Africa was associated with colonialism and European settlement, the Japanese movement grew against a background of industrialization and modernization following the beginning of the Meiji period in 1868 without European colonization. Rochdale co-operative stores were first established in

Tokyo and Osaka in 1879. Drawing upon German legislation, the Japanese Parliament passed the Industrial Co-operative Law in 1900 to encourage co-operatives. This legislation provided a favorable climate for Japanese co-operatives, with the formation of the Central Union of Co-operative Societies of Japan in 1905 to promote co-operatives and co-ordinate their activities (Patmore and Balnave, 2018, p. 105).

The international nature of the co-operative movement was highlighted by the formation of the ICA, which held its first Congress in London in August 1895 with participants from a range of countries, including Argentina, Australia, Denmark, Italy, Germany, India and the US, with the largest number being from the UK. The British domination of the ICA executive continued until the 1920s, reflecting the support of the British co-operative movement for the ICA and the high travel costs for other representatives outside Britain. At the outbreak of the First World War, the ICA was dominated by consumer societies with working-class sympathies, particularly from Britain, but that insisted on political autonomy from socialist parties and trade unions (Patmore and Balnave, 2018, pp. 105–107).

World Wars, the Great Depression and the Rise of Totalitarianism

The co-operative business model spread even further throughout the world from 1914 to 1945, but faced major challenges – two world wars, the economic impact of the Great Depression and the rise of totalitarianism in the form of Communism and Fascism. One estimate indicates that by 1937, there were worldwide at least 810,512 co-operative societies, with 50,279 being consumer co-operatives (Cole, 1944, p. 353).

The First World War generally strengthened European consumer co-operative movements, because of government reliance on co-operatives for the distribution of essential commodities and the production of goods for the military. The German consumer co-operative movement expanded its coverage beyond the working-class, with governments permitting civil servants to join socialist-led co-operatives and middle-class Germans joining to increase their opportunities to obtain food supplies. German co-operatives benefitted from a large increase in members' savings due to the scarcity of goods and very high wages. The growing consumer co-operative movement in France gained the first comprehensive legislation in May 1917, which recognized the Rochdale principle of member equality and provided through the Ministry of Labor loans at 2 percent interest to assist co-operative development (Patmore and Balnave, 2018, pp. 116–117).

While the British consumer co-operatives' membership grew from 3,054,000 in 1914 to 4,131,000 in 1919 with 10 percent of the total sales of food and household goods by 1918, there were difficulties. The co-operative movement, unlike private traders, did not engage in war profiteering and, whenever possible, used its market power to restrain the price rises by private traders. The CWS purchased large amounts of agricultural land to contribute to food supplies and became the largest farming enterprise in Britain. Consumer co-operatives faced hostility, with the Asquith Liberal Government deciding to tax the trading surpluses of co-operatives to prevent profiteering and a new coalition government's clumsy implementation of food rationing, which was administered by local Food Control Committees where private retailers were overrepresented. The consumer co-operatives decided that they needed a voice in Parliament and rejected political neutrality by formally entering politics in 1917 and forming the Co-operative Party to counter the rise of political opposition by independent shopkeepers to co-operatives and calls by them for a boycott of retail co-operatives (Patmore and Balnave, 2018, pp. 117–118).

There were also changes in Northern Europe. In Finland, the consumer co-operatives that wished to ally themselves with the Socialists split from the 'politically neutral' *Suomen Osuuskauppojen Keskuskunta* in 1916, supporting proportional representation for the larger urban co-operatives and forming their own co-operative union and wholesaler *Suomen Osuustukkukauppa* in 1917, a division that would hinder future capital accumulation and the development of manufacturing facilities (Hilson, 2017, pp. 131–133). In neutral Scandinavia, the British blockade on shipping intensified negotiations over the formation of a joint buying organization with *Nordisk Andelsforbund* (NAF), a joint Danish, Norwegian and Swedish wholesaling co-operative being formed in 1918, with Finland later joining in 1928 and Iceland after the Second World War. While the Scandinavian co-operatives were not given a preferential position in the distribution of supplies during the First World War, they did not face government opposition like their British counterparts and did not see the need to politicize (Friberg, 2017, p. 211).

From the end of the First World War in 1918 until the onset of the Great Depression in 1929, there was a continued expansion of the European consumer co-operatives, though with some setbacks. Many Italian consumer co-operatives faced bankruptcy after 1921 because while they grew during the War, they did not develop the management and technical skills to deal with the postwar challenges of high inflation and unemployment. There was a split in 1919 between the Catholic and Socialist co-operatives and the Italian fascists incorporated consumer co-operatives into the State. The Government appointed managers with Fascist sympathies and developed a regimented form of co-operation interwoven into the fabric of the corporate state and economy (Patmore and Balnave, 2018, pp. 122–123). In the USSR, following the Russian Revolution a decree in September 1918 forced *Centrosoyus*, the All Russian Union of Consumer Societies founded in 1904, and co-operatives to have state representatives on their boards with the right of veto. All consumer co-operatives in March 1919 were transformed into consumer communes, which had a compulsory membership and absorbed the functions of credit and agricultural co-operatives. However, under the New Economic Policy in May 1923, with the end of the Russian Civil War and the Bolshevik desire to reduce peasant resistance, co-operatives became voluntary and self-governing again (Heaton, 1936, pp. 497–498, 729–730; Patmore and Balnave, 2018, p. 123; Rhodes, 1995, pp. 95–100). The German consumer co-operatives also faced difficulties with hyperinflation, with an estimated 50 percent of German consumer co-operatives being close to bankruptcy in 1924 (Prinz, 2003, pp. 25, 27; Prinz, 2017, p. 251).

There was also increasing competition from chain stores and the rise of 'dime stores', associated with the expansion of the US retailer Woolworth, particularly in Germany and the UK, and clones such as the *Cinq and Dix* in France, which had low prices on mass produced goods, were well lighted, decorated with bright colors and played background music (Furlough, 1991, pp. 266–268). Despite this, by 1929 there were 6,169,000 members in Britain, 4,000,000 members in Germany and 3,500,000 members in France. Ten percent or more of the population belonged to consumer co-operatives in Hungary, Switzerland, Czechoslovakia, Denmark and Finland (Cole, 1944, p. 372; Heaton, 1936, p. 729).

While the Great Depression brought challenges for some European co-operatives, by 1937 those in democratic countries recovered.[4] Consumer co-operatives faced a decline in demand, production and capital. Between 1929 and 1933, the turnover of consumer co-operatives declined by 50 percent in Germany, 38 percent in Poland, 31 percent in Hungary, 20 percent in Finland and 15 percent in Austria. In Britain, turnover and the value of goods produced by co-operatives fell respectively 29 and 24 per cent in 1931–1932, while share capital fell by 23.8 per cent (Krasheninnikov, 1988, pp. 90–91). The Co-operative Bank failed in France in 1933 and the Labor Bank failed in Belgium in 1934, placing further financial pressures on co-operatives. The co-operatives also faced political challenges from small private retailers who were concerned at the rising competition from department stores, chain stores and co-operatives (Patmore and Balnave, 2018, p. 123). Private traders in the UK persuaded the Government to impose further taxation on the co-operatives in 1933.[5] In the UK, while sales per member fell, the membership of the consumer co-operative movement grew during the 1930s from 6.4 million in 1930 to 8.6 million in 1939, with the movement capturing 11 percent of the total retail trade in 1938 and taking a major share of the market in staples such as milk, coal and bread (Birchall, 1994, p. 134; Cole, 1944, pp. 305, 371–372).

The shift toward totalitarianism in Europe during the 1930s Depression led to greater state control of co-operatives. With the accession of the Nazis to power in Germany, an order was issued on 15 May 1933 placing all consumer co-operatives under the leadership of the German Labor Front, and legislation capped the dividend in 1934 at 4 percent to limit the consumer co-operative's appeal (Prinz, 2017, p. 252). The consumer movement lost its democratic and voluntary character with elected co-operative leaders being replaced by Nazis, who the co-operatives were forced to elect. In May 1935, a decree repressed consumer co-operatives by forbidding the creation of new consumer co-operatives, outlawing the opening of new branches, amalgamating all associations in the one location and by dissolving consumer co-operatives once their assets could be liquidated (Aschhoff and Henningsen, 1986, pp. 31–32). These measures were also implemented following the annexation of Austria in 1938 and Czechoslovakia in 1939 into Germany.[6] Similar trends followed elsewhere with Stalin in 1935 dissolving the USSR urban co-operatives, with their stores becoming state enterprises.[7]

The Second World War disrupted the European consumer co-operative movement. Besides the physical destruction of co-operative facilities and the persecution of co-operative leaders, the countries invaded by Germany and its allies saw some co-operative facilities being handed over to private traders or placed under government control. The consumer co-operative movement was destroyed by decree in Germany and Austria in 1941, with all assets being transferred to the state and local consumer co-operatives becoming state chain stores (Aschoff and Henningsen, 1986, p. 31). As in the First World War, there was recognition by the occupying powers that co-operatives could play a useful role in the rationing and distribution of goods in Belgium, Serbia, Denmark, Czechoslovakia, France, the Netherlands and Poland (Digby, 1948, pp. 46–47, 53). The British consumer co-operative movement supplied a quarter of the civilian population with their food commodities and, as in the First World War, supported rationing and protested profiteering by private retailers (Robertson, 2009, pp. 225–226).

There was the continued development of co-operatives in Japan, with a push for the middle and working-class to form citizens' consumer co-operatives to distribute daily necessities at affordable prices. Sukazo Yoshino, a democracy advocate, and Toyohiko Kagawa, the Christian social reformer, separately established new co-operatives such as the Katei Kobai Co-operative in Tokyo in 1919, the Nada Co-operative in 1921 and the Kobe Co-op in 1921 (Kurimoto, 2003, pp. 56–57). The Government also passed the Industry Co-operative Law in 1921 and established a Central Industry Co-operative Bank in 1923. Co-operative Household Associations were founded at Kobe in 1924 and Nada in 1929, which were voluntary organizations without specific rules that produced many women activists in the Japanese co-operative movement. However, as Japan militarized in the 1930s, government control over co-operatives increased. Consumer co-operatives, particularly those associated with the political left, either went bankrupt or faced destruction due to staff being conscripted into the military and allied bombing (Grubel, 1999, pp. 306–307; Takamara, 1995, pp. 262–263).

The co-operative movement in the Americas further developed in this period. While Argentina did not participate in the First World War, its economy boomed through the export of agricultural produce which left it without debt for the first time in its history. By 1921 the movement was dominated by rural co-operatives, with consumer co-operatives numbering 43 of 218 co-operatives and approximately one-quarter of the total co-operative membership. The EHO supported the first congress of Argentinian co-operatives in 1919, and in 1923 set up a credit union, where the funds of approximately 20 workers societies were deposited and became a central feature of the growth of the EHO. Following the example of the EHO, workers in the growing center of Bahia Blanca formed the Cooperativa Obrera Limitada (CO) in October 1920. The CO aimed to fight the rising price of bread by establishing a bakery and later moved into pasta manufacturing. Consumer co-operatives in 1932 established their own federation *Federación Argentina de Cooperativas de Consumo*, which from 1940 moved into wholesaling (Vuotto, Verbeke and Caruana, 2017, pp. 486–492). After several attempts, Argentinian national co-operative legislation was passed in 1925 based on Rochdale principles, and by 1940 there were 76 consumer co-operatives (Delom, 1943, p. 42). In Canada, there developed the Antigonish movement, which arose from the extension department at the Catholic Antigonish University in Nova Scotia established in 1930. Catholic priests Jimmy Tompkins and Moses Coady believed that the economic misery associated with the Great Depression would strengthen radicalism at the expense of Judeo-Christian values and organized all types of co-operatives, including consumer co-operatives, to address this misery (Macpherson, 1979, pp. 130–133).

The consumer co-operative movement in Australia and NZ tended to fluctuate in their fortunes, with peaks following the First World War and the Great Depression. Rochdale consumer co-operatives also became a feature of rural areas of Australia, particularly in fruit-growing or poultry-breeding districts or in towns at important railway junctions such as Junee in the Riverina region of NSW. By 1923, there were 152 consumers' societies in Australia with a membership of 110 000. The postwar boom in the NZ co-operative formation reached its peak in 1921. However, commercial competitors, such as chain stores, undercut the NZ co-operatives through price competition and many co-operatives went into liquidation (Patmore and Balnave, 2018, p. 140).

While the Depression of the 1930s initially weakened Rochdale consumer co-operatives in both countries, they grew in the recovery that followed. There were overseas influences with the Japanese co-operator Kagawa visiting Australia and NZ in 1935 and Australians promoting the Antigonish movement locally. In early 1934, there were six consumer co-operatives in NZ, with overall membership totaling 1,500. By August 1937, the movement had 26 co-operatives and 8,000 members. There was an expansion of women's guilds in Australia and NZ, with the Australian women's guilds forming a national organization in 1936. While there was an expansion of the activities of the NSWCWS in NSW, a drive to establish a co-operative wholesaler in NZ was less successful, and collapsed in 1938 as some manufacturers refused to supply it and many consumer co-operatives did not support it (Patmore and Balnave, 2018, p. 140–141).

While its congresses and executive meetings were disrupted by the two World Wars, the ICA continued to function and diversify its activities. At its peak in 1932, 40 countries were represented covering 99,600,000 members, and by 1938 it had representatives from 34 countries covering 168,672 co-operatives and 72,384,164 members (Parker and Cowen, 1944, p. 35). Membership by 1937 had extended beyond Europe to include Argentina, India, Japan and Palestine. The ICA Executive was transformed in 1921 from a purely British group to having representatives from the leading co-operative countries. The ICA developed a close relationship with the International Labour Organisation (ILO), which was an agency of the newly created League of Nations that established a Co-operative Service to assist the international development of co-operatives. The International Co-operative Women's Guild was established in 1924 and became an advocate for the political rights of women, world peace and international disarmament (Patmore and Balnave, 2018, p. 144).

The ICA clarified and reinforced the co-operative identity. It reviewed the ICA co-operative principles with the 1937 Paris Congress adopting seven principles of which four were obligatory for any co-operative – open membership, democratic control, dividends on purchases and limited interest on capital. To highlight the international significance of co-operatives, the Executive Committee in 1923 declared the first Saturday in July to be International Co-operative Day and in 1925 formally adopted the Rainbow Flag as its official ensign (Shaffer, 1999, pp. 14, 120–122).

The ICA had to confront the rise of totalitarian states and their implications for co-operatives and ICA membership. The Stockholm ICA Congress of 1927 reduced the influence of the USSR and other large movements by amending the rules, so that one country had no more than 20 percent of the Congress votes and that the USSR be counted as one country. The ICA refused to recognize the co-operative movements that arose in Fascist Italy and Nazi Germany (Patmore and Balnave, 2018, p. 145).

The Postwar Period

The international consumer co-operative movement faced two major challenges from the end of Second World War to the early 1990s – sustained economic growth and prosperity in Western industrial countries followed by a period of economic uncertainty and the international divisions underlying the Cold War. In general, despite concerns about the reappearance of another depression, Western economies responded well to the shift from wartime to a peacetime economy following the conclusion of the Second World War. Assertive governments became involved in directing economic development along the lines of Keynesian economic theory. Pent-up demand from the scarcities of the war fed the consumer binge that would became a hallmark of Western industrialized countries until the 1970s. Consumer co-operatives faced increased competition as rival retailers took advantage of the development of supermarkets, mass advertising and supply chain management. The high standard of living generated by this period of growth weakened the traditional support for consumer co-operatives as prices fell and goods became relatively plentiful, forcing consumer co-operatives to reconsider their appeal to a more affluent population (Patmore and Balnave, 2018, p. 155).

The postwar boom came to an end with the 1975 global recession and stagflation, triggered by an oil shock. The following decades witnessed major fluctuations in the world economy, with further global recessions in 1982 and 1991. Globalization meant that severe economic and financial disruptions in certain countries had profound effects on others. By the end of the 1970s, the philosophy of 'economic rationalism' was emerging among economists to replace Keynesian economics. Economic rationalism promoted neoliberal policies and values: deregulation, a free market economy, privatization of state-owned industries and a reduction in the size of the welfare state. The rise of neoliberalism began in the UK in 1979, with the election of the Conservative government led by Margaret Thatcher (Patmore and Balnave, 2018, pp. 187–188).

In retailing, the inflationary pressures of the 1970s increased the costs of holding stocks on the premises and improvements in delivery techniques reduced the need for on-site warehousing leading to a 'chain store revolution'. Large supermarket chains developed Regional Distribution Centres or centralized depots. Technological developments at the cash register, such as price scanning, allowed better supply forecasting and an emphasis on 'demand pull' rather than 'supply push'. The headquarters of the chain store supermarkets became responsible for buying and negotiated on behalf of all stores in the chain. These developments paved the way for large cost savings, increased efficiency and productivity of operations and cheaper prices (Ekberg, 2012, p. 1006; Hallsworth and Bell, 2003, pp. 306–311).

While the Western economies faced both economic prosperity and uncertainty, the Cold War divided the world. The extension of Soviet influence into Eastern Europe and Asia brought challenges to a co-operative movement that valued democracy, economic autonomy and freedom of speech with co-operatives being generally parastatal. In the Eastern Block, governments such as the German Democratic Republic supported consumer co-operatives in the postwar period, not least for reasons of food supply. However, co-operative societies were allowed only in rural areas in the USSR and Czechoslovakia, while in urban/industrial areas, state-owned retailers became responsible for food distribution (Neunsinger and Patmore, 2017, p. 734). Cold War politics led to conflict within the ICA, and raised concerns among conservatives in Western countries that collectivities such as co-operatives and trade unions were agents of Communist influence and even ideology (Birchall, 1997, pp. 187–189).

Consumer co-operative movements in Western Europe experienced mixed fortunes in the postwar period. While some could survive or strengthen their market share, others went into decline. Consumer co-operatives in France, for example, were relatively slow in their uptake of self-service and supermarkets. While in 1959 one in six people was a member of a consumer co-operative, the regional nature of the movement meant that they had multiple branches and, like their counterparts in other countries, were not structured to deal with large-scale distribution. As supermarkets were established outside cities, the co-operatives struggled, with only a few small societies remaining by 1985. Paralleling the decline of the traditional French co-operative movements were the rise of new 'organic co-operatives', the first appearing in Lyon in 1971 that promoted natural organic products and services and were linked to environmental concerns (Birchall, 1997, p. 91; Lambersens, Artis, Demoustier and Mélo, 2017, pp. 111–117).

In contrast, the British consumer co-operative movement was a leader in self-service and supermarkets in the postwar period. By 1950, the movement had 11 million members and a 10 percent market share (Secchi, 2017, p. 535). It was also leading the way in modernization, and by 1950 had 40 percent of the supermarkets and 90 percent of all self-service shops (Birchall, 1997, p. 84). However, its growth had stalled by the late 1950s, as other retail stores adopted self-service, with downward pressures on the level of co-operative dividends due to competition. There were also structural weaknesses with over 1,000 societies, which had many small stores and a lack of integration with their wholesalers compared to the competing chain stores. While from 1958 there was recognition of the need to centralize, local societies defended their independence. The movement's fragmentation and reluctance to embrace structural reform contributed to a significant decline in the British consumer co-operative movement between 1964 and 1984, with membership falling from close to 13 million to 8 million and the market share decreasing from nearly 11 percent to 4.2 percent (Birchall, 2011b, p. 54; Secchi, 2017, pp. 534–536, 540).

The UK co-operative movement began to regain its strength from the late 1970s. The CWS merged with the SCWS in 1977 and successfully responded to consumer concerns over issues such as Fair Trade. There was an emphasis on buying out marginal and small consumer co-operatives, with the takeover of the movement's largest society, the London Co-operative Society, in 1982, highlighting widespread corruption and accelerating the closure of many stores to mitigate financial losses. This led to a new era in the UK consumer co-operative movement. For the first time since 1963, co-operative membership grew in 1989 (Secchi, 2017, pp. 538–544).

While the British movement struggled, other co-operative movements adapted and prospered. The Italian consumer co-operative movement achieved success from the mid-1970s. Networks of consumer co-operatives led to the adoption of unified strategies for thousands of small co-operatives and the creation of a group of not more than 100 co-operatives with the same brand. There were also favorable legislative measures that recognized their economic and social role and contributed to their institutional viability. Finally, the Italian movement adapted to the changing needs and wants of consumers, shifting its values and objectives since the 1980s from the protection of worker purchasing power to the promotion of responsible consumption and the protection of consumer health (Battilani, Balnave & Patmore, 2015). Similar success occurred in the Nordic countries, with the Swedish movement beginning structural reorganization by merging local societies into larger units and becoming "the most dynamic and innovative of all the European sectors" (Birchall, 2011, p. 56).

Two examples of expanding consumer co-operative movements in Asia were Japan and South Korea from the 1970s. Following the Japanese surrender, the economy was in crisis due to the destruction of war, and many of the Japanese urban populations faced food shortages and rampant inflation. Buying groups were formed in neighborhoods or workplaces, with more than 6,500 co-operatives of this kind operating in 1947. However, most were short-lived due to ineffective management and support systems, as were the worker-led consumer co-operatives established by trade unions in the 1950s. Against the background of rapid economic growth, which in Japan began in the late 1950s, and the coinciding changes in consumption and distribution, consumers became increasingly concerned with the price and quality of food and with ecological issues such as pollution. 'Citizen's co-ops' backed by housewives were established in each prefecture in the 1960s in response to these concerns. These consumer co-operatives expanded rapidly during the 1960s, and had grown to a membership of 2 million by 1970 and 14 million by 1990. They also took on a distinctive style, namely the Han system and joint buying through home delivery, which continued to expand from the 1970s (Kurimoto, 2010, pp. 4–6, 12–13). The Consumer Co-operative Law of 1948, which recognized the co-operative principles and provided tax relief, provided a legal framework for postwar consumer co-operatives in Japan and contributed significantly to the distinctive traits of the Japanese consumer co-operative movement such as a ban on sales to nonmembers. There was also a ban on consumer co-operatives establishing wholesale societies that was not lifted until 1954 (Birchall, 1997, p. 180; Kurimoto, 2017, pp. 672–673).

As in Japan during the 1970s, a strong network of well-educated South Korean housewives interested in conscious consumption for reasons of food safety and environmental protection emerged in the late 1980s. In April 1987, the Hansalim Community Consumer Co-operative (now Seoul Hansalim), a door-to-door delivery system based on units of 5 households, was formed by 350 households in Seoul and Gwacheon. The political democratization movement also allowed the right of assembly in the late 1980s, and a significant number of civic organizations emerged in South Korea, including consumer co-operatives (Hyung-Mi, 2017, pp. 371–375).

In the Americas, consumer co-operatives in Canada and Argentina faced serious challenges by the 1990s. While there were over 400 consumer co-operatives on the Prairies and in British Columbia by the late 1960s and the merger of 4 provincial co-operative wholesalers into Federated Co-operatives Limited (FCL) by 1970, which gave the consumer co-operatives greater access to capital and the buying power necessary to compete with the supermarket chains, consumer co-operation struggled in Quebec, Atlantic Canada and Ontario. Economic uncertainty with widely fluctuating interest rates in the 1980s undermined efforts by consumer co-operatives to meet the challenges of growing chain store competition and the increasing concentration of agro-food industries on the supply side (Patmore and Balnave, 2018, pp. 170–171, 198–199).

Despite these issues, there were significant developments within the Canadian consumer co-operative movement with the growth of indigenous co-operatives in the Canadian North, particularly in the Arctic region among the Inuit from 1959, and a shift toward organic food stores. Canadians protested the North American agro-food industry's use of chemicals in the production of crops and the traditional way in which stores, including traditional retail co-operatives, were managed. In Canada, the largest concentration of these food stores was found in British Columbia in the 1980s, with them organizing their own wholesales, including the one called 'The Fed Up Co-op Wholesale', whose title was a satirical criticism of the FCL (MacPherson, 2017, pp. 446, 450, 452).

In Argentina, there were problems for consumer operatives. From 1980, economic policy was aimed at reducing state intervention in the economy and controlling inflation, with trade opening to foreign investment. This allowed multinational food retail chains to enter the country and 64,000 food stores to disappear along with almost 125,000 jobs between 1984 and 1993. Despite expansion by the EHO in the 1980s, hyperinflation and deregulation of the currency in 1991 led the EHO to suspend its savings bank operations and hold a meeting of creditors to avoid bankruptcy (Vuotto, Verbeke and Caruana, 2017, pp. 498–504).

Rochdale consumer co-operatives in Australia and NZ generally failed to exploit the potential of the economic buoyancy of the postwar era and survive the challenges that followed the postwar boom. Increased competition from capitalist chain stores, and a failure of many consumer co-operatives to adopt self-service and modernize, meant many consumer cooperatives in smaller rural communities lost business to larger regional or urban centers, where there was the volume of business to justify large supermarkets. The populations of smaller rural communities grew only marginally and even declined, and in the coal mining communities where the co-operatives had been sustained, mines closed and the working-class aspect of these towns evaporated. There were also problems with high levels of credit, particularly in rural areas, and cases of mismanagement. Even in larger centers, consumer co-operatives struggled, with the Adelaide Cooperative an early casualty, going into liquidation in February 1962 after 94 years of trading. The most spectacular collapse of an Australian consumer co-operative was the Newcastle and Suburban Co-operative, which reached a peak membership of 95,000 in 1978 and closed in 1981. A subsequent investigation of the collapse found there were problems such as overstaffing and inadequate accounting practices. There were also problems on the wholesaling side, with the NSWCWS closing business in 1979. In NZ, the Manawatu Cooperative, which had 34,000 members in June 1981, went into receivership in February 1988. The co-operative covered growing losses by selling off property and borrowing to invest in property development. However, rising interest rates eroded returns, while the share market crash of October 1987 thwarted plans for financial restructuring. The surviving Rochdale consumer co-operatives in Australia overcame the lack of a co-operative wholesaler by combining the Rochdale model with franchising. As in France and Canada, while the established consumer co-operatives were facing decline, a small number of local food co-operatives developed that focused on local and organic food such as Alfalfa House in Sydney (Patmore and Balnave, 2018, pp. 175, 207–209).

The ICA's international standing expanded in the decades following the Second World War. The ICA's Relief Fund assisted refugees and the rebuilding of the co-operative movements in Germany, Italy and Austria. While the Cold War produced tensions and distrust within the ICA over the issues of political neutrality and democratic autonomy, the ICA began to expand geographically with a development fund established in May 1953 to promote co-operation and bilateral links established with developing countries, particularly in Asia and Africa. By 1960, the number of non-European countries exceeded the number of European countries for the first time. It also further extended beyond consumer co-operatives with the admission of housing and fishing co-operative federations and greater coverage of agricultural and financial co-operatives. The ICA set up its first regional office for Southeast Asia in New Delhi, India, in

1960, and in 1968 it established its first African regional office in Moshi, Tanzania. The ICA shifted its headquarters in 1982 from London to Geneva, which was near the ILO and a center of United Nations (UN) activity (Patmore and Balnave, 2018, pp. 177–178, 214).

Conclusion

Consumer co-operatives arose from the inequities of the industrial revolution in the UK, with workers concerned over the quality and price of the food and the need to circumvent company stores. While the issues of quantity and price have remained an important issue for the formation of consumer co-operatives, they also became part of a movement that addressed the market failures of the capitalist system and even promoted an alternative vision of modern society – the Co-operative Commonwealth. The CWS in the UK highlights how consumer co-operatives can expand their activities to include wholesaling, manufacturing, banking, insurance and international trade as well as the promotion of co-operative ideal through the CU and the WCG. The spread of the consumer co-operative movement throughout the world and the formation of the ICA signifies the value of consumer co-operatives in a range of national political and economic contexts.

While the consumer co-operative movement successfully spread throughout the world, there were tensions. There were concerns about whether consumer co-operatives should engage in politics as this could undermine their broad appeal, with the consumer co-operatives aligning with socialist parties in France, Belgium and Finland, for instance, and the consumer co-operatives forming their own political party in the UK to fight opposition from private retailers. The notion of 'consumer sovereignty', whereby consumers rather than workers played a dominant role in consumer co-operatives and their economic activities, became the ethos of the CWS influenced by failures of producer co-operatives. Finally, while consumer co-operatives faced challenges in the postwar period in terms of competition from other retailers, their decline was not inevitable as some consumer co-operative movements such as Italy and Japan thrived. Further, continued market failures in terms of retailers failing to meet the growing consumer environmental concerns led to the growth of local food co-operatives in Australia, Canada and France. The next chapter will focus on the US consumer co-operative movement against the background of these international developments.

Notes

1 *The Co-operator*, 1 May 1828, p. 1.
2 *The Co-operative Magazine and Monthly Herald*, June 1826, pp. 194–199, July 1826, pp. 226–227.

3 *Empire*, 26 August 1858, p. 3.
4 *Monthly Labor Review* (hereafter *MLR*), August 1944, p. 309.
5 *MLR*, August 1944, p. 320.
6 *MLR*, April 1941, pp. 901, 908–909.
7 *MLR*, April 1941, pp. 901, 905, August 1944, p. 321.

References

Aschhoff, G. and Henningston, E., 1986, *The German Co-operative System. Its History, Structure and Strength*, Frankfurt am Main, Fritz, Knapp, Verlag.

Bamfield, J., 1998, "Consumer-Owned Community Flour and Bread Societies in the Eighteenth and Early Nineteenth Centuries," *Business History*, 40 (4), pp. 16–36.

Battilani, P., Balnave, N. and Patmore, G., 2015, "Consumer Co-operatives in Australia and Italy," In Jensen, A., Patmore, G., and Tortia, E., eds., *Cooperative Enterprises in Australia and Italy. Comparative analysis and theoretical insights*, Florence, Firenze University Press, pp. 57–73.

Birchall, J., 1994, *Co-op: the people's business*, Manchester, The University of Manchester Press.

Birchall, J., 1997, *The international co-operative movement*, Manchester, The University of Manchester Press.

Birchall, J., 2011, *People-Centered Businesses. Co-operatives, Mutuals and the Idea of Membership*, Houndsmills, Palgrave Macmillan.

Christiansen, N.F., 2012, "Denmark's road to modernity and welfare: The co-operative way," In Hilson, M., Markkola, P., and Östman, A., eds., *Co-operatives and the Social Question. The co-operative movement in northern and eastern Europe, c. 1880–1950*, Cardiff, Welsh Academic Press, pp. 25–40.

Cole, G.D.H., 1944, *A Century of Co-operation*, Manchester, CU.

Delom, B., 1943, "The Co-operative Movement in Argentina", In ILO, ed., *The Co-operative Movement in the Americas. An International Symposium*, Montreal, ILO, pp. 41–44.

Digby, M., 1948, *The World Co-operative Movement*, London, Hutchinson's University Library.

Durr, A., 1988, "William King of Brighton: Co-operation's Prophet?", In Yeo, S., ed., *New Views of Co-operation*, London, Routledge, pp. 10–26.

Earle, J., 1986, *The Italian Cooperative Movement. A Portrait of the Lega Nationale delle Cooperative e Mutue*, London, Allen & Unwin.

Ekberg, E., 2012, "Confronting three revolutions: Western European consumer co-operatives and their divergent development," *Business History*, 54 (6), pp. 1004–1021.

Eklund, E., 2007, "Retail Co-operatives as a Transnational Phenomenon: Exploring the composition of Australian colonial society and culture," *Journal of Australian Colonial History*, 9, pp. 127–145.

Friberg, K., 2017, "A Co-operative Take on Free Trade: International Ambitions and Regional Initiatives in International Co-operative Trade", In Hilson, M., Neunsinger, S., and Patmore, G., eds., *A Global History of Consumer Co-operation since 1850: Movements and Businesses*, Leiden, Brill, pp. 201–225.

Furlough, E., 1991, *Consumer Co-operation in France. The Politics of Consumption, 1834–1930*, Ithaca, Cornell University Press.

Gide, C., 1922, *Consumers' Co-operative Societies*, New York, Alfred A Knopf.

Graff, M., Kenwood, A.G. and Loughheed, A.L., 2013, *Growth of the International Economy, 1820–2015*, New York, Routledge.

Grubel, P., 1999, "The Consumer Co-op in Japan: Building Democratic Alternatives to State Led Capitalism," In Furlough E., and Strikwerda C., eds., *Consumers against Capitalism? Consumer Co-operation in Europe, North America and Japan, 1840–1990*, Lanham, MD, Rowman and Littlefield, pp. 303–330.

Hallsworth, A., and Bell, J., 2003 "Retail Change and the United Kingdom Co-operative Movement – New Opportunity Beckoning?" *The International Review of Retail, Distribution and Consumer Research*, 13 (3), pp. 301–315.

Heaton, H., 1936, *Economic History of Europe*, New York, Harper & Brothers.

Hilson, M., 2017, "Consumer Co-operation in the Nordic Countries, c. 1860–1939," In Hilson, M., Neunsinger, S., and Patmore, G., eds., *A Global History of Consumer Co-operation since 1850: Movements and Businesses*, Leiden, Brill, pp. 121–144.

Hyung-Mi, K., 2017, "The Experience of the Consumer Co-operative Movement in Korea: Its Break off and Rebirth," In Hilson, M., Neunsinger, S., and Patmore, G., eds., *A Global History of Consumer Co-operation since 1850: Movements and Businesses*, Leiden, Brill, pp. 353–378.

Krasheninnikov, A.I., 1988, *The International Co-operative Movement. Past, Present and Future*, Moscow, Centrosoyus.

Kurimoto, A., 2003, "The Institutional Change and Consumer Co-operation: Japanese vs. European Models", In Amsab-Institute of Social History, ed., *Consumerism versus Capitalism? Co-operatives Seen from an International Comparative Perspective*, Ghent, Amsab-Institute of Social History, pp. 53–75.

Kurimoto, A., 2010, "Evolution and Characteristics of Japanese-style Consumer Co-ops," In Consumer Co-operative Institute of Japan, ed., *Toward Contemporary Co-operative Studies: Perspectives from Japan's Consumer Co-ops*, Tokyo, Consumer Co-operative Institute of Japan, pp. 3–26.

Kurimoto, A., 2017, "Building Consumer Democracy: The Trajectory of Consumer Co-operation in Japan," In Hilson, M., Neunsinger, S., and Patmore, G., eds., *A Global History of Consumer Co-operation since 1850: Movements and Businesses*, Leiden, Brill, pp. 668–697.

Lambersens, S., Artis, A., Demoustier, D. and Mélo, A., 2017, "History of Consumer Co-operatives in France: From the Conquest of Consumption by the Masses to the Challenge of Mass Consumption," In Hilson, M., Neunsinger, S., and Patmore, G., eds. *A Global History of Consumer Co-operation since 1850: Movements and Businesses*, Leiden, Brill, pp. 99–120.

MacPherson, I., 1979, *Each for All: A History of the Co-operative Movement in English Canada, 1900–1945*, Toronto, Macmillan

MacPherson, I., 1999, "Of Spheres, Perspectives, Cultures and Stages: The Consumer Co-operative Movement in English-Speaking Canada, 1830–1980," In Furlough, E., and Strikwerda, C., eds., *Consumers against Capitalism? Consumer Co-operation in Europe, North America and Japan, 1840–1990*, Lanham, MD, Rowman and Littlefield, pp. 331–357.

MacPherson, I., 2017, "Patterns, Limitations and Associations: The Consumer Co-operative Movement in Canada, 1828 to the Present," In Hilson, M.,

Neunsinger, S., and Patmore, G., eds., *A Global History of Consumer Co-operation since 1850: Movements and Businesses*, Leiden, Brill, pp. 431–455.

Neunsinger, S. and Patmore, G., 2017, "Conclusion: Consumer Co-operatives Past, Present and Future", In Hilson, M., Neunsinger, S., and Patmore, G., eds., *A Global History of Consumer Co-operation since 1850: Movements and Businesses*, Leiden, Brill, pp. 729–751.

Parker, F.E., and Cowan, H.I., 1944, *Cooperative Associations in Europe and their Possibilities for Post-War Reconstruction*, Bulletin No. 770, Washington DC, US Department of Labor.

Patmore, G. and Balnave, N., 2018, *A Global History of Co-operative Business*, Abingdon (UK), Routledge.

Potter, B., 1891, *The Co-operative Movement in Great Britain*, London, Swan Sonnenschein.

Prinz, M., 2003, "The Structure and Scope of Consumer Co-operation in the 20th Century Germany in the English Mirror," In Amsab-Institute of Social History, ed., *Consumerism versus Capitalism? Co-operatives seen from an International Comparative Perspective*, Ghent, Amsab-Institute of Social History, pp. 15–50.

Prinz, M., 2017, "German Co-operatives: Rise and Fall 1850–1970," In Hilson, M., Neunsinger, S., and Patmore, G., eds., *A Global History of Consumer Co-operation since 1850: Movements and Businesses*, Leiden, Brill, pp. 243–266.

Purvis, M., 1986, "Co-operative retailing in England, 1835–1850: developments beyond Rochdale," *Northern History*, 22 (1), pp. 198–215.

Purvis, M., 1998a, "Societies of Consumers and Consumer Societies: Co-operation, Consumption and Politics in Britain and Continental Europe *c.* 1850–1920," *Journal of Historical Geography*, 24 (2), pp. 147–169.

Purvis, M., 1998b, "Stocking the Store: Co-operative Retailers in North-East England and Systems of Wholesale Supply circa 1860–1877," *Business History*, 40 (4), pp. 55–78.

Redfern, P., 1913, *The Story of the CWS. The Jubilee History of the Co-operative Wholesale Society Limited. 1863–1913*, Manchester, CWS.

Redfern, P., 1938, *The New History of the CWS*, London, J.M. Dent & Sons.

Rhodes, R., 1995, *The International Co-operative Alliance During War and Peace. 1910–1950*, Geneva, ICA

Robertson, N., 2009, "Co-operation: The Hope of the Consumer? The Co-operative Movement and Consumer Protection, 1914–1960," In Black, L., and Robertson, N., eds., *Consumerism and the Co-operative Movement in Modern British History. Taking Stock*, Manchester, Manchester University Press, pp. 222–239.

Secchi, C., 2017, "Affluence and Decline: Consumer Co-operatives in Postwar Britain," In Hilson, M., Neunsinger, S., and Patmore, G., eds., *A Global History of Consumer Co-operation since 1850: Movements and Businesses*, Leiden, Brill, pp. 527–547.

Shaffer, J., 1999, *Historical Dictionary of the Co-operative Movement*, Scarecrow Press, Lanham, MD, USA.

Strikwerda, C., 1999, "Alternative Visions and Working Class Culture: The Political Economy of Consumer Co-operation in Belgium, 1860–1980," In Furlough, E., and Strikwerda, C., eds., *Consumers against Capitalism?*

Consumer Co-operation in Europe, North America and Japan, 1840–1990, Lanham, MD, Rowman and Littlefield, pp. 67–91.

Takamara, I., 1995, *Principles of Co-operative Management*, Kobe, Co-op Kobe.

Thompson, D.J., 2012, *Weavers of Dreams. Founders of the Modern Co-operative Movement*, 2nd ed., Davis, CA, Twin Pines Press.

Thornes, R., 1988, "Change and Continuity in the Development of Co-operation, 1827–1844," In Yeo, S., ed., *New Views of Co-operation*, London, Routledge, pp. 27–51.

Vuotto, M., Verbeke, G. and Caruana, M., 2017, "Consumer Co-operation in a Changing Economy: The Case of Argentina," In Hilson, M., Neunsinger, S., and Patmore, G., eds., *A Global History of Consumer Co-operation since 1850: Movements and Businesses*, Leiden, Brill, pp. 481–506.

Wilson, J., 1995, *British Business History, 1720–1994*, Manchester, Manchester University Press.

Wilson J., Webster A. and Vorberg-Rugh R., 2013, *Building Co-operation. A Business History of the Co-operative Group*, 1863–2013, Oxford, Oxford University Press.

3 Consumer Co-operatives in the US before 1993

This chapter looks at the fortunes of the broader consumer co-operative movement in the US until the demise of the CCB in 1993 to provide a broader picture of the CCB experience. It examines the history of the US consumer co-operatives in terms of three periods. It will first look at the various experiments with consumer co-operatives during the nineteenth century. This paper then explores the first half of the twentieth century when the consumer co-operative movement reached its peak in the US. The final section of the paper focuses on the developments from the end of the Second World War until the early 1990s, when the established consumer co-operative movement went into decline. There was a slight resurgence of consumer co-operatives in the late 1960s and 1970s, arising from the protest movement on a range of issues, including the Vietnam War and the environment. While the US consumer co-operatives did not become a dominant player in US retailing, they did capture support as part of a broader co-operative movement of three Presidents and fluctuating support from the labor movement. Consumer co-operatives played an important role in certain communities and regions of the US. They gained a national profile through organizations such as the Co-operative League of the USA (CLUSA) and the National Co-operatives Inc. (NC).

The Nineteenth Century

The interest in the notion of co-operation first appeared in the US in the 1820s. Against the background of an economic depression and a general economic collapse with the panic in 1819, Cornelius Blatchley, a Quaker pharmacist, in 1822 advocated the idea of co-operation to transform society and achieve social justice. Blatchley, strongly influenced by the experiences of religious communes such as the Shakers, Harmony and the Moravian Brotherhood, founded the Society for Promoting Communities in New York in 1820. He drew upon the ideas of Owen and invited Owen to the US. Owen saw the US in the wake of the American Revolution as being a more favorable location for the values of liberty and equality that underpinned his beliefs and he gained a favorable reaction when he gave speeches at the House of Representatives in Washington DC (Curl, 2012, pp. 37, 284, 286; Hillquit, 1971, p. 54; Oved, 1987, p. 109).

Owen in 1825 founded New Harmony in Indiana as an example of a co-operative community. Over 900 people, mainly urban workers, settled on 20,000 acres, which included farm land, a co-operative silk factory, woolen mill, brickyard, distillery, oil mill and die works. Members of the co-operative had to balance debits from the community store with work credits on an annual basis (Curl, 2012, pp. 36–37, 287). Individuals could only join if they had the majority support of an assembly of members. The community's land was held in perpetuity and could not be sold to outsiders, with anyone leaving the community receiving compensation for any real estate they purchased at a value to be determined by the community. There were efforts to influence behavior through, for example, a ban on the sale of alcohol in the community and members could be "dismissed" from the community for "misconduct" and "idleness."[1]

Owen's ideas and New Harmony received nationwide publicity, with Owen embarking on US national speaking tours. There were at least nine other similar communities in the US formed along similar lines, such as Valley Forge in Pennsylvania and Franklin in New York. One notable co-operative community was Nashoba in Tennessee, a slave state, founded in 1825 on 2,000 acres of land. Frances Wright, a Scottish-born early suffragist (Hillquit, 1971, p. 66), was critical of the then US ideal that all men were "born free and equal," particularly in relation to its "citizens of colour."[2] Wright applied Owen's ideas to the liberation of black slaves, viewing the co-operative communities as an alternative to a violent uprising, and freed slaves living in the community. These mixed communities of black and white would produce for their common needs and use surpluses to found new colonies and liberate more slaves (Curl, 2012, pp. 37, 286–287, 295).

Owen tried to make New Harmony into a more democratic community, with each member receiving benefits as per need rather than receiving benefits as per the work performed. This sparked conflict among the diverse range of members, which included urban workers and middle-class intellectuals, and New Harmony split into at least five groups and the experiment failed by 1827. Capital was an issue with banks generally owning the land and the members having to pay a large mortgage. A further economic downturn in 1828–1829 depressed wages and restricted credit, making it difficult for workers to establish more co-operatives. With the demise of New Harmony, the movement dissipated with all the co-operative communities eventually collapsing. Nashoba, which succeeded for three years and resisted hostility from local racists, was unable to meet its land payments to the bank as the economy worsened (Curl, 2012, pp. 287–289, 295). While Owen left for England and returned briefly to the US on three further occasions after the failure of New Harmony, his son Robert Dale Owen stayed in the US and continued to promote his fathers' ideas through publications such as the *Free Inquirer*, which he published with Frances Wright. Robert Dale Owen went on to serve two terms in the US Congress and drafted legislation under which the Smithsonian Institution in Washington was established (Hillquit, 1971, pp. 54–56).

There was some early interest in consumer co-operatives in the US. Robert Owen's store at New Harmony was an early example of a co-operative store, with time credits for work performed in the form of labor notes being exchanged for goods at the store. Joseph Warren, who lived at New Harmony, organized a similar store in Cincinnati, Ohio, known as the 'Time Store' in 1827, but closed despite some success three years later. There were also stores established in Philadelphia and New York in 1829, with one of the latter organizers being Bryan, a former storekeeper of the Brighton Co-operative in England and a disciple of King. Bryan continued to correspond with his compatriots in Brighton and encouraged their children to come to the US. The New York co-operative never had more than 40 members and had collapsed by 1830 (Curl, 2012, pp. 37–38; Parker, 1956, p. 3; Thompson, 2012, p. 14).

There was a resurgence of interest in consumer co-operatives in the 1840s. John Kaulback, a Boston tailor and member of the New England Association of Mechanics, promoted the idea of a buying club to procure basic goods in 1844 to increase attendance at Association meetings. This led to a store being opened in 1845 and ultimately the formation in January 1847 of the Workingmen's Protective Store, which had 12 stores. While the founders knew little about Rochdale principles, there was adherence to the principles of equal voting and cash sales. The movement by October 1852 had become the New England Protective Union, covering both farmers and workers, with 403 stores. There was even a Protective Store wholesaler, called the Central Agency. These Protective Stores declined in the face of internal discord, competition from non-cooperative retailers and the disruption arising from the US Civil War. However, three of these stores were still in operation in 1888 (Patmore, 2017, p. 508).

The ideas of the Rochdale movement began to attract interest in the US from the 1850s. One significant influence was the work of Holyoake, whose pamphlet entitled *Self-Help by the People: History of Co-operation in Rochdale* was first produced in a summary form in the *New York Tribune* before the Civil War. US co-operators saw advantages regarding the Rochdale approach. While the Protective Union approach relied on membership fees, the Rochdale consumer co-operatives accumulated capital through the sale of shares to members. There were an estimated 100 stores opened for business during the Civil War, with many of them drawing from the Rochdale principles (Leikin, 2005, pp. 205–206).

Following the Civil War, there were movements among farmers and workers, which encouraged consumer co-operatives. In rural areas, railway construction assisted the development of agriculture and settlement, allowing farmers and their co-operatives access to wholesalers and manufacturers. The Patrons of Husbandry or the Grange Movement, which was founded in Washington DC in December 1867, aimed to remove middlemen and bring consumers, farmers and manufacturers into "direct and friendly relations." They became strongly influenced by the Rochdale principles and there were reciprocal visits by the CWS and the Grange between 1874 and 1876. While the Grange unsuccessfully explored the idea of setting up an Anglo-American Co-operative Company to provide for the reciprocal trade of US agricultural goods for CWS manufactured goods, the Grange sponsored Rochdale co-operative stores and they spread throughout New England, the Midwest, the South and across to the Pacific Coast. Their efforts at co-operation spread to manufacturing, grain elevators, banking and insurance. There were issues relating to the insistence on cash transfers, with farmer members withdrawing because of the failure to provide credit. Where credit was given, this created serious financial liabilities for the co-operatives. There were also problems attracting immigrant farmers and objections to extension of membership beyond farmers who worked their own land. While some stores continued to operate, the Grange movement had lost its momentum by the mid-1880s (Keillor, 2000, pp. 38–39; Knapp, 1969, pp. 51–54; Parker, 1956, pp. 10–15; Vale, 1966).

There were also labor organizations that encouraged co-operatives such as the Knights of St. Crispin and the Knights of Labor. While the focus of the Knights of Labor shifted from 1884 to a "co-operative industrial system," its 1878 constitution called for "distributive co-operatives." By 1883, the Knights of Labor had organized between 50 and 60 co-operative stores. While they operated generally on Rochdale principles, they were closed organizations that admitted and traded only with members of the Knights. Stores were organized particularly in towns where the only retailer was a company store. While the Knights of Labor collapsed in the 1890s, some of its co-operative stores continued to operate (Parker, 1956, pp. 15–21).

Another organization that encouraged consumer co-operatives was the 'labor exchange' movement, which began in Missouri in 1889. Members were asked to bring any "product of labor" such as a handicraft to the labor exchange, where they would receive a check for its estimated wholesale value. The check could be used to buy any article on display, such as food, clothing and home wares. While the national leadership of movement opposed conventional co-operation, these exchanges developed into Rochdale consumer co-operatives in California and Washington State. The labor exchange, organized in Dos Palos, California, in 1896, became the Dos Palos Rochdale Co. in 1899, remaining in business until 1920 (Parker, 1956, p. 22).

There was an attempt to establish a national body for co-operatives in the 1890s. Cooperatives formed the Co-operative Union of America in September 1895 at Cambridge, Massachusetts, to act as an educational and coordinating body for local co-operatives. The Co-operative Union joined the ICA and issued a newspaper. It only had 14 members in the North-Eastern US and faced financial difficulties. Following the dissolution of the Cambridge Co-operative Association, which was its major sponsor, it collapsed in 1899 (Parker, 1956, pp. 23–24).

While the broader attempts to establish consumer co-operatives failed in the nineteenth century, there were a number of independent consumer co-operatives in various locations that operated for varying periods. The Union Co-operative Association No. 1 in Philadelphia, the first known co-operative store in the US based on Rochdale principles, was organized in December 1862, with its first store opening in April 1864 with 23 members. Thomas Phillips, one of the founders, obtained directly from the Rochdale Pioneers in England their constitution and other relevant documents. The Co-operative increased the number of stores from one to three, but membership and sales did not match the expansion's expenditure, and the store closed in November 1866. More successful was the Philadelphia Industrial Co-operative Society, also based on Rochdale principles, which operated from 1874 to 1890. The Lonaconing Co-operative in a western Maryland coalfield operated from 1874 to 1921, when an economic downturn led members to dissolve the co-operative, with each member receiving the full value of their shares plus a bonus of 20 percent. On the Pacific Coast, the first consumers' co-operative in California was organized in San Francisco in 1867 called the Co-operative Union Store, but only lasted a short time (Parker, 1956, p. 29; Patmore, 2017, p. 510).

Despite some local successes, the future of consumer co-operatives in the US did not look very promising at the end of the nineteenth century. Edward Bemis (1895, p. 377), from the University of Chicago, in a report on the US to the first ICA Congress in August 1895 noted, "there are probably ten failures to one success, and even the successful organizations, with few exceptions, are not growing much." Bemis (1895, p. 377) further stated that the "lack of the co-operative spirit, the stimulus to individualism, the migratory character of our people, and the failure thus far to appreciate the importance of small economies, probably account for the weakness of distributive co-operation in America." Limited data from the US Bureau of Labor Statistics indicates that there were only 96 consumer co-operatives in 23 US states in 1900. Of these, they were primarily found in Massachusetts (20), Kansas (10), Minnesota (10), California (6) and Texas (6). While there was a move to establish a co-operative wholesaler in California, there were no co-operative wholesalers or federations elsewhere. Consumer co-operatives tended to run their own small retail business with virtually no contact with other co-operatives (Parker, 1956, pp. 34–35).

1900–1945

There were fluctuations of interest in US consumer co-operatives during the first half of the twentieth century. There was a gradual expansion of interest in co-operatives between 1900 and 1910. There was criticism of the high prices set by monopolies. Socialist and farmer groups promoted them as means to redressing injustice end eliminating waste. The movement, however, remained uncoordinated with 343 co-operatives in 1905, 138 in the Midwest and 98 in the far west of the US. One example of enthusiasm for retail co-operatives was the Pacific Coast Co-operative Union formed in November 1899 at Oakland, California, to study and promote co-operative ideas. It purchased a small warehouse in San Francisco and renamed it the Rochdale Wholesale Company. New stores averaged 9 per year, and by 1906, there were almost 100 throughout California. Attempts to co-ordinate wholesaling operations did not produce good financial results and by 1913, fewer than 30 of the co-operative stores remained. There was a further attempt to revive interest with the formation in 1913 of the Pacific Co-operative League (PCL), which encouraged consumer co-operatives through the establishment of buying clubs. Stores could only be established if they met certain capital and membership requirements. The Rochdale Wholesale Company eventually became a subsidiary of the PCL. Another organization called the Right Relationship League (RRL), which was formed in Minneapolis in 1905 and organized on a regional basis, encouraged locals to get enough members and capital and then buy an existing store to eliminate start-up costs and not increase the level of competition. The owner of the old store generally became the manager. By January 1908, the RRL had 47 stores located in western Wisconsin and Minnesota. There were financial management issues and the League discontinued operations in 1915 (Patmore, 2017, pp. 511–512).

One particularly notable feature of this period was the role of ethnic groups such as the Finns in Michigan, Minnesota and Wisconsin in actively promoting co-operation. While there were political differences within the American Finn community, they were more radical than most other immigrant communities and strongly influenced by socialist ideals. They arrived too late to obtain the best homestead land and were further radicalized through having to find work in mines and lumber camps. They played an active role in strikes such as the Mesabi Iron Range strike in 1907, which led to many of them being blacklisted and forced to farm marginal land to survive. An example of a Finnish co-operative was the Farmers' Co-operative Company, which was founded at Hancock Michigan in 1914 following their participation in a copper mining strike. Finns formed the Co-operative Central Exchange (CCE), a Wisconsin-based wholesaler, in 1917. One of the long-term issues for these co-operatives was the replacement of Finnish by English as the language of co-operative business as more non-Finns joined them (Patmore, 2017, p. 512).

While there were some problems with the survival of co-operatives at the local level, there were continued efforts to establish a national organization that could co-ordinate co-operatives. Dr. James and Agnes Warbasse held a meeting in their Brooklyn home in January 1916 that launched CLUSA to promote co-operative education and bring together the co-operative movement. James Warbasse was President of the League from 1916 to 1941 and Agnes served as educational director from 1916 to 1928. Early CLUSA leaflets warned against the dangers of co-operatives giving credit to their members and warned co-operative members of the pitfalls of shopping at other stores to obtain cheap bargains for future financial health of the co-operative.[3] CLUSA published *The Co-operative Consumer* and organized its first national conference in September 1918 that attracted 185 delegates from 386 co-operatives. CLUSA joined the ICA in 1921 and in 1922 adopted the Circle Pines or Twin Pines seal, showing two pines surrounded by a circle (Parker, 1956, pp. 56–58,108; Warbasse, 1936, p. 16).[4]

The establishment and growth of CLUSA was assisted by the impact of the First World War. The co-operatives also found support from both unions and farmers. Unions were particularly concerned about rising prices, profiteering and a declining standard of living. The American Federation of Labor (AFL) at its November 1916 Convention appointed a committee to investigate co-operatives, which reaffirmed its support for co-operation at the AFL 1917 Convention and called for the appointment of a lecturer for one year to promote consumer co-operatives. While affiliates did not provide sufficient funds for the appointment of the lecturer, the AFL lobbied the federal government to exempt co-operatives from income tax on accumulated savings (Patmore, 2017, pp. 512–513).

Unionists played a key role in organizing co-operatives between 1917 and 1922. Coalminers and railway workers were particularly active in organizing consumer co-operatives, with very successful co-operatives being formed by the United Mine Workers in Illinois, Ohio and Pennsylvania. In 1918, Seattle workers formed the Seattle Consumers Co-operative Association, which claimed 1,460 members, eight grocery stores, a coal yard and two tailor shops in October 1919. Financial management issues and inadequate capitalization aided its demise in 1920. There was also a push toward co-operative wholesaling, with five regional wholesalers being organized between 1915 and 1919 and a National Co-operative Wholesale Association being formed in 1919. The high point of interest in co-operatives was the Farmer-Labor Conference held in Chicago in November 1919, which brought together representatives from farm organizations, unions and co-operatives. It adopted a National Co-operative Manifesto and appointed a joint board for developing co-operatives. A second conference in February 1920 aimed to bring together co-operative consumers and eliminate speculators. The All-American Co-operative Commission was formed at these conferences, but failed to gain endorsement from the AFL and received a lukewarm response from CLUSA. Despite this, it is estimated that there were 2,200 consumer co-operatives in active operation by the end of 1920 (Frank, 1994, pp. 145–152; Patmore, 2017, p. 513).

Despite the optimism at the end of the First World War, the consumer co-operatives faced major challenges during the 1920s. There was a postwar economic recession, which had a devastating impact on Seattle's co-operatives according to Frank (1994, p. 145). Unions faced increased challenges in an increasingly anti-union environment, with employers establishing company unions to supplement bona fide unions (Patmore, 2016, ch. 4). There were also scandals involving bogus co-operatives, whereby private promoters used co-operatives as a means of obtaining money for their own purposes, and disillusionment among organized workers with the number of co-operative failures. Even when prosperity returned in the mid-1920s, consumers were turning to installment plans or hire purchase to buy goods and co-operative store members demanded more access to credit, forcing co-operatives to increase their financial liabilities (Consumer's League of New York, 1922, pp. 16–18; Parker, 1956, pp. 93–99).

Against this background, there was a decline in the number of the co-operatives and the general collapse of co-operative wholesaling in the early 1920s. Many regional wholesalers and the National Co-operative Wholesale Association went into liquidation, as did many of the local co-operatives associated with them. The PCL in California, for example, had developed by 1921 into a total of 47 societies in California, New Mexico, Nevada and Arizona with a membership of approximately 15,000. There were criticisms of the PCL for being centralized and too autocratic, with ultimate power resting in the hands of three individuals. Only 20 percent of the business of the local co-operatives was being channeled through the PCL. There was a drive to raise $50,000 to overcome financial liabilities and a new body, the Pacific League Co-operative Stores (PLCS), was organized to act as operating manager of the whole chain. The PLCS, however, breached the Rochdale principles by having voting according to the number of shares, with the three leading individuals of the PCL becoming trustees of the PLCS and given 51 percent of the total stock for past services. Controversy led to the PLCS' permit to do business being revoked and going into bankruptcy in February 1922 (Parker, 1956, pp. 81–89). While some local co-operatives did continue to trade for a short period, the bankruptcy of the PCL destroyed "most of the co-operative activity" in California (Neptune, 1977, p. 6).

By 1930, it was estimated that there were approximately 1,800 distributive co-operatives in the US, of which 1,400 were general and grocery stores. Other distributive co-operatives included petrol stations, bakeries and restaurants. The movement was strongest in Minnesota, Michigan and Wisconsin, which reflected the influence of immigrant groups such as the Finns. The second strongest region was the North-East, with the New England states, New York and New Jersey. There was a negligible presence of consumer co-operatives in California, following the collapse of the PCL, and the Southern States. There were also four regional co-operative wholesalers. CLUSA continued to promote the co-operative movement's general interests (Long, 1930, pp. 53–54).

The co-operative movement faced both political and economic challenges during the 1930s Depression. There had been Communist interest since 1921 in capturing the co-operative movement, but Warbasse was opposed to Communism and strictly followed the Rochdale principle of political neutrality. The issue came to a head at the 1930 CLUSA Congress, after a Communist organizer openly attacked Warbasse and CLUSA, and the Communist delegates withdrew not only from the Congress but also from the co-operative movement. While there were some splits at a regional level and some co-operatives joined the Communists, the bulk of the co-operative movement remained committed to the principle of political neutrality. In Wisconsin, the CCE, whose BD had rejected a Communist Party request for funds, responded to the Communists by altering its name to the Central Co-operative Wholesale (CCW), changing its label from the red star to the twin pines and encouraging non-Finns to join. The Communists formed their own wholesaler, the Workers' and Farmers' Co-operative Unity Alliance (WFCUA). While by 1934 the CCW had 34 stores in Wisconsin, the WFCUA only had 4 (CLUSA, 1932, pp. 31–32; Keillor, 2000, p. 311; Knupfer, 2013, pp. 22–23; Parker, 1937, p. 97).

Despite the wage cuts, work rationing and unemployment, the collapse of co-operatives was not as great as it was in the early 1920s, with members of some co-operatives voting to leave any surplus funds in the co-operative to ensure financial stability. Although sales fell sharply initially, sales increased by 24.3 percent in 1934 and 20.3 percent in 1935. Between 1929 and 1934, CLUSA estimated that the membership of consumer co-operatives grew 40 percent from 1929 to 1934, with its membership growing from 155 societies with 77,826 members in 1927 to 1,500 local associations and over 750,000 members in 1935. E.R. Bowen, a former sales executive for a farm machinery company, became CLUSA's chief executive on 1 January 1934, and broadened CLUSA to embrace the farmers' purchasing associations, increased publicity for the co-operative cause and improved its financial position, reducing its dependency on Warbasse's philanthropy. CLUSA also developed the Rochdale Institute, which was formed in 1937, to provide educational and business training courses (Patmore, 2017, pp. 515–516; US Department of Labor, 1940, p. 9).

The co-operative movement also consolidated its position during the early 1930s. Six regional associations combined to form NC in February

1933, a joint buying organization that became sole trade mark owner and custodian of the CO-OP label, as the first step toward a national organization. There were also new regional wholesalers formed in Texas, Washington and Illinois. There were also central associations of local co-operatives and regional federations of co-operatives, such as the Consumers Co-operative Association (CCA) in Missouri, formed to market bulk items, including petrol and developing the CO-OP label to highlight the quality of their goods, echoing the Rochdale Pioneers concern with eliminating adulteration. The co-operative movement also encouraged youth leagues and women's guilds to encourage young people and women to join the movement. African Americans in urban areas formed co-operatives in locations such as Chicago and Harlem, which was also the headquarters for Young Negroes' Co-operative Leagues. There were also external influences with a visit to the US by the Japanese Christian Co-operator Kagawa, which attracted considerable interest, and publicity surrounding the co-operative educational work of the Antigonish movement in Canada. The Great Depression generally encouraged criticism of the prevailing business system and the search for alternatives based on service rather than profit (Knapp, 1973, p. 440; Parker, 1956, pp. 155–157; Patmore, 2017, pp. 515–516).

The co-operative movement also faced favorable political support from President Roosevelt and renewed interest from the labor movement. Roosevelt set up a Consumers Advisory Board, which included Warbasse, in June 1933 to protect consumer interests under the Codes of Fair Competition of the National Industrial Recovery Act (NIRA). Roosevelt's New Deal posed an early problem for the consumer co-operatives. Under the NIRA codes, there were prohibitions against rebates and discounts as they were an unfair trade practice. Following protests from the co-operative movement, President Roosevelt issued an Executive Order on 23 October 1933 exempting all "bona fide and legitimate cooperative organization" from the code prohibitions, providing the patronage refunds were paid out of actual earnings rather than as a discount at the time of purchase (Knapp, 1973, pp. 377–378). Roosevelt also supported the broader co-operative cause by backing the 1934 Federal Credit Union Act, which recognized that credit unions had fared well during the 1930s Depression and provided an opportunity for all citizens to organize credit unions, and the establishment of the Rural Electrification Administration, which encouraged rural electricity co-operatives (Curl, 2012, p. 173; Moody and Fite, 1971, ch. 7).

Roosevelt sent a mission to Europe in July 1936 to report on co-operative developments in Europe. Roosevelt (1938, pp. 226–227) was particularly interested in co-operatives as a "middle way" in Sweden, where co-operatives "existed happily and successfully alongside private industry..." When the report of the mission was released, it was an anticlimax. While it recognized the economic and social benefits of co-operation in Europe, it doubted whether consumer co-operatives would be a panacea for the US. While there were no specific recommendations for government assistance in the report, the Mission did recommend a survey of consumer co-operatives and the establishment of an agency to assist consumer co-operatives (Knapp, 1973, p. 391).

The co-operative movement also found a renewed level of support from the trade unions. The AFL welcomed the resurgence of the consumer co-operative movement, noting the benefits of co-operatives for workers in cutting out the middleman, ensuring the quality of goods and reducing prices by minimizing waste. Bowen addressed the November 1936 AFL Convention in Tampa, Florida. The AFL published a pamphlet *An Idea Worth Hundreds of Dollars* in 1937, promoting the Rochdale principles and encouraging members to contact CLUSA. Unions at local level also played a crucial role in organizing some consumer co-operatives. In Racine, Wisconsin, Herbert Katt, a former garage proprietor and activist for the local unemployed, initiated the movement toward a consumer co-operative in July 1934. The voluntary organizing committee included unionists, and union members purchased over half the initial shares in the co-operative. The Racine Consumers' Co-operative was incorporated on 24 October 1934 and it began operations as a petrol station on 1 February 1935 with Katt as the manager. By May 1937, services to members expanded to include a coal department, a garage, groceries and home appliances such as refrigerators and washing machines. The co-operative had a benefit for the unions, in that it was a closed union shop and union wage rates were observed. The co-operative also assisted during industrial disputes through donations of petrol and food (Patmore, 2017, p. 517). While the co-operatives did receive labor support, business groups such as the Chamber of Commerce of the United States (1936, p. 3) watched the growth of consumer co-operatives with concern, noting that it was "improper for government agencies to extend preferential treatment" to them as they were "but another form of competitive force" seeking to win the patronage of consumers.

One area where the US co-operative movement differed from the UK co-operative movement was women's guilds. There were examples of active local women's guilds in Minneapolis and Waukegan, north of Chicago (Knupfer, 2013, pp. 19, 25). The Northern States Co-operative Women's Guild, which was formed in 1930, was the only guild organization in the US on a regional basis. The guilds initially had all Finnish members and were found primarily in Minnesota, Michigan and Idaho. An attempt to form a National Guild was unsuccessful and the main activity focused on the Women's Committee of CLUSA, which was established by the 1942 CLUSA Congress. There were also several co-operative women's associations that focused on co-operative education, but they were not organized along the lines of the women's guilds (Patmore, 2017, pp. 518–519).

The consumer co-operative movement on the entry of the US into the Second World War reached unprecedented levels of influence and membership. President Roosevelt continued his public support of co-operatives, praising their potential role in international postwar reconstruction through bringing relief to victims of "Axis aggression"[5] and appointing the CLUSA President to the UN Food Conference in 1943.[6] CLUSA estimated in 1942 that there were 3,100 co-operative stores in the US, with a membership of 485,000 and a total turnover of $129,650,000. There was also a major change in the CLUSA leadership. Warbasse conflicted with Bowen, particularly over the extension by Bowen of the definition of consumer co-operative to include co-operative purchasing by farmer's organizations. This change broadened the League through the inclusion of farmer wholesale co-operatives and shifted the League membership majority from industrial workers to farmers. It also led to factions built around Bowen and Warbasse. Warbasse ultimately resigned as CLUSA President in 1941. Murray Lincoln, who had a background in the farmers' distributive co-operatives and was a founder of what is now the Nationwide Insurance Group, became the new President and remained in that post until 1965 (Patmore, 2017, p. 519).

The Second World War brought forward the same opportunities and challenges for consumer co-operatives as other businesses such as labor shortages and difficulties with of obtaining goods such as gasoline. The United Co-operative Society of Manyard, Massachusetts, moved toward self-service supermarkets as a way of overcoming wartime labor shortages.[7] The co-operatives supported nation-wide rationing to ensure an equitable distribution of goods and assisted in drives for war bonds. One form of wartime consumer co-operatives that developed were transitory co-operatives in the Japanese American War Relocation Camps, which arose from President Roosevelt's Executive Order 9066 that relocated and interned all people of Japanese descent living in California, Oregon, Washington and part of Arizona, and the Civilian Public Service camps for conscientious objectors. At the War Relocation Camp at Manzanar, California, the co-operative in June 1943 had 7,150 members, with services that included a canteen, clothing shop, beauty shops and a newspaper.[8] There were also developments in wholesaling. NC, which strengthened its position as a national buying association during the War, entered manufacturing in 1943 with the purchasing of a chemical products company, which manufactured cosmetics and polishes, and a milking machine manufacturer. The CCA during 1944 purchased the National Refining Company's oil refinery at Coffeyville, Kansas.[9] By 1945, NC had taken over much of the promotional work for co-operatives that had been done formerly by CLUSA. CLUSA also gained considerable kudos for its assistance to war-ravaged Europe through a Freedom Fund and later the Co-operative for American Remittances to Europe (CARE – subsequently the E stood for Everywhere)

(Knapp, 1973, pp. 497–498, 531; Parker, 1956, pp. 166–167; Wollenberg, 2008, p. 106).[10]

The co-operatives continued growth attracted further concern in the established business community with the formation in 1943 of the well-resourced National Tax Equality Association (NTEA), which attacked co-operatives as "tax dodgers" and suggested they were "unpatriotic" (Knapp, 1973, pp. 521–525). The NTEA continued to be a major problem for the US co-operative movement after the War with one CLUSA officer in 1949 describing Vernon Scott, the executive vice-president of the NTEA, as being "the co-operative movement's worst enemy in America ...,"[11] and the NTEA producing anti-cooperative movies in the mid-1950s.[12]

From 1945 to 1993

From the high point of the 1940s, consumer co-operatives in the US, as in a number of countries such as Australia, NZ and France, generally went into decline. The postwar prosperity with its relatively low levels of unemployment and inflation removed the main economic factor that had driven individuals to form and maintain co-operatives. Co-operatives were also caught up in the immediate postwar anti-Communism in the US, which cast doubts over the loyalty of collective organizations such as co-operatives and unions to American values. CLUSA, for example, in 1959 called for recall of a high school economic textbook produced by the Council for the Advancement of Secondary Education that mentioned the role of co-operatives in the Soviet economy and even the Nazi economy, but made no reference to their roles in the US and UK economy.[13] There was also increased competition from non-cooperative chain stores, which offered consumers a wider range of goods at competitive prices without the need to wait for a dividend, but less service. Co-operatives in smaller rural communities lost business to larger regional or urban centers, where there was the volume of business to justify large supermarkets. Residents, attracted by the spread of urban advertising, had greater mobility to shop elsewhere due to the availability of automobiles and better roads. The populations of smaller rural communities grew only marginally and even declined (Patmore, 2017, pp. 520–521).

Co-operatives in larger communities managed to continue and even prosper. The Ithaca Consumer Co-operative Society (ICCS), which was established during the 1930s in a university town in upper state New York, grew to over 2,000 members during the 1950s. It opened a supermarket in 1949 and a shopping center in 1958 that expanded to include services such as a laundry, a pharmacy and a beauty salon. There was support for community organizations and the promotion of consumer education with a full-time educational director appointed in

1946.[14] However, financial issues arose from its expansion, with the co-operatives' assets and liabilities nearly equal by 1967 as members withdrew their capital. Like many consumer co-operatives, tensions increased as the co-operative grew, with membership involvement declining and the BD gaining more control. Some major decisions were taken without a membership vote such as building a shopping center. The refusal of the co-operative to support a boycott of nonunion grapes and lettuce in support of Caesar Chavez and the United Farm Workers Committee in California on the grounds of political neutrality led to the picketing of the co-operative's store and car park. The co-operative also had to pass on losses to members following declining sales in 1973 through higher prices (Knupfer, 2013, pp. 47–63).

There were new urban co-operatives such as the Harlem River Consumer Co-operative (HRCC), which opened in June 1968 in a predominately African American Manhattan neighborhood. Founder Cora Walker, a Harlem lawyer, established the co-operative to combat high prices, reject inferior products and provide more choices, particularly ethnic food, with the first 10,000 shares at $5 each being sold by teenagers going to door-to-door. The co-operative reached 4,000 members by 1971 and became the spearhead for a program to set up similar co-operatives in 26 poverty areas in New York, which were to be known collectively as the Headstart Food Co-operative and funded by the New York Community Training Institute, an anti-poverty organization. The co-operative faced major labor issues with the Local 338 of the Retail, Wholesale and Chain Store Food Employees Union over the issue of a union shop, which nearly bankrupted the co-operative and brought successful legal action by the HRCC against the union. The union agent, L. Joseph Overton, had a conflict of interest in promoting the 18-month strike with picketing to pressure the HRCC into using food products promoted by a company in which he had a financial interest, with Overton being jailed for six months and fined $10,000 (Nembhard, 2014, pp. 137–138).[15]

At the national level, CLUSA in August 1946 broadened its focus to organize all types of co-operatives including credit unions, housing co-operatives and medical co-operatives with a proposed Co-operative Federation of America. Jerry Voorhis, who lost his Californian seat in the US House of Representatives to the future US President Richard Nixon in 1946, replaced Bowen as CLUSA General Secretary in 1947 and held that office until 1967.[16] Despite its broader membership, CLUSA tried to improve the efficiency of the retail co-operatives by conducting forums on business management for the board members and managers of local co-operatives and running training institutes for consumer co-operative employees. CLUSA sponsored the formation of a professional Consumer Co-operatives Managers' Association in June 1959.[17] Co-operatives expanded the variety of CO-OP-labelled goods with CO-OP fish balls being imported from KF, the Swedish co-operative wholesaler, in 1947 and increased sales of electrical appliances, such as refrigerators and vacuum cleaners, to match growing consumer demand following the War.[18] By 1954, there were approximately 1,050 consumer co-operatives with 600,000 members and a turnover of approximately $110,000,000. The co-operative sector, however, was a small and declining sector of all food sales in the US, with their proportion of all food sales falling from 0.45 percent in 1948 to 0.28 percent in 1954. By 1969, there were only 430 stores with approximately 450,000 members. There was consolidation of co-operative wholesalers with NC merging with United Co-operatives in November 1972 to form Universal Co-operatives (CLUSA, 1954, p. vi, 1969; Patmore, 2017, p. 521).[19]

These problems occurred against the background of a weakening of the level of political and industrial support for the co-operative movement following the Second World War. There was a peak of active support by the AFL and Congress of Industrial Organizations (CIO), which later merged to form the AFL-CIO in 1955, for the co-operative movement in the late 1940s, with unions such as those covering iron ore miners and steelworkers encouraging members to join co-operatives and in a few cases providing union funds to assist co-operatives. The 1949 Convention of the American Federation of Teachers, for example, passed resolutions endorsing co-operatives and calling upon members to become active in co-operatives, while the Illinois State Federation of Labor condemned the NTEA.[20] Co-operatives reciprocated by giving aid to striking iron ore miners in Michigan, Minnesota and Wisconsin in 1946. There was continued political controversy raised particularly by the Republicans over whether co-operatives should receive aid through tax concessions and direct financial assistance. With the exception of the Democrat President Harry Truman, who was sympathetic to the co-operative movement,[21] subsequent Presidents did not champion the co-operative movement during the postwar economic boom as did Roosevelt (Patmore, 2017, p. 524; US Department of Labor, 1947, pp. 26–27).

With the end of post-prosperity in 1973 and the economic instability that followed in the 1970s and 1980s, the established consumer co-operatives began to struggle faced with inflation and high interest rates. The ICCS faced a rival co-operative, the Ithaca Real Food Co-operative (IRFC), which was founded in 1971 and whose members criticized the ICCS for failing to commit to co-operative principles or to healthy food. ICCS sales fell and Mid-Eastern Co-operatives, the wholesaler, cut off trade credit in 1975 because it could not pay its bills. Finances deteriorated and ICCS closed in 1982 (Knupfer, 2013, pp. 64–66). While the HRRC continued to trade until at least 1975, it collapsed by 1976 in the face of harsh competition from local non-cooperative chain stores (Nembhard, 2014, pp. 138–139). The collapse of the ICCS and the HRRC were overshadowed by the dissolution in 1991 of the Greenbelt Co-operative in Maryland, which had a peak membership of 116,018 in

1986 (Cooper and Mohn, 1992). A small number of co-operatives continued to operate into the early twentieth century (Patmore and Balnave, 2018, p. 280; Knupfer, 2013, p. 69), with older consumer co-operatives in Hanover, New Hampshire, and Adamant, Vermont, still operating by 2019 (Knupfer, 2013, chs. 5–6).

Amidst this decline of the older consumer co-operatives, there were some positive developments. Following lobbying from CLUSA, the Congress in 1978, with the support of Democrat President Jimmy Carter, established the federally funded National Consumer Co-operative Bank (NCCB) to provide cheap finance to co-operatives. The administration of President Ronald Reagan moved to close the NCCB as part of budget cuts, but agreed to privatize the NCCB in 1981 after the co-operatives raised close to $200,000,000 in capital for the Bank (Patmore, 2017, p. 524).[22] One of the early tasks of the NCCB was to sustain ailing consumer co-operatives such as the ICCS, which the NCCB informed in May 1981 that it was in foreclosure as it was unable to pay interest on its mortgage (Knupfer, 2013, p. 66).

Disillusionment with capitalism during the late 1960s and 1970s led to the formation of new consumer co-operatives. Protestors against the Vietnam War, environmentalists, community control advocates and civil rights activists saw co-operatives as a symbol of the counterculture. Some of these co-operatives, as in Australia, Canada and France, have been able to prosper by specifically focusing on organic foods and locally produced goods. Examples of still trading include the New Pioneer Food Co-operative in Iowa City, founded in 1971, and the Green Star Co-op in Ithaca, which incorporated the bulk item IRFC's Grain Store. Both the Ithaca and Iowa City co-operatives provide an opportunity for members to work in the store and receive a discount on their purchases. The growth of these consumer co-operatives followed the earlier pattern of establishing regional associations and then eventually forming the National Co-operative Grocers' Association (NCGA) in 1999 (Knupfer, 2013, pp. 66–67; Patmore, 2017, pp. 524–525).

Despite all the problems for the US consumer co-operatives since the Second World War, CLUSA survived. It became the National Co-operative Business Association (NCBA) in 1985 and its membership still covers all forms of co-operatives. It conducts education programs and lobbies Congress on behalf of co-operatives. In 1991, the NCBA successfully lobbied Congress to establish the Rural Co-operative Development Grants program to encourage new co-operative businesses in rural areas (Patmore, 2017, p. 525).

Conclusion

While the early US consumer co-operatives did develop their own co-operative models, the Rochdale model became the dominant form, being imported through literature and immigration. The model that evolved was based on regions with a national co-operative wholesaler and a national league to co-ordinate the co-operatives and lobby the Government. While CLUSA was initially dominated by urban co-operatives, farmer co-operatives from the 1930s became more dominant, leading to frictions within the organization. There were also long-standing issues relating to 'political neutrality', particularly in dealing with radical groups such as Communists. While there were women activists in the consumer co-operative movement such as Agnes Warbasse, the organization of women's guilds was weak and a national organization could not be sustained as in the UK.

The growth of co-operatives was linked to issues such as the deterioration of real wages and disillusionment with the prevailing economic order. Immigrant groups such as the Finns imported their radical political philosophies and encouraged co-operatives, particularly in the mid-Northern states. For varying periods, the consumer co-operatives obtained allies in the Democratic Party and the trade union movement. However, the tax concessions given to them provoked opposition in business groups such as the NTEA and the Republican Party.

The collapse of the US consumer co-operative movement in the decades after the Second World War was against the background of a less favorable political and economic climate. With the end of the Truman administration, the co-operatives had few allies at the national level until the presidency of Jimmy Carter, who at CLUSA's urging established the NCCB. The enthusiasm of the labor movement also weakened with the postwar prosperity. While there were examples of co-operatives that massively expanded such as the Greenbelt Co-operative, internal political divisions, poor management and an increasingly competitive supermarket industry contributed to their demise. While there was a burst of enthusiasm for co-operatives in the late 1960s and the 1970s it came too late to sustain the older consumer co-operatives. As noted in the previous chapter, this collapse was not inevitable, as co-operative movements in some countries were able to prosper and even reverse the decline. The next chapter will now begin the specific focus of the book on the history of the CCB.

Notes

1 *The Co-operative Magazine and Monthly Herald*, January 1826, pp. 15–16, October 1826, pp. 301–306.
2 *The Co-operative Magazine and Monthly Herald*, April 1828, p. 74.
3 Envelope, 'Co-operative League of America. Miscellaneous Pamphlets, 1916–1917'. HD 3446, United States Department of Labor Library, Washington, DC.
4 *New York Times* (*NYT*), 24 February 1957, p. 85.
5 Co-operative News League, Press Release, 27.01.1944. CLUSA, Box 47, File – 'Co-op League, Reconstruction. Folder 2.' Truman Presidential Library and Archives, Independence, Missouri, USA (TPLA).

6 *Co-op* (Chicago), April 1945, p. 17.
7 *The Co-op Messenger* (Maynard, MA), April 1943, p. 1.
8 Letter from J. Bruce to C.J. McLanahan, 9 June 1943. CLUSA, Box 58, File – 'Coop League New Service, Miscellaneous copy.' TPLA.
9 *Co-op* (Chicago), January 1945, p. 14
10 *Co-op Magazine* (Chicago), May 1946, pp. 5, 7.
11 Letter from W.J. Campbell to F. Toothill, 26 August 1949. CLUSA, Box 71, File – 'Foreign countries, England Folder 2.' TPLA.
12 *Co-op News* (*CN*), September 1956, p. 4.
13 *CN*, July-August 1959, p. 5.
14 *Co-op Magazine* (Chicago), July 1946, p. 8.
15 *NYT*, 8 February 1971, p. 25, 5 June 1971, p. 31, 14 April 1972, p. 25, 25 April 1972, pp. 1, 25, 7 June 1972, p. 4, 27.03.1972, p. 21; 'Walker, Cora T' at https://www.encyclopedia.com/education/news-wires-white-papers-and-books/walker-cora-t accessed 26 February 2018.
16 *Co-op* Magazine (Chicago), April 1947, p. 5; Letter from W.J. Campbell to G.F. Folley, 18 June 1947. CLUSA, Box 70, File – 'Foreign co-ops, International Co-operative Alliance Folder 2.' TPLA; *NYT*, 12 September 1984, p. B6. Typescript, 'Structural Chart of the Organization of the Consumer-Purchasing Co-operative Movement in the USA'. CLUSA, Box 43, File – 'Coop Congress – mimeographed material issued.' TPLA.
17 Memo from J. Voorhis, n.d., Carton 2 Folder 24. BANC MSS 90/140 c. CCB Records, UCB BL.
18 *Co-op Magazine* (Chicago), April 1947, p. 20, June 1947, p. 11, November 1947, p. 16.
19 *CN*, 16 October 1972, p. 1.
20 Secretary's Report to the BD of the Co-operative League, 15 November 1949. CLUSA, Box 46, File – 'Coop League – Board Meetings.' TPLA.
21 Letter from Harry S. Truman to Howard A. Cowden, 17 November 1949. CLUSA, Box 58, File – 'Cowden, Howard A. Folder 2.' TPLA
22 *NYT*, 14 July 1978, pp. D1, D9

References

Bemis, E.W, 1895, "The United States," In ICA, *Report of the First International Co-operative Congress Held in the Hall of the Society of Arts on 19th, 20th, 22nd, and 23rd August 1895*, London, ICA, pp. 376–381.

Chamber of Commerce of the United States, 1936, *Co-operative Enterprises Operated by Consumers*, Washington, DC, Chamber of Commerce of the United States.

Consumer's League of New York, 1922, *Consumers' Co-operatives in New York State*, New York, Consumer's League of New York, New York.

CLUSA, 1932, *Second Yearbook. The Co-operative League of the U.S. of America. A Survey of Consumers' Co-operatives in the United States 1932*, New York, CLUSA.

CLUSA, 1954, *1954 Co-op Yearbook*, Chicago, IL and Washington, DC, CLUSA.

CLUSA, 1969, *Co-operatives U.S.A. Facts and Figures 1969*, Chicago, IL, CLUSA.

Cooper, D.H. and Mohn, P.O., 1992, *The Greenbelt Co-operative: Success and Decline*, Davis, CA, Centre for Co-operatives, University of California, Davis.

Curl, J., 2012, *For All the People: Uncovering the Hidden History of Co-operation, Co-operative Movements, and Communalism in America*, 2nd ed., Oakland, CA, PM Press.

Dana Frank, 1994, *Purchasing Power. Consumer Organizing, Gender and the Seattle Labor Movement, 1919–1929*, Cambridge, Cambridge University Press.

Hillquit, M., 1971, *History of Socialism in the United States*, 5th ed., New York, Dover Publications.

Keillor, S., 2000, *Co-operative Commonwealth: Co-ops in Rural Minnesota, 1859–1939*. St. Paul, MN, Minnesota Historical Society Press.

Knapp, J.G., 1969, *The Rise of American Co-operative Enterprise 1620–1920*, Danville, IL, The Interstate Printers and Publishers.

Knapp, J.G., 1973, *The Advance of American Co-operative Enterprise: 1920–1945*, Danville, IL, Interstate Printers & Publishers, Inc.

Knupfer, A.M., 2013, *Food Co-ops in America. Communities, Consumption and Economic Democracy*, Ithaca, NY, Cornell University Press.

Leikin, S., 2005, *The Practical Utopians. American Workers and the Co-operative Movement in the Gilded Age*, Detroit, MI, Wayne State University Press.

Long, C., 1930, "Consumers' Co-operation in the United States of America," In Alanne, V.S., ed., *The First Yearbook. The Co-operative League of the U.S. of America. A Survey of Consumers' Co-operation in the United States. 1930*, New York, CLUSA, pp. 52–61.

Moody, J.C. and Fite, G.C., 1971, *The Credit Union Movement. Origins and Development, 1850–1970*, Lincoln, University of Nebraska Press.

Nembhard, J.G., 2014, *Collective Courage. A History of African American Co-operative Economic Thought and Practice*, University Park, The Pennsylvania State University Press.

Neptune, R., 1977, *California's Uncommon Markets. The Story of Consumers Co-operatives 1935–1976*, Richmond, CA, Associated Co-operatives.

Oved, Y., 1987, *Two Hundred Years of American Communes*, New Brunswick (US), Transaction Publishers.

Parker, F.E., 1937, "Consumers' Co-operation in the United States," *Annals of the American Academy of Political and Social Science*, 191 (1), pp. 91–102.

Parker, F.E., 1956, *The First 125 Years: A History of the Distributive and Service Co-operation in the United States, 1829–1954*, Superior, Wisconsin Co-operative Publishing Association.

Patmore, G., 2016, *Worker Voice. Employee Representation in the Workplace in Australia, Canada, Germany, the UK and the US 1914–1939*, Liverpool, Liverpool University Press.

Patmore, G., 2017, "Fighting Monopoly and Enhancing Democracy: A Historical Overview of US Consumer Co-operatives," In Hilson, M., Neunsinger, S., and Patmore, G., eds., *A Global History of Consumer Co-operation since 1850: Movements and Businesses*, Leiden, Brill, pp. 507–526.

Patmore, G. and Balnave, N., 2018, "Controlling Consumption: A Comparative History of Rochdale Consumer Cooperatives in Australia and the United States," In Patmore, G., and Stromquist, S., eds., *Frontiers of Labor. Comparative Histories of the United States and Australia*, Champaign, University of Illinois Press, pp. 266–286.

Roosevelt, F.D.R., 1938, *The Public Papers and Addresses of Franklin D. Roosevelt with Special Introduction and Explanatory Notes by President Roosevelt, Volume Five, The People Approve, 1936*, New York, Random House.

Thompson, D.J., 2012, *Weavers of Dreams. Founders of the Modern Co-operative Movement*, 2nd ed., Davis, CA, Twin Pines Press.

US Department of Labor, 1940, *Consumers' Co-operatives 1939*, Washington DC.

US Department of Labor, 1947, *Developments in Consumer' Co-operatives Movement in 1946*, Washington DC.

Vale, V., 1966, "An Anglo-American Co-operative Project of the 1870s: The Mississippi Valley Trading Company," *Bulletin (British Association for American Studies)*, 12/13, pp. 42–60.

Warbasse, J.P., 1936, "A Brief History of the Co-operative League of the U.S.A," In CLUSA, *Third Yearbook. The Co-operative League of the U.S. of America. A Survey of Consumer Co-operation in the United States*, Minneapolis, MN, CLUSA, pp. 19–23.

Wollenberg, C., 2008, *Berkeley. A City in History*, Berkeley, CA, University of California Press.

4 The Origins and Early Years of the Berkeley Co-operative until 1947

This chapter explores the specific context of the formation of the CCB and its early years. It examines the early history of Berkeley and then proceeds to look at the factors that assisted the establishment of the CCB during the 1930s such as Upton Sinclair and the 'End Poverty in California Movement' (EPIC) campaign in 1934 and the visit by the Japanese Christian co-operator, Toyohiko Kagawa, to the Bay Area. It traces the journey of the co-operation of Berkeley from a buyers group in 1937 to the CCB in 1939. It then explores the management of the early co-operative exploring issues such as governance, the stresses of the Second World War, early attempts to set up branch stores and the merger with the Finnish BCU in 1947. It then examines the relationship of the co-operative to its members, employees, the local community and the broader co-operative movement, particularly co-operative wholesaling.

Berkeley before 1947

The early inhabitants of Berkeley were the Huichin Indians, part of a larger Ohlone or Costanoan linguistic group that occupied the area from the Central San Francisco Bay area south to Monterey. They lived in groups of several hundred individuals in well-defined territories relying upon acorns, fish and game for food. They left their mark on the landscape with the indentations in rock formations that can still be seen in Mortar Rock Park in North Berkeley where generations of Huichin women ground seeds and nuts. Their life was disrupted with the arrival in 1769 of the Spanish, who cleared the East Bay of Indians and moved them to Mission Dolores in San Francisco. By 1820, there seems to be no more native people in present-day Berkeley. The Huichin faced a series of epidemics, including measles, cholera and smallpox that reduced their numbers, with the survivors drifting south after Mexico which had gained independence from Spain in 1821 broke up the missions in 1833. The Spanish and later the Mexican Government sent few settlers to California, and it was not until 1820 when Don Luis Peralta, who had long service with the Spanish Army, was given a land grant on the East Bay that covered Berkeley and 1841 when the first European style dwelling was built in Berkeley by his son Domingo who grazed cattle on his rancho for cattle hides and tallow to be sold in markets in the Eastern US and Britain (McCardle, 1983b, pp. 35–38; Wollenberg, 2008, pp. 1–9).

With the annexation of California by the US in 1847 and Californian gold rush, the character of Berkeley began to change with the arrival of more US citizens and other immigrants to the Bay Area. The Peraltas had to deal with squatters and continual legal challenges over their landholdings with Francis Kitteridge Shattuck, a disappointed gold seeker from upstate New York, and his partners each filing 160-acre land claims in November 1856 on what is now central Berkeley. There was also development in Ocean View or West Berkeley on Bay Shore north and south of the mouth of Strawberry Creek, where Captain James Jacobs, a Danish merchant seafarer and later gold seeker, purchased land in 1853 and built a wharf that became the commercial center of Berkeley, with a starch mill opening in 1855 and a lumberyard in 1856. There was a further boost to development in 1877 when the Central Pacific Railroad (CPRR) opened the transcontinental railway along the Berkeley shore with the first overland train in September 1878, giving the West Berkeley businesses direct access to the national railway network. Retail businesses grew along San Pablo Avenue and Western University Avenue and West Berkeley gained a post office in 1878. The population grew from 668 in 1880 to 1,544 in 1900, with a diverse working-class community that included Scandinavians, Mexicans, Irish Catholics, Germans, Chinese and a small population of African Americans (Ferrier, 1933, pp. 32–33, 116, 118–19; Jorgensen-Esmaili, 1983a, pp. 67–68; Jorgensen-Esmaili, 1983b, pp. 81–82; Wollenberg, 2008, pp. 9–23; Weis, 2004, p. 3).

While West Berkeley developed, the growth of East Berkeley was shaped by the foundation of the UCB. The origins of UCB lie in Congregationalists receiving a charter for the College of California, previously Contra Costa County Academy, in Oakland in 1855 under the presidency of Reverend Henry Durant. Durant, who saw Oakland as too rowdy a place for a liberal arts education for young gentlemen that emphasized classical studies and Christian morality, and fellow Congregationalist Reverend Samuel Willey, who had initially proposed the idea of the College, persuaded the College's Board of Trustees by the end of 1857 to purchase land five miles north of Oakland that possessed great views of the Gold Gate and water supplied by Strawberry Creek. While there was a ceremony in 1860 to dedicate the new campus at a rocky outcrop, now known as Founders Rock, the College did not have the funds required for the move from Oakland. The State of California in 1868, however, acquired the College of California, taking advantage of the federal 1862 Morrill Land College Act that provided federal land to states to fund colleges that would teach practical courses such as agriculture and engineering as well as liberal arts, as the basis for the University of California (UC), with the new campus commencing operations in 1873.

Retail businesses and housing developed around the campus, named Berkeley in 1866 after George Berkeley, the deceased English Bishop of Cloyne and early patron of college education in the US, with a railway being completed from the CPRR West Oakland depot and ferry terminal, which provided San Francisco services, to Shattuck Avenue in 1876 and Vine Street in 1878, encouraging residential and commercial development in North Berkeley. A rivalry developed between middle-class East Berkeley and working-class West Berkeley and conflicts developed over the Strawberry Creek water supply and prohibition of alcohol consumption. Residents of both communities, however, grew dissatisfied with the level of services provided by Alameda County, which had jurisdiction over unincorporated areas, and joined forces to have the City of Berkeley incorporated on 1 April 1878. By 1900, Berkeley's total population grew to 13,214 with farms and most of its streets still unpaved (Burk and Jury, 1983, pp. 133–36; Ferrier, 1933, pp. 37, 60–64; Starr, 2005, p. 108; Wollenberg, 2008, pp. 22–47).

Berkeley underwent massive growth in the first two decades of the twentieth century, reaching 40,434 in 1910 and 56,036 in 1920, with it being the fourth largest growing city in the US in the first decade of the twentieth century. Major contributors to this urbanization were the 1906 San Francisco earthquake, the Key System of urban transport and the growth of UCB. Refugees from the San Francisco earthquake fled to Berkeley and East Bay, which were relatively unaffected, with thousands staying on in Berkeley and contributing to a post-earthquake housing boom. The quake also encouraged business to move from San Francisco to Berkeley, with 37 new factories being built in the four months after the quake. The Key System arose from the consolidation of all streetcar operations in the East Bay by Francis Smith, who had earned his fortune through borax mining. He provided competition to the Southern Pacific Railroad, which acquired by lease the CPRR, by having small streetcars as feeders for an interurban train system that provided connections through a wharf at Emeryville by fast propeller-driven ferries to San Francisco. The development from 1903 of the Key System, which allowed Berkeley residents to commute to work in Oakland and San Francisco, was associated with land development in areas such as Claremont, with the Claremont Hotel resort opening in 1915, Elmwood and the north campus business district along Euclid Avenue. The Berkeley community became more complicated as it also became dormitory suburb for commuters (Trimble, 1977, pp. 25–28; Wollenberg, 2008, pp. 47–58). The number of students on the Berkeley campus grew from 2,241 in 1900 to 10,887 in 1920 (UCB Office of Vice Chancellor of Finance, 2019). This growth was associated with Benjamin Wheeler, UC President from 1899 to 1919, and Phoebe Hearst, one of its greatest benefactors and UC's first female member of the Board of Regents, which consisted largely of the Governor of California appointees and oversaw the administration of the UC. The UCB's reputation for excellence spread, with the construction of many UCB landmarks, including the Campanile, the Hearst Greek Theatre, Wheeler Hall and the Sather Gate (Manning, 1983, pp. 202–205; Wollenberg, 2008, pp. 58–63).

Alongside this urbanization, Berkeley also gained a reputation for Bohemianism in the area known as 'Nut Hill', which was a hillside area north of campus and East of Euclid Avenue, associated with individuals such as Charles Keeler, the poet and naturalist, and Bernard Maybeck, the architect. While Republicans dominated local government from 1903 to 1947, Berkeley did elect a Socialist Mayor, J. Stitt Wilson, who served from 1911 to 1913. The growth was also accompanied by the development of restrictive covenants in Berkeley, which were provisions whereby developers prevented buyers of houses from subsequently selling or renting their homes to 'undesirable' individuals, which meant Asians and African Americans, who generally lived south of Dwight Way and west of Grove Street (Burnett, 1983, pp. 279–282; Weinstein, 2008, pp. 52–72, 114; Wollenberg, 2008, pp. 64–73).

While Berkeley continued to expand during the 1920s, which saw a major fire in 1923 that destroyed 580 buildings to the north of campus and the population grew to 82,000, the city faced major challenges during the 1930s. While UCB weakened the impact of the Depression of the local economy, the industries in West Berkeley suffered and there was an increase in working-class unemployment, which increased the worker militancy and eventually led to the union organization of Berkeley's largest employers such as Colgate-Palmolive. The City attracted New Deal projects that, for example, developed Tilden Park in the hills above Berkeley, constructed the Rose Garden in Euclid Avenue and undertook major improvements in the UCB Botanical Gardens. There was a growth in student activism at UCB among a significant but vocal minority of students which championed worker rights and the anti-war movement. Harry Kingman, the director of the University Young Men's Christian Association, was crucial in establishing in 1933 the University Students' Co-operative Association (USCA), which began with 10 students sharing a small rooming house and has provided affordable student accommodation at UCB to this day. Despite efforts by the UCB to restrict freedom of speech by both staff and students, academics such as physicist J. Robert Oppenheimer supported leftist causes such as the Spanish Civil War Relief and discussed Marxism. While there was left-wing activism in Berkeley, the city voted Republican in the 1932 Presidential and the 1934 Californian Governor's elections, and in 1932 there were 10,885 registered Democrats compared to 30,073 Republicans in Berkeley. Berkeley fostered a vigilante committee that beat supporters of the 1934 San Francisco General Strike, with members of the Cal football team volunteering as strikebreakers. The liberal policies of International House at UCB, which opened in 1930, and its students from a variety of nationalities and races attracted racist criticism and even concerns about interracial marriage between male and female students (Jury, 1983, p. 340; McCardle, 1983a, p. 382; Smith, 2014, pp. 10–38; Weinstein, 2008, p. 123, Wollenberg, 2008, pp. 85, 96–103; Illustration 4.1).

The Second World War created an economic boom in Berkeley and the Bay Area, with increased demand for everything from toothpaste to shipbuilding. The military-built Camp Ashby in Berkeley for a segregated unit of African American military police and the Savo Island housing project for married personnel in South Berkeley. Labor shortages encouraged the migration of African American workers to Berkeley

Illustration 4.1 Berkeley Rose Garden, September 2019. Courtesy of Helen Warner, Photographer.

and created a crisis in housing in Berkeley, with the city council refusing to co-operate with the federal government on a public housing project as it would attract 'undesirable elements' to Berkeley. The federal government went ahead without local participation and built the Codornices Village, which was barrack-like accommodation on the Berkeley boundary with nearby Albany, with about 25 percent of the units reserved for African American families. Berkeley residents also faced extensive federal wartime regulations that included rationing and shortages of goods and services, including gasoline and meat,[1] and controls on prices, wages and rents. At UCB, enlistments led to a decline in student numbers from 17,870 in 1939 to 11,028 in 1944, with special military training programs offsetting the decline in enrolments to some degree. Oppenheimer, fellow physicist Ernst O. Lawrence, who was the first UCB academic to win a Nobel Prize, and other UCB scientists played a crucial role in nuclear research that led to the development of the atomic bomb with the Lawrence radiation laboratories being moved to their current location on the hill above the campus (UCB Office of the Vice Chancellor of Finance, 2018; Wollenberg, 2008, ch. 7).

One dark aspect of the War for Berkeley was the relocation of approximately 1,400 individuals of Japanese descent to internment camps under President Roosevelt's Executive Order 9066 between 28 April 1942 and 1 May 1942 with Kurasaburo and Kikuyu Fujii shuttering their University laundry, which was sold at a large loss, and renting out their house while interned. George Yasukochi, later a CCB employee, escaped internment with assistance of co-operative activists, by being relocated to the East where he studied at the Rochdale Institute in New York and later worked at consumer co-operatives in Chicago until he returned in 1945. Some Berkeley residents formed a Fair Play Committee to protest the internment and UC President Robert Sproul calling upon the federal government to allow Japanese Americans to finish their college education. Church groups helped find internees places to store their belongings and house their pets, which they could not take with them (BHS, 1995, pp. 8–15; Weinstein, 2008, pp. 129–131; Wollenberg, 2008, pp. 107–108; Yamada, 1983, pp. 415–421).

While Berkeley attracted a wide variety of immigrant groups by the end of the Second World War, one significant group for the development of co-operatives were the Finns, who settled in West Berkeley. While they were not a dominant part of the population, they organized visible community organizations. The Finnish population in Alameda County grew from 140 in 1900 to 1,153 in 1920, primarily from Finns moving across the Bay from San Francisco after the Finnish enclave was destroyed in the 1906 San Francisco earthquake. They either came directly from Finland or via the northern-Wisconsin-Minnesota-Michigan-area route, where, previously noted, they played an important role in establishing consumer co-operatives, to make the Berkeley Finnish community the second largest in the US. The Berkeley Finns built several Lutheran churches and the Finnish Hall, which was constructed by the Finnish Comrades Association, a radical political organization, and opened in October 1908. The local lodge of the Finnish Brotherhood, the United Kaleva Lodge of Brothers and Sisters No. 21, established in April 1911 to provide financial support in illness and death opened a hall in 1932. As elsewhere in the US, there were divisions within the Finnish community on ideological lines, with dissidents splitting in support of the Industrial Workers of the World (IWW) in 1911 and holding meetings at Holtz Hall (Mannila, 1984, p. 1; Neptune, 1977, p. 12; Watkins, 2019).

The Origins of the Berkeley Co-operative

Following the collapse of the PCL in California, co-operatives had virtually disappeared by the beginning of the Great Depression. By 1934, there were only three surviving consumer co-operatives, with one being in a timber cutting and fishing village of Fort Bragg on the Mendocino coast, where Finns formed the Fort Bragg Co-operative Mercantile Corporation in 1923. In California, there were several factors that assisted the revival of consumer co-ops in the Great Depression. In 1932, the Californian unemployed organized self-help co-operatives to trade labor for food, clothing and housing, which received federal and state financial assistance from 1933 to 1938. Upton Sinclair, the author and Democratic candidate, was inspired by the network of self-help co-operatives and barter clubs that had developed in the Los Angeles area in 1932 and 1933 and ran for Governor in 1934 on the EPIC platform. EPIC solved unemployment by taking over unused farms and disused factories and setting up self-production units where the unemployed would regain their jobs. There developed EPIC clubs throughout the State, of which there were nearly 300 by February 1934, to support the campaign. While the campaign failed in the face of a well-funded and established media-supported Republican campaign, the clubs became an outlet of dissatisfaction with the economic system and fueled the formation of buying clubs and co-operatives. Most of the EPIC buying clubs, such as New Day Co-operative in Oakland, which ceased operations in November 1935, only lasted a few weeks but provided future members and leaders for the emerging co-operative movement. There also arose from EPIC the short-lived Co-operative Councils formed in the Bay Area and Los Angeles, with the buying agency of the latter evolving into the Co-operative Wholesale Association of Southern California. CLUSA was optimistic about the developments in California and appointed a representative in that state. EPIC supporters were however unsuccessful in the Californian legislature in securing the passage of co-operative legislation (Gregory, 2015, pp. 55–56; Jones and Schneider, 1984; Neptune, 1977, pp. 11–12; Parker, 1956, p. 193; Randall and Daggett, 1936, pp. 155–170).

The visit by Japanese Christian co-operator Kagawa to the Bay Area, which was cosponsored by the Federal Council of Churches, also influenced Christians to look at co-operatives as a Christian alternative to the existing system of distribution. The trip gained a great deal of publicity, as the US Federal Health Service detained Kagawa on Angel Island in San Francisco Bay upon arrival in December 1935 because he had trachoma, an infectious eye disease, but was released following direct intervention by President Roosevelt on the condition that he be accompanied by a doctor or nurse to ensure that there was no contagion (Schildgen, 1988, pp. 182–3). A group that held regular study meetings at the First Methodist Church in Oakland decided after Kagawa's visit to focus on examining how co-operatives work and form a buying club to pool their grocery buying and reduce costs. Roy Wilson, an Alameda Methodist clergyman, from December 1935 operated the buying club with members ringing him twice a week to place their orders and Wilson then buying a master order for distribution among the members. In the following year, Wilson and his volunteers delivered about $12,000 worth of groceries to more than 100 families and established contacts with producers and wholesalers.[2] There was a net charge of 10 percent for overheads, but the group saved from 5 to 10 percent off the prices they would have paid to their local chain store. The membership expanded to include a wide range of viewpoints, including EPIC activists, Humanists, Catholics, Mormons and agnostics and occupations, including professors, laborers, clerks and executives. The buying club established local depots and meeting places in East Oakland, Alameda, central Oakland and Berkeley (BHS, 1996, p. 3; BHS, 1983a, p. 6; Neptune, 1977, pp. 9–12).

In the Bay Area, these buying groups formed the Pacific Co-operative Services (PCS), which was incorporated on 8 January 1937,[3] as an umbrella-buying organization that provided liability protection. As business grew, the PCS members decided to employ Robert Neptune as full-time manager. Neptune had just finished his studies at UCB, where he majored in economics, merchandising and retailing and was enthusiastic about co-operatives through his involvement in the Wesley Foundation, which was part of the Berkeley Trinity Methodist Church, where the Reverend George Burcham and his wife Margaret Burcham encouraged his interest. He also attended Kagawa's lectures when he visited the Bay Area. The PCS moved away from the idea of a 10 percent surcharge on prices to following the co-operative practice of charging competitive prices and then providing patronage refunds or dividends. The growth of business led to a move first to new premises in Hobart Street in Oakland and then to Franklin Street in Oakland (BHS, 1996, pp. 2–4, 6; Neptune, 1977, p. 11; Illustration 4.2).

The PCS in August 1937 rented a small store with Charles Best, who had been an EPIC activist,[4] and later Neptune as manager from October

Illustration 4.2 Robert Neptune and Early Berkeley Store. Courtesy of Berkeley Historical Society.

1937 in Shattuck Avenue, Berkeley, as part of a plan to decentralize the PCS with self-governing units that had 'democratic control' and autonomy for educational and business activities. Besides Berkeley, there were self-governing units at Oakland, Allendale and Alameda. The PCS, which pooled buying for the stores, would be a policy-making organization with a delegate assembly elected annually by the membership, with representation in proportion to each unit's membership. Subject to the Delegate Assembly, a BD, with one director elected by each unit, would oversee the operations with meetings on a more frequent basis (PCS, n.d.).

The PCS (n.d.) through a leaflet promoting the Berkeley store appealed to those individuals "fed up with high pressure salesman-ship, misleading advertising, mis-branding and high prices for goods of poor quality..." The PCS (n.d.) reminded readers that co-operatives as "practical" method of consumer control had been "founded nearly a century before" and cited Rochdale principles, including "'one member – one vote', 'cash trading' and reserves for education'." The Berkeley store raised capital through members purchasing shares and certificates of interest and each unit monitored the quality of its goods through quality committee, which investigated the more popular brands to obtain a laboratory rating. The PCS held social events such as dinners, with one on 2 August 1937 at the USCA's Barrington Hall attracting 220 participants and Herman Korby, the manager of the Fort Bragg co-operative, talking about the reasons for its success. It also granted a charter to a Women's Guild in Berkeley to promote co-operation among women and advocate lower prices. From January to July 1937, the Berkeley membership grew from 21 to 54.[5]

The Berkeley store was successful and gained the support of the local Finnish community, whose support was crucial in its survival, with 97 members by 1 February 1938. The growth in demand led to a move in January 1938 to a larger store at 175 University Avenue near McGee Avenue with hours being extended from 10 am to 8 pm, Monday to Saturday, from 14 February 1938. Even though there were packaged items available, a low-cost philosophy encouraged the decision to include many bulk items such as brown sugar and rice. The Berkeley Unit also increased its capital by encouraging members in February 1938 to invest their dividends in $5 certificates of interest at 4 percent.[6] The staff grew to three employees, and by the end of 1938 annual sales reached $16,856 with net savings of $412 (Neptune, 1977, pp. 12–13). Berkeley developed its own speakers program, with Professor Clark Kerr from the UCB Department of Economics talking about co-operative economics in August 1938, and appointed an Education Committee. Its quality committee, besides monitoring quality of goods, also checked prices through comparison with chain store competitors. The Berkeley store also collectively bargained with local suppliers to obtain a variety of good and services for members, including furniture and paint. It also engaged in political lobbying for stronger consumer protection laws in February 1938, by calling upon members to write to members of Congress calling for the expansion of the Food and Drug Act to protect consumers against misleading advertising and harmful products. A notable early activist was J. Stitt Wilson, Berkeley's only Socialist Mayor, who had subsequently fallen out with the Socialists, but retained a key interest in progressive issues, supporting Sinclair in 1934 (Burnett, 1983, p. 282; Curl, 2012, p. 193; Gregory, 2015, p. 59).[7]

Paralleling these developments was a co-operative initiative by the Finns of Berkeley. In 1937, the local lodge of the Finnish Brotherhood, the United Kaleva Lodge of Brothers and Sisters No. 21, appointed a co-operative committee. This committee in April 1937 assembled a group of about 30 interested people and after a long discussion they decided to open a service station. The committee held several meetings and ultimately adopted a set of bylaws. Korby, the Fort Bragg Co-operative manager, encouraged the formation of the co-operative and became the first member of the new co-operative with a $10 full membership at the inaugural meeting on 11 February 1938. The name registered was the Berkeley Co-operative Union (BCU) and there was a grand opening on 16 April 1938 at a rented site on the corner of Bancroft Way and San Pablo Avenue, Berkeley. They had over 100 members and there was an initial capital outlay of $1,099. The BCU continued to raise funds, and through loans from members purchased a lot on the corner of University Avenue and Acton, where they opened a new service station in April 1939 (BCU, 1941, pp. 3–5; Neptune, 1977, pp. 12–13).

Eugene Mannila, who became the manager in April 1940, was a Finnish American and later served in the US military during the Second World War for two and half years. He had worked in co-operatives upon leaving high school in Minnesota and receiving training in co-operative business practices. Through his father, he had also been exposed to IWW radicalism and had a strong belief in equal opportunity for all, particularly regarding race. His fluency in Finnish was an important reason for being appointed manager (BHS, 1983b, pp. 5–13, 47; Mannila, 1984, p. 4).

There was a growing move within the Berkeley Unit of the PCS to gain even further autonomy through separate incorporation. There were some who supported greater centralization such as Carroll Melbin, the Chair of the Berkeley Unit Council. Those who supported greater autonomy argued that the other units were not as financially strong as the Berkeley Unit and were concerned that would become liable for the debts of the other units. The Berkeley store generated a surplus of $423.13 in the first quarter of 1939 and $185.01 in the second quarter of 1939, with the latter figure being lower due to wage increases. Membership had also grown from 170 in 1938 to 236 in 1939. There was also concern that the management committee of the PCS met too infrequently to ensure effective supervision of the units. Some believed that the Berkeley Unit would have to expand further to meet growing demand and that it would be unfair for the debt required for the expansion to be imposed on the other units. A secret ballot of Berkeley members at a membership meeting in August 1939 revealed that members were willing individually to invest a total of $5,750 at an interest rate of 5 percent in a new store in University Avenue. There was also interest in closely working with the BCU, which was a potential new source of new members, with only a 15 percent overlap of membership in September 1939. The proposed new store was to be built on a site adjacent to the BCU gas station. A Berkeley store members' meeting on 6 September 1939 resolved to incorporate separately and retain their assets. The PCS agreed and the Berkeley store was separately incorporated on 8 November 1939, with the PCS transferring all Berkeley area assets and members to the CCB. With the Allendale Unit also withdrawing from the PCS, only the Oakland Unit, which had merged with the Alameda Unit in June 1938, continued to function under the PCS (BHS, 1996, p. viii; Neptune, 1977, pp. 13, 191).[8]

Managing the Co-operative

The AGM elected the volunteer BD, who in turn elected the CCB officers. At the Members Meeting in February 1940, nine directors and three alternative directors were elected, two of whom were unsuccessful in the election for the board positions. These alternatives could replace directors who left the board during their term of office. By November 1940, three directors were elected for three years, three for two years and three for one year depending on their relative votes. Candidates could be selected by a nominating committee or by members at the AGM. Carroll Melbin served as President from 1939 to 1940 and from 1942 to 1944 (Neptune, 1977, 185). Women served on the BD and held key positions such as CCB Secretary, with Katherine Smallwood, S.G. Zane and Virginia Holmgren, respectively, filling that position from 1939 to 1940, 1941–1942 and 1943–1945. The BD set up specialist committees to oversee the operations of the CCB. There were five committees in November 1939: education, management, membership and transfer, quality and wholesaling. This was eventually reduced to three main standing committees: finance, membership and education. In 1945, the finance and membership committees were combined to form a management committee in the interest of efficiency to counter a decline in the CCB's finances. The War did disrupt the level of member involvement in CCB governance, with three directors leaving Berkeley to undertake war duties by September 1942. While there were calls for tighter scrutiny of management decision-making and the Board in September 1941 did require the manager to introduce new lines of products only with their approval; the CCB BD generally supported the 'judgement of the manager', claiming that the Board was unable to scrutinize every detail of the store (Neptune, 1977, pp. 183–6).[9]

Robert Neptune continued to manage the CCB after incorporation. Neptune, although manager and not elected to the Board, served as CCB treasurer from 1940 to 1943. The CCB faced some difficulties after Neptune resigned from the manager's position in February 1943 to become manager of the co-operative wholesaler, Associated Co-operatives of Northern California (ACNC). Robert March, who in March 1943 succeeded Neptune as general manager, served as treasurer and manager of the University Avenue Store. The BD was concerned about poor sales figures, and in April 1944 declared the position of General Manager open to fresh applications, with George Nash, who the Board believed had the training and experience to meet the needs of a growing co-operative, but without co-operative retailing experience, being appointed General Manager in May 1944. There were protests by some members about Nash's lack of co-operative experience and his increased salary. Against a background of complaints that included the breaching of wartime price controls and 'chain store' advertising standards, Nash was relieved of his duties in August 1944 and the position of General Manager was again declared open with any applications by March and Robert Fogarty, another senior employee who replaced March as Treasurer, not to be considered, but the BD decided to appoint Fogarty as General Manager in November 1944, with March resigning to join ACNC. Further concerns about financial performance led the BD to declare again in May 1945 the position of General Secretary open to find someone "capable of doing the job."[10]

During this period of confusion, the Board also asked Neptune to be an acting part-time General Manager, while continuing his duties at ACNC, on several occasions. Neptune initiated a plan in June 1945, whereby store managers were autonomous regarding sales and expenses, but subject to centralized bookkeeping and central buying until the appointment of a permanent General Manager, which was delayed due to finances. The CCB BD also adopted in August 1945 a set of policies to guide managers and ensure consistent management practices. While Don Hillberg, who had been manager of the Colusa branch store, became the manager of the main University Avenue store in September 1945, Neptune continued in his role as Acting General Manager. With the closure of the last branch store in March 1946, Hillberg became in effect the General Manger of the CCB, even though there were calls for the appointment of one. Hillberg also faced controversy when the CCB was fined by the Office of Price Administration for breaching wartime regulations by linking the price of eggs with margarine in February 1946 following complaints by members, with Neptune personally calling for the severe censure and dismissal of Hillberg if it happened again for breaching co-operative principles.[11]

The CCB opened its new food store at 1414 University Avenue next to the BCU gas station in July 1940, with more space and an attractive building with a Co-operative sign on the front in bold letters. Within several months, the BD decided to expand the range of products to include meat and hired a butcher (Neptune, 1979, p. 13). The CCB also introduced daily deliveries in September 1940. The CCB looked at providing other services to members. In May 1942, the BCU, with the support of the CCB, founded the Co-op Center Federal Credit Union (CCFCU) to provide financial services to co-operative members and employees, which by August 1945 could accept deposits of up to $500 and provide loans of up to $350 per person for a range of purposes, including the purchase of CO-OP electrical appliances from the BCU. The CCFCU operated at the BCU's electrical and hardware store. While by 31 October 1945 the CCFCU had made 56 loans to the value of $6,631, it had only 94 members or 7 percent of its membership base in the CCB and the BCU due to a lack of demand for loans arising from shortages of electrical appliances (Mannila, 1984, p. 10; Tworek, 2008, p. 26).[12] Lotte Mohr, the CCFCU treasurer called upon members "to put your savings to work in the Co-operative Movement!" so that the credit union could provide more financial assistance (Illustration 4.3).[13]

With the wartime shortages and rationing of tires and gasoline that followed US entry into the Second World War, the CCB found it necessary to stop deliveries to members in September 1943[14] and open branch stores. There was criticism of the branch proposal, with Robert March preferring improvements to the delivery system and warning the BD of the dangers of an "expensive and risky" investment in a branch store.[15] Food branch stores, which had assistant managers, were opened on Ashby Avenue, near College Avenue, in August 1942 and in Colusa Avenue in September 1943 to bring service closer to members. There were problems in maintaining these stores and wartime labor shortages

Illustration 4.3 CCB Delivery Truck. Courtesy of Berkeley Historical Society #2566.

made it difficult to find suitable staff to operate them. Two women managed the Ashby Avenue store for varying periods, one of whom was Sylvia Mannila, the wife of Eugene Mannila. By March 1945, a modified delivery system was reintroduced, whereby if customers packed their own boxes in store they would be delivered from the stores on certain days. Despite this, the Colusa Avenue branch closed when the lease expired in September 1945, with the CCB reluctant to open another branch in the area due to high rents and the branch's losses. The Ashby branch was also unsuccessful and closed in March 1946 with the CCB again focusing its activities on the University Avenue store, which was rearranged to provide more space to display goods and provide a more pleasant atmosphere for customers (Neptune, 1977, p. 14). The CCB continued the PCS interest in food quality. In June 1941, the BD rejected a proposal from the meat manager to sell lower quality meat and instructed Neptune to obtain a federal government pamphlet for distribution to members on the grading of beef by quality.[16]

As Table 4.1 indicates, CCB turnover increased from 1941 to 1944 but declined in 1945 and 1946. It also faced losses in 1944 and 1945 and its first drop in member equity in 1945. There were problems for the CCB in obtaining essentials such as meat and gasoline and competition from nearby stores. Labor costs also increased with 10 percent of employee's time being spent on rationing administration and member complaints about the quality of produce, the pricing policy and employee service. The cessation of the delivery service weakened demand with purchases being made from convenient alternative stores. While the branch stores were supposed to overcome the suspension of the delivery service, they increased expenditure without increasing revenue and added to the deficit in 1944 and 1945.[17]

The CCB made calls for members to increase their capital contribution and ensure the financial viability of the co-operative. From the outset, members were encouraged to use their dividends to purchase

Table 4.1 CCB Finances 1939–1946 (Neptune, 1977, p. 191)

Year	*Turnover – Dollar Volume*	*Net Savings () Loss*	*Member Equity*
1939	29,652	1,594	1,893
1940	28,149[a]	472[a]	2,204
1941	91,914	2,205	5,677
1942	181,500	1,950	6,350
1943	198,500	588	7,345
1944	221,249	(1,070)	7,876
1945	187,000	(2,198)	6,980
1946	136,180	4,542	11,617

a Nine months only due to change in fiscal year

certificates of interest. The leadership aimed to have membership investment as two-thirds of total assets. By September 1944, the figure was only 44 percent. In February 1945, an appeal was made to the 574 members with an equity of less than $10 to bring their investment up to that amount. The CCB did not issue patronage refunds or dividends for 1944–1945 to retain earnings. Despite the continued drop in turnover in 1946, these measures and economies gained from decisions such as closing the branch stores helped the CCB return to profit.[18]

There was a push to merge the BCU and the CCB. Against the background of concerns that the rationing of gasoline and auto parts may threaten the viability of the service station, the BCU in December 1941 opened a hardware store on University Avenue just east of the CCB store using the building of a small family store that had gone out of business. While the BCU had hoped to stock electrical appliances and heavy hardware items, wartime shortages led it to focus on paint, insecticides, light hardware and variety-store goods. Labor shortages led to the use of volunteer labor to keep the store open. The BCU also decided to lease its petrol station from 19 June 1945 until 1 March 1946, to overcome wartime regulations that favored leasing over private ownership and ensure a sufficient supply of gasoline. Given the proximity of the BCU's hardware store and petrol station to the CCB's University Avenue retail store, there was an overlap of membership and there were Finns and non-Finns on the CCB and BCU BD, with the Finnish American Arvid Nelson serving as Secretary of both co-operatives. The CCB targeted the Finnish community to increase membership with gatherings at private homes, where there was coffee, movies, picnics and even bingo. There increasingly grew a discussion over a possible merger, and the two co-operatives merged on the 1 January 1947 with a BD elected from a roster of nominees from the two predecessor organizations. Mannila, who returned to be BCU manager after his military discharge on 1 March 1946, became the General Manager of the merged co-operative, as Hillberg did not want to manage the amalgamated co-operative, but did stay on as food store manager (Mannila, 1984, p. 3; Nelson, 2005, p. 29; Neptune, 1977, pp. 16–17).[19]

Members, Employees and Community

As Table 4.2 highlights, CCB membership continued to grow from 1939 to 1945, with a decline in 1946 being explained by the removal of inactive members from the membership register. The CCB to retain and attract members continued to use the Rochdale principles, including democratic control, cash trading and political and religious neutrality. They also highlighted that CCB had lower prices than most of its main competitors. It sought membership opinions on crucial issues such as the maintenance of the branch stores through mail-in questionnaires. The

Table 4.2 Number of Members 1939–1946 (Neptune, 1977, p. 191)

Year	*Number of Members*
1939	236
1940	365
1941	567
1942	840
1943	925
1944	1030
1945	1,113
1946	920

Education Committee tried to make AGM and quarterly members' meetings, which could approve changes in CCB Bylaws, more interesting, by showing movies such as a film on Kagawa and Japanese co-operatives in April 1940, organizing exhibits and arranging panel discussions. The CCB also targeted prospective members with literature highlighting the benefits of co-operative membership, and in March 1941 set up a complaints box to monitor member grievances. There were study groups, branch store advisory councils and with the initial support of the BCU, the CCB launched the monthly *CN* in February 1945, which replaced an irregular bulletin produced on a Gestetner, to communicate with members and promote co-operation. While the Berkeley women's guild was still active in August 1943, reports on their activities are absent from the CCB minutes after this date.[20]

The CCB also encouraged the formation of neighborhood groups, which focused on educational programs and social activities, with the first being formed in March 1944. By 1945, there was a coordinator for the groups and a focus on increasing sales, to reverse the CCB's financial problems, and the promotion of peace with the end of the War. There were in November 1945 five neighborhood groups, which met monthly with a 'potluck' dinner, where every individual brings a dish for dinner. While there was a focus on social activities, the Ashby Neighborhood Group's protests over the appointment of Fogarty, who they viewed as financially incompetent and "lukewarm" on co-operatives, as manager of the Ashby store in October 1945 led to Fogarty's resignation at the request of the BD.[21]

There were issues with member participation beyond a small group of activists. At the first quarterly Members Meeting in February 1940, there were 15 candidates for 9 directors, but only 38 members voted. Before November 1943, the quarterly Members Meeting only met the requirement for a 10 percent quorum on two occasions. While at the 31 May 1945 membership meeting failed to meet quorum with only 75 members present, there was a lively discussion over the future of branch stores and coffee and cookies provided as refreshments. Generally, there was concern among the BD at the members' "lack of spirit" by April 1945.[22]

The CCB developed member education programs. By 1945, every month a commodity such as a fruit or a processed item was picked for members to highlight the value of the product, with the *CN* carrying articles describing the value of the product. There was a special project to acquaint members with audiovisual equipment such as a movie projector, so they could promote the CCB among interested groups. The CCB also established circulating libraries in its stores, which primarily carried material on co-operatives, but also economics and fiction.[23]

The CCB had only a small workforce during this period with 3 full-time employees in January 1940 and 12 by November 1943, of whom 7 were women,[24] but still faced wartime labor problems like other businesses. They lost experienced labor due to military enlistment and had to pay higher wages due to competition with defense industries. There were also concerns within management about the level of enthusiasm and morale among employees.[25] With the end of the War, the situation began to improve with the return of enlisted personnel experienced in retailing. Teruo Nobori, a Japanese American, become the head of the CCB produce department. He had run his own grocery, fruit and meat business in Berkeley before being sent to a Japanese Internment Camp and then volunteering for the US Army, with distinguished service in Northern France as a radio operator, including the Bronze Star. His experience with purchasing quality fruit and vegetables was linked with improving sales in the produce department. The CCB's appointment of Nobori broke an informal ban by Berkeley businesses on the employment of Japanese Americans, and other local businesses followed. The BD in March 1946 announced that racial discrimination in employee recruitment would not be tolerated (Tworek, 2008, pp. ix–x; Yamada, 1995, p. 20).[26]

Generally, the CCB was sympathetic to labor unions. While the PCS ensured that a milk delivery service to members initiated in August 1937 was delivered by union drivers, the PCS depots such as Berkeley did not pay union rates to their employees, but aimed to raise wages toward union rates as business increased. A Membership Meeting in February 1940 criticized these low wages and voted to pay bonuses of $120 to Robert March and $180 to Robert Neptune, the two permanent employees, but not as a precedent.[27] The Retail Clerks International Association (RCIA), which a labor union founded in 1888 to cover retail employees or shop assistants (Harrington, 1962, p. 6), tolerated this situation while the Berkeley store remained small, but the opening of a new food store in 1940 led the union to negotiate its first contract with the CCB which provided for a 54-hour week, a retail clerks pay of $24 per week and a managers scale of $27.50. The CCB also signed a contract with the union covering meat cutters with the opening of the meat department. It became a closed union shop, with one employee in March 1942 refusing to pay the RCIA initiation fee and being forced to leave the CCB. The

CCB also hired part-time employees through the RCIA and its good relationship with the union helped avoid strikes during contract negotiations that occurred at competitors such as Safeway (Neptune, 1977, p. 14).[28]

Volunteer labor by members played an important role in the CCB. In 1945, members provided market intelligence for the CCB by visiting 15 competitors to undertake an elaborate market basket survey of 27 items to challenge claims that CCB prices were too high, with CO-OP brand prices only being beaten by one competitor. A similar survey in 1946 found that the CCB's prices were higher than its competitors, forcing the BD to instruct the manager to reduce the prices of staple groceries. Volunteers performed other roles such as maintaining membership records, stocktaking and helping set up the new store in July 1940.[29]

The CCB played an active role in the local community. It donated co-operative books to local libraries and money to local causes such as the Albany volunteer police. CCB volunteers staffed the Information Center of Berkeley's Civil Program in March 1942.[30] Neptune, as manager, supported the affiliation of the CCB to the Berkeley Chamber of Commerce to highlight the co-operative's "friendliness and constructiveness" and highlight that they were "not a group of wild haired radicals trying to ruin the business structure ..."[31] Following advice from CLUSA, the affiliation did not proceed forward. There was also reluctance to engage in local politics, with the Berkeley Better Citizenship League being allowed to use its facilities in April 1941, but a ban being placed on any political literature being placed in the Store. The CCB BD did narrowly vote by four to three in December 1943 to endorse the principles of the California Farmer Labor Consumer Committee to Combat Inflation, which included subsidies for farmers and support for government action against food profiteering and black markets. There was lobbying of politicians by the CCB on issues such as tax simplification, a fairer tax system and the imposition of the taxes on luxury items.[32]

Berkeley and the Co-operative Movement

The Bay area co-operatives entered wholesaling with the formation in Californian Co-operative Wholesale (CACW) in August 1936, with significant supporters being the Fort Bragg Co-operative, whose manager Korby became the first CACW president, the PCS[33] and the UCSA. The CACW was not a financial success with one of its first ventures being the purchase of a syrup kitchen, with bottling equipment and formulas for making maple syrup. Its products included canned goods produced by a self-help co-operative in Los Angeles sold under the 'Cal-bart' brand. The CACW's turnover in 1937 was only $3,300 and its net earnings were $350. The initial BD resigned and a new BD elected in February 1938 with Larry Collins, the UCSA buyer-manager as president. The new board decided to close the CACW warehouse and operate the wholesale in three divisions: a petroleum division operated by the manager of an Oakland service station co-operative; a grocery division handled by the manager of the Berkeley Co-operative; and a service division to carry on organization, promotion and education. At the back room of the Berkeley Store, there was one pile of groceries for Berkeley and one pile for the CACW. The CACW paid no salaries and any earnings were to be used to offset the CACW debts (AC, 1944, pp. 3–4; BHS, 1996, p. 12; Neptune, 1977, pp. 20–21; US Department of Labor, 1939, p. 11).[34]

With a growing number of co-operatives in the Bay Area, including the BCU, the CCB and the Palo Alto Co-operative (PAC), which had been incorporated in March 1935, the CACW changed its name to the ACNC in November 1939 to match the Associated Co-operatives of Southern California (ACSC) in Los Angeles and signify a working relationship between the two wholesalers. The number of retail co-operatives dealing with the wholesaler grew from 2 in January 1939 to 13 in January 1940.[35] The ACNC in 1940 rented a warehouse on 40th St. in Oakland, where it consolidated its grocery, petroleum and service activities under the management of Park Abbott, who was replaced by Neptune in 1943. By 1940, the major items handled in terms of turnover were gasoline and kerosene (45 percent), groceries (34 percent), tires and auto accessories (9 percent) and electrical appliances (7 percent). The ACNC successfully applied in October 1941 for membership of NC, which allowed the ACNC to use the CO-OP brand on products which it purchased locally, the first example being roasted coffee that was obtained from a San Francisco supplier. It sourced its CO-OP labelled goods, including canned goods and auto supplies, from the CCA in Missouri and canned goods from the Blue Lake Producers Co-operative, whose farmer members had purchased a cannery in May 1938 in West Salem, Oregon. The ACNC became a member of CLUSA in October 1942 and purchased its own warehouse at 815 Lydia St. in Oakland in 1943 (Mabey, 2015; Neptune, 1977, p. 22; Parker, 1942, p. 7; US Department of Labor, 1941, pp. 14–15).

The wartime rationing of goods, such as petroleum and tires, curtailed further overall growth in the Californian co-operative wholesaling, with some gains being made for the ACNC through the Japanese internment camp co-operatives. Even before the outbreak of the War, the ACSC struggled compared to the ACNC, with the turnover of the former being $9,987 and the latter being $190,431 in 1941. The ACSC faced further difficulties with the outbreak of war in obtaining goods and ceased wholesaling operations in 1942. The ACNC began making deliveries to South California in February 1943, and within a few months 8 of the 12 South Californian consumer co-operatives were members of the ACNC. In February 1944, the ACNC also expanded its operations by deciding to supply farmers in California, Nevada and Arizona, and on 1 July 1944 became the regional distributor of the CO-OP Universal Milking Machine for NC. With the demise of the ACSC, the ACNC dropped the 'Northern' and became Associated Co-operatives (AC) in 1944. The AC expanded into insurance services in March 1945. In June 1946, the AC set up a scheme whereby members could deposit excess funds with them at an interest rate of 2 percent, and in September 1946 expanded its support to local co-operatives by providing an accounting service to co-operative members. By 1947, the AC had 43 members and $1,033,265 in turnover (AC, 1944, pp. 5–6; Mabey, 2015; Neptune, 1977, pp. 147, 190; US Department of Labor, 1943, p. 11; US Department of Labor, 1944, p. 5; US Department of Labor, 1945, p. 8; US Department of Labor, 1947, p. 17).[36]

While the ACNC and later the AC became an important supplier of goods to CCB, which voted in August 1941 to loan the ACNC $100 and then $25 for every month after to expand its wholesaling activities, there were tensions. The CCB joined the PAC in May 1940 in condemning the ACNC for loaning $500 to a Sacramento Co-operative and encouraging co-operatives to expand on credit beyond their means without sound educational programs to promote co-operatives. There were concerns in May 1942 that the ACNC's growing practice of purchasing goods on credit rather than by cash would expose the regional co-operative movement to undue risk. The CCB in June 1940 refused to endorse an ACNC pamphlet on 'Co-operatives and the War' for potentially dividing the membership on a controversial issue. The CCB showed a willingness to look at multiple wholesalers by examining in December 1944 the possibility of linking up with the Independent Grocers' Association, but eventually signing up with United Grocers because of lower prices.[37]

The Berkeley co-operators were involved in the moves to establish a co-operative association for California. While a Southern California Co-operative League was established to coordinate co-operatives and promote the co-operative ideal, the Northern Californian co-operatives lagged. There was by August 1937 a Northern California Co-operative Council (NCCC), which included representatives from CCWA, UCSA, PCS and PAC, and made the *Northern Californian Co-operator* its official publication in January 1938 to promote its activities. The NCCC was consolidated with the CACW in 1939 in the ACNC. There was a Californian Convention of co-operatives in Los Angeles in July 1938 with PCS representatives that organized a new state Co-operative League and elected Stitt Wilson as state organizer (Neptune, 1977, p. 23).[38]

The leaders of the Southern and Northern Californian co-operatives held the first of several joint conferences in Fresno, California, in January 1939, which strengthened the network of co-operators, many of whom had religious backgrounds and similar social views, and led to the formation of a legislative committee, which lobbied the Californian legislature on issues such as whether it was appropriate for consumer co-operatives to be considered corporations and whether funds invested back in co-operatives should be considered profits for taxation purposes.

There was also a committee that promoted health co-operatives and criticized the California Medical Association for trying to stop these co-operatives. The consumer co-operatives supported an unsuccessful proposal by Democratic Governor Culbert Olson for compulsory health insurance, which permitted individuals to gain medical and health insurance from a co-operative health insurer if they wished. Stitt Wilson played a prominent role as chair of these early conferences (Dimmitt, 2007, pp. 12–13; Neptune, 1977, pp. 23–4).[39]

One the outcomes of these meetings was the development of a summer camp at Camp Sierra, a summer conference ground 60 miles east of Fresno from 1939. The Camp was operated by a nonprofit organization that was partially subsidized by the Methodist Church. Russell or 'Rusty' Proffitt, a co-operative activist, Oakland attorney, Kagawa enthusiast and Methodist played an important role in persuading the Methodist Church to allow the co-operatives to use the Camp. Camp Sierra provided an opportunity for co-operative activists and their families to come for a low-cost vacation and participate in an annual clearing house for the exchange of ideas and co-operative philosophy. The Camp in July 1940, for example, had 167 registrants, including 19 children and 12 participants from the CCB. The Camp featured study or interest groups discussing a wide range of issues, including accounting, credit unions, women's guilds, peace and the problems of 'bigness' for co-operatives. Camp Sierra in 1940 also began publishing its own newsletter, *Pine Knots*. One of the highlights of the 1941 Camp was a sampling of CO-OP brand canned and bottled goods. The Camp featured talks by co-operative leaders such as Merlin Miller, CCA educational director, in 1940, on 'the business challenge of co-operative ideals', and Dr. Michael Shadid, a founder of the health co-operative movement in the US, in 1945. Camp Sierra was not held during 1942 and 1943 due to the Second World War (Collins, 1979, pp. 34–35; Neptune, 1977, pp. 24, 178; Patmore and Balnave, 2018, p. 172; Thompson and Awner, 1979, p. 21; Illustration 4.4).[40]

While the CCB was involved in the broader co-operative movement, it helped develop and promote other co-operatives. The CCB encouraged members to join Books Unlimited, which was founded in 1940 as a co-operative for book and magazine readers and assisted buying clubs in the East Bay. At the request of the PCS store at Oakland, the CCB took over the management of the financially troubled co-operative in August 1941 for three months, as there were concerns that its failure would weaken support for the co-operative movement generally.[41] While the store had 221 members, of which only 125 were fully paid up, there was an operating deficit of $595 for the six months ending 30 June 1941 and there was "no educational program or sense of solidarity."[42] Despite the CCB's efforts and the involvement of the Consumers Co-op Stations, which ran gas stations in Oakland, the Oakland store ceased

Illustration 4.4 Camp Sierra Lecture. Courtesy of Berkeley Historical Society.

operations in April 1942. The early success of the CCB led to other requests for assistance, with a request by the ACNC for the services of employee Robert March to work at the Port Huntley Co-operative for sixty days being turned down in November 1941 due to labor turnover at the CCB.[43]

Conclusion

This chapter highlights several important points about the early development of Berkeley and the CCB. While Berkeley is mainly associated with UCB, it was a more diverse community with working-class West Berkeley and being part of the commuter belt for workers in Oakland and San Francisco. While Berkeley become synonymous with Bohemianism and briefly flirted with a Socialist Mayor, the town was conservative with Republicans dominating political life. Berkeley became increasingly ethnically diverse, with a Finnish community that had strong co-operative tradition, Japanese Americans and African Americans attracted by the growth of industry during the Second World War.

The CCB was born out of the Californian experience of the 1930s with the EPIC movement and the search for alternatives as highlighted by the influence of Kagawa. While the CCB initially prospered, it faced many challenges exacerbated by the onset of the Second World War.

The departure of its first manager Neptune was followed by a period of turmoil, with managers losing the confidence of the BD as the CCB struggled with poor financial performance. The decision to set up branch stores, a feature of the future CCB growth strategy, exacerbated financial and management problems with their eventual closure. While there was membership apathy in these early years, there was a small group of activists who believed in the co-operative and in one instance, played a significant role in the downfall of a manager who was "lukewarm" toward co-operatives. The CCB also developed a very close relationship with the labor unions, which sheltered the CCB from industrial disputes at competitors such as Safeway. While there were tensions, the CCB was fortunate that there developed a strong wholesaler through the ACNC and later AC. After the merger with the BCU, the CCB now faced a period of postwar prosperity and began its first steps toward resuscitating a branch network.

Notes

1 Report President to the BD, November 1943, p. 2, Carton 1 Folder 5. BANC MSS 90/140 c. CCB Records, UCB BL.
2 *Pacific Co-operative Services Inc. News Letter*, 19 January 1937.
3 Letter R. Neptune to W.J. Campbell, 20 February 1937. CLUSA, Box 111, File – 'Local and Regional Co-operatives. Associated Co-operatives.' TPLA.
4 Interview of Bob March by Therese Pipe, 2 May 1987. Transcript. BHS.
5 *News Notes* (PCS), 9 June 1937, 22 July 1937, 6 August 1937, 20 August 1937; PCS, Berkley Branch, Circular, 1 June 1937. PCS, leaflet, 31 March 1938. BHS; *Pacific Co-operative Services Inc. News Letter*, 19 January 1937. Proceedings of Second Quarterly Conference of Consumer Co-operatives, Fresno, California, 22–23 April 1939. Letter R. Neptune to W.J. Campbell, 20 February 1937. CLUSA, Box 111, File – 'Local and Regional Co-operatives. Associated Co-operatives.' TPLA.
6 Berkeley Co-operative Store, Leaflet, 1 March 1938. BHS; *Coop News* (Berkeley), February 1938, p. 1; *Co-op News* (PCS), 1 May 1938; Letter R. Neptune to W.J. Campbell, 20 February 1937. CLUSA, Box 111, File – 'Local and Regional Co-operatives. Associated Co-operatives.' TPLA; PCS, Berkeley Branch, *Dividend Vouchers*, 25 February 1938. PCS, leaflet, 31 March 1938. BHS.
7 Berkeley Co-operative Store, Leaflet, 1 March 1938, Berkeley Unit Notice, 25 August 1937. BHS; Berkeley Unit Membership, 17 July 1939, Berkeley Unit Council, 2 August 1939, Carton 1 Folder 1. BANC MSS 90/140 c. CCB Records, UCB BL; *Co-op News* (PCS), 1 May 1938; Proceedings of Second Quarterly Conference of Consumer Co-operatives, Fresno, California, 22–23 April 1939. CLUSA, Box 111, File – 'Local and Regional Co-operatives. Associated Co-operatives.' TPLA.
8 Berkeley Unit Council, 17 May 1939, 17 July 1939. Berkeley Unit Membership Meeting, 17 July 1939, 6 September 1939, 25 October 1939. Special Meeting Notice, 6 September 1939, Carton 1 Folder 1. BANC MSS 90/140 c. CCB Records, UCB BL; *Co-op News* (PCS), 6 July 1938.
9 BD, 29 November 1939, 20 March 1940. Membership Meeting, 28 February 1940, 29 November 1940, Carton 1 Folder 1. BD, 18 August 1941,

Adjourned BD, 29 September 1941, Carton 1 Folder 2. BANC MSS 90/140 c. CCB Records, UCB BL; CCB Newsletter, 22 September 1942, p. 1; *CN*, February 1945, p. 2, November 1945, p. 1, December 1945, p. 3.

10 BD, 22 February 1943, 25 October 1943, Carton 1 Folder 4. CCB Circular, 10 June 1944. BD, 23 May 1944, 26 September 1944. Finance Committee, 28 February 1944. Letter from Charles Thurmond to Robert March, 24 April 1944. Management Committee, 8 May 1944. Petition to BD and President of the CCB, 23 May 1944. Report of the Board of Managers, November 1943. Special BD, 10 May 1944, Carton 1 Folder 5. Special Directors, 6 May 1945, Carton 1 Folder 6. BANC MSS 90/140 c. CCB Records, UCB BL; Interview Bob March by Therese Pipe, 2 May 1987. Transcript. BHS

11 BD Minutes, 24 October 1944, Carton 1 Folder 5. BD Minutes, 22 May 1945, 26 June 1945, 28 August 1945, Letters, Don Hillberg to the BD, 20 March 1946, Robert Neptune to Earle Fuller, 16 March 1946, Management Committee minutes, 21 August 1946, Carton 1 Folder 6. BANC MSS 90/140 c. CCB Records, UCB BL; *CN*, September 1945, p. 1, November 1945, p. 2.

12 *CN*, May 1945, p. 2; August 1945, p. 3, September 1945, p. 1, December 1945, p. 3, January 1946, p. 1; Report Manager to BD, 24 July 1940, 16 September 1940, Letter Clarke M. George to BD, 14 December 1941, Carton 1 Folder 1. BANC MSS 90/140 c. CCB Records, UCB BL.

13 *CN*, December 1945, p. 3

14 BD Report, November 1943, Carton 1 Folder 5. BANC MSS 90/140 c. CCB Records, UCB BL.

15 Letter Bob and Vivienne March to BD, 2 February 1942. Report Manager to BD, 17 August 1942, Carton 1 Folder 3. BANC MSS 90/140 c. CCB Records, UCB BL.

16 BD, 16 June 1941, Carton 1 Folder 2. BANC MSS 90/140 c. CCB Records, UCB BL; *CN*, March 1945, p. 1, September 1945, p. 1, October 1945, p. 5, November 1945, p. 3, October 1946, p. 1.

17 *CN*, May 1945, p. 2, July 1945 p. 2, November 1945, p. 2. Membership Meeting, 28 February 1940, Carton 1 Folder 1, BD, 25 October 1943, Carton 1 Folder 4. BD Report, November 1943, Carton 1 Folder 5. BANC MSS 90/140 c. CCB Records, UCB BL.

18 *CN*, February 1945, p. 1, February 1946, p. 3; Membership, 28 February 1940, Carton 1 Folder 1. BANC MSS 90/140 c. CCB Records, UCB BL.

19 *CN*, July 1945, p. 1, August 1945, p. 4, March 1946, pp. 1, 3.

20 BD, 17 April 1940, 15 June 1940. Management Committee, 5 August 1940. Members Meeting, 28 August 1940, Carton 1 Folder 1, BD, 17 March 1941, Carton 1 Folder 2, Board of Education Minutes, 4 August 1943, Carton 1 Folder 4. Board of Education Minutes, 17 January 1944. Carton 1 Folder 5. BANC MSS 90/140 c. CCB Records, UCB BL; *CN*, April 1945, pp. 1–2, May 1945, p. 1, June 1945, pp. 2–3, July 1945, p. 1, October 1946, p. 1.

21 BD, 28 March 1944, Carton 1 Folder 5. BD, 23 October 1945. Letter Cecilia Weaver to BD, 1 October 1945, Carton 1 Folder 6. BANC MSS 90/140 c. CCB Records, UCB BL; *CN*, November 1945, p. 7.

22 Members Meetings, 28 February, 28 August 1940, Carton 1 Folder 1. BD, 17 March 1941, Carton 1 Folder 2, BD Report, November 1943, Carton 1 Folder 5. BD, 24 April 1945, Carton 1 Folder 6. BANC MSS 90/140 c. CCB Records, UCB BL; *CN*, June 1945, pp. 2–3.

23 *Co-op Magazine* (Chicago), January 1946, pp. 9–10; *CN*, February 1946, p. 1

24 BD, 31 January 1940, Carton 1 Folder 1. BD Report, November 1943, Carton 1 Folder 5. BANC MSS 90/140 c. CCB Records, UCB BL.

25 *CN*, November 1945, p. 2.

26 *CN*, November 1945, p. 2, May 1946, p. 1; Letter Earle Fuller to Carl Neilsen, 20 March 1946, Carton 1 Folder 7. BANC MSS 90/140 c. CCB Records, UCB Bancroft Library.
27 Berkeley Unit Meeting Notice, 25 August 1937. BHS; Letter from R. Neptune to W.J. Campbell, 20 February 1937. CLUSA, Box 111, File – 'Local and Regional Co-operatives. Associated Co-operatives.' TPLA; Membership Meeting, 28 February 1940, Carton 1 Folder 1. BANC MSS 90/140 c. CCB Records, UCB BL.
28 BD, 21 October 1940, Carton 1 Folder 1. Manager's Report, 20 January 1941, Carton 1 Folder 2, Managers' Report to BD, 16 March 1942, Carton 1 Folder 3. BANC MSS 90/140 c. CCB Records, UCB BL.
29 BD, 31 January 1940, 17 April 1940, Report of Manager to BD, 24 July 1940, Carton 1 Folder 1, Committee on Records, Auditing and Finance Minutes, 9 December 1941, Carton 1 Folder 2. BANC MSS 90/140 c. CCB Records, UCB BL; *CN*, July 1945, p. 1, August 1946, p. 1
30 BD, 17 August 1942, Managers' Report to BD, 16 March 1942, Carton 1 Folder 3. BD, 28 March 1944, Carton 1 Folder 5. BANC MSS 90/140 c. CCB Records, UCB BL; *CN*, February 1946, p. 1.
31 Manager's Report, 20 January 1941, Carton 1 Folder 2. BANC MSS 90/140 c. CCB Records, UCB BL.
32 BD, 21 April 1941, 19 May 1941, Carton 1 Folder 2. BD, 28 December 1943, Letters Maurice Howard to BD, 26 November 1943, Virginia Holmgren to John Tolan, 29 April 1944, Carton 1 Folder 5. BANC MSS 90/140 c. CCB Records, UCB BL.
33 *News Notes* (PCS), 26 May 1937.
34 *Northern California Co-operator*, January 1938, p. 2, February 1938, p. 4
35 Minutes of Fresno Meeting of Associated Co-operatives of Northern California and Associated Co-operatives of Southern California, Harts' Cafeteria, 24 and 25 February 1940. CLUSA, Box 111, File – 'Local and Regional Co-operatives. Associated Co-operatives.' TPLA.
36 Memo Robert Neptune to All Co-operatives, 12 June 1946, Carton 1 Folder 7. BANC MSS 90/140 c. CCB Records, UCB BL.
37 BD, 15 May 1940, 5 June 1940, Carton 1 Folder 1, BD Adjourned Meeting, 25 August 1941, Carton 1 Folder 2, Letter Carroll Melbin to ACNC BD, 21 May 1942, Carton 1 Folder 3, BD, 13 December 1944, 23 January 1945, Carton 1 Folder 6. BANC MSS 90/140 c. CCB Records, UCB BL.
38 *Co-op News* (PCS), 6 July 1938, p. 2; North Co-operative Council Minutes, 26 April 1938, 12 July 1938. CLUSA, Box 111, File – 'Local and Regional Co-operatives. Associated Co-operatives.' TPLA; *News and Notes* (PCS), 6 August 1937; *Northern California Co-operator*, February 1938, p. 3.
39 Proceedings of the Conference of Consumer Co-operatives, Fresno, California, 21 and 22 January 1939. Proceedings of the Second Quarterly Conference of Consumer Co-operatives, Fresno, California, 22 and 23 April 1939. CLUSA, Box 111, File – 'Local and Regional Co-operatives. Associated Co-operatives.' TPLA.
40 *CN*, 5 June 1957, p. 3; *Pine Knots*, 14 July 1940, 16 July 1940, 18 July 1940; Proceedings of the Second Quarterly Conference of Consumer Co-operatives, Fresno, California, 22 and 23 April 1939. CLUSA, Box 111, File – 'Local and Regional Co-operatives. Associated Co-operatives.' TPLA.
41 BD, 18 August 1941, Letter Russell Proffitt to T. Ahonen, 4 August 1941. Management Committee, 7 August 1941, Carton 1 Folder 2, BD, 26 April 1943, Carton 1 Folder 3. CCB Records. BANC MSS 90/140 c. UCB BL; *CN*, October 1946, p. 3; *Pine Cones*, Summer Issue 1962, p. 1.

42 'Proposal on the Operation of the Oakland Store by the Berkeley Co-operative Store, for a Limited Period', 4 August 1941, Carton 1 Folder 2. BANC MSS 90/140 c. CCB Records, UCB BL.
43 Adjourned BD, 3 November 1941, BD, 27 November 1941, Carton 1 Folder 2. Report Manager to BD, 20 April 1942, Carton 1 Folder 3. BANC MSS 90/140 c. CCB Records, UCB BL.

References

AC, 1944, *Year Book – 1944*, Oakland, CA, AC.

BCU, 1941, *Building a Foundation for Future*, Berkeley, CA, BCU.

BHS, 1983a, *Catherine Best Nollenberger. The Consumers Co-operative of Berkeley – Its Founding and Philosophy*, Berkeley, CA, BHS.

BHS, 1983b, *Eugene Mannila. A Finnish Pioneer of the Consumers Co-operative of Berkeley*, Berkeley, CA, BHS.

BHS, 1995, *A Conversation with George Yasukochi. Controller of the Consumers' Co-operative of Berkeley, 1956–1982*, Berkeley, CA, BHS.

BHS, 1996, *A Conversation with Robert Neptune – Pioneer Manager of the Consumers Co-operative of Berkeley, and Long-Term Manager at Associated Co-operatives*, Berkeley, CA, BHS.

Burk, B. and Jury, F., 1983, "Incorporation," In McCardle, P., ed., *Exactly Opposite the Golden Gate. Essays on Berkeley's History 1845–1945*, Berkeley, CA, BHS, pp. 133–138.

Burnett, J.T., 1983, "J. Stitt Wilson," In McCardle, P., ed., *Exactly Opposite the Golden Gate. Essays on Berkeley's History 1845–1945*, Berkeley, CA, BHS, pp. 133–138.

Collins, L., 1979, "How Co-op Label Came to the Sierra," In Thompson, D. and Awner, M., eds., *A Rainbow on the Mountain. Cooperators Celebrate Forty Years of Camp Sierra*, Richmond, CA, AC, pp. 34–35.

Curl, J., 2012, *For All the People: Uncovering the Hidden History of Co-operation, Co-operative Movements, and Communalism in America*, 2nd ed., Oakland, CA, PM Press.

Dimmitt, M., 2007, *Ninety Years of Health Insurance Reform Efforts in California*, Sacramento, California Research Bureau.

Ferrier, W.W., 1933, *Berkeley, California. The Story of the Evolution of a Hamlet into a City of Culture and Commerce*, Berkeley, CA, Author.

Gregory, J.N., 2015, "Upton Sinclair's 1934 EPIC Campaign: Anatomy of a Political Movement," *Labor*, 12 (4), pp. 51–81.

Harrington, M., 1962, *The Retail Clerks*, New York, John Wiley.

Jones, D.C. and Schneider, D.J., 1984, "Self-Help Production Co-operatives: Government Administered Co-operatives During the Depression," In Jackall, R., and Levin, H.M., eds., *Worker Co-operatives in America*, Berkeley, University of California Press, pp. 57–84.

Jorgensen-Esmaili, K., 1983a, "The Growth of Ocean View," In McCardle, P., ed., *Exactly Opposite the Golden Gate. Essays on Berkeley's History 1845–1945*, Berkeley, CA, BHS, pp. 279–282.

Jorgensen-Esmaili, K., 1983b, "Ocean View's Social and Ethnic Diversity," In McCardle, P., ed., *Exactly Opposite the Golden Gate. Essays on Berkeley's History 1845–1945*, Berkeley, CA, BHS, pp. 80–84.

Jury, F., 1983, "How the City Weathered the Cruelest Depression Year," In McCardle, P., ed., *Exactly Opposite the Golden Gate. Essays on Berkeley's History 1845–1945*, Berkeley, CA, BHS, pp. 332–354.

Mabey, K.F., 2015, "Jack and Beanstalk connection brought Hollywood to Area Cannery," *Statesmen Journal* (Salem, Oregon), 18, p. 7

Mannila, E., 1984, *The Finns and the Bay Area Co-operative Movement*, Berkeley, BHS.

Manning, S., 1983, "Benjamin Ide Wheeler and Phoebe Hearst," In McCardle, P., ed., *Exactly Opposite the Golden Gate. Essays on Berkeley's History 1845–1945*, Berkeley, CA, BHS, pp. 202–205.

McCardle, P., 1983a, "J. Robert Oppenheimer," In McCardle, P., ed., *Exactly Opposite the Golden Gate. Essays on Berkeley's History 1845–1945*, Berkeley, CA, BHS, pp. 378–383.

McCardle, P., 1983b, "The Costanoan Indians," In McCardle, P. (ed.), *Exactly Opposite the Golden Gate. Essays on Berkeley's History 1845–1945*, Berkeley, CA, BHS, pp. 35–38.

Nelson, A., 2005, *The Nelson Brothers. Finnish-American Radicals from the Mendocino Coast*, Ukiah, CA, Mendocino County Historical Society.

Neptune, R., 1977, *California's Uncommon Markets. The Story of Consumers Co-operatives 1935–1976*, 2nd ed., Richmond, CA, Associated Co-operatives.

Parker, F.E., 1942, *Consumers' Co-operatives in 1941*, Washington DC, US Department of Labor.

Parker, F.E., 1956, *The First 125 Years: A History of the Distributive and Service Co-operation in the United States, 1829–1954*, Superior, Wisconsin Co-operative Publishing Association.

Patmore, G. and Balnave, N., 2018, *A Global History of Co-operative Business*, Abingdon, Routledge.

PCS, n.d., *Consumer Co-operation in Berkeley*, Berkeley, CA, PCS.

Randall, H.J. and Daggett, C.J., 1936, *Consumers' Co-operative Adventures. Case Studies*, Whitewater, Wisconsin Whitewater Press.

Schildgen, R., 1988, *Toyohiko Kagawa. Apostle of Love and Social Justice*, Berkeley, CA, Centenary Books.

Smith, H.L., 2014, *Berkeley and the New Deal*, Charleston SC, Arcadia Publishing.

Starr, K. 2007, *California. A History*, New York, The Modern Library.

Thompson, D. and Awner, M. (eds.), 1979, *A Rainbow on the Mountain. Cooperators Celebrate forty years of Camp Sierra*, Richmond, CA, AC.

Trimble, P.C., 1977, *Interurban Railways of the Bay Area*, Fresno, Valley Publishers.

Tworek, C.J., 2008, *Background for an Exhibit. The Creation and Development of the Co-operative Center Federal Credit Union*, MA History Project Proposal, California State University East Bay.

UCB Office of the Vice Chancellor of Finance, 2019, "Our Berkeley. Enrolment History Since 1869," available at https://pages.github.berkeley.edu/OPA/our-berkeley/enroll-history.html (accessed 14 April 2019).

US Department of Labor, 1939, *Consumers' Co-operatives in 1938*, Washington DC.

US Department of Labor, 1941, *Operations of Consumer Co-operatives, 1940*, Washington DC.

US Department of Labor, 1943, *Consumers' Co-operation in the United States in 1941*, Washington DC.

US Department of Labor, 1944, Operations of *Consumers' Co-operatives in 1943*, Washington DC.

US Department of Labor, 1945, *Developments in Consumer' Co-operatives Movement in 1944*, Washington DC.

US Department of Labor, 1947, *Developments in Consumer' Co-operatives Movement in 1946*, Washington DC.

Watkins, T., 2019, "When West Berkeley Was Finntown," available at www.sjsu.edu/faculty/watkins/finntown.htm (accessed 19 October 2019).

Weinstein, D., 2008, *It Came from Berkeley. How Berkeley Changed the World*, Layton UT, Gibbs Smith.

Weis, E., 2004, *Berkeley. The Life and Spirit of a Remarkable Town*, Berkeley, CA, Frog Ltd.

Wollenberg, C., 2008, *Berkeley. A City in History*, Berkeley, CA, University of California Press.

Yamada, T.R., 1983, "Japanese Internment," In McCardle, P., ed., *Exactly Opposite the Golden Gate. Essays on Berkeley's History 1845–1945*, CA, Berkeley, BHS, pp. 415–421.

Yamada, T.R., 1995, *The Japanese Experience. The Berkeley Legacy, 1895–1995*, Berkeley, CA, BHS.

5 Gaining a Foothold

1947–1961

While the population of Berkeley declined slightly in the 1950s, there were opportunities for the CCB to grow with the spread of suburbia into new areas such as Walnut Creek. The CCB expanded continuously in this period, but took a cautious approach to expansion by linking any new stores to the level of membership in any locality outside Berkeley, with the first major expansion being Walnut Creek in 1957. It also moved further into the area of co-operative education and hired a home economist in 1955 to help with the maintaining the quality of its merchandise and educate members on nutrition. The home economists, who were women, were to play a major role in the growing consumer activism of the CCB. The growth of the CCB raised concerns about membership communication and participation with experiments involving a parliament. The CCB continued to build its links with the co-operative movement within California, the US and internationally.

Berkeley 1947–1961

While there were fears that there would be a slump at the end of the Second World War with the end of war production and the demobilization of military personnel, the US economy emerged as the dominant player in the postwar international economy compared to economies that had been damaged and destroyed by the War. With the beginning of the Cold War, the US government began to rearm very soon after the end of the War to meet the threat of international Communism. Between 1945 and 1960, the Gross National Product increased by 250 percent, from $200 billion to over $500 billion. Berkeley shared the postwar boom with pent-up consumer demand being released with the end of wartime rationing and shortages. Low interest rates encouraged consumer spending and housing construction (Brinkley, 2003, p. 800; Wollenberg, 2008, pp. 120–121).

While Berkeley, Oakland and San Francisco saw a decline in their population during the 1950s, Berkeley's population fell relatively slightly from 113,805 in 1950 to 111,268 in 1960. There was an exodus away from the established Bay Area cities to the growing suburban periphery, particularly of white middle-class families. Between 1950 and 1960, the proportion of whites in Berkeley fell from 86.4 percent to 73.8 percent. Suburban expansion was fueled by growth of the ownership of automobiles and public investment in highways. Government housing agencies provided low-interest loans to middle-class white families in favor of new suburban homes rather than buying or renovating homes in mixed-race urban communities. It was not until the Kennedy administration in the 1960s that racial discrimination was outlawed in Federal Housing Authority loan programs (Bay Area Census, 2018; Wollenberg, 2008, pp. 120–121).

Walnut Creek, which is connected to Berkeley by the Caldecott Tunnel to the east, experienced suburbanization, growing from 2,420 in 1950 to 9,903 in 1960 with a white population of 98.4 percent. Walnut Creek saw its retailing profile expand with the opening of the Broadway Shopping Centre, with its 1,500 car parking places, in October 1951, and its role as a transportation hub established, with the opening of a major state freeway in March 1960. As early as 1951, Walnut Creek officials were aware of plans to build a suspended monorail service from their community to Walnut Creek to San Francisco, which was the foundation of the construction of the Bay Area Rapid Transit (BART) system in the late 1960s (Bay Area Census, 2018; Rovanpera, 2009, pp. 94–95, 106–107).

The decline in the white population in Berkeley was to some degree offset by the growth of the African American population, which as a proportion of the population grew from 11.7 percent in 1950 to 19.6 percent in 1960. With capital accumulated as part of war work and desire to fulfill the American dream of home ownership, African American families bought well-maintained and affordable homes on the Berkeley flatlands, with some unscrupulous speculators engaging in "block busting" by scaring white families to sell with fear that a racial minority-dominated neighborhood would reduce land values. By 1954, the overwhelming majority of residents of the wartime Codortnices Village were poor and African American, including the later Black Panther Party leader, Bobby Searle, who grew up there as a child. The Berkeley and nearby Albany City Councils opposed public housing and refused to take over the Village from federal authorities. The federal government announced the closing of the project in March 1954 and evicting tenants with a termination date set for 30 June 1956. Despite some resistance by residents, the Village was demolished, with the UCB intervening and saving some of the housing for married students, and residents purchasing modest homes on the Berkeley flatlands. By the 1950s Berkeley was becoming increasingly segregated, with African Americans dominating large parts of the Berkeley flatlands and whites dominating the Berkeley hills and the UCB campus area (Bay Area Census, 2018; Johnson, 1996, pp. 229–230; Rorabaugh, 1989, pp. 5–6; Wollenberg, 2008, pp. 122–123).

While there was a shift to the suburbs from Berkeley, the UCB continued to play a key role in sustaining the local economy. The UCB's enrolments increased from 18,262 in 1945 to a peak of 25,852 in 1948, with the GI Bill providing financial aid to veterans to attend college. While there was a decline in enrolments following the postwar surge of veterans, UCB enrolments again increased to 25,946 by 1961. There was a continued expansion of the UCB campus into Telegraph Avenue, with the opening of the Student Union in March 1961 on a block formerly occupied by local businesses on the north of Bancroft Avenue. Speculators also took advantage of the expansion to divide single-family homes into apartments or tear down old homes to hastily build new apartments to provide cheap student rentals near the campus. There was opposition by local landlords to the university building student dormitories, but in 1960 UCB opened two student residence halls. While these dormitories eased the student housing shortage, they intensified the postwar strain on the services provided by the City of Berkeley by taking land of the tax rolls (Berkeley Student Housing, 2018; Lyford, 1982, p. 17; Rorabaugh, 1989, p. 6; UCB Office of the Vice Chancellor of Finance, 2019; Wollenberg, 2008, p. 124).

UCB also became embroiled in the anti-Communism in the US. The UC Board of Regents in 1940 had prohibited the hiring of Communist faculty members, although this was softened during the War because of the alliance with the USSR. Before Senator Joe McCarthy began his campaign against Communists in Washington, Senator Jack Tinny of the Californian legislature in the state capital Sacramento held hearings from 1946 to 1948 accusing UCB professors and students of treason, even casting a shadow over the noted physicist Oppenheimer. The UC Board of Regents responded in May 1949 with an oath for UC employees requiring them to state that they were not Communist Party members. This sparked mass protests at the UCB Greek Theatre by both staff and students and the Academic Senate led by the distinguished psychology professor Edward Tolman, which called upon the Board of Regents to revoke or revise the oath. Staff who refused to take the oath were fired, with 31 members of UCB staff, including Tolman, losing their jobs in the "August expulsions" of 1951. Other staff quit in protest and research was disrupted. Despite a change of opinion by UC President Sproul, the Board of Regents insisted the oath continue. The dismissed employees successfully sued UCB with the State Supreme Court in 1952 ruling it as unconstitutional as it singled out one class of employee, with Tolman and his colleagues being reinstated. The Californian legislature passed the Levering Act to extend the oath to all state employees, with the US Supreme Court ruling in 1967 that the Levering Act and loyalty oaths were unconstitutional. Anti-Communism also had an impact outside UCB, with Berkeley school teachers required to take the oath and the notable case of Doris Walker, a clerk at Cutter Laboratories, who was dismissed because of her leftist political beliefs (Weinstein, 2008, pp. 142–143; Wollenberg, 2008, pp. 125–127).

While anti-Communism was an important political issue in Berkeley during the 1950s, there was a shift toward the left in the community. Lewis Hill, a pacifist, founded KPFA, the first US listener-sponsored radio station, and during the 1950s, except for a temporary shutdown in 1951 due to financial reasons, became an important arena for the discussion of leftist viewpoints. Demographics did not favor conservative Republicans with often conservative whites moving to the suburbs, and the rising African American population and new young university-affiliated families tending to vote Democrat. The Berkeley Democratic Club (BDC), which had been set up in 1934 to support Upton Sinclair's unsuccessful campaign for governor, attracted liberals and affiliated to the liberal Californian Democratic Council. The BDC was an active supporter of Adlai Stevenson's unsuccessful campaign for President in 1952 and Pat Brown's successful campaign for Californian Governor in 1958. There was political activism among the growing African American community in Berkeley led by D.G. Gibson, an African American Berkeley business owner, who from the 1920s organized a voting bloc of East Bay African Americans and shifted from the Republicans to the Democrats due to the growing African American support for Roosevelt and the New Deal. Coalitions of liberals, African Americans and unionist activists achieved notable successes in 1948, with election of African American pharmacist William Byron Rumford for the State Assembly seat that covered a large part of Berkeley, and in 1958, the election of labor leader Jeffrey Cohelan to the Congress seat covering Berkeley (BHS, 1989, p. 9; Grillo, 1978; Weinstein, 2008, pp. 142–145; Wollenberg, 2008, pp. 127–129).

On the BCC, there were barriers to change. There was a Californian nonpartisan ballot system, that prohibited candidates for city office running under party labels, so that the election could not be simply reduced to a Republican versus Democrat contest. Liberals tended to scatter their organizing efforts and funds among several candidates, while a well-financed ticket of candidates was organized by the pro-business Republicans and endorsed by the conservative *Berkeley Gazette*. Liberal Democrats achieved success in 1947, with the election of Presbyterian Reverend Laurance Cross to the post of Berkeley Mayor following a scandal over parking meters. While Cross remained Mayor until 1955 and took controversial stands on issues, his one vote posed no threat to the conservative majority. By the 1955 City elections, the local Democrats developed a basic structure known as the "Berkeley Caucus" to coordinate liberal candidates at each election through shaping the platform, endorsing a small ticket of candidates and provide financial and grassroots support to the endorsed candidates. As many as 300–400 Berkeley residents were involved in the two or three sessions of the Berkeley Caucus that preceded each election. One issue that Democrats focused on was on low wages of City employees and the need to increase them to attract and retain staff. The liberal Democrats finally won a majority on the BCC with five out nine members and the School Board in 1961 with the first two African American office holders in Berkeley history – Wilmot Sweeney on Council and Reverend Roy Nichols on the School Board (BHS, 1989, p. 10; Kent, 1978, pp. 80–82; Lyford, 1982, pp. 16, 18; Nathan and Scott, 1978, pp. 486–488; Rorabaugh, 1989, p. 6; Weinstein, 2008, p. 164; Wollenberg, 2008, p. 130).

Managing the Co-operative

During this period, there was no turnover in the position of general manager compared to the previous period, with Mannila remaining in the position. The BD encouraged him to appoint an assistant general manager, particularly after Mannila suffered a mild heart attack in February 1955, to help administer the growing co-operative and provide a backup if Mannila had further health issues. Thomas Flynn, who was the merchandise organizer in hardware and had worked at the rival Safeway, became the new assistant general manager on 1 April 1956. He was succeeded in March 1958 by Robert Lee, who also worked at Safeway and had a Stanford Master's Degree in Business Administration.[1]

By contrast, there were several presidents, most notably the UCB economics professor Robert Aaron Gordon, who served two terms from 1955 to 1956 and from 1958 to 1960 (BHS, 1987b, p. 23; Neptune, 1977, pp. 185–186). Mannila later recalled that Gordon "asked hard questions," and if the board meeting "went off on to any tangent" he "would simply look at the clock and tell them, we have this much business and we've got all this to go through" (BHS, 1983, pp. 32–33). Gordon also helped Mannila develop his skills in inventory control and budget management and a strong friendship developed between the two of them. Gordon did not favor rapid expansion and believed that new stores should only be opened after careful planning. He was succeeded by George Little, who had been a chair of the Finance and Membership Committees in 1961. Little was a certified public accountant and Assistant Treasurer at the States Steamship Company (BHS, 1984, p. 13; Neptune, 1977, p. 185).[2]

The BD came from a variety of backgrounds, largely white collar. The December 1954 BD consisted of a housewife, UCB professor, credit investigator, office manager, auto repairer, salesman, corporation officer, traffic agent and dry cleaner. Dr. Waino Soujanen, another UCB economist, who had done store surveys for the rival Safeway and gave advice to CCB on its expansion plans, served on the BD from 1956 to 1958. Tauno Ahonen, a CCB director until 1949 and then from 1953 to 1957 and a leader of the Berkeley Finnish community, successfully advocated that the CCB should own rather than lease its stores. While the BD was dominated by men, Ann Dorst chaired several committees, including Members Relations, and was on the BD from 1956 to 1961. The BD continued to be assisted by committees, including from May 1954 a Future Plans Committee, with Robert Neptune from AC as chair, to review its long-range goals. Neptune advocated the expansion of the CCB as it assisted the expansion of AC (BHS, 1987a, pp. 1–2; BHS, 1987b, pp. 25–26, 28; Neptune, 1977, pp. 183–185).[3]

There were few disagreements on the Board, which were quickly settled, and no organized factions battling for control (BHS, 1984, p. 16). This did not mean that Board meetings were not arduous, with a meeting on February 1959, for example, commencing at 7.40 pm and ending at 11.40 pm, with Gordon casting his vote as chair on three occasions to break tied votes. There were also efforts to promote leadership through retreats with members holding positions on the Board, committees and other units attending a special weekend retreat in November 1956 in the redwood forests of the Canyon Elementary School in the Berkeley Hills on the theme of how to transform shoppers into co-operators. There was also some sensitivity by Mannila about the circulation of sensitive Board and Management Committee minutes, with the Management Committee in May 1948 assuring Mannila that his concerns could be addressed by "tasteful wording."[4]

The CCB developed and expanded its Berkeley operations by purchasing adjoining properties when they became available. The University Avenue food store floor space was tripled in October 1948, incorporating a bakery, with members being offered child minding or "corralling" over the opening weekend while they inspected the enlarged premises. There was a major transformation of the store into a modern supermarket with an official opening on 2 December 1953. One feature of the new supermarket was a permanent Kiddie Korral, where young children were supervised while their mothers went shopping. Children played in a fenced area with toys, picture books and a blackboard available at no charge. The CCB consulted with the Akron, Ohio, consumer co-operative about a similar service. The upgraded supermarket included a larger parking lot, using the gas station space arising from its move to the corner of University Avenue and Sacramento Street in February 1951. The CCFCU was provided with space in a back building facing the parking lot. This transformation of University Avenue store involved the use of mortgage finance, which was endorsed by a membership meeting in March 1953, as the CCB leadership believed that member capital was insufficient to fund the growth. A new CCB hardware variety store with Ed Hagelberg as manager, next to the University Avenue Store, was opened in December 1955, replacing an old and unattractive building (Mannila, 1984, pp. 5–6). While there was some interest in reinstituting a home delivery service, this was rejected by the BD in 1949 (Illustration 5.1).[5]

Illustration 5.1 Arvid Nelson, Member #2 breaking ground for remodeling of University Avenue Store, April 1953. Courtesy of Berkeley Historical Society #2216.

While there was an initial reluctance to open new branch stores due to the disappointing wartime experience, one factor that encouraged new branches was the movement by Berkeley members to the suburbs such as Walnut Creek. By 1953–1954, the membership, investment and patronage outside Berkeley and adjacent Albany was respectively 33.2, 32.6 and 22.8 percent, with Oakland, El Cerrito, Richmond and San Francisco having significant concentrations of members. There was growing pressure on the University Avenue store, which had expansion problems because of Lees Florist and Nursery, whose owner, Homer Lee, rejected CCB offers to purchase or exchange land. The Walnut Creek members continued to shop at Berkeley, bringing with them new shoppers and prospective new members. The Walnut Creek members began agitating for the opening of a branch from May 1951and held a meeting with management the following month. They brought signs to CCB meetings calling for a Walnut Creek Store. The CCB Future Plans Committee presented a report to the December 1954 CCB Annual Meeting supporting general expansion. The BD in February 1955 set some conditions for expansion, which included an initial membership of 500 members and that new members must raise $50,000 in capital investment. The Diablo Valley, which included Walnut Creek, was the preferred area for expansion with Walnut Creek and its surrounding area having 182 members by July 1956. The move toward expansion by the BD was overwhelmingly supported by a members' annual meeting in December 1955. The CCB opened its 1510 Geary Road, Walnut Creek store in October 1957, with Robert Ballew as manager, a members' advisory committee, specialist member's committees on issues such as consumer information, a supermarket, a Kiddie Korral, a gas station and CCFCU offices. The volume of sales and growth of membership arising from the Geary Road matched the predictions of the studies that underlay the CCB's decision to open the branch (BHS, 1996, pp. 23–24; Mannila, 1984, p. 7; Neptune, 1977, p. 40).[6]

A third Co-operative Center was opened at 1550 Shattuck Avenue, Berkeley, in December 1959, to also ease the strain on the University Avenue store with a supermarket and co-operative/mutual organizations such as the CCFCU, Co-op Travel, Mutual Service Insurance Companies of St. Paul (MSI) and Arts and Crafts Co-operative Inc. (ACCI), which had been organized in 1957. The Kiddie Korral at Shattuck by April 1961 operated for 28.5 hours per week with 450 children. The Shattuck Avenue store also had a pharmacy department, with Adolf Kamil as manager, which was the first pharmacy in California not to be operated from stand-alone premises and created controversy particularly with the California State Board of Pharmacy. Val Linton, previously the manager of the University Avenue store, became the manager of the new store (Mannila, 1984, p. 7; McCarthy, 2007; Neptune, 1977, p. 148; Illustration 5.2).[7]

Even with the opening of the new center in Shattuck Avenue, the BD faced further demands for expansion. By June 1960, the CCB had significant groups of members and interest in Marin County, San Francisco and Hayward. The BD in June 1960 laid down revised guidelines for expansion, which included any center being within a 25-mile radius of the University Avenue Center, a potential membership of 500 families and $50,000 invested at the time of opening, with undertaking by the promoters to raise these figures to 1,000 and $100,000 within a year of opening.[8]

As Table 5.1 indicates, the CCB grew from 1947 to 1961. Growth was assisted by the opening of new stores in Berkeley and the extension into Walnut Creek in 1957. Members received patronage refunds throughout this period, with 2.7 percent for 1947–1948 and 4.04 percent for 1960–1961. As Table 5.2 indicates, during the 1950s patronage rates fluctuated between 1.2 percent and 3.36 percent, while the interest rate on shares was generally 4 percent. The CCB also actively encouraged members to finance its expansion through greater investment in co-operatives shares, including the "plow-back" of patronage refunds and interest on

Illustration 5.2 Shattuck Avenue Site, 1959. Courtesy of Berkeley Historical Society.

shares into capital investment. The Finance Committee in May 1947 sent letters to all members urging them to invest in the CCB and activists visited and phoned over half the members in the East Bay. While the CCB continued to issue patronage refunds, the refunds for 1946–1947 were only paid in cash to those members who held $50 or more in shares. Those who did not have this amount of CCB shares had their patronage refunds credited toward additional shares if the added investment came to $5 or more. This allowed the CCB to build up sufficient funds to finance the enlarging of the University Avenue food store in 1948. A proposal to require members to have $100 rather than $50 in CCB shares before they received patronage refunds and capital interest payments was rejected at a semi-annual meeting in June 1949. This resolution was submitted by the Board to members again in May 1951, with reference made to the PAC where the minimum amount was $210. While the majority voted for the resolution, it failed to meet the two-thirds majority

Table 5.1 CCB Finances 1947–1961 (Neptune, 1977, p. 191)

Year	*Volume ($)*	*Net Savings ($)*	*Member Equity ($)*
1947	313,530	14,414	61,715
1948	479,195	16,273	101,327
1949	754,110	18,931	132,520
1950	959,232	32,499	166,227
1951	1,171,877	40,656	233,461
1952	1,320,364	29,513	284,216
1953	1,347,465	37,297	306,326
1954	2,099,516	55,745	379,228
1955	2,658,416	109,565	471, 576
1956	3,591,880	150,982	699,700
1957	4,312,508	221,425	923,500
1958	6,621,455	231,709	1,139,300
1959	7,928,554	338,607	1,420,323
1960	9,215,232	437,867	1,710,828
1961	11,081,588	664,318	2,078,808

Table 5.2 CCB Interest on Shares and Patronage Refunds 1951–1961 (BHS, 1995, p. 50)[9]

Year	*Interest (%)*	*Patronage Refund (%)*
1951	4.0	2.56
1952	4.0	1.20
1953	3.33	1.57
1954	3.86	1.79
1955	4.0	3.25
1956	4.0	2.90
1957	4.0	3.36
1958	4.0	2.22
1959	4.0	3.05
1960	4.0	3.20
1961	4.0	4.04

required by the rules. Only 12 percent of members by April 1951 had more than $100 invested in shares. A further motion to increase the minimum amount to $200, with only 6.2 percent of members fulfilling the requirement in September 1953, was again submitted to members in December 1953 but amended to require only $100. Members were also encouraged to borrow money from the CCFCU at low interest rates to purchase shares and the CCB borrowed money from the CFFU at more favorable rates than the banks. By April 1955, the CCB was free of external debt by paying off its mortgages. The BD authorized in October 1956 a further finance drive of $250,000 by 1 May 1957 to fund expansion in Berkeley and Walnut Creek through increased shareholdings and the purchase of certificates of deposit with interest rates varying from 4 percent to 4.5 percent, depending on maturity. The target of $250,000, however, was not achieved until September 1957; a drive for $500,000 by April 1960 commenced in March 1958. The December 1956 Annual Meeting authorized the Board to obtain mortgage finance for the expansion by a vote of 701 to 67. Subsequent requests by the BD for further mortgage finance were also approved.[10]

The growth of CCB led to some tensions within the management. Robert March, who returned to the CCB in 1953 and became grocery manager at the Walnut Creek store, disagreed with the manager, Robert Ballew, over his proposal to match a tactic of the CCB's competitors in Walnut Creek that allowed loss leaders on items such as sugar to undercut CCB revenue. March went directly to Mannila and persuaded him to adopt the tactic of co-operative education rather than below-cost pricing as a way to attract members. The BD in February 1957, however, dropped a policy of "fair trade prices" in favor of "meeting competition wherever possible at management's discretion," which was put into effect in April 1957 after some opposition from the Member Relations Committee. The management in February 1957 was also given discretion to accept discounts and rebates from suppliers to assist competition with other stores after a vote of five to three. Director Stan Brown, a credit investigator, supported these changes and hoped to see the CCB change from being a price follower to price leader. Mannila saw these changes as necessary to combat changes from discount houses, particularly in the hardware and variety department, and obtained BD protection for CCB managers from prosecution from suppliers, under fair trade legislation, who opposed discounters. Conflicts with Assistant General Manager Robert Lee over pricing led to March's resignation in July 1959, as he faced a transfer from Grocery Department to the lower status gas station manager at Walnut Creek gas station. Further controversy arose in the BD in March 1961 when three directors presented a petition against the management's policy of "loss leaders."[11]

Members

As Table 5.3 indicates, the CCB grew every year reaching 19,630 members by 1961. Following the merger with the BCU, Finns remained a significant part of the membership and leadership. Their co-operative culture was important for sustaining the CCB and providing a platform for growth. Membership meetings initially were carried on in the Finnish tradition with refreshments accompanied by polka music and dancing. The Finnish Brotherhood Hall was a focal point for membership meetings and other events such as employee Christmas parties. The CCB held national and UN day celebrations. There was a strong presence of Finns on "Finnish Day" with Finnish national costume and food. Food

Table 5.3 CCB Number of Members 1947–1961 (Neptune, 1977, p. 191)

Year	*No. of Members*
1947	1,495
1948	1,690
1949	2,187
1950	2,668
1951	3,282
1952	3,753
1953	4,157
1954	5,188
1955	6,019
1956	7,493
1957	8,900
1958	11,878
1959	13,667
1960	16,947
1961	19,630

was often imported from Finland for the event. Finns continued to play a key role in the CCB with, for example, Mannila as general manager, Ahonen and Laurie Lehtin on the BD and Paul Padi, a local Finnish builder, being the building superintendent of the expansion of the University Avenue store. Highlighting the Finnish influence on the CCB, Yrjö Kallinen, a noted Finnish co-operative educator, addressed CCB and CCFCU board and committee members in June 1951 (BHS, 1987b, p. 26; Mannila, 1984, pp. 4–6; Illustration 5.3).[12]

The growth in membership encouraged the CCB to examine ways of improving the process of keeping membership records and processing the receipts required for patronage refunds through electronic data processing (EDP) to reduce costs and labor time. The CCB cashiers wrote the member numbers of their receipt stubs, which were then sorted into member number groups for processing. The first steps to automating this process began in 1959 with the keypunching of members purchases on tabulating cards. These cards were processed at the end of each financial year for the calculation of dividends or patronage refunds and the issuing of statements and checks. New cash registers were introduced into the University Avenue store in March 1959 that printed the member's number on the receipt stub. The CCB decided in May 1961 to join with the AC and CCFCU in setting up a joint EDP facility.[13]

There was a continued emphasis on promoting cooperation and member loyalty. There were articles in the *CN*, films and speakers. Shadid, a founder of the health co-operative movement in the US, was promoted as a speaker at Oxford Hall in March 1948 and Voorhis, CLUSA General Secretary, addressed the December 1949 AGM. The Member Relations

Illustration 5.3 CCB UN Day, 21 October 1961. Courtesy of Berkeley Historical Society.

Committee inaugurated an annual members' picnic on 2 August 1953 at the Laurel Picnic Area in Tilden Regional Park. While the CCB provided paper plates, napkins and wooden utensils, participating members were expected to contribute to a potluck lunch, with activities including baseball, which was played between a members and employees' team, horseshoe pitching and guessing contests. The CCB also introduced "Welcome Wednesday" nights with coffee and deserts in January 1954 to induct new members. There was a revival of interest in the formation of neighborhood groups with a new Neighborhood Groups Committee in 1955, with six groups by July engaging on discussions on issues such the CCB expansion and organizing potluck dinners in members' homes. There were also other social groups, including a choir and an "Unattached" group for CCB single adult members and their guests to engage in social activities. While there was an unsuccessful attempt to reform a women's guild in 1949, the Members Relations Committee established a Youth Group in 1958 for high school students to engage in discussions, social groups and projects, with a part-time youth worker being appointed for six months in 1959.[14]

The CCB formally initiated in December 1948 an education program with a full-time educational director. Charles Davis, who commenced work in the CCB as a food store clerk, became the first educational director. Davis clashed with many of the volunteers who had undertaken the work previously and resigned in January 1950 after less than a year. He was succeeded in March 1950 by Emil Sekerak, who had worked at Ohio Farm Bureau Co-operatives, with Murray Lincoln, who became CLUSA president, and as an AC field organizer in Northern California.[15]

Sekerak shaped the CCB's education activities. One of his initial tasks was to put a counter in the front of the store to sign up members, encourage investment, promote a co-operative community, listen to complaints and pass on suggestions. His other activities included running an educational program,[16] the publication of the *CN*, employing education assistants in each of the centers and supervising the Kiddie Korral Program, which Sekerak later noted became "a kind of pre-nursery experience for the kids, who learned to socialize sometimes for the first time."[17] Sekerak played a significant role in the later Center Councils, membership meetings and committees, such as member relations, consumer information and public relations (Neptune, 1977, p. 87).[18]

The education program activities led the CCB to become a center for consumer activism through providing a home economist service and lobbying governments on consumer issues (Neptune, 1977, p. 87). Later dismissed by 1970s feminist scholarship for their emphasis on preparing "women for the miserable life of a housewife" (Goldstein, 2012, pp. 282–283), the CCB female professional home economists played an important role in educating members about consumer rights. The CCB hired its first home economist Mary Gullberg on a part-time basis in 1955 to help with maintaining merchandise quality and educating members on nutrition. One early task for Gullberg involved preparing a letter to members of Congress following a CLUSA appeal supporting a Bill that prohibited manufacturers adding chemicals to food without government approval. Betsy Wood joined CCB as a second part-time home economist in 1956 while Gullberg was on summer vacation. By December 1957, Wood was employed on a quarter-time basis. With the CCB's expansion to Walnut Creek, Gertrude Ascher was appointed home economist there on a quarter-time basis, with duties including consulting with "homemakers" and demonstrations on subjects such as turkey roasting and stuffing. The CCB also lobbied politicians for the banning of subliminal advertising in 1958.[19]

The CCB Consumer Information Committee, which was formed in 1950 and operated for varying periods and reestablished as the Consumer and Information Protection Committee (CIPC) in 1961, played an important role in raising member awareness of the advantages and disadvantages of products such as dried skim milk and cheese through demonstrations of the product. It also organized speakers to talk about nutrition, including Adelle Davis, a noted author of several cookbooks and consultant nutritionist, to speak on "Good Nutrition – Good Health" in April 1952.[20]

While the CCB was growing, a smaller percentage of members were participating in meetings and there were smaller turnouts for CCB elections. The CCB management encouraged members to attend meetings with refreshments, co-operative movies such as the British "Men of Rochdale" in May 1947 and child care.[21] There were, in addition to regular meetings, special meetings of members to discuss issues such as the finance strategies for expansion. From 1951, there developed "buzz sessions," where groups would break off from membership meetings to discuss and report back to the meeting on issues such as housing.[22]

Despite these efforts to encourage member participation, they became ineffective because of a lack of quorums (Curl, 2012, p. 194). A crucial semi-annual meeting in May 1949 to vote on changes in the bylaws that would increase member capitalization was abandoned because of the lack of a quorum of 10 percent of members. At a subsequent meeting in July, the proposals were defeated and returned to the Finance Committee for reconsideration. The CCB in 1956 adopted new rules that allowed a mail ballot before members' meetings with the mail votes to be counted in determining the quorum. While there were state legislative changes in 1957, which the CCB lobbied for, and subsequent rule changes endorsed by CCB members that reduced the requirement for a quorum to 5 percent, the problem persisted. A Semi-Annual Meeting in May 1961, which was to discuss obtaining additional finance of $650,000 through mortgaging the stores, failed because only 153 of the required 250 members attended. The agenda items were subsequently submitted to a mail ballot of members, with members voting by 571 to 36 to approve the mortgage plan.[23]

The BD experimented with the idea of a Co-op Parliament to promote member participation. The CCB was aware of this idea as early as 1954,[24] when similar debates about membership participation in a growing organization occurred in the Greenbelt Co-operative in Maryland, which eventually established a Co-op Congress in 1955. The Greenbelt Co-operative drew its inspiration from large consumer co-operatives in Europe, particularly Sweden, and the district organization of US farmer co-operatives. The foundation of the Greenbelt Congress was a local organization for members of the co-operative store or shopping center they patronized. The members in each area would elect representatives to a local council, with all representatives being members of the Congress, which would develop and recommend candidates for the direct election to the BD by members (Cooper and Mohn, 1992, pp. 131–132, 247). A resolution calling for a committee to examine the idea of a Congress was defeated at a CCB Annual Meeting in December 1954, with opponents arguing that the existing governance structure was meeting member needs. The CCB Board Directors eventually in October 1956 endorsed an experiment of an Advisory Committee with the principle of geographic representation to increase democratic control over policy-making.[25]

The CCB Members elected Parliamentary representatives in March 1958 and met quarterly from April 1958. There was criticism of the Berkeley voting constituencies for the Parliament, which were initially not based on geographical areas but on districts based on surnames – A, B and C, for example. Critics claimed that this electoral system was designed to prevent interest groups forming.[26] This was confirmed by CCB Director Dorst, who noted that the alphabetical system arose from a wish not to carry "into the Parliament any racial or economic divisions already in Berkeley."[27] Some members forwarded a petition of protest to the BD, but it confirmed an alphabetical system at its December 1957 meeting. The Parliament was restricted in its powers compared to the BD, but could pass resolutions on behalf of members for consideration of the Board and make recommendations to the Board. Key committees such as Member Relations preferred to remain under the jurisdiction of the BD rather than Parliament as the BD had the CCB legal authority. The BD rejected in January 1959 any proposal for sharing control of its staff or committees, with Parliament noting that they could not "serve two masters."[28]

While initially the Parliamentary meetings provided an opportunity for members to express their complaints, they did provide a means of communication between the membership, directors and employees and had some safety valve benefits. The Parliament discussed a wide range of issues. The June 1958 Parliament, which attracted 51 representatives and was held in the Finnish Brotherhood Hall, set up a committee of inquiry to relay to the BD the Parliament's views on the hardware variety store, which was criticized by representatives for running out of significant items, poor customer relations and the lack of a directory to assist members find items. There was a call for an appeal by Dr. Albert Schweitzer, the Nobel Peace Prize winning humanitarian, calling for ending of nuclear testing to be circulated to members. There were concerns expressed that this would breach the co-operative principle of political neutrality, and instead it was proposed that there be a symposium held that examined the case for and against nuclear testing. There was also a discussion of the effect of radiation on produce and Strontium-90 on milk. The Parliament successfully recommended to the BD that the CCB support legislation for the regular inspection and testing of foods for radioactivity (Neptune, 1977, p. 86).[29]

There were calls for Parliament to extend its powers and direct member referendums on key issues. In November 1959, Parliament sought to nominate the candidates for the BD, to designate the nominees it preferred for elections and require the BD and senior management to attend Parliament on request to answer questions. These and other proposals that would have led to a more permanent role for the Parliament were, however, defeated in a membership vote in May 1960 by 289 to 254, with a turnout of less than 4 percent.[30] Some CCB leaders were skeptical of the need for a Parliament, with George Little claiming that "The experimental Parliament has not yet demonstrated the need for such a body."[31] Members also called for referendums, with some Walnut Creek members petitioning against a liquor department at their store in November 1960 and unsuccessfully requesting a referendum on the issue.[32]

The BD began to restructure the Parliament. It decided in June 1960 to base the next Parliamentary elections for all members on shopping centers and geographical districts in outlying areas. There were 11 districts with University Avenue, Shattuck Avenue and Walnut Creek each having 13, 14 and 12 representatives, respectively. The other eight districts, which included Richmond, El Cerrito, Oakland, Marin County and San Francisco, had a total of 15 representatives. Parliament was renamed Congress, which continued with same functions, along the lines of the US political system as of October 1960. Despite these moves to greater member participation, apathy remained a problem, with only 10 percent of members voting in the 1960 CCB Congress elections. Congress also added to the growing organizational complexity of the CCB with a Committee on Committees meeting in May 1961 to streamline the organization. An issue could be dealt with by five committees with the BD making decisions before the issues had been dealt with by all the relevant committees.[33]

There were a variety of methods used to obtain members' opinions. From May to November 1950, the CCB suggestion box attracted 244 notes with major issues being calls for a new brand, item or size (58 percent), quality complaints (12 percent) and price complaints (5 percent). The CCB also conducted member surveys to find out shopping habits, as with the case of members who did not patronize the CCB in 1947. A random sample survey of 200 members during 1950 was conducted to find out how they felt about the co-operative and suggest changes. George Leavitt, a director with a background in psychology, suggested to Sekerak the idea of conducting a survey. UCB graduate students were paid to take the 84-item questionnaire to the members' homes. It was found that one reason members did not shop as much as the CCB as they would like was that they thought it was too far away. This fueled the idea in the CCB that would be good to open more stores in Berkeley and Walnut Creek. Other findings included a strong support by members of the Rochdale principles, and approximately 50 percent of members spent more than $100 at the CCB during 1949. A subsequent questionnaire sent to all members in September 1952 to find out how the CCB could better serve their members was a failure, with only 75 members responding.[34]

There were member concerns about the expansion program. Concerns focused on the use of mortgage finance to fund the remodeling of the University Avenue store. Some members, including the Finns, believed that growing reliance on external finance would lead to the CCB's demise despite its endorsement by a members' meeting. These fears led to an increase in requests for the redemption of share capital at a rate that threatened the capitalization of the CCB. The BD in May 1953 responded by declaring a moratorium on the withdrawal of share capital, except in the case of dire emergencies, with some redemptions approved from October 1953 as revenue improved. With the increase in sales arising from the store remodeling, the fears and requests for redemption subsided and the CCB finances were stabilized (Mannila, 1984, p. 6).[35]

Employees and Community

The CCB workforce expanded during this period, with 133 full-time and 53 part-time employees by September 1958, and the CCB continued to generally support labor unions. The *CN* was produced by union labor, and CCB Education Committe members in 1948 visited labor union local meetings and invited union members to come to CCB meetings. The CCB also donated groceries to San Francisco workers involved the 1948 International Longshore and Warehouse Union (ILWU) Strike. In the 1949 contract negotiations, it met the demands of the RCIA for wage increases ahead of other employers on the understanding if the wage increases were not agreed to by other retailers they could revert to the original pay scale. The CCB avoided a potential strike by its employees. The CCB established a Labor Advisory Committee with union members of the CCB in 1960 to ensure good relations. There were occasional tensions with the RCIA over, for instance, "carry-out boys" going beyond their duties of carrying purchases to shoppers' cars, though a new contract signed in 1960 permitted them to bag groceries for customers. The CCB was also caught up in disputes between its building contractors and their workers, as occurred for 40 days during the expansion of the University Avenue store in July 1953, and was subject to picketing by ILWU members in November 1956 arising from a jurisdictional dispute with the Teamsters Union over the coverage of a CCB wholesaler United Grocers' warehouse in nearby Richmond. The CCB placed signs in its store windows challenging the statements of the picketers' placards. The CCB rejected an ILWU request in October 1961 to withdraw all Colgate-Palmolive products due to a labor dispute at their Berkeley factory, but did agree to identify at point of purchase that these products were being produced at a plant where there was a strike. The CCB took the view that it was for the individual member to decide which of its products to boycott due to labor issues, but it focused on purchasing from suppliers with good labor relations.[36]

The CCB faced problems with labor turnover and implemented several strategies to maintain worker morale and commitment. The December 1949 AGM called on the BD to establish a special committee to examine personnel problems in the CCB after 10 of 26 employees had left during the year.[37] A new Personnel Committee was established in 1950 with Robert March, who was then working for AC and not CCB, as chair. Besides dealing with personnel issues, the Committee "was to focus on the ways and means for employees to enhance the role of co-ops among our members and within the community."[38] The BD in February 1951, on the recommendation of the Personnel Committee, agreed to offer incentive payments for superior employees' performance at the discretion of the General Manager following consultation with Department Heads. Following complaints about the handling of grievances by the management, the BD in September 1955 asked the Personnel Committee to hear grievances by employees against management in the future. At the 1949 AGM, the CCB handed out gold twin pines service pins to five employees with more than ten years' service in the co-operative movement, including Mannila, and bronze service pins to ten employees with more than one year service. Silver pins were also subsequently handed out for employees with five years' service. The CCB sent employees and their families to Camp Sierra to participate in both the educational and recreational activities and underwrote the 1953 Christmas dinner for employees, with each employee being given a canned ham for Christmas. Employees in 1956 formed the Berkeley Co-operative Employees' Association (BCEA), which received financial assistance from the CCB to organize social events and store discounts for BCEA members for items over $50. The CCB Board Directors to encourage longer service approved in May 1956 a retirement Deferred Savings Program to supplement social service benefits for employees retiring at 65 years of age or later with more than three years' service. A regular payment was made by the CCB into the fund supplemented by a proportion of CCB net savings in years when economic performance was particularly good. Employees by June 1957 were meeting monthly without management to discuss their work and the CCB. The CCB preferred to promote from within, with managers in 1961 being rotated between stores for experience.[39]

While CCB tried to promote employee morale and loyalty to the co-operative, there were limitations. The BD accepted a Committee of Management recommendation in April 1949 that employees were not entitled to staff discounts as it would create an unfair advantage compared to members and was inconsistent with co-operative "ideals and principles." There were restrictions on employees' rights as CCB members. There was a management 'consensus' that employees were not allowed to be voting members of the BD, the Nominating Committee or any of the specialist committees such as finance due to a conflict of interest and the potential undermining of management. The CCB Parliament voted by 20 votes to 18 in November 1959 to deny employees their eligibility to stand for Parliament.[40]

The CCB continued to diversify its workforce. African American workers were underrepresented in Berkeley grocery stores, constituting an estimated 1.5 percent of the workforce in 1958 (Lemke, 1987, p. 47). Matt Crawford, the first CCB African American employee, was hired as a food store apprentice in July 1948. Crawford worked for the CIO and the National Negro Congress, which consisted of labor and community groups concerned with advancing the civil rights of African Americans. Crawford, who was a CCB member since 1937, was attracted to working at the CCB because of its commitment to workers being members of labor unions and believed that the co-operative movement provided more opportunities for African Americans and other minority groups to express their "own desires." Crawford eventually left the CCB to work as a loans officer at the CCFCU in 1959. The CCB hired George Yasukochi, who following his return to Berkeley worked at USCA and was an AC director, as an accountant in September 1956 and eventually became Controller before retirement in 1982 (BHS, 1993, pp. 1–4; BHS, 1995, pp. v, 15–18; Neptune, 1977, p. 182; Tworek, 2008, p. 28). While the CCB had progressive hiring policies, it rejected a request in February 1950 by the Congress of Racial Equality (CORE) to boycott of Carnation Milk Products due to its discriminatory hiring practices against minorities. There was a suggestion at the Management Committee that if this policy was adopted for all employers there would little merchandise in the store.[41]

Volunteer labor continued to play an important role in the CCB. The *CN* in April 1949 called for volunteers to telephone members about forthcoming meetings and to price check other stores to ensure that the CCB was competitive. Members were encouraged to leave their details and information about their skills for volunteer work at the CCB office. Following the opening of the remodeled supermarket in December 1953, volunteers beautified the new parking lot with plants and later staffed an information booth in the store. Mary Gullberg initially volunteered as the CCB home economist in November 1954. The CCB in 1957 organized the volunteers into a group known as the "Rochdale Recruits." Occasional tensions flared between employees and volunteers, with employees successfully objecting to a proposal that volunteers be given gift of a potted plant for participation in CCB UN Day Celebrations in 1960.[42]

As the CCB grew, it became a focal point for community groups to promote various causes. Management refused to allow posters and signs to be put up in the food or hardware stores as they could create an "unsightly appearance." By June 1949, groups could put posters of a limited size in a specified place on the front of the gas station. By November 1951, there was a similar notice board outside the food store. The lobby of the remodeled University Avenue store after its opening in December 1953 became a place for local community organizations such as the Children's Community Center Co-operative Nursery School to hold events such as bake sales. The CCB took no position on the loyalty oath controversy at UCB in 1950 and declined to donate funds to those opposing it. While the CCB did not directly engage in BCC politics, it encouraged members to take an active interest in issues such as withdrawing rent controls in Berkeley and attend a City Council meeting to voice their opinions in July 1951. The CCB sent delegates to a Conference on World Disarmament and Economic Development held at UCB in 1956. Donations were given to community organizations such as the Berkeley YMCA and CCB teams played in local sporting competitions. There were also economic links with other Berkeley businesses such as Kaufman's Drapery Store, where members in 1959 could obtain discounts and credit toward patronage refunds. Mannila became active in the local business community and became President of the University Avenue Merchants Association in 1953 and the East Bay Food Dealers Association in 1961. While CCB joined the Berkeley Chamber of Commerce in 1951, its membership was not continuous and it was critical of the Chamber's recommendations concerning the vote in November 1958 on Proposition 18 in California, which aimed to outlaw compulsory labor unionism in collective agreements, with the BD endorsing a CCB Parliament resolution calling for distancing the CCB from the Chamber because of co-operative political neutrality. There were other tensions with local community organizations, with the Walnut Creek Methodist Church protesting in July 1957 against the issuing an off-sale beer and wine license to the new adjacent Walnut Creek store.[43]

Berkeley and the Co-operative Movement

The CCB remained affiliated to AC, and in 1959 passed the PAC in terms of sale volumes and became the most significant AC affiliate. As Table 5.4 highlights, the AC suffered a general decline in membership from 43 in 1949 to 9 in 1961 with a peak of 52 in 1950, but saw a major growth in turnover with fluctuations from 1,463,404 in 1948 to 5,629,080 in 1961. Reflecting a broader trend for US consumer co-operatives, many smaller rural consumer co-operatives such as Madera in California failed during the 1950s, while the larger consumer co-operatives in larger centers such as PAC and CCB generally grew in terms of membership, turnover and their significance for the AC's survival. As wartime shortages eased, some co-operatives outside the Bay Area ceased dealing with the AC, as they found that they could source goods locally and save freight (BHS, 1996, pp. 64, 66; Neptune, 1977, pp. 37–38, 40, 174–176; Patmore, 2017, pp. 520–521).

The AC was faced with changing patterns of consumption, uncertainty over its role and a decline in membership in the 1950s, and looked at a variety of ways to ensure growth and survival. The greater availability of alternative sources of supplies for farmers from 1949 and the unwillingness of farmers' co-operatives to join and finance the AC, which they saw as dominated by urban consumer co-operatives, led the AC to sell its

Table 5.4 AC Membership and Financial Performance 1947–1961 (Neptune, 1977, p. 190)

Year	*No. of Members*	*Turnover*	*Net Savings*
1947	43	1,033,265	17,342
1948	46	1,463,404	30,606
1949	51	1,331,438	(63,241)
1950	52	924,361	10,456
1951	51	785,954	15,017
1952	45	795,333	9,588
1953	38	734,567	9,107
1954	25	849,631	14,473
1955	22	981,060	9.050[a]
1956	20	1,217,358	10,609[a]
1957	12	1,560,533	3,744[a]
1958	11	2,140,691	4,122[a]
1959	11	2,500,968	4,605[a]
1960	9	4,583,515	3,922[a]
1961	9	5,629,080	3,922[a]

a Amount of Net Savings Determined by Cost-Plus Contracts

farm supply and building materials business to Central Co-operative of Modesto, California, and focus primarily on groceries and automobile accessories. Poor finances in 1949 also forced AC to reduce its organizing and education work by dismissing its field organizers and terminating its publication, *Associated Co-operator.* A California Co-operative League was established to continue the educational work of the AC, with the educational directors of the PAC and the CCB sitting on its management committee and membership being encouraged on an individual basis. The AC also faced competition from another co-operative wholesaler, United Co-operatives, which opened a facility in San Francisco in 1949 and took business away from AC.[44]

While there were discussions as early as 1950, the AC in 1954 adopted a Cost-Plus method for handling transactions like that used by some co-operative wholesalers on the East Coast. Merchandise is billed to the stores at the AC's cost prices. AC then billed the co-operatives separately for a proportion of budgeted overhead costs based on their purchases from the AC, with quarterly adjustments made for actual expenditures occurred. The stores were also expected to provide investment capital for AC's operations, as the Cost-Plus billing program did not provide earnings for capital investment, through a Working Funds Agreement. In October 1954, eight of the AC members, including CCB, agreed and Cost-Plus came into effect in November 1954 (BHS, 1989, p. 3; BHS, 1996, p. 15; Neptune, 1977, pp. 34–39). Later, Neptune (1977, p. 39) would argue that managers had an incentive to increase their business with AC as it increased the returns of their investment, and in 1955 "the volume of the warehouse" increased 24 percent and the "expense ratios were materially reduced."

The AC moved to a new warehouse in Berkeley in December 1955, which it leased and used new warehousing methods such as pallet racks to increase efficiency. There was further expansion with AC, more than doubling its warehouse facilities in March 1959, and expanding its stock beyond CO-OP products to include health and beauty aids in December 1959. The CCB, besides being an investor in the AC, also encouraged its employees to stock and members to buy AC CO-OP labelled goods. CCB members also were encouraged to purchase AC insurance services, with CCB members eligible for the patronage refunds. The AC in 1958 sold its insurance business to MSI, which operated as a co-operative and established its Pacific Region headquarters in Palo Alto. The CCB voted to join the MSI in July 1958, and the MSI became a significant source of finance for the CCB with $150,000 being borrowed in February 1960. The buying power of the AC helped reduce prices for CCB members, with the Fort Bragg Co-operative and the CCB persuading the AC to become a franchisee for one power tool manufacturer, leading to a 25 percent reduction in power tool prices (Neptune, 1977, pp. 40–41, 150).[45]

There were also calls for the CBB, PAC and AC to work more closely together. There were occasional tensions, with the CCB criticizing the AC in November 1948 for increasing competition for investment funds for publishing an advertisement in the *Associated Co-operator* by PAC inviting investment. The AC commenced a short-lived supervisory service with the CCB, PAC and the San Jose Co-operative in April 1948, to improve the flow of information on the business activities by providing a supervisor who moved between the three retail co-operatives and report on issues such as the types of commodities in the stores, displays and sales data. There were exchanges of information between PAC and CCB with a joint meeting of their public relations committees in Palo Alto in October 1954. The two co-operatives engaged in the joint buying of goods, but this "did not work out" and was discontinued in 1958.[46]

With the growing volume of business for CCB, PAC and AC, the AC prepared a report on a possible merger between the organizations in late 1959. A three-day planning conference of the three co-operatives' general managers and their assistants in the Carmel Valley in 1960 unanimously called for the merger. Neptune supported the merger, arguing that their buying strategies were inefficient in the face of increasing competition and the merger would lead to better management. There were reservations on the CCB BD about the merger, and in January 1960 it initially rejected a proposal to employ a management consultant to examine the issue and supported a joint committee to explore how co-ordination could be improved with PAC and AC. The CCB BD did eventually agree in April 1960 to AC employing a management consultant, subject to certain conditions such as employing a local firm, and a consultant's report was presented to the joint meeting of the three boards of directors on April 1961. It found that there were few tangible benefits for CCB arising from joint management or merger and there were obstacles to a merger between PAC and CCB, including the current level of savings and different operating methods. Uniformity of management and further growth of the two co-operatives was needed before more advantages of a merger could be attained. No further action was taken with agreement that the matter would be reexamined in the future, if the operating efficiencies and net savings of PAC and CCB came closer together (Neptune, 1977, pp. 36, 79–80, 176).[47]

While the CCB remained committed to the AC, deciding in May 1948 to purchase all AC items, it explored other wholesaling arrangements as the AC could not meet the CCB demand for a variety of products. The board voted in 1949 to join the California Hardware Retail Association, even though it was a member of the anti-cooperative NTEA, to gain access to its surveys on hardware prices. It joined the United Grocers wholesaler in 1951.[48] With nine other grocers, the CCB launched the Gold 'N Rich Dairy Corporation in Berkeley in 1956 to provide fresh milk and milk products for the stores. Initially, ten retailers participated with a capital investment of $20,000 and commitment to purchase their milk from the new organization. Gold 'N Rich built a pasteurizing and bottling plant close to the processing plant of the Challenge Cream and Butter Association, a marketing co-operative, which contracted to supply Gold 'N Rich with milk and provided Gold 'N Rich with a loan of $150,000 (Neptune, 1977, p. 106).

The CCB participated in the annual conferences for co-operative managers run by CLUSA and other co-operative organizations. Mannila attended a co-operative managers' conference sponsored in May 1951 by a consumer co-operative in Akron, Ohio, with Murray Lincoln from CLUSA being a keynote speaker and topics discussed, including co-operative expansion programs and the relationship between co-operative boards and managers. The CCB and PAC jointly hosted this Conference in 1954. There was also a conference for co-operative educational and organizational directors in June/July 1959 in East Lansing, Michigan, which was attended by Sekerak.[49]

The CCB played a role in the support and formation of other co-operatives. There was the Californian Co-operative Finance Corporation incorporated in 1948 to assist co-operatives with building finance, but dissolved in 1953 due to its inability to raise sufficient capital. Books Unlimited, which became incorporated bookseller in 1951 and reincorporated as a co-operative bookseller in 1961, had floor space in the CCB stores. The CCB helped form the ACCI. Artists initially had held sales of art produced by them and by co-operatives in other countries as an adjunct to the activities of the Member Relations Committee, but eventually formed their own independent co-operative with corporate status in 1959.[50] The CCB assisted the ACCI by providing the employee dining room at the University Avenue store as a venue for its early meetings and providing gallery space upstairs (McCarthy, 2007). It moved to establish a co-operatively controlled organization savings and loan association, eventually to be known as the Twin Pines Federal Savings and Loan Association. The idea was first discussed following the AGM of CCFCU in 1959. The idea was taken up by the CCB Future Plans Committee in 1960, with a detailed application for registration being prepared and filed on 7 April 1961. The first Twin Pines BD had a wide range of experience that included mortgage banking and co-operatives. The registration application was approved, subject to the pledging of $50,000 being held by the Federal Home Loan Bank of San Francisco to guarantee against any losses, and that a minimum of 400 persons would subscribe $500,000 to be deposited in the new association, of which 90 percent was to be from individuals and not corporations. The CCB provided a loan for the guarantee fund and pledges for support, particularly from CCFCU depositors. The doors were opened for business on 1 July 1962 (Neptune, 1977, p. 142). The CCB encouraged members interested in organic food in 1957 to form a group to purchase these products and opened in September 1958 an Organic Foods Co-op (OFC), which operated a small store near the University Avenue store and claimed to be the first in the Bay Area. The CCB also contributed to CLUSA providing an affiliation fee of ten cents per member in January 1950 and provided loans to the CCFCU, Santa Monica Co-operative and the UCSA to help their activities. The CCB continued play an important role in Camp Sierra, with Sekerak having a prominent role in organizing the program (Neptune, 1977, p. 155; Tworek, 2008, pp. 26–27). The CCB acted to protect co-operative businesses by reporting to the government bogus co-operatives that wrongly used the term "co-operative" in their business activities (Illustration 5.4).[51]

The CCB, however, found it could not assist all co-operative activity. The San Gabriel Co-operative near Los Angeles approached the CCB, CLUSA, PAC and AC for a $5,000 gift or loan to help it deal with financial difficulties in 1956. The Californian co-operatives rejected this approach because all funds were committed to local needs, and the San Gabriel Co-operative's survival "was not urgent for the overall co-operative program in Southern California."[52] The San Gabriel Co-operative ceased operations by at least 1960 (Neptune, 1977, p. 176).

The CCB also developed international links. Kagawa again visited Berkeley in December 1950. In 1959, the PAC and the CCB accepted two executives for training from the Japanese Consumers' Co-operative Union (JCCU) at the request of Kagawa, who was JCCU President and later died in Tokyo on 26 April 1960. CLUSA organized the visits through its Fund for International Co-operative Development. Shigeru Fukuda, who was Chief Secretary of the Management Guidance

Illustration 5.4 Books Unlimited, University Avenue Store, 1960. Courtesy of Berkeley Historical Society.

Department at the JCCU stayed at CCB for five months and the policies and practices of the CCB were an influence on the Japanese movement. The CCB was also visited by co-operators from a variety of countries, including Malaysia, Egypt, Finland, India, the UK and West Germany. There were fundraising events for overseas co-operatives such as India Day on 3 April 1954, which involved Indian products, music and curries, and raising $250 toward the purchase of a jeep station wagon for the Indian co-operative movement. Members would also report on their visits to co-operatives overseas in the *CN*, with one member reporting in November 1954 of a six-month trip to England that included visits to about 20 co-operative stores and conversations with numerous co-operators (Ohya, 1992, p. vi).[53]

The CCB and AC supported a proposal by Governor Pat Brown to appoint a Consumer Counsel, who would advise the Governor on legislation necessary to promote and protect the Californian consumer. Helen Nelson, resident of Mill Valley in Marin County, an economist and CCB member, was appointed to the new position in 1959 and served until January 1967, when she was asked to resign by the incoming Republican Governor Ronald Reagan, who wanted the review of the continuation of the Counsel. Helen Nelson was employed at the Division of Labor Statistics and Research in the Californian Department of Industrial Relations and had been previously employed at the Federal Bureau of Labor Statistics. Nelson was a special guest speaker at the CCB AGM in January 1960. The CCB and AC also supported the formation of the Californian Consumer Association in July 1959, which arose from a Consumers' Conference held in June 1958. The Association, which monitored the Consumer Counsel and consumer legislation, included labor unions, co-operatives and credit unions.[54]

Conclusion

The period from 1947 to 1961 is one of steady expansion for the CCB with an additional center at Berkeley and the Walnut Creek Centre. There was a caution about expanding, as the CCB faced growing demand for stores in other Bay areas such as Marin County. While there were disagreements over issues, the Board was not factionalized and faced stable leadership with Mannila as General Manager and Gordon as President for several years. The period saw the foundation of a strong education program with home economists fueling a movement toward consumer activism. The CCB remained sympathetic to organized labor and tried to promote the loyalty and morale of its staff. The relationship with the AC and the broader co-operative movement continued to strengthen. There were some issues that were starting to emerge that could destabilize the co-operative. These included the growing organizational complexity of the CCB with increasing oversight of management by the BD with a growing number of member committees, including a Personnel Committee that could hear employee grievances. There were restrictions on participation by employee members and member apathy, which continued despite ideas such as the CCB Parliament. The CCB now faced further rapid growth and political upheaval as it entered the 1960s with major divisions in US society over civil rights and the Vietnam War.

Notes

1 Acting Managers' Report to BD, 25 February 1955, Carton 2 Folder 17. BANC MSS 90/140 c. CCB Records, UCB BL; *CN*, March 1956, p. 1, March 1958, p. 1; Interview Bob March by Therese Pipe, 2 May 1987. Transcript. BHS.

2 *CN*, 1 February 1961, p. 1.

3 AC Manager's Report to AC BD, 1 December 1951, Carton 1 Folder 12, CCB, Application before the Department of Investment, Division of Corporations of the State of California, 11 December 1954, Carton 2 Folder 17. BANC MSS 90/140 c. CCB Records, UCB BL; CCB Annual Report (AR), 1953–1954, p. 5.

4 *CN*, 1 November 1956, p. 4, March 1959, p. 2; Management Committee, 17 May 1948, Carton 1 Folder 9. BANC MSS 90/140 c. CCB Records, UCB BL.

5 *CN*, October 1948, May 1949, February 1951, November 1952, April 1953, December 1953, September 1954, November 1954, December 1954.

6 BD, 28 May 1951, 23 July 1951, Carton 1 Folder 11. BD Special, 6 December 1954, Carton 1 Folder 13. UCB, 'Statistical Data by Location 1953–1954', Typescript, Carton 2 Folder 17. BANC MSS 90/140 c. CCB Records, UCB BL; *CN*, October 1948, July 1951, December 1954, March 1955, June 1955, January 1956, p. 1, August 1956, p. 1, October 1957, p. 1; Interview Emil Sekerak by Therese Pipe, 6 February.1987. Interview Carroll Melbin by Therese Pipe, 21 February 1988. Interview Bob Arnold by James Mass, 18 April 1987. Transcript. BHS.

7 *CN*, March 1958, p. 2, 4 December 1959, p. 8, 8 April 1961, p. 7; Interview Adolph Kamil by Greg Patmore, 26 February 2013. Transcript. Author; Education Director's Report to the BD, 28 April 1958, Carton 2 Folder 22. BANC MSS 90/140 c. CCB Records, UCB BL.

8 *CN*, 11 July 1960, p. 1.

9 CCB, AR, 1951–1952, p. 1; Memo to CCB Members, 1 October 1960, BANC MSS 90/140 c, Carton 13 Folder 21. BANC MSS 90/140 c, CCB Records, UCB BL.

10 *CN*, 1 February 1948, September 1948, January 1949, June 1949, August 1949, 20 April 1951, June 1951, August 1951, October 1951, 28 October 1953, December 1953, April 1955, 1 November 1956, pp. 1, 4, 20 December 1956, p. 1, 3 September 1957, p. 6, August-September 1958, p. 9, June 1959, p. 1, 15 December 1961.

11 BD, 25 February 1957, 25 March 1957, 22 April 1957, Carton 1 Folder 13, BD, 27 March 1961, Carton 2 Folder 19. Supplementary Managers' Report to Board of Directors, 25 February 1957, Carton 2 Folder 19, Managers' Report to Board of Directors, 23 December 1957, Carton 2 Folder 23, Managers' Report to Board of Directors, 27 July 1959, Carton 2 Folder 24. BANC MSS 90/140 c. CCB Records, UCB BL; *CN*, 3 May 1957, p. 1, 6 October 1959, p. 4; Interview Bob March by Therese Pipe, 2 May 1987. Transcript. BHS.

12 *CN*, 20 April 1951, June 1951, July 1955; Interview Emil Sekerak by Therese Pipe, 6 February 1987. Transcript. BHS.

13 *CN*, July-August 1959, p. 5; Finance Committee, 19 January 1959. Managers' Report to BD, 23 March 1959, Carton 2 Folder 24. Finance Committee, 18 May 1961, Carton 2 Folder 27. CCB Records, UCB BL.

14 BD, 19 December 1949, Carton 1 Folder 10. BANC MSS 90/140 c. CCB Records, UCB BL.

CN, 15 March 1948, July 1953, August 1953, January 1954, February 1954, July 1955, August-September 1958, p. 3, March 1959, pp. 1, 4, 4 December 1959, p. 7.

15 *CN*, January 1949, February 1950, March 1950; Interview Emil Sekerak by Therese Pipe, 6 February 1987. Transcript. BHS.
16 *CN*, December 1952.
17 Interview Emil Sekerak by Therese Pipe, 6 February 1987. Transcript. BHS.
18 Interview Emil Sekerak by Therese Pipe, 6 February1987. Transcript. BHS.
19 *CN*, October 1955, March 1956, p. 4, June 1956, p. 4, 16 December 1957, p. 4; Education Director's Report to the BD, 25 October 1957, 25 November 1957, 24 February 1958, Carton 2 Folder 22. BANC MSS 90/140 c. CCB Records, UCB BL.
20 *CN*, July 1950, April 1952, November 1954, 27 December 1966, p. 3.
21 *CN*, May 1947, November 1949.
22 *CN*, September 1951.
23 CCB, AR 1955–1956, p. 8; BD, 22 July 1957, Carton 1 Folder 13, Letter E. Sekerak to B. Rumford, 26 February 1957, Carton 2 Folder 19, Education Director's Report to the BD, 23 December 1957, Carton 2 Folder 22. BANC MSS 90/140 c. CCB Records, UCB BL. *CN*, June 1949, August 1949, October 1949, 3 June 1961, pp. 1, 3, 24 July 1961, p. 1.
24 *CN*, March 1954.
25 Annual Meeting, 2 December 1954, Carton 12 Folder 21. BANC MSS 90/140 c. CCB Records, UCB BL; *CN*, 1 November 1956, p. 4.
26 *CN*, October 1957, p. 7.
27 *CN*, 16 January 1958, p. 10.
28 *CN*, 16 January 1958, pp. 3, 11; Member Relations Committee, 2 April 1959, Carton 2 Folder 24, BD, 26 January 1959, Carton 2 Folder 25. BANC MSS 90/140 c. CCB Records, UCB BL.
29 CN, July 1958, p. 3.
30 *CN*, 4 December 1959, p. 8, 6 June 1960, p. 1.
31 *CN*, 6 June 1960, p. 2.
32 Petition, "Protest Against the Sale of Hard Liquor by the Co-op", no date. Walnut Creek Centre Committee, 14 November 1960. Letter Eugene Mannila to D.E. Phelps, 15 November 1960, Carton 3 Folder 27. BANC MSS 90/140 c. CCB Records, UCB BL.
33 BD, 19 December 1960, Carton 2 Folder 25. Committee on Committees, 10 May 1961, Carton 3 Folder 27. BANC MSS 90/140 c. CCB Records, UCB BL; *CN*, 11 July 1960, pp. 1–2, 6 September 1960, p. 1.
34 *CN*, October 1950, February 1951, March 1951, September 1952; Interview Emil Sekerak by Therese Pipe, 6 February 1987. Transcript. BHS; Management Committee, 17 May 1948, Carton 1 Folder 9. BANC MSS 90/140 c. CCB Records, UCB BL.
35 *CN*, June 1953, November 1953, January 1954.
36 BD, 22 November 1948, Carton 1 Folder 9. BD, 23 October 1961, Carton 1 Folder 9. Letter Eugene Mannila to J.C. Sergeant, 18 December 1959, Carton 3 Folder 26, Report of General Manager to the BD, 26 November 1956, United Grocers Circular, 1 November 1956, Carton 2 Folder 19, Report of General Manager to the BD, 29 September 1958, Carton 2 Folder 23. BANC MSS 90/140 c. CCB Records, UCB BL; *CN*, 15 October 1947, 15 March 1948, October 1949, July 1951, July 1953, August 1953, 5 February 1960, p. 1, 7 March 1960, p. 2, 14 November 1960, p. 3.
37 *CN*, December 1949.
38 *CN*, January 1950.
39 BD, 26 February 1951, Carton 1 Folder 11, BD, 23 April 1956, Carton 1 Folder 13, Press Release, "Co-op Rotates Managers", n.d., Carton 2 Folder 27. BANC MSS 90/140 c. CCB Records, UCB BL; *CN*, December 1949, July

1952, December 1953, June 1954, October 1955, March 1956, p. 2, May 1956, p. 7, June 1956, pp. 3, 5, 5 June 1957, p. 7.

40 BD, 25 April 1949, Management Committee, 18 April 1949, Carton 1 Folder 10. Management Committee, 21 September 1959, Carton 2 Folder 24. Member Relations Committee, 1 October 1959, Carton 3 Folder 25. BANC MSS 90/140 c. CCB Records, UCB BL; *CN*, 4 December 1959, p. 8.

41 BD, 25 July 1949. Management Committee, 20 February 1950, Carton 1 Folder 10. BANC MSS 90/140 c. CCB Records, UCB BL; *CN*, October 1956, p. 1.

42 BD, 25 November 1954, Carton 1 Folder 13, BD, 19 December 1960, Carton 2 Folder 25. BANC MSS 90/140 c. CCB Records, UCB BL; *CN*, April 1949, January 1954, February 1954, April 1954, November 1954, February 1955, March 1956, 3 April 1957, p. 3, 3 May 1957, p. 1; Interview Emil Sekerak by Therese Pipe, 6 February 1987. Transcript. BHS.

43 BD, 28 August 1950, 25 September 1950, Carton 1 Folder 10, BD, 22 October 1951, Carton 1 Folder 12, BD, 25 August 1953, Carton 1 Folder 13, Letter S. Avakian to E. Mannila, 19 August 1957, Carton 2 Folder 19. BANC MSS 90/140 c. CCB Records, UCB BL; *CN*, June 1949, July 1951, November 1951, 28 October 1953, December 1953, March 1954, March 1956, p. 3, May 1958, p. 9, October 1958, pp. 1, 7, 12, 3 September 1959, p. 1, 8 March 1961, p. 3.

44 *CN*, May 1949, August 1949, September 1949, October 1949, November 1950.

45 BD, 26 October 1959, Carton 2 Folder 25. Report of General Manager to the BD, 28 April 1958, Carton 2 Folder 19, Finance Committee, 20 October 1960, Carton 3 Folder 27. BANC MSS 90/140 c. CCB Records, UCB BL; *CN*, November 1949, 16 January 1957, p. 11, August-September 1958, p. 6.

46 AC Memo, Robert Neptune, 2 April 1948, BD, 1 November 1948, Carton 1 Folder 9, BD, 27 December 1948, Carton 2 Folder 20. BD, 26 May 1958, Carton 1 Folder 10. Joint All Committee Meeting, 5 October 1954. Carton 2 Folder 17. BANC MSS 90/140 c. CCB Records, UCB BL.

47 BD, 23 November 1959, 25 April 1960, Carton 2 Folder 25, CCB Parliament, 15 November 1959, Carton 3 Folder 26. BANC MSS 90/140 c. CCB Records, UCB BL; *CN*, 4 December 1959, p. 4, 5 February 1960, p. 2, 6 May 1960, p. 2.

48 BD, 24 May 1948, Carton 1 Folder 9, BD, 26 November 1951, Carton 1 Folder 12. BANC MSS 90/140 c. CCB Records, UCB BL; *CN*, August 1949.

49 CN, August 1953, June 1954, July-August 1959, p. 3.

50 BD, 26 July 1948, Carton 1 Folder 9, BD, 23 March 1953, Carton 1 Folder 13. BANC MSS 90/140 c. CCB Records, UCB BL; *CN*, May 1959, p. 1; Interview Eva Goodwin by Bob Larsen, 22 October 1987, 29 October 1987. Transcript BHS; *Pine Cones*, Summer 1962, p. 1.

51 *CN*, February 1950, May 1955, May 1956, p. 7, 5 June 1957, p. 1, September 1957, p. 7, February 1958, p. 8, August-September 1958, p. 5, 3 September 1959, p. 5, 18 October 1965, p. 1; Interview Emil Sekerak by Therese Pipe, 6 February 1987. Transcript. BHS; Letter J.R. Johnston to F.W. Collins, 24 July 1957, Carton 2 Folder 19. BANC MSS 90/140 c. CCB Records, UCB BL.

52 BD, 26 March 1956, Carton 1 Folder 13. BANC MSS 90/140 c. CCB Records, UCB BL.

53 *CN*, January 1951, June 1951, August 1951, February 1952, April 1952, August 1952, April 1954, November 1954, 3 September 1959, p. 1, 6 May 1960, p. 1.

54 *CN*, February 1959, p. 1, July-August 1959, p. 3; 3 September 1959, p. 8; 6 October 1959, p. 1, 3 February 1960, p. 1, 6 February 1967, p. 3, 20 February, p. 2.

References

Bay Area Census, 2018, available at www.bayareacensus.ca.gov (accessed 14 June 2018).

Berkeley Student Housing, 2018, available at www.lib.berkeley.edu/uchistory/general_history/campuses/ucb/housing.html (accessed 14 June 2018).

BHS, 1983, *Eugene Mannila. A Finnish Pioneer of the Consumers Co-operative of Berkeley*, Berkeley, CA, BHS.

BHS, 1984, *Margaret Shaughnessy Gordon. Past President of the Consumers Co-operative of Berkeley, Research Economist, and Community Leader*, Berkeley, CA, BHS.

BHS, 1987a, *George G. Little. The President of the Consumers Co-operative of Berkeley in the 1960s*, Berkeley, CA, BHS.

BHS, 1987b, *Laurie Leonard Lehtin. A Finnish Leader's Perspective on the Co-operative movement*, Berkeley, CA, BHS.

BHS, 1989, *William Taylor (Zach) Brown. A Discussion of his Life in Berkeley City Politics and in Consumers Co-operative Movement*, Berkeley, CA, BHS.

BHS, 1993, *Matt Crawford: Reflections on the Cooperative Center Federal Credit Union of Berkeley, and the Consumers Co-operative of Berkeley*, Berkeley, CA, BHS.

BHS, 1995, *A Conversation with George Yasukochi: Controller of the Consumers Co-operative of Berkeley, 1956–1982*, Berkeley, CA, BHS.

BHS, 1996, *A Conversation with Robert Neptune – Pioneer Manager of the Consumers Co-operative of Berkeley, and Long-Term Manager at Associated Co-operatives*, Berkeley, CA, BHS.

Brinkley, A., 2003, *American History. A Survey. Volume II: Since 1865*, 11th ed., New York, McGraw-Hill.

Cooper, D.H. and Mohn, P.O., 1992, *The Greenbelt Co-operative: Success and Decline*, Davis, CA, Centre for Co-operatives, University of California.

Curl, J., 2012, *For All the People: Uncovering the Hidden History of Co-operation, Co-operative Movements, and Communalism in America*, 2nd ed., Oakland, CA, PM Press.

Goldstein, C.M., 2012, *Creating Consumers: Home Economists in Twentieth Century America*, Chapel Hill, University of North Carolina Press.

Grillo, E., 1978, "D.G. Gibson: A Black Who Led the People and Built the Democratic Party in the East Bay," In Nathan, H., and Scott, S., eds., *Experiment and Change in Berkeley. Essays on City Politics 1950–1975*, Berkeley, CA, Institute of Government Studies, UCB, pp. 1–7.

Johnson, M.S., 1996, *The Second Gold Rush: Oakland and the East Bay in World War II*, Berkeley, University of California Press.

Kent, T.J. Jr., 1978, "Berkeley's First Liberal Democratic Regime, 1961–1970. The Postwar Awakening of Berkeley's Liberal Conscience," In Nathan, H., and Scott, S, eds., *Experiment and Change in Berkeley. Essays on City Politics 1950–1975*, Berkeley, CA, Institute of Government Studies, UCB, pp. 71–104.

Lemke, G., 1987, *Afro-Americans in Berkeley 1859–1987*, Berkeley, CA, BHS.

Lyford, J.P., 1982, *The Berkeley Archipelago*, Chicago, IL, Regnery Gateway.

Mannila, E., 1984, *The Finns and the Bay Co-operative Movement*, Berkeley, CA, BHS.

McCarthy, K., 2007, "History of the Arts & Craft Co-operative, Inc," available at www.accigallery.com/history-of-acci.html (accessed 30 August 2018).

Nathan, H. and Scott, S, eds., 1978, *Experiment and Change in Berkeley. Essays on City Politics 1950–1975*, Berkeley, CA, Institute of Government Studies, UCB.

Neptune, R., 1977, *California's Uncommon Markets. The Story of Consumers Co-operatives 1935–1976*, 2nd ed., Richmond, CA, AC.

Ohya, M., 1992, "Preface," In Fullerton, M., ed., *What Happened to the Berkeley Co-op? A Collection of Opinions*, Davis, CA, Center for Co-operatives, University of California.

Patmore, G., 2017, "Fighting Monopoly and Enhancing Democracy: A Historical Overview of US Consumer Co-operatives," In Hilson, M., Neunsinger, S., and Patmore, G., eds., *A Global History of Consumer Co-operation since 1850: Movements and Businesses*, Leiden, Brill, pp. 507–526.

Rorabaugh, W.J., 1989, *Berkeley at War. The 1960s*, New York, Oxford University Press.

Rovanpera, B., 2009, *Walnut Creek. An Illustrated History*, Walnut Creek, CA, Walnut Creek Historical Society.

Tworek, C.J., 2008, *Background for an Exhibit. The Creation and Development of the Co-operative Center Federal Credit Union*, MA History Project Proposal, California State University East Bay.

UCB Office of the Vice Chancellor of Finance, 2019, "Our Berkeley. Enrolment History Since 1869," available at https://pages.github.berkeley.edu/OPA/our-berkeley/enroll-history.html (accessed 14 April 2019).

Weinstein, D., 2008, *It Came from Berkeley. How Berkeley Changed the World*, Layton, UT, Gibbs Smith.

Wollenberg, C., 2008, *Berkeley. A City in History*, Berkeley, University of California Press.

6 Politics and Expansion
1962–1971

This chapter examines the rapid growth of the CCB during the 1960s. The growth was assisted by expansion into new areas such as Marin County. The second aspect of growth involved the taking over of private stores such as the five Sids chain stores in 1962, which provoked controversy within the CCB. There was internal controversy about the CCB's involvement in political issues, such as the protests over Governor Ronald Reagan in 1969 ordering the Californian Army National Guard (CANG) into Berkeley to end the protests in the People's Park at UCB, and the rise of factional politics that reflected the broader political divisions in Berkeley. The CCB strengthened its role as a center for consumer activism. It called for labeling standards, published a low-cost cookbook in 1965 and introduced organic produce in 1970. The CCB continued to recognize labor unions and in 1968 supported the struggles of Californian farm workers for a union by boycotting nonunion grapes.

Berkeley and Beyond

While Oakland and San Francisco declined in population during the 1960s, between 1960 and 1970 the population of Berkeley slightly increased from 111,268 to 116,716. The White population in Berkeley continued to decline from 73.8 percent to 66.7 percent, while the African American population grew from 19.8 percent to 23.5 percent. Other areas of the Bay Area continued to benefit from suburbanization, with Walnut Creek dramatically growing from 9,903 to 39,844 and Marin County, north of San Francisco and linked directly to the East Bay by the opening of the Richmond-San Rafael Bridge in 1956, growing from 146,820 to 206,038. Walnut Creek and Marin County had white populations of 98.1 percent and 90.5 percent by 1970 (Bay Area Census, 2018).[1]

The UCB student numbers fluctuated during the 1960s. There were 27,740 and 27,712 students, respectively, in 1962 and 1971, with a peak year in 1964 with 30,032 students (UCB, 2019). Younger students, less likely to have family responsibilities than Second World War veterans, were assured of reasonably well-paid jobs on graduation. Clark Kerr, who became UC President in 1958, was a liberal Democrat and sympathetic to student concerns. He relaxed some rules governing political activities on campus, with political identities being allowed to speak on campus for the first time since the 1930s, but still prohibited political groups from raising money or holding demonstrations on campus property (Rorabaugh, 1989, pp. 9, 11; Wollenberg, 2008, pp. 136–138).

The UCB became a center of radical politics in the US during the 1960s. The radicalism was fueled by the campaigns for civil rights, opposition to the Vietnam War, calls for alternative education that challenged the status quo and the development of a counter culture. An early example of student activism was Toward an Active Student Community (TASC), which began in 1957 and opposed racial segregation in student housing and supported participatory educational projects. TASC in 1958 formed a new student political party, Slate, which achieved a primary goal in 1961, when the UC Board of Regents abolished compulsory Reserve Officers' Training Corps program on UC campuses in 1962. Berkeley students also protested the San Francisco meetings of the House Un-American Activities Committee in 1960. The Free Speech Movement (FSM), led by philosophy student Mario Savio, started protesting an administrative decision to ban political activity on Sproul Plaza at UCB in September 1964. This led to the greatest mass arrest in California history on the night of 2–3 December 1964 of 750 students engaged in a sit-in at Sproul Hall. The protests at Berkeley and other UC campuses assisted the election of Ronald Reagan as Governor in 1966 on an anti-student protest platform and paved the way for the dismissal of Kerr by a Reagan-dominated Board of Regents in 1967. Reagan and the UC Board of Regents' attitude to Kerr were influenced by the FBI Director, J. Edgar Hoover, who disliked Kerr's liberal politics. Despite this, conflict persisted at UCB with 3,000 students turning out to protest UCB's refusal to shut down for the Moratorium Day in 1969, and protests, walk-outs and mass teach-ins over the next two years over the War and the UCB's relationship with the military (Starr, 2007, pp. 328–329; Weinstein, 2008, pp. 151–153, 166–169; Wollenberg, 2008, pp. 136–138, 149–150).

The conflict reached a peak in February 1969 when Governor Reagan declared a "state of extreme emergency" in the City of Berkeley in response to a UC plea for help in dealing with continued campus unrest. The Governor's decree authorized the use of the CANG to assist local law authorities, if requested (Balnave and Patmore, 2017, p. 19). Reagan was frustrated at the UCB's "continued unwillingness to take the firm action necessary to protect the rights of students and faculty which are being so flagrantly violated."[2] According to official estimates, the conflict between protestors and the state over the use and fencing of People's Park on 15 May 1969, which was land owned by UCB that it planned to use as sports fields rather than open space, resulted in the death of a bystander by the police, 43 non-law enforcement casualties largely from shotgun pellets, 48 arrests and 103 police officers injured. Protestors in contrast claimed that the police shot 110 people. The CANG intervened the following day leading to skirmishes between protesters and armed government forces, with a national guard helicopter indiscriminately dispensing tear gas on 20 May into the Sproul Hall Plaza, and a further proclamation by Governor Reagan on 22 May enforcing a curfew in various locations in Berkeley and banning meetings, assemblies or parades of more than six people. Reagan justified his action in terms of substantial damage to UCB property and assaults on law enforcement officers (Balnave and Patmore, 2017, pp. 19–20). He referred to the People's Park as "an all night orgy center" and "garbage dump ...,"[3] and noted that "part of the lush greenery planted to make the lot a so-called sylvan glade turned out to be marijuana."[4] During the unrest, the Quakers distributed 30,000 daisies, which the protestors handed out to CANG members, who put the flowers on their bayonets and in their rifle barrels. CANG members talked to residents, particularly women, and many began to sympathize with the residents over the occupation of their city (Rorabaugh, 1989, p. 165). The state of emergency remained in effect until 2 June 1969 (Balnave and Patmore, 2017, p. 20).

The upheavals on the UCB campus were also reflected in a shift to the Left in Berkeley. Between 1962 and 1971, the number of registered Democrats rose from 31,650 to 67,151, while the number of registered Republicans fell from 17,455 to 15,550. Berkeley attracted progressives with the Red Family commune, which operated from 1969 to 1973 in Elmwood and included New Leftists such as Tom Hayden, who helped create Students for a Democratic Society (SDS) and later became a state senator. The Blue Fairyland, a radical parent-participation nursery school in Elmwood, attracted actress Jane Fonda and her daughter. Fonda would shop at the local CCB outlet and eventually married Hayden. Telegraph Avenue, with its street merchants and homeless people, became a focal point for conflict between police and counterculture advocates such as hippies in 1968 and 1969, with a rally outside Cody's bookshop on 28 June 1968 honoring the French student revolt against De Gaulle the previous month leading Berkeley police to use tear gas for the first time and some protesters responding with rocks. Huey P. Newton and Bobby Searle founded in 1966 the Black Panther Party, which was initially headquartered in South Berkeley and later Oakland. The Black Panthers became a focus of militant African American protest and rhetoric in the Bay Area for the next decade. There was also a surge of interest in women's liberation from 1968, with the Liberated Women of Berkeley supporting the 1969 protests concerning the People's Park. The counterculture created its own media with the *Berkeley Barb*, a notable example, commencing publication in August 1965 (Rorabaugh, 1989, pp. 121–122, 132–133, 159; Weinstein, 2008, pp. 165, 172–174; Willes, 2000, pp. 99–100; Wollenberg, 2008, pp. 143, 146).[5]

The new liberal Democratic BCC reflects the shift to the Left with city development and civil rights. It supported a grassroots campaign, whose leaders included Catherine Kerr, the spouse of Clark Kerr, to stop the filling and development of the Berkeley tidelands, with the BCC limiting the future fill to what is now the Berkeley marina, with an emphasis on parkland and recreational facilities. The BCC passed an ordinance banning housing discrimination, which a citizens' committee appointed by the BCC found to be endemic, in January 1963. It was rejected by a BCC referendum vote in April 1963 of 22,750 votes to 20,456, in a campaign that featured racism and threats by local realtors not to sell homes to African Americans in the Berkeley Hills. Republican Wallace Johnson, who supported the referendum, won the 1963 Mayoral race and held that position until 1971. While a similar initiative was introduced at the state level by Rumford and passed, it was also rejected in a state referendum, with Berkeley voters now supporting fair housing. The state referendum was eventually ruled invalid by the US Supreme Court in 1967 and the law again enforced. Mayor Johnson also joined with the liberal democrats to ensure that Berkeley community was not divided by the construction of BART, which was approved by 60.8 percent of voters in San Francisco, Contra Costa and Alameda Counties in November 1962. Berkeley residents in October 1966 voted with an 80 percent majority for a bond issue to ensure that it was built as a subway rather than above ground. Despite this, the construction of the North Berkeley station had an impact on the business at CCB's University Avenue store, as many long-standing members' homes were demolished (Daniels, 2013, p. 333; Healy, 2016, pp. 95–103; Johnson, 1978, pp. 193–201; Weinstein, 2008, p. 146; Wollenberg, 2008, pp. 130–133).[6]

The liberal Berkeley School Board in 1964 also moved to end the desegregation of schools starting with the junior high schools. Berkeley had only one high school and was integrated, but ability tracking meant classes remained segregated. The South Berkeley flatland schools predominantly had African American students, while the Berkeley Hills had white students. While there was an attempt to stop the integration of junior high schools in 1964, the recall campaign against board members failed by more than a two-thirds majority. The process was completed in elementary schools in April 1968 with the two-way busing of African American children to the Hills and white children going to the flatlands. Berkeley became the first city with more than 100,000 residents in the US to desegregate its schools voluntarily without a court order. While white families hostile to school integration left the district, the white enrolment in Berkeley schools was sustained by white parents sympathetic to school integration moving into Berkeley (Rorabaugh, 1989, p. 68; Weinstein, 2008, pp. 147–151; Wollenberg, 2008, pp. 133–134).

Politics in Berkeley became polarized between anti-Vietnam War radicals and liberal pro-War Democrats. The Berkeley Women for Peace

(BWP) sent 100,000 Christmas cards in 1965 to Lyndon Johnson's White House demanding peace, while the Berkeley Medical Aid Committee sent supplies to the Vietcong. There was a fracturing of the Democratic Party in Berkeley with the disappearance of the Party's precinct organization, the demise of the Party's local newspaper and Democratic Clubs either splitting or becoming inactive. Cohelan, the local liberal US Congress representative, who supported Johnson's Vietnam policy, was challenged in 1966 by Robert Sheer, who saw the War as a make-and-break issue. Ron Dellums, a radical anti-War BCC member, successfully defeated Cohelan in the Democratic Primary 1970. Radical Warren Widener, Berkeley's first African American Mayor, was elected in 1971 by 49 votes and the leftist April Coalition Slate won seats on the BCC (Kent, 1978, pp. 97–98; Weinstein, 2008, pp. 146, 165–166; Wollenberg, 2008, pp. 150–151).

Managing the Co-operative

From 1962 to 1971, there were signs of growing turmoil in CCB management. Robert Lee, an Assistant General Manager, resigned on 31 July 1966, citing the "harassment and abuse of management" and complaining about the erosion of management authority while being held responsible for financial performance.[7] Mannila continued to serve as General Manager until December 1971, despite health issues in January 1969. He gave six months' notice of his early retirement to give the BD time to find a replacement. Mannila grew frustrated with many BD directors being unable to understand financial statements and some showing a greater willingness to pursue issues that were not of importance to the CCB's financial position. There were five presidents during this period, with George Little continuing in the role until 1967. After this, there was a regular turnover of presidents reflecting the growing factionalism of the BD, with Robert Arnold serving from 1968 to 1969 (Mannila, 1984, p. 25; Neptune, 1977, pp. 185–186).[8]

Two notable directors were Margedant Hayakawa and Robert Treuhaft. Hayakawa had extensive co-operative experience before joining the CCB in 1955. In Chicago, she was on the boards of South Shore Co-operative and the Hyde Park Co-operative, where she became President from 1954 to 1955. She edited from 1942 to 1947 the Midwest newspaper, *Co-op News*. After her arrival in the Bay, she was a promoter of the expansion of CCB into Marin County. She served on BD during 1963–1968, including a period as CCB Vice President. She was the wife of English Professor Samuel Hayakawa, a noted linguist who served as President of San Francisco State University and later become a Republican Senator for California. Hayakawa was strongly opposed to consumer co-operatives to entering politics, believing they were "sunk" if they became a "political battleground." Treuhaft served on the BD during 1964–1969. He was a lawyer, a Communist Party member from the mid-1940s until 1957, leaving after Nikita Khrushchev's revelations in 1956 about the horrors of Stalin, and husband of the author Jessica Mitford. Treuhaft was a lawyer for the FSM and among those arrested in December 1964. He first became active in the East Bay Memorial Association, being elected to its BD in September 1955. This organization, which aimed to provide simple and dignified funerals at a reasonable cost, received initial financial assistance from the CCB in April 1955. While Treuhaft criticized the BD prior to 1968 for mismanagement in terms of expansion and declining patronage refunds and for employment discrimination against African Americans, he saw the CCB as playing a political role, arguing that the Vietnam War was the most important issue facing consumers (BHS, 1987b, pp. 47–48; BHS, 1990, pp. 29–30, 53–60, 70–71, 79; BHS, 1996b, p. 24; Curl, 2012, p. 196; Neptune, 1977, pp. 183–184; Rorabaugh, 1989, p. 42).[9]

The major question that divided the BD was the question of political neutrality. There were clashes between those who saw the co-operative as a business and those who saw it as a platform for political issues. As early as 1964, two opposing factions appeared on the BD that became known as the Moderates and the Progressives. This division mirrored the factions within the Berkeley Democratic Party, with the former linked to the liberals and the later to the radicals. Little and Hayakawa were examples of Moderates, while Treuhaft and Arnold were Progressives. Treuhaft was critical of Little as President, and when he was nominated for the BD in January 1964, he claimed that Little weakened BD unity by "brusquely" treating dissenting opinions. The Moderates attempted to stop Treuhaft running for the BD in 1967, when the Nominating Committee refused to endorse him because of his radical politics, even though he was no longer a Communist Party member. Tensions increased with Treuhaft and the Progressives, but Treuhaft gained a position on the ballot with the support of a petition signed by approximately 1,200 members. The Treuhaft household was turned into a campaign headquarters, with Mitford helping as an organizer, and Treuhaft was reelected. Arnold and others formed a Member Action Committee in the wake of the 1967 BD elections, which aimed to deal with the CCB's "urgent" problems and produced a critical newsletter. When the Progressives won the BD, they alienated liberal shoppers and vice versa. The Progressives controlled the BD from 1968 to 1969 and 1972. There was a rule that since 1955 allowed the three alternate directors to fill vacant positions in the absence of regular directors, and their votes created further instability in a factionalized political environment. The voting was close with a faction holding a five to four margin when they were in power. When a Moderate member was absent at a BD meeting on 28 December 1970, a temporary Progressive majority drafted a tough affirmative action policy, which was reversed at the next meeting. The changes in BD leadership led to dramatic changes in policy for management, staff confusion, declining staff morale, a lack of information for members and the replacement of key personnel. One of the reasons for Mannila's early retirement in 1971 was the shifting policy according to which faction was in power, which he later claimed was one of the "most difficult things" working at the CCB. The conflict within the CCB BD over politics reflected widespread distrust of professionalism and leadership in Berkeley during the 1960s, which placed further pressure on CCB managers. Managers, for example, found that their 1967–1968 budget was not approved until after the beginning of the financial year due to concerns about issues, such as the accuracy of their past revenue forecasts and the value of education expenditure. There were also similar internal divisions in other Berkeley organizations, where radicals played an important role such as the Berkeley Free Clinic and radio station KPFA (BHS, 1983, pp. 36–37; BHS, 1987a, p. 17; BHS, 1987b, p. 29; BHS, 1990, p. 70; BHS, 1996b, p. 20; Curl, 2012, p. 196; Kresy, 1980, pp. 2–3, 5–6; Lyford, 1982, p. 240; Neptune, 1977, pp. 112–113; Ohya,1992, p. vii; Rauber, 1992, p. 14; Illustration 6.1).[10]

Illustration 6.1 CCB Board, 1964. Seated from left: Jessie Coles, Maudelle Miller, George Little, Clinton White, Margedant Hayakawa. Standing from the Left: Edward Barankin, Robert Treuhaft, Robert Arnold, Hans Lescke, Tom Farris, Earle Fuller. Courtesy of Berkeley Historical Society #10455.

The view that the CCB should not engage in politics had been a dominant view up until the early 1960s drawing on the early Rochdale principles. The BD rejected a proposal in March 1959 to support a proposition for school boards bonds in Berkeley as it did not wish to "violate a Co-op Principle of political neutrality."[11] The CCB Board of Directors in June 1960 adopted policy that it should only take a stand on legislative issues if they related to consumer protection, affected CLUSA affiliates and Rochdale co-operatives, including the CCB, or where endorsed by CLUSA.[12]

There was shift toward a political role in the 1960s. The BD in March 1963 decided to support the BCC Fair Housing Ordinance in the April referendum. While the BD claimed that fair housing was an extension of co-operative principles and therefore nonpolitical, Mannila claimed that the BD's position would lead to the politicization of the CCB as it was a party-political issue. The DB also gave support to the Rumford legislation on fair housing and opposed the initiative to repeal it. Against a background of condemnation by UC staff of the use of CANG on the Berkeley campus in May 1969, the DB unanimously demanded the immediate withdrawal of the CANG and Sheriff's forces in Berkeley and called for the end of the state of emergency. There was a division by five to four on a resolution to join a protest march against the presence of the CANG in Berkeley and close all the Berkeley stores to allow employees to participate. While there were concerns about a quorum, similar resolutions of protest were passed at the Semi-Annual Meeting of members in May 1969. The CCB faced criticism and resignations by some members who objected to the CCB taking a "political stand" on Reagan's action.[13] Dissident BD members in a letter to the *CN* argued that the BD should refrain from "taking a position on controversial matters which are not conducive to the economic growth and stability of the Co-op."[14] The BD also decided by five votes to four on 28 October 1969 to close the CCB stores before noon on 14 November 1969 in support of a second nationwide Vietnam Moratorium. Dissident BD members issued a circular calling upon CCB members to protest the decision, with some members resigning or reducing their capital investment in the CCB over the issue. Data for the 53 weeks ending 4 October 1969 indicates that 117 or 4.9 percent of members leaving the CCB gave the CCB's stance on public issues as their major reason. For the 13 weeks ending 1 January 1970, there were 59 or 10.2 percent of members leaving over politics, the largest proportion after "moved, deceased or divorced" at 64.8 percent.[15]

While there were divisions on the BD, the growth of the CCB presented challenges to the management. Mannila maintained the practice of weekly meetings of store and department managers to discuss member concerns and improve efficiency. As the CCB grew, the management ranks expanded with the appointment of specialists. Following the resignation of Assistant Manager Lee in July 1966, Controller Yasukochi had the added title of Assistant to the General Manager and Robert Satake, supervisor of the garage and service stations, became Operations Manager. Center managers were also given greater local authority and responsibility. The CCB added a personnel director to assist with the management of a growing workforce. The Progressives, when they won power in 1968, hired for the first time external consultants, Arthur D. Little Inc., to review CCB management, reflecting their criticism of CCB management. The Little report was also critical of the CCB management structure. The BD adopted recommendations, including "differential merchandising," where each Center would reflect on local marketing conditions and provide goods and services to meet local demands, a management performance measurement system and the creation of a Corporate Development and Financial Manager, a position filled by Barry Solloway, who commenced in July 1969 to assist long-term planning (Neptune, 1977, p. 112).[16]

As Table 6.1 indicates, while the volume of CCB sales continually increased from 1962 to 1971, there were financial issues appearing in the late 1960s as political issues split the BD. Net savings peaked in 1965, with a general decline leading to loss in 1971, the first since 1946. Member equity also peaked in 1968 and went into decline, falling by 2.7 percent between 1968 and 1971.

There were two strategies that underlay the growth of sales. There was continued expansion into new areas such as El Cerrito in June 1963 and Marin County in March 1967. The El Cerrito Center included a gas station, supermarket, a pharmacy, a children's clothing store, which along with one at the University Avenue store was closed in 1970 due to poor sales, an in-store bakery that was later expanded to supply baked goods to other CCB Berkeley stores and offices for the CCFCU and the MSI. The El Cerrito Center was also innovative in EDP, as new cash registers had optical readers that allowed data concerning membership numbers and purchases to be forwarded to a computer for processing.

Table 6.1 CCB Finances 1962–1971 (Neptune, 1977, p. 191)

Year	*Volume ($)*	*Net Savings ($)*	*Member Equity ($)*
1962	16,018,645	522,814	2,475,474
1963	19,626,000	422,500	2,841,600
1964	22,747,700	796,400	3,262,800
1965	23,321,400	890,600	3,662,800
1966	23,723,700	671,000	3,910,100
1967	26,540,700	473,600	4,021,200
1968	27,875,700	485,000	4,023,900
1969	29,813,500	430,00	3,969,000
1970	34,280,600	396,600	3,912,900
1971	40,208,800	(73,200)	3,912,100

It also introduced a service that allowed individuals or their doctors to mail their prescriptions to the pharmacy and receive their medicines at home by first-class mail on the following day. The Marin Buying Group was formed in 1951 and applied, with 140 members, for CCB membership in January 1957. CCB members undertook a drive in 1960 to obtain sufficient members and capital to have a CCB center. The CCB took option on land for a possible center site in December 1960, which spurred another organizing effort, but its application for rezoning of land to commercial was defeated by a unanimous decision of the Corte Madera Council in March 1961. There was strong opposition from existing retailers to planning approval.[17] When the Marin Center opened in Corte Madera, it included a food store and a range of diversified services operated by lessees, including a restaurant, a laundromat and a camera shop. There were issues for the CCB in managing a large shopping center, with some of the initial lessees closing due to insufficient turnover and some stores vacant for several months while new tenants were sought. The Center was not to be fully occupied for another three years (Neptune, 1977, pp. 51–52). The CCB also opened in Berkeley a garage in Shattuck Avenue in February 1964, a new Shattuck Avenue hardware-variety-pharmacy center on the corner opposite the Shattuck Avenue Center in January 1967 and a new garage on University Avenue in January 1968 (Illustration 6.2).[18]

Illustration 6.2 Home Economist Nancy Bratt at Marin Center, 1967. Courtesy of Berkeley Historical Society #10460.

The second aspect of growth involved the taking over of non-cooperative five Sids chain stores in 1962. This strategy for rapidly increasing growth had been advocated by other US co-operators. On a CCB visit in February 1961, CLUSA President Lincoln told management that co-operatives were not growing fast enough and needed to grow through "buying out some chains."[19] There were other co-operatives, such as the Co-operative Enterprises of Akron, Ohio, in 1960, that had expanded their stores through the purchase of supermarkets belonging to a private chain.[20]

Sid Wallace, the owner of Sids Stores, had become involved with the CCB through his participation in the Gold 'N Rich Corporation. Three of his stores were in Berkeley, one in Walnut Creek and one in Castro Valley. All these stores and their fixtures were leased rather than owned and Wallace's recent expansion into Walnut Creek and Castro Valley had created financial difficulties for him. He approached several supermarket chains for possible purchase and eventually turned to the CCB (BHS, 1990, p. 62; Neptune, 1977, p. 45).

The CCB management saw the purchase as a major opportunity to grow sales, reduce the warehouse operating costs, increase operating margins, recruit new members and establishing its presence in other areas. The CCB was planning to move into areas such as Telegraph Avenue and the Castro Valley. As the stores were leased, the capital investment would be small and would be required for fixtures and inventories with a cash outlay of $591,000 for the stock shares in Sids Stores. The CCB also picked up the chain's subleases and concessions and CCB services such as the Kiddie Korral, and the home economists were extended to the new stores. The CCB BD held several special sessions with major secrecy because of fears that a premature public discussion would adversely impact on relations with Sids employees and suppliers. Wallace was also concerned that if the CCB turned down his offer, then the publicity would undermine his chances of a sale to other possible buyers. The CCB took control of Sids stores in March 1962 (Neptune, 1977, pp. 45–46; Illustration 6.3).[21]

While most of the stores were incorporated into the CCB, the Vine Street store, located near the CCB Shattuck Avenue Center, operated briefly as a convenience store for members, but was closed in October 1965 and the lease terminated. The Sids University Avenue store, which was near the CCB University Avenue store, was subleased to a private operator. The initial operator and his successors went bankrupt and the property became a drain on the finances of CCB, which converted the store into a Natural Foods store in May 1971 with organic foods and bulk products. While the OFC faced internal conflicts, there was a growing demand for organic produce with the Berkeley Neighborhood Food Conspiracy, a nonprofit buying club, operating in 1970 to provide organic produce to low-income consumers, and the CCB introducing organic produce into all its stores in April 1970. The success of the Natural

Illustration 6.3 The Art of Kiddie Korral Children, February 1965. Courtesy of Berkeley Historical Society.

Foods Store, which the OFC blamed for its demise in December 1971, led to another one being opened in the CCB Marin Center in December 1971. The Telegraph Avenue store became CCB Center on 31 May 1962 and soon became the second largest store in terms of turnover, earning a surplus of $1,034,000 until 1967. The lease, however, linked rents to sales. As sales increased at the Telegraph Avenue store so did the rent, and the owner was reluctant to sell the store to the CCB as it provided a good rent income. The Castro Valley store, which was the largest in the Sids chain, became a CCB Center on 5 July 1962, but because of high costs lost $592,644 until 1967. The introduction of a discount price structure, which matched prices at rival commercial discount outlets, in February 1969 for Castro Valley and the Walnut Creek stores increased the sales volume at the Castro Valley Store; by 1971, its sales volume had reached a level of $55,000 per week, despite heavy competition from the nearby Lucky and Safeway stores. The success of the discount pricing approach, with increases in volume as high as 37 percent on a weekly basis, led to the extension of discount pricing in five other CCB stores in February 1970, accompanied by a shift from newspaper to radio advertising, with sales volume increasing 20–30 percent in those stores. This marked a shift in the CCB from a relatively high-priced retailer with an appeal to an affluent clientele to a lower price and high-volume retailer with an appeal to the broader community. There were also initially difficulties with the Sids South Main store in Walnut Creek, which the CCB Walnut Creek Center Committee favored selling, with a dramatic drop in initial sales from $40,000 to $16,000 and unsuccessful efforts to sublease the property. There were concerns that the new store, located in an area of little support for the CCB, would take away business from the existing nearby CCB store in an area of intense competition. The store finally gained Co-op identification on 29 November 1962, but lost $246,341 up to 1967. Sales gradually increased to more than $50,000 per week by 1971. Both the South Main and Castro Valley stores were vulnerable to competitors with promotions based on gambling games, such as Safeway's Bonus Bingo, which gave prizes up to $5,000, affecting the sales in these stores in 1966. One implication of the purchase of Sids Stores is that it delayed the expansion into Marin County by diverting capital away and weakening the early efforts of Margedant Hayakawa and others to promote the CCB where there was strong local co-operative interest (BHS, 1987a, p. 24; BHS, 1990, p. 63; Neptune, 1977, pp. 46–47, 53–54, 61).[22]

The Sids purchase became of source of controversy for the CCB for the rest of its history. While a Semi-Annual Meeting of members in May 1962 endorsed the purchase, the BD was criticized for making a significant decision to expand without the knowledge or participation of members. The decision fueled a growing dissension among CCB members. The Progressive faction saw the purchase of Sids as a major error of the Moderates. The purchase of Sids included its debts and customers, who were not CCB members and not necessarily loyal to the co-operative ideal. The Sids customers gave up a blue stamp loyalty program and were not familiar with CO-OP-labelled goods and the CCB democratic practices. There were also issues with Sids employees who did not have a co-operative orientation (Curl, 2012, p. 196; Mannila, 1984, p. 8; Neptune, 1977, pp. 46, 128).[23]

The CCB developed other services for its members. After the BD agreed to cosponsor a charter trip to Europe with Books Unlimited in September 1967, the first tour flight departed from Oakland to Amsterdam in May 1968, leading to further charter tours for CCB members. The CCB also participated in the US Department of Agriculture food stamp program initiated by the 1964 federal legislation, which allowed low-income families to shop at the El Cerrito and Geary Road Centers by January 1966. The CCB participated in its extension into Alameda County on 1 August 1968 and finally to all stores in April 1969 with the extension into Marin County. The federal food stamp program constituted 7 percent of all CCB food sales by September 1970. The BD approved the use of Master Charge credit cards for nonfood purchases in June 1969 subject to an educational program on the use of credit cards. An amendment to the CCB bylaws, which followed the traditional Rochdale principle of cash-only sales, to allow the use of credit cards, however, was overwhelmingly defeated at the CCB Annual Membership Meeting in January 1970. The CCB from 1971 provided legal services to members through the Consumers Group Legal Service (Neptune, 1977, pp. 151–153).[24]

Members

As Table 6.2 indicates, while membership grew in the 1960s, there was drastic decline after 1968 in member equity of a per capita basis, increasing the need to obtain outside mortgage finance. There was also a stagnation of membership in 1967–1968 with a gain of only 200 members. While interest payments on shares remained at 4 percent until 1967, financial difficulties forced the payment to fall below 4 percent from 1968 to 0 in 1971. There was also in 1968 a new CCB bylaw limiting share interest payments to one-quarter of net savings after taxes. Members were encouraged to convert shares into certificates of interest, which could return 6 percent in 1968 and further raised to maximum of 7 percent in December 1969. Patronage refunds did not match the peak of 4.04 percent in 1961, with fluctuations reflecting increased operating costs, and from 1968 deteriorated to the point that no refund was paid in 1971 when the CCB made a loss. Both the declining interest rate on shares and patronage refunds were justified on grounds that members were paying less after 1970 with the adoption of discount pricing. The membership outside Berkeley became more significant, with the three Berkeley shopping centers covering 46 percent, the Walnut Creek Centers providing 17 percent and the Marin Center 7 percent, respectively, of the

Table 6.2 Number of Members 1962–1971 and Member Per Capita Equity, Interest on Capital and Patronage Refund (BHS, 1995, pp. 50, 67; Neptune, 1977, p. 191)[25]

Year	*No. of Members*	*Member Per Capita Equity ($)*	*Interest (%)*	*Patronage Refund (%)*
1962	24,531	101	4	2.64
1963	30,500	93	4	1.50
1964	34,700	94	4	2.50
1965	37,200	98	4	2.70
1966	39,500	99	4	1.85
1967	43,000	94	4	1.06
1968	43,200	93	3.32	1.10
1969	46,800	85	3	0.92
1970	54,100	72	2.96	0.75
1971	61,400	63	0	0

membership in June 1967. The Finnish influence in the CCB declined as membership in size and location increased and the Finns got older. There was also dissatisfaction with the CCB political infighting and concerns about the political views of the Progressives, with Finns shopping elsewhere and withdrawing their capital. The departure of Mannila in 1971 highlighted the end of significant Finnish role in shaping the CCB (BHS, 1987b, p. 32; Mannila, 1984, p. 9; BHS, 1996b, pp. 20–21).[26]

There were continued efforts to attract new members and encourage social activities. There was "Bring A Neighbor Week" in April 1964 to coincide with the 27th anniversary of the CCB. Members were encouraged to bring their nonmember neighbors with them to look at the CCB shopping facilities, where there were special low prices and activities such as CCB historical exhibitions and a Punjabi cooking demonstration at the Shattuck Avenue Center. The El Cerrito Center had a hootenanny, a children's fashion parade and a magic show. There were 65 special activity groups and classes, ranging from languages to cake decorating, and 70 special events, including UN week, Japanese Week and cooking demonstrations, in 1965. There were family outings to San Francisco Giants baseball games. A membership drive in September 1969 provided an individual incentive with each member receiving a ten-pound turkey for every seven new members they signed up.[27]

Despite these efforts, membership participation remained an issue in the CCB. The participation in the BD elections fluctuated between 8.53 percent in 1965 and 25 percent in 1967 during a factionalized election campaign. Less than 300 members attended the Semi-Annual Meeting in May 1962 that endorsed the purchase of Sids Stores. A March-April 1964 membership poll, which supported CCB pricing policy with loss leaders and specials, only attracted a 2.7 percent response. A crucial Semi-Annual Meeting in May 1966 to consider a BD request for a $1.2 million mortgage authorization lapsed for the want of a quorum. A subsequent ballot of members succeeded in June 1966 for a lesser amount of $800,000 by 1,099 to 191 votes.[28]

The growth of CCB centers led it to consider expanding the role of Center Councils. Since May 1962, Walnut Creek had an elected Council, while other centers and groups organizing new CCB centers had volunteer unelected Councils. The CCB in 1963 established experimental Center Councils, which met monthly, with representatives elected directly by members shopping at that center. There were nine members on each Center Council with staggered terms and three alternate representatives. The Centers were to be the basis for a revamped Co-op Congress with one Center representative for each 350 members. The Co-op Congress would meet four times a year to discuss in greater depth than the BD major policy issues, consider questions referred to it by the BD and make recommendations to the BD.[29] The Center Councils were designed with the growth of the CCB to "increase membership participation, understanding and control."[30] The first Center Council elections in July 1963 saw the election of 89 representatives for seven Centers, but with a disappointing 5 percent turnout of members.[31]

There was support by member Irv Rautenberg, who served as chair of the Members Relations Committee and Shattuck Avenue Center Council (SACC), and Maudelle Shirek, who served on the BD from 1963 to 1968, for a greater role for the Center Councils at the expense of the BD, management and the factions. While the Center Councils, however, remained advisory bodies without real powers, they could take initiatives such as SACC producing a newsletter in 1966. The Center Councils were also given a legislative lobbying role by the BD in February 1965, when a legislative chair was appointed at each Center to monitor the activities of the Consumer Counsel in Sacramento and help organize writing campaigns and deputations to Sacramento by Center members. The Center Councils provided a focus of a discontent with the BD. SACC in 1966 circulated pamphlets protesting the possible acquisition of a new store in North Oakland while improvements were needed in the existing shopping centers. This campaign led the BD to omit the North Oakland proposal from the loan authorization approved by ballot in June 1966. The BD placed restrictions on Center Council activities prohibiting them in October 1964 from endorsing candidates in BD elections and generally banning the use of any CCB funds for candidate campaigns. There was a push to strengthen the role of the Center Councils, with the Co-op Congress resolving in June 1965 that the BD end the experimental status of Congress and the Center Councils and amend the CCB bylaws to include them. The Congress also wanted all matters referred to the BD considered within 30 days and nonvoting representation on the BD and the Management Committee, but BD referred these matters back to the Congress in September 1965. Following a Congress recommendation, the BD renamed the Congress the 'Congress of Center Councils' (CCC) in January 1966, with all Center Council representatives now Congress representatives, but not did give the CCC a permanent status. The CCC served as an interchange of ideas between Center Councils and could initiate policy recommendations to be forwarded to the BD. The CCC continued to meet until August 1967, when only 17 of the 120 representatives attended, and no further meetings occurred as the focus shifted to the Center Councils directly raising issues with the BD through a Committee of Council Chairman established in May 1968 (Curl, 2012, p. 196),[32] which became increasingly frustrated at the inability of the BD to hear their concerns and in December 1970 called upon the BD to increase its meetings to twice a month to strengthen membership control. The BD agreed to the request on an experimental basis for six months.[33]

The CCB continued the educational program, but there were concerns about cost and disruption by the BD factional conflicts. The *CN* became weekly in January 1964 with more space to publish members' letters and promote co-operation with savings arising from the elimination of external advertising with advertising in the *CN*. By 1967, the Education Department employed 15 home economists and education assistants with a budget of $250,000, with one notable event being Lorne Greene from the popular television series *Bonanza* narrating a CLUSA film "This is a Co-operative" at Castro Valley in September 1967. While Mannila was increasingly concerned about the education department's costs and unsuccessfully proposed a plan in early 1968 that included the removal of home economists and education assistants at each center, the Progressives challenged Sekerak, who supported political neutrality, as part of their desire to change the CCB's direction. The BD in April 1968 set up an Education Committee with all current directors as members to oversee the education program, which was later extended to include interested members, and the Education Director reporting to the Committee rather than Mannila on the education program. The BD placed Sekerak on a one-year leave of absence in May 1968 and finally removed Sekerak in February 1969, replacing him with Don Rothenberg from a field of over 150 applicants for Education Director. Rothenberg, who commenced work on 1 July 1969, was a former Communist Party member and had been the political organizer for African American Tom Bradley in his 1969 unsuccessful Democratic primary campaign for Los Angeles Mayor. Sekerak as a CCB member later openly supported the successful Moderates in the 1970 election campaign, who placed the education program back under the control of the General Manager in March 1970 (BHS, 1990, pp. 77–80; Kaufmann, 2004, pp. 69–70; Neptune, 1977, p. 87).[34]

The CCB continued its focus on consumer activism. It called for labeling standards and the CCB home economists issued advocacy statements, the first one in 1964 calling for all ingredients to be listed on ice cream labels. While the CCB produced a cookbook to celebrate its 25th anniversary in 1962, it published a low-cost cookbook in 1965, which was an initiative of the Telegraph Avenue Center Council (TACC), and used members' recipes with a focus on inexpensive main dishes and enough protein for good nutrition. The low-cost cookbook was subsequently reprinted eight times. The Shattuck Avenue Center in May 1965 placed signs obtained from the British Ministry of Health on the dangers of cigarettes in the store. After several attempts by cigarette sales representatives to remove the signs, Nan Reidenbach, the Shattuck Avenue education assistant, obtained more copies and placed them out of reach of the visiting sales representatives. The CCB ordered similar signs for other centers. The CCB banned smoking in all shopping and checkout areas in September 1971. During 1968, the CCB and the PAC introduced into all departments unit pricing, whereby the customer could see the price for the packet and the price per pound for items. In 1970, it banned the sale of hazardous pesticides in its stores and joined other organizations in a legal brief opposing electricity price increases by Pacific Gas and Electricity or PG&E. The CCB played an active role in the Consumer Federation of America (CFA), which arose from a Consumer Assembly in 1966 and became the largest consumer lobbying group in Washington. CCB home economist Gullberg was elected to the CFA Board in 1969 and was appointed to President Richard Nixon's Food Safety Panel of the White House Conference on Food, Nutrition and Health, which aimed to tackle hunger and led to increased funding for food stamps. The CCB sponsored a talk by consumer activist Ralph Nader in April 1971 at Walnut Creek, which attracted 2,500 people, and began selling nitrate-free hot dogs in September 1971. The CCB lobbied extensively for Fair Packaging and Labeling Act that US Congress passed in 1966 and the Cereal Enrichment Law in California, which became effective on 1 February 1972 and allowed beneficial additives in bread such as B vitamins and Iron. While the CCB was unsuccessful through a petition campaign in 1970 for Californian legislation to allow refunds for bottle returns to encourage recycling, the CCB with local ecology groups introduced recycling for tin cans, aluminum cans, glass and newspaper, a first for Berkeley. However, the BD decided in April 1971, despite its recycling initiative, to replace paper bags with clear plastic bags for produce, despite the recognized pollution problem, to reduce a growing shoplifting problem. Not all the CCB local initiatives were successful. It packaged meat in 1965 so the customer can see the fattier or worst side of the meat before making a purchase to highlight that the CCB was an honest retailer. However, the idea backfired with a decline in meat sales and it was discontinued. There was also controversy over a CIPC educational campaign in 1964 on the pros and cons of fluoridation of the water supply, which faced opposition from the CCB members involved in the East Bay Committee Against Fluoridation Inc., with one member describing the campaign as "political" as there was a referendum in the issue in June 1964 (BHS, 1996a, pp. xi, 16, 75, 78; CCB, 1962; CCB, 1965, p. 2; Fullerton, 1992, pp. 94–95; Illustration 6.4).[35]

Employees and Community

The CCB employed approximately 400 full-time and 150 part-time employees by January 1969 and continued to maintain good relations with labor unions with a Labor Co-operative Coordination Committee briefly operating from 1961 to 1963. The CCB began a gradual move to supporting workers involved in labor disputes in 1962 by placing information cards on Colgate-Palmolive products to highlight that workers were on strike and giving members the right to choose whether they would purchase these products or not. The BD went further in October 1963 by agreeing to boycott goods produced by employers where strikes were endorsed by the Alameda County Central Labor Council.

Illustration 6.4 Recycling at CCB. Courtesy of Berkeley Historical Society #10472.

The vote was five for and two against, with two abstaining. CCB members would be informed by labels on the shelves and in the *CN*, but stock, including that held at the AC warehouse, remaining on the shelves until sold out. There was, however, opposition to consumer boycotts by members who did not believe that the co-operative should be involved in politics, claimed that it was a matter of individual choice and were concerned that outside organizations rather than the BD would dictate CCB policy. Correspondence by members indicated by February 1964 that there was strong opposition with 113 members opposing any boycotts, 21 supporting boycotts concerning strikes and civil rights issues, 17 favoring boycotts concerning strikes only and 1 favoring civil rights boycotts only. The BD moved in July 1968, following unilateral action by Mannila in response to "innumerable requests," to an outright boycott of nonunion grapes in support of the United Farm Workers (UFW), which were not available until June 1970 when the first grapes produced by union labor became available. These struggles had their origin in the 1965 Delano strike, where Mexican and Filipino farm workers in the San Joaquin Valley walked out and resulted in their leader Cesar Chavez becoming a national figure. Shelf-labeling could be extended to other issues. The BD on 27 February 1967 instructed management to place notices on all shelves identifying products made by Dow Chemical and to post statements by members critical of the Company over its production of napalm, which was used in the Vietnam War, and a Dow Chemical response. This followed the BD receiving a legal opinion that a January 1967 Annual Meeting motion favoring the shelf marking of boycotted products was advisory not binding, but receiving two petitions with 2,087 signatures supporting the notices and statements on Dow Chemical products. While some moderate older members left the CCB over boycotts and other actions against companies, it attracted radical university student members, who possessed less capital (BHS, 1990, pp. 68–69, 81; Wollenberg, 2008, pp. 143–144).[36]

Labor turnover, morale and training remained key issues for the management of CCB employees. During 1965, there was a growing level of employee and member comments about feelings of dissatisfaction and injustice among employees. The CCB Congress in March 1965 called upon the BD to investigate the level of labor turnover among CCB employees. The SACC requested the BD in April 1965 to improve employee relations at the CCB by employing a personnel manager and an ombudsman to hear employee grievances in confidence independently of management. The BD responded, with advice from George Strauss from the UCB Institute of Industrial Relations (IIR) and UCB Visiting Professor Joel Seldman from the University of Chicago, by establishing a Personnel Committee in April 1965 at a meeting attended by approximately 100 members and employees. The Committee included former directors, such as Robert Gordon, and Strauss. Employees were encouraged to take their grievances through their labor union and the CCB appointed a personnel director in September 1965. The Personnel Committee initiated a grievance procedure for nonunion issues, reformed the employee evaluation process to provide for employee involvement, placed a stronger emphasis on fair employment practices and called for the reform of Kiddie Korral employment practices, emphasizing that Center managers in future should consider the opinions of Kiddie Korral attendants about issues such as overcrowding and safety. CCB employees continued to be paid to go to Camp Sierra to further their knowledge about the cooperative movement, with nine attending in 1965. There was a review of staff training by a subcommittee of the Personnel Committee chaired by Strauss in 1970 and the CCB inaugurated in 1971 a training program, with classes held most weeks that taught employees about their jobs and the CCB (Neptune, 1977, p. 112). Reflecting changing trends of fashion, BD decided in July 1968 that male employees were no longer required to be "clean shaven." While employees could not be on the BD, the BD permitted and encouraged employee members to sit on the CCB committees and in April 1970 allowed them to run for Center Council elections, but limited the number of regular and alternate delegates to three for each Council in August 1971. While there was a reluctance to allow employee representation on the DB, there were also growing concerns about employee performance and honesty. The CCB Management also hired Commercial Services Systems, a shopping service, from April 1971 to check on a regular basis employee interaction with customers to rate individual performance and remove dishonest employees.[37]

The CCB's progressive approach against discrimination in employment shielded it from public opposition to the hiring practices of its competitors. By November 1963, the CCB was requesting labor unions to add antidiscrimination clauses in their contracts with the CCB and directly seeking African American applicants through civil rights groups and the African American press. The CCB's leadership also gave support to the broader campaigns for civil rights by raising funds from CCB members in 1964 and 1965 to support the efforts of the Council of Federated Organizations, based in Jackson, Mississippi, to ensure African American voter registration in the South. CCB fair employment policy was reinforced internally through conferences and memos to center and department managers. Ray Thompson, an African American chair of the TACC and later CCB Vice President and Director, promoted the African American employment and CCB membership. The Lucky's stores had the lowest percentage of African American employees of any Bay Area grocery chain. Berkeley demonstrators, inspired by the local chapter of CORE, targeted the Lucky's supermarket in Telegraph Avenue in February 1964 with a 'shop-in', whereby protestors filled up their shopping trolleys with good and had the retail clerks ring up the bill, but walked away saying they could not pay the bill. This tactic brought the supermarket to a standstill, with Lucky workers requiring several hours overtime to return the items to the shelves. When the Lucky management withdrew shopping trolleys and bags to stop the CORE activists, tensions arose with CCB when the CORE activists purchased CCB bags and used CCB shopping trolleys without CCB management approval to continue their protest. The protest eventually persuaded Lucky to change its employment practices. The CCB by March 1965 had 15 percent Asian, 3.8 percent Latin American and 11.1 percent African American employees. The CCB's African American employees continued to agitate for better working conditions, with the Black Employees of the Consumer Co-operative group in June 1968 calling for a boycott of the CCB store unless a range of policies included more favorable hiring and management training were introduced. Larry Bailey in 1968 became the first African American center manager at the University Avenue Center. The BD in April 1969 voted to set a percentage minimum targets for the employment of African Americans of 20 percent by the end of the 1968–1969 financial year and 25 percent by the end of the 1969–1970 financial year (BHS, 1990, p. 75; Neptune, 1977, p. 185; Rorabaugh, 1989, p. 73; Wollenberg, 2008, p. 138).[38]

The BD also began to examine gender discrimination in the CCB with the commissioning of a report in August 1970 to examine the status of women employees, following concerns raised by director Anne Frentz. Against the background of protests and lobbying by female employees and feminist groups, the BD in October and November 1970 adopted a range of fair employment practices, including a requirement that all women will comprise a minimum of 40 percent of employees in all job categories and in-service training on fair employment for managers involved in recruiting staff. The BD went further in December 1970, when the Progressives controlled the BD in the absence of a Moderate member, and adopted an affirmative action program, whereby that until the community composition regarding ethnicity and gender is reached the CCB would favor where possible women and members of minority ethnic groups in hiring, transfer, promotion and training. The Moderate faction, regaining control at the next meeting, changed the policy and adopted 'a general affirmative action' program, with a detailed policy accepted by the BD on 31 March 1971 that forbade discrimination in hiring, promotion and retention of employees on the basis of sex, religion, race or place or national origin. The DB also required the personnel director to provide specifically quarterly goals on the employment of women and minorities leading to employment levels that reflected the composition of the working age population of the community. Female and minority staff would be given preference in training for higher positions until the affirmative action goals were met. Feminist groups put further pressure on the CCB by obtaining the day after the BD March decision an investigation of the CCB by the State Fair Employment Practices Commission. The Moderate policy switch angered the women's groups and helped the Progressives win control of the BD in January 1972.[39]

Volunteer labor by members continued to play a role in the CCB operations. Over 100 volunteer members participated in the Telegraph Avenue and Castro Valley openings in 1962, acting as hosts and hostesses for the former Sids customers, providing refreshments and information on the CCB. They played a role in the 1963 capital raising campaigns by ringing members to ask for additional CCCB investment and conducted price surveys in the CCB stores for management without the knowledge of employees. The CCB in 1964 also ran an 'interest and skills bank', where members could list their qualifications and interests, including accounting, advertising, consumer testing and typing, for service in a range of activities, including specialist committees.[40]

While the BD reflected the political divisions in Berkeley, the CCB provided a forum for political and social debates of the 1960s and contributed to the local community. The CCB established 'free speech tables' in January 1962 for community literature and petitions, but there was continued controversy about allowing community groups to present their ideas at the CCB store entrances, with management fearing a loss of sales. There were limitations with the BD disallowing in September 1964 material relating to political parties and candidates, but from

April 1965 allowing groups to use the tables to solicit donations. The tables also highlighted political differences between radical Berkeley and the more conservative "country" Centers. South Main Center Council refused a request for a table at its entrance by the Port Chicago Peace Vigil Group protesting at a nearby nuclear weapons depot, due to member complaints and declining patronage, but a sit-in at the CCB Berkeley stores in March 1967 reversed that position. While there was a high level of interest in politics in Berkeley, in the more conservative Castro Valley local community fundraising was more significant. In 1962, the CCB and PAC provided support to the public television station, KQED in San Francisco, by providing 13 weeks' finance for the weekly panel discussion program 'Profile – Bay Area', which was hosted by Casper Weinberger, later President Reagan's Secretary of Defense. The CCB in July 1964 donated $300 to the JF Kennedy School in Oakland for program to help high school dropouts and suspended students continue their education and gain employment. Other donations included the Walnut Creek Civic Center, the Oakland Symphony Orchestra, local sporting teams and the Richmond Festival of the Arts. Center Councils were also allowed to make donations to local community groups, receiving $300 each in May 1967. The CCB in 1969 donated food to children's breakfast programs organized by the Black Panthers, which prompted some letters of complaints in CN and resignations over engagement in politics and claims that the Black Panthers would undermine "racial peace." The CCB also contributed to debates relating to the impact of BART on Berkeley, by proposing that the redeveloped land above BART be used for a public park in the first instance or otherwise co-operatively owned low- and medium-rental apartments (BHS, 1990, p. 69; Curl, 2012, p. 197; Rauber, 1992, p. 13).[41]

The CCB in November 1966 faced protests over its prices from housewives and UCB students. The BWP, Campus Committee for New Politics, SDS, the Berkeley-based Consumers League for Lower Prices and the El Cerrito-Richmond Housewives League for Lower Prices distributed leaflets calling for a boycott of CCB stores as well as the non-cooperative chains stores, with demands for reduction of prices by 10 percent. This was part of a national protest about high food prices and supermarket promotional games (Cohen, 2004, pp. 367–368). The movement involved CCB members, with a petition reportedly signed by 500 CCB members and picketing of the CCB Berkeley stores. The CCB members' requests included a call for the CCB to reconsider the status of the loss making South Main and Castro Valley Centers and conversion of the University Avenue store into a discount operation. The protesters argued that the population around the University Avenue store was changing from middle-class whites to African Americans and working-class whites, who were more interested in lower prices than CCB services such as education. The boycotts were suspended after the

CCB agreed to refer the issue of lower prices to a CCB committee that included representatives from two of the protesting organizations. Treuhaft accused the 'conservative majority' on the BD of delaying tactics, while Sekerak criticized the CCB members for not following the CCB's democratic practices. The CCB subsequently reduced prices on 1,203 items to remain competitive with other stores that reduced prices following the protests.[42]

The CCB relationship with the local business community varied according to the faction in control. The moderates favored affiliation with local Chambers of Commerce, as occurred in all locations by March 1968. Treuhaft led an attempt in June 1965 to disaffiliate from the Berkeley Chamber of Commerce after its decision to allow its affiliates to be represented by employees only and complaints that CCB representatives were not receiving meeting notices. The matter was referred to the CCB Public Relations Committee so that it could meet with the Chamber's President, after which the CCB continued its affiliation with the Chamber accepting the nominated CCB representatives. A further attempt to disaffiliate by Treuhaft was defeated by five votes to four in November 1965. The BD in January 1967 decentralized the decision to Center Councils to affiliate with their local Chamber of Commerce. The Progressive-controlled BD in March 1968 voted not to renew affiliation with the Chambers, arguing that they supported legislation that was hostile to consumer interests and supported questionable business practices. An appeal by Center Council chairs to rescind the resolution was rejected by the BD. The Moderates reversed BD policy in July 1970 by allowing Center Councils to affiliate to local Chambers of Commerce provided they funded it.[43]

CCB and the Co-operative Movement

The CCB continued its close relationship with AC. As Table 6.3 indicates, while the number of co-operatives affiliated to AC remained small with a peak membership of 12 in 1970, turnover almost quadrupled during the period. The AC relied heavily on CCB and PAC for sales, with the CCB being its largest purchaser with 82 percent of its business in 1969. The AC faced a major setback in June 1962 with the loss of its warehouse, IBM EDP system and its inventory due to fire. The CCB provided a temporary office for the AC and a new warehouse in the Golden Gate Industrial Park at Port Isabel in Richmond was opened in September 1963 with finance from MSI. Neptune, the AC General Manager, continued to be a supporter of growth for the Bay Area consumer co-operatives to achieve economies of scale for AC, as the industry wholesalers consolidated and competitors such as Safeway and Lucky Stores, with their own warehouses, increased sale volume (Neptune, 1977, pp. 47–50).[44]

The AC warehouse extended its EDP facilities in 1968 to include a Digitronics tape receiver that allowed stores to transmit orders over the

Table 6.3 AC Membership and Financial Performance 1962–1971 (Neptune, 1977, p. 190)

Year	*No. of Members*	*Turnover*	*Net Savings*
1962	8	5,809,120	3,638[a]
1963	8	6,613,980	3,638[a]
1964	9	8,664,120	3,273[a]
1965	10	9,497,914	5,500[a]
1966	10	10,192,200	42,500[a]
1967	10	11,647,909	45,100[a]
1968	11	11,754,928	50,000[a]
1969	11	13,342,016	52,000[a]
1970	12	17,754,000	52,000[a]
1971	10	20,305,100	52,000[a]

a Amount of net savings determined by Cost-Plus contracts.

telephone for entry into the computer. After trials at CCB's El Cerrito store, the appropriate equipment was purchased for all stores, which allowed improved store inventory turnover, decreased turnaround time from order to store delivery to less than 24 hours and a reduction of the labor time required for key punching orders (Neptune, 1977, p. 81). According to Neptune (1977, p. 81), the "CO-OP stores were the first in the Bay Area to provide this kind of complete integrated ordering procedure for their markets."

The AC and the CCB integrated operations in other ways. By the end of 1968, there was joint buying of produce with produce purchase and delivery from the warehouse. There was a merging of the merchandising functions of the warehouse and retail stores, with AC buyers meeting with sales people and receiving presentations of new items and promotions. Decisions were jointly made on product purchasing by AC and CCB personnel. From 1968, there were weekly AC and CCB management staff meetings to review issues, particularly in relation to EDP. The Richmond facilities of the AC were renovated to allow the inclusion of the CCB administrative, education and accounting offices on a leasehold basis in November 1970 (Neptune, 1977, pp. 80–82).[45]

The AC encouraged co-operative formation and education leading to the establishment of the AC Development Department (ACDC) in 1964. After an initial approach to the CCB, the ACDC provided support for the Neighborhood Co-operative of San Francisco, which had its charter issued in May 1962, in the low-income Hunters Point-Bayview Area. African American leaders were concerned with the hiring practices, prices and product quality of the local independent stores. They opened a store in 1 July 1965 with the CCB Membership Committee donating $1,250 raised through the sale of secondhand paperbacks for member and public education. The new co-operative, however, failed to reach the sufficient volume to be viable. Despite assistance from Safeway, which helped with a wholesaling and staff supervisory program without interfering in membership control, and further assistance from the CCB, it closed in December 1971. The ACDC also worked to establish a co-operative presence in 1966 at Santa Rosa, which was 50 miles from the AC warehouse, purchasing land and finding a manager. This store, however, closed after only nine months due to insufficient capital and members. Another AC initiative was Bay Area Neighborhood Development Foundation (BAND), which was a nonprofit foundation formed in November 1964 and received federal funding. It primarily targeted major low-income areas over a four-year span with educational programs aimed at encouraging the formation of co-operatives with only four credit unions being developed for community residents. BAND was hampered by limited time to develop its program and a lack of qualified co-operative experts. Its work was taken over by the BAND Foundation, which was a privately financed separate entity, with its first donation being from the retailer J.C. Penny, and its focus shifting to economic development in African American communities (BHS, 1987b, p. 49; Neptune, 1977, pp. 55–56, 125, 131–137, 146–147).[46]

There was a further attempt to merge the Bay Area co-operatives. A committee, which consisted of presidents and managers of the main Bay Area co-operatives, including the CCB, presented a report on restructuring to the AC Annual Delegate Meeting in February 1968. It proposed five ten-year goals for the Bay Area co-operatives that included a "fully consolidated" Bay Area Co-operative in terms of ownership, financial responsibility, democratic control and patronage. The CCB BD, now controlled by the Progressives, opposed the proposal and proceeded to hire an attorney to find if it could gain direct ownership control of the AC. Treuhaft, who served on the AC Board, was critical of the AC for allowing the CCB only one vote on the AC Board when it provided the overwhelming proportion of capital and business for the AC. The CCB attorney concluded that there was no practical way the CCB could unilaterally take control of the AC and recommended negotiation. The CCB BD did not proceed further with the takeover, despite an offer in June 1969 by PAC to sell its interest in the AC to the CCB, and further efforts by the AC to push toward a merger in 1971 went no further (BHS, 1990, p. 83; Neptune, 1977, pp. 82–83; Neptune, 1992, p. 5).

There were other tensions with the co-operative movement. Allegations appeared in the general press in February 1967 that the Central Intelligence Agency (CIA) funded CLUSA co-operative development projects in Africa, Asia and South America provided by the Fund for International Co-operative Development (FICD). While FICD was separate from CLUSA, Stanley Dreyer served both as President of CLUSA and Secretary-Treasurer of FICD. Dreyer responded to AC and

CCB requests for information by claiming that FICD had not knowingly received any money from an entity associated with the CIA. The Moderate-controlled BD passed a resolution in June 1967 calling upon CLUSA and FICD to stop receiving funds from the CIA and other secret government sources. Treuhaft, as a delegate to the CLUSA Biennial Congress in Kansas City in October 1968, had a motion ruled out of order that stated that CLUSA's reliance on government funding, including the CIA, violated Rochdale principles of freedom from government control and political neutrality and calling upon CLUSA in future to organize its international projects through the UN. Treuhaft later claimed that Sekerak's reluctance to criticize CLUSA's use of CIA funds weakened his credibility and helped the BD move against him as Education Director. There was also tension between the Progressives and MSI against a background of members' complaints about the MSI's handling of insurance policies. Treuhaft, who criticized MSI for being a mutual rather than co-operative as policy holders signed their voting rights over to a proxy when taking out a policy, obtained in August 1968 a review of CCB's relationship with MSI citing racial and political discrimination in its policies, poor "consumer orientation" and inadequate co-operative representation on its governing bodies. MSI admitted charging higher premiums in West Berkeley, which had a high proportion of African American and low-income families, by claiming that other insurance companies would not provide insurance policies there. The BD established a committee to review the relationship with MSI and its report in June 1969 recommended the "phasing out" of the special relationship with MSI and the CCB look for an alternative co-operative insurance provider. The BD in July 1969 decided to confirm the continuation of the MSI relationship before any alternative was found, which never eventuated (BHS, 1990, pp. 77–80).[47]

The CCB also assisted other co-operatives. The PAC, facing a series of losses, approached the CCB in October 1963 about a possible merger, with the CCB entering a contract with PAC in 1964 to provide management services. Val Litton, who had managed CCB stores and worked for Safeway, became resident manager to supervise day-to-day operations. While Litton, who was recalled by the CCB in 1968 to become retail operations manager, reduced costs, improved labor efficiency and increased sales volume, the operating losses continued, totaling $769,899 from 1961 to 1969 (Neptune, 1977, pp. 52–53).[48] The *CN* was also a joint publication of the CCB and the PAC for a short period in 1968. The CCB also supported other local co-operatives such as USCA, Taxi Unlimited and the short-lived Berkeley Newspaper Co-operative.[49]

The CCB maintained its links with the international co-operative movement. A CWS delegation led by James Peddie, chair of the UK Co-operative Party, visited the CCB in August 1962. There were visitors from co-operators in other countries, including Iraq, Sweden,

Tanganyika and NZ, with an interest in CCB initiatives such as the low-cost cookbook and the Kiddie Korral. The CCB supported the World-Wide Co-op Partners from 1962, which provided aid to overseas co-operatives as well as co-operatives serving disadvantaged communities in the South and the Neighborhood Co-operative in San Francisco. The BD in November 1965 agreed to adopt Nadakobe Consumers Co-operative in Japan as a sister co-operative. Mary Gullberg, a CCB home economist, represented the US at the 1965 ICA Congress in Switzerland. Nils Thedin, chief of the Swedish KF publications department and later chair of UNICEF, was the CCB guest speaker at the dinner after its Semi-Annual Meeting in May 1968. The CCB also held a two-week Skandia festival in May 1968 to promote goods produced by Nordic co-operatives, which had an office of the wholesaler NAF in San Francisco for the purpose of importing Californian agricultural goods. Ray Thompson, CCB Vice President, went on an 11-day study tour in 1968 to Sweden as a guest of the KF.[50]

Conclusion

Despite an increase in membership and sales volume by the end of the 1971, the CCB faced significant challenges. Reflecting the political climate of Berkeley and the US, the BD became factionalized and there was a growing question of management authority, with the relationship between the BD and CCB management deteriorating to the point where Mannila, the long-standing manager, decided to retire early. Participation remained an issue as factions dominated the BD and earlier initiatives such as Parliament became moribund. The Center Councils became a new forum for local member participation, with criticism of the BD that it was unresponsive due to its focus on factional politics. There was generational change with the Finns, who had played an important role in founding the CCB no longer playing a significant role, due to retirement and concerns about the political stance of the Progressives. While the more radical stance of the CCB DB attracted younger members, some more moderate members either resigned or ran down their capital due to disagreements with the CCB policy.

The expansion of the CCB, particularly through the Sids purchase, and growing industry competition placed further pressure on the traditional Rochdale consumer co-operative model. While the Sids purchase delivered the profitable store in Telegraph Avenue, it brought problems, including several unprofitable stores, the weakening of the Walnut Creek Center by the opening of another nearby CCB Center and delaying the grassroots initiative for a CCB Center in Marin County. The poor performance of the Walnut Creek and Castro Valley Store and intense competition led the CCB to adopt discount prices. All these developments contributed to two major aspects of Rochdale co-operative model – payment on share capital and a dividend on purchases – delivering a zero return to CCB members by 1971. While the CCB offered certificates of interest and encouraged members to shift their shareholding investment to this more lucrative form of investment with higher interest rates, the rate of capitalization per member was in decline. Co-operative and consumer education remained an important feature of the CCB, but concerns over cost and performance led to a major upheaval in 1968 with the replacement of Sekerak. There was a reluctance to embrace credit cards due to support for the Rochdale principle of cash trading.

There were tensions with labor, community and the broader co-operative movement. While relationship with organized labor remained good and the CCB was willing to support striking workers in their suppliers through shelf notifications and boycotts, there were issues concerning employee morale and the treatment of minorities and women employees. The idea of worker participation by 1971 was limited to Center Councils, which were advisory, and a traditional employment relationship between workers and managers persisted in the CCB with the professionalization of personnel management. While the CCB through its 'free speech tables' provided an important forum for community debate and gave financial support to community groups, these endeavors created controversy among its membership. The CCB was faced with community boycotts over its pricing and 'free speech table' policies. There was conflict with the local business community due to the Progressives hostility to the local Chambers of Commerce. The Progressives also challenged the CCB's relationship with the broader co-operative through its criticism of CLUSA and the MISC. They questioned the relative voice of the CCB in AC compared to its investment and purchases and considered a takeover of the AC. As the CCB moved further into the 1970s, the financial problems and governance tensions intensified.

Notes

1 KPIX-TV, 1956. "Richmond-San Rafael Bridge Opens"," 2 September, available at https://diva.sfsu.edu/collections/sfbatv/bundles/189372 (accessed 8 November 2018).
2 Letter Ronald Reagan to A. Watkins, 3 February 1969, folder "Research File Education – Campus Unrest – Berkeley, 1969 (1/2)", Box GO 156, Ronald Reagan Governor's Papers, Ronald Reagan Library (hereafter RRGPRRL).
3 Speech Transcript, Music Center, Independent Educators, 23 May 1969, folder "Education. Campus Unrest – General, 1969 (3/3)," Box GO 156, Research Files (Molly Sturgis Tuthill), RRGPRRL.
4 Speech Transcript, Commonwealth Club, San Francisco, 13 June 1969, folder "Education. Campus Unrest – General, 1969 (3/3)," Box GO 156, Research Files (Molly Sturgis Tuthill), RRGPRRL.
5 *Berkeley Barb*, 13 August 1965, p. 1.
6 CN, 5 June 1967, p. 7.

7 *CN*, 1 August 1966, p. 1.
8 *CN*, 12 February 1968, p. 1
9 BD, 25 April 1955, Carton 1 Folder 13. BANC MSS 90/140 c. CCB Records, UCB BL; *CN*, August 1955, October 1955, 4 April 1960, p. 1, 12 February 1968, p. 2; *CN*, 15 December 1962; Interview Emil Sekerak by Therese Pipe, 6 February 1987. Transcript. BHS; *NYT*, 16 January 1971, p. 41.
10 BD, 27 January 1964, Carton 3 Folder 25. BANC MSS 90/140 c. CCB Records, UCB BL; *CN*, 27 December 1966, p. 16, 17 April 1967, p. 11, 16 October 1967, p. 1, 30 October 1967, p. 1, 18 March 1968, pp. 1–2, 4 January 1971, p. 2, 1 February 1971, p. 1; Interview Emil Sekerak by Therese Pipe, 6 February 1987. Transcript. BHS; *Member Action Committee Report*, 8 May 1967, Carton 1 Folder 1. BANC MSS 94/220. RLP, UCB BL; *NYT*, 16 January 1967, p. 41.
11 Letter from E. Sekerak to William Rentz, 25 March 1959, Carton 2 Folder 24, *Marin Memo*, 20 October 1961, Carton 13 Folder 22. BANC MSS 90/140 c. CCB Records, UCB BL.
12 *CN*, 11 July 1960, p. 2.
13 BD, 26 May 1969, Carton 6 Folder 46, Memo from Eugene Mannila to BD, 25 March 1963, Carton 3 Folder 30. BANC MSS 90/140 c. CCB Records, UCB BL; *CN*, March 1963, p. 2, 13 January 1964, p. 3, 23 June 1969, pp. 1–2, 30 June 1969, pp. 1–3; *NYT*, 25 May 1969, E13.
14 *CN*, 9 June 1969, p. 2.
15 *CN*, 3 November 1969, p. 1, 10 November 1969, p. 1, 17 November 1969, p. 2; Memo D. Rothenberg to Education Committee, 12 March 1970, Carton 6 Folder 49. 'Reasons for Membership Withdrawal, 53 weeks ending 10/4/69', Typescript, Carton 6 Folder 48, Semi-Annual Membership Meeting, 23 May 1969, Carton 12 Folder 25. BANC MSS 90/140 c. CCB Records, UCB BL.
16 *CN*, 13 January 1964, p. 2, 11 October 1965, p. 1., 1 August 1966, p. 1, 6 January 1969, p. 1, 12 May 1969, p. 1, July 14, 1969, p. 1.
17 BD, 28 January 1957, Carton 1 Folder 13, Management's Report to the Board of Directors, 29 January 1962, Carton 3 Folder 28. BANC MSS 90/140 c. CCB Records, UCB BL; *CN*, April 1954, 4 April 1960, p. 1, 7 January 1961, p. 1, 1 February 1961, p. 1, 8 March 1961, p. 1.
18 *CN*, 3 May 1963, pp. 4–5, 18 January 1965, p. 3, 23 January 1967, p. 1, 13 March 1967, p. 1, 29 January 1968, p. 1, 30 December 1968, p. 3, 29 June 1970, p. 1, 3 December 1979, p. 1.
19 *CN*, 8 March 1961, p. 3.
20 Co-operative Enterprises of Akron, Press Release, 24 February 1960, Carton 3 Folder 25. BANC MSS 90/140 c. CCB Records, UCB BL.
21 *CN*, May 1962, p. 4; Interview Emil Sekerak by Therese Pipe, 6 February 1987. Transcript. BHS.
22 *Berkeley Daily Gazette*, 21 December 1971, p. 3; BD Special Meeting, 23 April 1962, Carton 3 Folder 25. Letter Margedant Hayakawa to George Little, 18 September 1962. Management Committee Minutes, 20 August 1962, Carton 3 Folder 27, Memo Marin Pre-Center Committee to members of Board Committees and Center Committees, n.d., Carton 13 Folder 22. Special Committee – Walnut Creek Sids Store, 20 July 1962. Carton 13 Folder 24. BANC MSS 90/140 c. CCB Records, UCB BL; *CN*, 6 June 1966, p. 1, 12 September 1966, p. 5, 11 December 1967, p. 3, 24 February 1969, p. 1, 12 January 1970, p. 2, 9 March 1970, p. 9, 23 March 1970, p. 2, 6 April 1970, p. 2, 13 April 1970, p. 1, 11 January 1971, p. 3.
23 *CN*, 14 September 1964, p. 7; Semi-Annual Meeting, 25 May 1962, Carton 12 Folder 5. BANC MSS 90/140 c CCB Records, UCB BL.

24 *CN*, 24 January 1966, p. 3, 25 September 1967, p. 2, 5 February 1968, p. 8, 5 August 1968, p. 1, 14 April 1969, p. 1, 8 December 1969, p. 7, 9 February 1970, p. 1, 11 January 1971, p. 7.
25 *CN*, 3 January 1972, p. 8.
26 *CN*, 27 December 1966, p. 4, 17 July 1967, p. 8, 7 October 1968, p. 1, 6 January 1969, p. 6, 29 December 1969, p. 1, 7 December 1970, p. 1; Memo, 'Distribution of Members by Center', 20 June 1967, Carton 5 Folder 42. BANC MSS 90/140 c. CCB Records, UCB BL; *NYT*, 16 January 1967, p. 41.
27 *CN*, 27 April 1964, p. 1, 7, 27 December 1965, p. 8, 6 September 1966, p. 3, 15 September 1969, p. 1.
28 *CN*, June 1962, p. 3, 4 May 1964, p. 2, 3 August 1964, p. 2, 6 June 1966, p. 1, 5 July 1966, p. 1, 6 February 1967, p. 1; Interview Emil Sekerak by Therese Pipe, 6 February1987. Transcript. BHS; Memo E. Sekerak to BD and Candidates for the Board, 27 January 1965, Carton 12 Folder 25. BANC MSS 90/140 c. CCB Records, UCB BL.
29 *CN*, May 1963, pp. 6–7; Interview Emil Sekerak by Therese Pipe, 6 February1987. Transcript. BHS.
30 *CN*, May 1963, p. 6.
31 *CN*, September 1963, p. 2.
32 Co-operative Congress minutes, 19 October 1965, Carton 4 Folder 38. BANC MSS 90/140 c. CCB Records, UCB BL; Interview Emil Sekerak by Therese Pipe, 6 February 1987. Transcript. BHS; *CN*, 22 June 1964, p. 2, 20 July 1964, p. 1, 8 September 1964, p. 1, 26 October 1964, p. 2, 23 February 1965, p. 1, 28 June 1965, p. 1, 27 September 1965, p. 2, 24 January 1966, p. 2, 14 February 1966, p. 1, 6 June 1966, p. 1, 13 June 1966, p. 1, 22 August 1966, p. 3, 17 July 1967, p. 1, 28 August 1967, p. 1, 6 January 1969, p. 10.
33 Center Council Chairmen's Committee Meeting, 1 December 1970. Carton 7 Folder 51. BANC MSS 90/140 c. CCB Records, UCB BL; *CN*, 11 January 1971, p. 5, 1 March 1971, p. 1.
34 BD, 13 May 1968, Carton 5 Folder 43, Semi-Annual Membership Meeting, 18 May 1968, Carton 12 Folder 25. BANC MSS 90/140 c. CCB Records, UCB BL; *CN*, December 1963, p. 7, 11 September 1967, p. 1, 1 April 1968, p. 3, 15 April 1968, p. 1, 12 August 1968, p. 1, 10 March 1969, p. 1, 14 July 1969, p. 1, 5 January 1970, p. 2, 9 March 1970, pp. 1, 10; Interview Emil Sekerak by Therese Pipe, 6 February 1987. Transcript. BHS.
35 *CN*, 11 May 1964, p. 5, 8 June 1964, p. 1, 3 August 1964, p. 1, 16 September 1968, p. 1, 7 October 1968, p. 8, 4 May 1970, p. 1, 13 July 1970, p. 1, 28 September 1970, p. 7, 3 May 1971, p. 3, 4 October 1971, p. 1, 3 July 1976, p. 4.
36 BD, 28 October 1963, Carton 3 Folder 25. BD, 22 July 1968. Managers' Report to BD, 22 July 1968, Carton 5 Folder 44. BANC MSS 90/140 c. CCB Records, UCB BL; *CN*, March 1962, p. 4, November 1963, pp. 2–3, 5, 13 January 1964, p. 7, 9 March 1964, p. 1, 6 February 1967, p. 2, 13 February 1967, p. 2, 27 February 1967, p. 1, 13 March 1967, p. 2, 5 August 1967, p. 1, 6 January 1969, p. 3, 1 June 1970, p. 1; *The Dispatcher* (San Francisco), 1 June 1962, p. 1.
37 BD, 26 April 1965, Carton 3 Folder 36. BD, 22 July 1968, Carton 5 Folder 44, Memo V. Litton to Employees, 30 March 1971, Carton 7 Folder 52. BANC MSS 90/140 c. CCB Records, UCB BL; *CN*, 22 March 1965, p. 1, 3 May 1965, p. 8, 10 May 1965, pp. 3, 10, 7 June 1965, p. 2, 12 July 1965, p. 2, 19 July 1965, p. 2, 11 October 1965, pp. 1–2, 27 December 1965, p. 10, 14 November 1966, p. 3, 27 December 1966, pp. 18–19, 4 May 1970, p. 3, 11 January 1971, p. 5, 30 August 1971, p. 10.

38 Memo E. Mannila to employees, 13 June 1968, Carton 5 Folder 43. BANC MSS 90/140 c. CCB Records, UCB BL; *CN*, November 1963, p. 5, 9 March 1964, p. 3, 22 March 1965, p. 1, 29 March 1965, p. 3, 21 February 1966, p. 1, 22 July 1968, p. 1, 6 January 1969, p. 3, 5 May 1969, p. 8.
39 BD, 24 August 1970, Carton 7 Folder 50. BANC MSS 90/140 c. CCB Records, UCB BL; CN, 31 August 1970, p. 1, 2 November 1970, p. 3, 30 November 1970, p. 1, 4 January 1971, pp. 1–2, 1 February 1971, p. 1, 22 February 1971, p. 3, 12 April 1971, p. 1, 17 May 1971, p. 3; Interview Bob Arnold by James Mass, 18 April 1987. Transcripts. BHS.
40 *CN*, June 1962, p. 1, 5 April 1963, p. 1, 13 January 1964, p. 2, 28 December 1964, 1 June 1965, p. 2.
41 BD, 26 November 1962, Carton 3 Folder 25, DB, 24 May 1967, Carton 5 Folder 42. BANC MSS 90/140 c. CCB Records, UCB BL; *CN*, February 1962, p. 2, 30 March 1964, p. 2, 27 July 1964, p. 1, 28 September 1964, p. 1, 26 April 1965, p. 1, 28 June 1965, p. 7, 10 April 1967, pp. 1, 3, 16 October 1967, p. 7, 30 October 1967, p. 1, 5 May 1969, p. 8, 26 May 1969, p. 2, 9 June 1969, p. 2, 14 July 1969, p. 2.
42 *Berkeley Barb*, 11 November 1966, p. 1, 25 November 1966, p. 3; *CN*, 14 November 1966, p. 1, 21 November 1966, p. 2, 28 November 1966, p. 7, 26 December 1966, p. 2, 19 February 1968, p. 7.
43 Public Relations Subcommittee to Study the Chamber of Commerce Question, 8 July 1965. Letter S.L. Davenport to F. Christmann, 15 July 1965, Carton 4 Folder 36, BD, 8 November 1965, Carton 4 Folder 38, BD, 9 January 1967, Carton 5 Folder 40. BANC MSS 90/140 c. CCB Records, UCB BL; *CN*, 28 June 1965, p. 7, 27 September 1965, p. 2, 1 April 1968, p. 3, 15 April 1968, p. 1, 3 August 1970, p. 1.
44 *CN*, June 1962, p. 1, 17 July 1967, p. 2, 22 September 1969, p. 1.
45 *CN*, 12 October 1970, p. 1.
46 BD, 25 June 1962, Carton 3 Folder 25. BANC MSS 90/140 c. CCB Records, UCB BL; *CN*, 30 November 1964, p. 14, 21 July 1965, p. 1, 19 August 1968, p. 2.
47 R. Treuhaft 'Mutual Service Insurance Co. Disservice in the Co-op', Leaflet, n.d., Carton 5 Folder 44. BANC MSS 90/140 c. CCB Records, UCB BL; *CN*, 22 May 1967, pp. 1–2, 19 June 1967, p. 1, 3 June 1968, p. 1, 9 September 1968, pp. 1–2, 11 November 1968, p. 3, 14 July 1969, p. 3, 4 May 1970, p. 3.
48 BD, 28 October 1963, Carton 2 Folder 5. BANC MSS 90/140 c. CCB Records, UCB BL.
49 CN, 28 September 1964, p. 2, 14 December 1964, p. 2. 13 September 1965, p. 12.
50 *CN*, 18 September 1962, pp. 1, 5, April 1963, p. 3, 2 August 1965, p. 1, 9 August 1965, p. 1, 22 November 1965, p. 2., 15 November 1965, p. 1, 8 May 1967, p. 4, 6 May 1968, pp. 1, 11, 13 May 1968, p. 1.

References

Balnave, N. and Patmore, G., 2017, "The Labour Movement and Co-operatives," *Labour History*, 112, pp. 7–24.

Bay Area Census, 2018, available at www.bayareacensus.ca.gov (accessed 8 November 2018).

BHS, 1983, *Eugene Mannila. A Finnish Pioneer of the Consumers Co-operative of Berkeley*, Berkeley CA, BHS.

BHS, 1987a, *George G. Little. The President of the Consumers Co-operative of Berkeley in the 1960s*, Berkeley, CA, BHS.

BHS, 1987b, *Laurie Leonard Lehtin. A Finnish Leader's Perspective on the Co-operative Movement*, Berkeley, CA, BHS.

BHS, 1990, *Robert E. Treuhaft. Left-Wing Political Activist and Progressive Leader in the Berkeley Co-op*, Berkeley, CA, BHS.

BHS, 1995, *A Conversation with George Yasukochi: Controller of the Consumers Co-operative of Berkeley, 1956–1982*, Berkeley, CA, BHS.

BHS, 1996a, *A Conversation with Betsy Wood: A Home Economist's Perspective on the Berkeley Co-op*, Berkeley, CA, BHS.

BHS, 1996b, *A Conversation with Robert Neptune – Pioneer Manager of the Consumers Co-operative of Berkeley, and Long-Term Manager at Associated Co-operatives*, Berkeley, CA, BHS.

CCB, 1962, *Co-op 25th Anniversary Menu Book*, Berkeley, CA, CCB.

CCB, 1965, *The Co-op Low Cost Cook Book*, Berkeley, CA, CCB.

CCB, 1971, *Ralph Nader Speech*, Berkeley, CA, CCB.

Cohen, L., 2004, *A Consumers' Republic. The Politics of Mass Consumption in Postwar America*, New York, Vintage Books.

Curl, J., 2012, *For All the People: Uncovering the Hidden History of Co-operation, Co-operative Movements, and Communalism in America*, 2nd ed., Oakland, CA, PM Press.

Daniels, D.H., 2013, "Berkeley Apartheid. Unfair Housing in a University Town," *History Research*, 3 (5), pp. 321–341.

Fullerton, M., (ed.), 1992, *What Happened to the Berkeley Co-op? A Collection of Opinions, Centre for Co-operatives*, Davis, CA, Center for Co-operatives, University of California.

Healy, M.C., 2016, *BART. The Dramatic History of the Bay Area Rapid Transit System*, Berkeley, CA, Heyday.

Johnson, W.J.S., 1978, "Berkeley: Twelve Years as the Nation in Microcosm, 1962–1974," In Nathan, H., and Scott, S, eds., *Experiment and Change in Berkeley. Essays on City Politics 1950–1975*, Berkeley, CA, Institute of Government Studies, UCB, pp. 179–230.

Kaufmann, K.M., 2004, *The Urban Voter: Group Conflict and Mayoral Voting Behavior in American Cities*, Ann Arbor, University of Michigan Press.

Kent, T.J. Jr., 1978, "Berkeley's First Liberal Democratic Regime, 1961–1970. The Postwar Awakening of Berkeley's Liberal Conscience," In Nathan, H., and Scott, S, eds., *Experiment and Change in Berkeley. Essays on City Politics 1950–1975*, Berkeley, CA, Institute of Government Studies, UCB, pp. 71–104.

Kresy, G., 1980, "The Berkeley Co-op. An Economic and Political History 1964–1980 as seen by one individual," Unpublished typescript, Carton 49 Folder 13. BANC MSS 86/178c, Helen Nelson Collection (hereafter HNC), UCB BL.

Lyford, J.P., 1982, *The Berkeley Archipelago*, Chicago, IL, Regnery Gateway.

Mannila, E., 1984, *The Finns and the Bay Co-operative Movement*, Berkeley, CA, BHS.

Neptune, R., 1977, *California's Uncommon Markets. The Story of Consumers Co-operatives 1935–1976*, 2nd ed., Richmond, CA, AC.

Neptune, R., 1992, "Could the Failure of California's Uncommon Markets Have Been Avoided?" In Fullerton, M., ed., *What Happened to the Berkeley Co-op? A Collection of Opinions*, Davis, CA, Center for Co-operatives, University of California, pp. 1–10.

Ohya, M., 1992, "Preface," In Fullerton, M. ed., *What Happened to the Berkeley Co-op? A Collection of Opinions*, Davis, CA, Center for Co-operatives, University of California, pp. v–ix.

Rauber, P., 1992, "Decline and Fall of the Berkeley Co-op," In Fullerton, M., ed., *What Happened to the Berkeley Co-op? A Collection of Opinions*, Davis CA, Center for Co-operatives, University of California, pp. 11–17.

Rorabaugh, W.J., 1989, *Berkeley at War. The 1960s*, New York, Oxford University Press.

Starr, K., 2007, *California. A History*, New York, The Modern Library.

UCB Office of the Vice Chancellor of Finance, 2019, "Our Berkeley. Enrolment History Since 1869," available at https://pages.github.berkeley.edu/OPA/our-berkeley/enroll-history.html (accessed 14 April 2019).

Weinstein, D., 2008, *It Came from Berkeley. How Berkeley Changed the World*, Layton UT, Gibbs Smith.

Willes, B, 2000, *Tales from the Elmwood*, Berkeley, CA, BHS.

Wollenberg, C., 2008, *Berkeley. A City in History*, Berkeley, University of California Press.

7 Instability and Final Expansion

1972–1980

This chapter explores the growing instability for the CCB following the departure of Eugene Mannila, who had been general manager since 1947. A turnover of senior managers and continued BD faction fighting exacerbated poor decision-making and planning. Despite this the CCB continued to expand with the opening of the San Francisco North Point Shopping Centre and the leasing of the three Mayfair chain stores in Oakland in 1974, which expanded the CCB into less affluent areas of the Bay Area. The CCB continued to promote consumer protection and environmental awareness. These developments were set against the background of the end of postwar prosperity in 1973 and the challenges of inflation and higher interest rates. By August 1977, CCB only accounted for 3.4 percent of total retail grocery in the five Bay Area Counties compared to Safeway with 27 percent distributed among 117 stores and Lucky with 18.3 percent distributed among 61 stores.[1]

Berkeley

Berkeley, like Oakland and San Francisco, declined in population during the 1970s, with its population slightly falling from 116,716 in 1970 to 103,328 in 1980. BART contributed to a loss of housing units in downtown Berkeley, particularly for the older Finnish community that had been traditionally strong supporters of the CCB,[2] Oakland and San Francisco. The decline in the white population in Berkeley slowed, falling slightly from 67.7 percent to 66.9 percent. The African American population declined sharply after the postwar growth, falling from 23.5 percent in 1970 to 20 percent in 1980. This had an adverse effect on the CCB University Avenue store, located in an area with a large African American population, who viewed the CCB favorably because of its affirmative action policies. Neighboring Oakland by contrast saw an increase in the African American population from 34.5 percent to 47 percent. Other areas continued to benefit from suburbanization with Walnut Creek growing from 39,844 to 50,689 and Marin County growing from 206,038 to 222,568. Walnut Creek and Marin County had white populations of 94.5 percent and 92.8 percent by 1980 (Bay Area Census, 2019; Gordon, 1992, p. 61; Landis and Cervero, 1999, p. 6).

Berkeley's economy saw a decline in manufacturing in West Berkeley and the continued growth of the service sector. The Sealy Mattress Company, which moved their operations from Oakland to West Berkeley in 1959, sold the factory in 1972 to A.J. Bernard, who divided it into 35 spaces for uses that included artisan workshops, artists' studios and theaters. From 1963, leaders of the Berkeley business community proposed to redevelop much of West Berkeley into an industrial park, but this was successfully opposed by residents. Cultural and artistic businesses developed in Berkeley. Fantasy Records, which gained success from the local band Creedence Clearwater Revival, moved into new studios in West Berkeley in 1971. It expanded into film production, including the production of notable *One Flew Over the Cuckoo's Nest*, with the owner Saul Zaentz renting out office space and production facilities to other local filmmakers. Alice Waters, a former activist in the FSM, in 1971 opened the restaurant Chez Panisse opposite the CCB Shattuck Avenue Center. Chez Panisse helped create 'California Cuisine' and became the center of a culinary district – the North Berkeley 'Gourmet Ghetto'. The UCB increased its economic significance in the Berkeley with the student population that grew from 28,559 in 1972 to 30,883 in 1980 (BAHA and D. Thompson, 2019; Schuermann, 2018; Johnson, 1978, pp. 202–203; UCB Office of the Vice Chancellor of Finance, 2019; Weinstein, 2008, pp. 179–181; Wollenberg, 2008, pp. 156–162).

The radical mood of the 1960s began to weaken, despite events such as the Symbionese Liberation Army assassination of Marcus Foster, the Oakland school superintendent, and the kidnapping of heiress Patricia Hearst in 1974 from her Berkeley apartment. With the end of the Vietnam War and the adoption of radical ideas by mainstream politicians such as George McGovern, activists went in many directions, including rejoining the American middle class, shifting to rural communities or being victims of political repression, notably the FBI's COINTEL program. There were surviving expressions of the radical politics with the founding of the Center for Independent Living (CIL) by disability activists Ed Roberts and Phil Draper in 1972 (Wollenberg, 2008, pp. 148, 150).

At the BCC, the radicals' success in the 1971 elections prompted liberals and the business conservatives to form a coalition to oppose the radicals. Two local parties, completely unrelated to national politics, developed with Berkeley Citizens' Action (BCA) attracting the Left and the All-Berkeley Coalition or the BDC attracting the Right. While moderates generally controlled the BCC, progressives set the agenda through ballot initiatives. African Americans were a major swing vote between the two factions. Groups such as the Black Caucus, which was formed in 1969 to support BCC candidates, had raised concerns of African Americans about their treatment by Berkeley police with charges of police brutality. There was hostility toward the police for their role in dealing with political upheavals in Berkeley. The critics, including the Black Caucus and the Black Panthers, supported the community control of police, but a Berkeley proposal to control the police through elected neighborhood councils was defeated in April 1971. A later ballot initiative led to the establishment of a strong civilian police review board in 1973. Concerns over property development led to a neighborhood preservation ordinance in 1973, which slowed 'ticky-tacky' residential development, and a landmark preservation ordinance in 1974. The Berkeley Architectural Heritage Association (BAHA) and the BHS, founded in 1974 and 1978, respectively, highlighted a growing awareness of history and heritage in the community. A rent control initiative was passed in 1980, which reflected a growing demand for rental housing in Berkeley, as UCB failed to build more dormitory space for its growing student numbers and changing demographics with more single adults and families with fewer children (Hopkins, 1978, pp. 120, 126–127; Johnson, 1978, pp. 221–225; Rubenzahl, 1978, pp. 335–342; Weinstein, 2008, p. 157, 165; Wollenberg, 2008, pp. 151–154, 170).

Managing the Co-operative

As Table 7.1 highlights, sales volume increased in the period 1972–1980. The CCB faced a further loss in 1972, which undermined the ability of the CCB to obtain external loans from established financial institutions in 1973 due to their loss of confidence in the CCB. The CCB turned to MSI, which loaned the CCB $600,000 with a mortgage on the Shattuck Avenue Store. It endured additional losses from 1976 to 1978, when the worst deficit in the history of the CCB occurred. As losing operations for the two months ending on 26 November 1977 resulted in debt exceeding member equity by $101,000, CCB management were unable under the CCB bylaws to issue new certificates of interest or incur other debts until there was net equity or membership approval, which was obtained in January 1978. CCB was forced to seek external mortgage financing

Table 7.1 CCB Finances 1972–1980 (Neptune, 1977, p. 191; Neptune, 1982, p. 21)

Year	*Volume ($)*	*Net Savings ($)*	*Member Equity ($)*
1972	41,019,400	294,300	3,564,400
1973	46,465,100	216,700	3,629,000
1974	57,609,000	785,100	4,063,700
1975	69,188,900	396,100	4,421,900
1976	72,575,700	217,600	4,477,700
1977	72,286,800	359,600	4,132,700
1978	75,813,700	789,900	3,408,800
1979	78,513,900	45,400	3,272,100
1980	83,757, 800	762,500	3,935,400

and freeze the redemption of member shares from December 1977 until March 1979, when the real value of shares again matched the nominal value of $5. The CCB faced further difficulties when the Californian State Department of Corporations, concerned with the CCB's financial problems, did not renew the CCB's permit to sell shares in May 1978. While the CCB was permitted again to sell shares in January 1980, new members were restricted to one share and the Department required the CCB to provide prospective members with several documents, including an audited financial statement before they joined. The Department also prohibited the sale of additional shares and certificates to existing members. These restrictions were lifted on 1 January 1981 due to legislative reforms that allowed all Californian co-operatives to raise up to $100 per person without Department approval. The banks remained reluctant to provide major financing to the CCB, but improving finances led the NCCB to approve a million-dollar loan to the CCB in 1980. The CCB's financial difficulties led it to close the Kiddie Korrals at University Avenue, Telegraph Avenue and Castro Valley in October 1976. The Telegraph Avenue was reopened, after protests by angry parents and the TACC, with reduced hours being introduced for the other Kiddie Korrals still operating. All Kiddie Korrals were eventually shut in 1978. The CCB sold surplus property to raise cash, with the Walnut Creek Geary Street Store sold in September 1978 and then leased it back for 20 years, which injected $581,000 into the CCB. While there were fluctuations, member equity in the CCB fell from a peak in 1976, with a slight recovery to a lower level in 1980. There was a return to surplus in 1979 and 1980, with the latter being assisted by a sale of CCB housing near the University Avenue Center (BHS, 1987, p. 38, 1995, pp. 59, 61, 67; Brand, 1982, pp. 6–7; Schildgen, 1992, p. 43).[3]

Factions remained a feature of the BD, with the Progressives regaining control in 1972 in a campaign that included an attack on the Moderates' progress in an area of affirmative action for women and minorities. The Progressives were reelected in 1973, 1975 and 1976. The Moderates won power in 1974 and held power again from 1977 on a platform of "sound business practices," introducing a boycott policy in July 1978 that allowed products to be removed from shelves to protect the community's "health and welfare" or if there was a decline in sales, particularly after an informational campaign highlighting concerns about the product. The Moderates reorganized in 1979 as the Promoters of Active Co-operatism (PACT), with successful candidates in 1980 being Margaret Gordon, who was a former BCC member, a former UCB IIR Associate Directors and wife of the former CCB President Robert Gordon, and Helen Nelson, the former California Consumer Counsel. Emil Sekerak, the former Education Director, played a key role in organizing PACT. These factional shifts again created problems for management, as policies could shift depending who was in control of the BD. There was also growing controversy in 1974 over whether only the BD could make public statements on behalf of the CCB, but the BD resolved in June 1974 that CCB members if authorized by Center Councils and CCB committees could make statements that did not conflict with BD policy. Permission was also granted if there was no time for presentation of the statement to the BD and speaker made it clear they were not speaking for the BD. The BD also began from 1972 to meet in "executive sessions," which excluded both members and employees, leading to accusations that the BD was freezing out members and employees and reducing transparency. Against the background of management upheaval and poor financial performance, the *CN* stopped publishing regular summaries of BD minutes in October 1978, which some members argued weakened CCB democracy, leading to reports reappearing in July 1979. Edna Haynes, a personnel consultant, became the first female CCB President in 1974 and again in 1977. Jane Lundin and Linda Akulian served as CCB Presidents in 1975 and 1976, respectively. Curtis Aller, a Professor of Economics at the San Francisco University and a Rhodes Scholar, was elected by the BD as President in 1978, 1979 and 1980 (BHS, 1983, 1984, pp. 10–11, 17–18; Brand, 1982, p. 6; Neptune, 1977, pp. 114, 185).[4]

There was further instability with a high level of senior manager turnover. Val Litton, the CCB's retail operation manager, replaced Mannila as General Manager on 1 January 1972, after an exhaustive search process that began with 80 applications for the job. Barry Solloway, the CCB Corporate Development and Financial Manager, became the Assistant General Manager. The new Progressive majority on the BD objected to the Moderates' choice of Litton and appointed the Education Director Rothenberg rather than the General Manager as BD Secretary as had been traditionally the practice. The relationship between the BD and Litton further deteriorated, with Progressive President Larry Duga later accusing him of poor performance. Litton resigned in July 1972, claiming that he had lost the BD's confidence, with consultants Knight, Gladieux and Smith being brought in to assist the management during the transition to a new General Manager. Roy Bryant, who became the General Manager on 15 January 1973 after an extensive search process, had no co-operative experience, but had 25 years of experience in the grocery industry, with the last 18 months at the Mayfair Stores, where he was assistant general manager with territory covering Northern California and Northern Nevada. He took advantage of several senior management resignations, including Assistant General Manager Barry Solloway that occurred in the wake of Litton's departure, to reorganize operations and make several new external appointments. Bryant developed a good working relationship with Education Director Rothenberg and ensured that Rothenberg's concerns about the community and political climate were incorporated in management decisions. Bryant cancelled engaging a new bread supplier, Continental Breads, to reduce prices when he learnt from Rothenberg that the company was owned by AT&T, which had been linked to the overthrow of President Allende in Chile in 1974. While Bryant worked well with both factions on the BD, he submitted his resignation on 18 December 1975, but was given leave away from the stress of the job and unanimous support by the BD. Bryant's leave was accompanied by senior management criticism that there had been a breakdown in communication with the BD, with management being excluded from significant decisions and Bryant's concerns about a decision by the BD to enter into commercial relationship with the Consumer Trade Association, which provided discounts on goods such as automobiles and proved short-lived. Bryant eventually resigned in December 1976 to accept the position of Chief Executive Officer at the Greenbelt Co-operative (BHS, 1995, pp. 54–55; Neptune, 1977, p. 114).[5]

There was further turnover in the position of General Manager. Leonard Levitt became General Manager in May 1977 bringing with him extensive non-cooperative supermarket management experience, including Safeway. He, however, was unable to stop mounting losses and declining member investment. Levitt stopped the *CN* publishing letters that were critical but not "constructive," to promote patronage and discourage the polarization of membership. He cut services, including the education budget in August 1978. There were calls for the dismissal of Levitt and the circulation in September 1978 of a recall petition for four directors, including President Aller. Levitt left in September 1978 despite a five-year contract, with the BD buying him out of his contract. The BD approached Neptune, the AC General Manager, to be simultaneously CCB manager to replace Levitt. Neptune, who criticized the recall petitioners for "hassling" and encouraging new customers brought in by strikes at competitors stores to shop elsewhere, remained in these joint positions for two years. The CCB's finances showed a major improvement with a return to surplus in 1979 and 1980. Herbert Grevious, the first African American General Manager, replaced Neptune as General Manager in September 1980 with an international search firm assisting recruitment. Grevious was a Harvard MBA and had supermarket management experience in Philadelphia, but no co-operative management background (BHS, 1984, p. 18, 1995, p. 59, 1996b, p. 19; Neptune, 1977, p. 115; 1982, p. 6).[6]

The CCB continued to expand into new localities and offer a wider range of services. Despite the lingering concerns over the takeover of the Sids stores in 1961, the CCB leased three Mayfair chain stores in Oakland in 1974. The CCB had an established interest in developing co-operatives in low-income areas and had earlier examined East Oakland. Mannila was reluctant to expand into these areas with a large-scale investment until the residents committed themselves in advance to provide finance and active support. The BD authorized management in March 1970 to negotiate with the developer of the West Oakland Acorn Project about a new co-operative center following a feasibility study undertaken by Barry Solloway, the then CCB Corporate Development and Financial Manager. There were approaches to West Oakland residents, including tours of CCB facilities, to see if they were interested and would welcome a CCB Center in their neighborhood, with the BD agreeing in principle to establish a Center in June 1970. The project was delayed because the Acorn developer could not raise sufficient capital for the whole center. A further CCB study in March 1972 indicated that a new center would generate continued losses, and there were concerns by CCB directors and staff over whether they could change the long-standing shopping habits of the Acorn residents and whether the store would have a sufficient profile in the proposed shopping center. The BD in September 1972 decided not to proceed with the Acorn project, following a report by the consultants Knight, Gladieux and Smith that reinforced that it would be a loss-making concern and a survey of members in Oakland and Alameda revealing that 61 percent would not shop there and preferred to continue shopping in Berkeley. By August 1973, with improving finances and a growth of apartment and housing construction in the Acorn project despite the absence of shopping facilities, the BD instructed Bryant to hire a supermarket expert to look at the best type of supermarket for the Acorn project and potential patronage. Both the report and data provided by CCB management again saw the proposed store as viable and the BD approved Bryant's recommendation to proceed in September 1973, which included conditions such as an escape clause for the CCB if there were financial issues, with the BD finally approving a lease in October 1973 and a planning meeting held with potential shoppers at the Acorn Community Center in March 1974.[7]

While the proposed Acorn Center was progressing, the CCB moved into Oakland, when Mayfair Stores decided to discontinue their operations in Northern California with three Oakland stores. Bryant had worked for the Mayfair Stores and brought the leases to the BD's attention. He believed that they would increase the economies of scale for the CCB stores and reduce costs. Two of the Mayfair stores, North Oakland on Telegraph Avenue and the Broadway-Macarthur shopping center, were in locations that provided improved services to CCB members currently residing in Oakland, while the third in the Park Boulevard shopping area provided a new store in a central city location that would attract new members. The first store on Telegraph Avenue in North Oakland opened as a CCB store on 1 May 1974. The North Oakland Telegraph Store was only to provide a limited range of services, which included a current liquor license, as it was close to the existing Telegraph Avenue Center. However, as CCB members preferred the Telegraph Avenue store, they shifted back to the older store and CCB had to attract them back by providing a full supermarket service at the newer store to reduce congestion at the older store. However, the North Oakland store produced a financial loss with higher price items not selling. The Broadway-MacArthur shopping center and Park Boulevard stores, which were offered by Mayfair to the CCB in June 1974, were converted into CO-OP operations on 22 July 1974. Center Councils began functioning at all the new stores. While there was a similar argument to Sids in the case of North Oakland that the transaction had to be kept secret from members to forestall competitors, there was very little CCB opposition to the leasing of the Mayfair stores given the long-standing interest of expanding into Oakland, with Progressives supporting the Moderate-controlled BD decision because the new stores would be beneficial to low-income areas. The new Mayfair stores, however, were a financial drain on the CCB and the BD decided in June 1978 to close Park Boulevard, which ceased trading on 15 July 1978, and North Oakland, but reversed its decision on the latter store subject to the store meeting a minimum level of sales following North Oakland Center Council (NOCC) and community protests, which criticized the BD for favoring predominately white high-income areas and presented a petition of over 5,000 signatures opposing the closing of the store. The North Oakland store met the sales criteria only briefly after a neighborhood door-to-door campaign by local members to increase patronage and soon again returned losses. As with the earlier takeover of the Sid Stores, the new employees that came into the CCB were not familiar with co-operative practice and principles, and there were further concerns that the CCB prices were too high for residents. Despite the earlier enthusiasm for the Acorn Center, this project did not proceed as the sponsors were unable to meet a building schedule, and in February 1975 Bryant declared the project was "dead." When the possibility of reexamining of the Acorn proposal was again raised in October 1980, Grievous rejected the idea on the grounds of financial risk and negative impact on the sales of the existing CCB Oakland stores (BHH, 1995, p. 53, 1996a, p. xii; Curl, 2012, p. 201; Neptune, 1977, pp. 62–63; Rauber, 1992, p. 14; Schildgen, 1992, p. 42; Yasukochi, 1992, p. 27).[8]

The Oakland expansion was followed by the opening of the San Francisco North Point Shopping Centre, near Fishermen's Wharf, in August 1975. There had been a long interest in establishing a CCB center in San Francisco, with an approach by San Francisco members to the CCB Future Plans Committee for a store in January 1962 when there were 500 members, and then again in November 1964 when there were 735 CCB members in the City. One issue that complicated the expansion into San Francisco was CCB support for the failed Neighborhood Co-operative, with San Francisco members being encouraged in January 1965 to give support to Neighborhood Co-operative (Neptune, 1977, p. 63).[9]

Local San Francisco members formed in June 1974 the Committee for a San Francisco Co-operative. While some San Francisco members criticized the BD decision to purchase the Oakland Mayfair stores for undermining their approach of "ground up" growth led by CCB members rather than BD "down growth," the Committee held its first organizing meeting in October 1974. The Committee sought a good site for a store and CCB staff evaluated alternative sites. The leased store, a former Mayfair store operating as Budget Basket, was operating at a loss, but following the opening of the CCB store the sales volume doubled and new members joined the CCB. The organizing committee became the new Center Council. The store was financially successful, and in September 1976 the CCB opened a new Basic Food shop in the Northpoint Center to supply bulk and natural foods to its growing San Francisco membership, which was relocated to the main Northpoint store in August 1978. San Francisco, like the new Oakland stores, did not have all the CCB services such as a Kiddie Korral (Neptune, 1977, p. 63).[10]

There were other possibilities of absorbing the chain stores. John Niven, the previous operator of the San Francisco Northpoint store and owner of Northern California Supermarkets (NCS), which operated a chain of 14 stores, approached Bryant in September 1975 with a proposal that the CCB manage 12 of his stores. Niven would accept the CCB operating and merchandising program, which included AC CO-OP-labelled goods, and pay the labor costs needed to implement the program. The proposal gained the support of Neptune, who saw the benefits for the AC of increased economies, with the AC in 1974 deciding to sell CO-OP brands to non-cooperative stores to increase volume. Following meetings that included the CCB, PAC and AC, it was understood that the NAC stores should ultimately become community-owned stores. Opposition developed within the CCB to the proposal, with calls for CCB management to focus on CCB problems such as long delays in the refurbishment of the University Avenue Center. The BD eventually abandoned the idea in November 1975 on a recommendation by Bryant, who wanted to avoid a split in the CCB over the issue and concentrate on building the CCB. The BD agreed in March 1976 to a more limited NCS proposal focusing on its stores in Salinas and Monterey on the understanding that if local consumers organized a co-operative, then the store would be mutualized. NCS further requested that this agreement be extended to three more stores, but later withdrew its proposal (BHS, 1995, p. 55; Neptune, 1977, p. 64).[11]

The CCB introduced new services to members, but also withdrew from some local ventures. The CCB moved to allow credit cards at most nonfood facilities in March 1978 to attract sales, with one director, Bonnie Fish, arguing that the ICA had dropped the principle of cash trading in 1975. The CCB placed a greater emphasis on recreational goods with an expansion into wilderness and winter-related sports supplies. There was a new store opened for these goods in the Corte Madera Co-op Center in Marin County in April 1972, and in 1973 the Wilderness Department was transferred from the Shattuck Avenue hardware variety store to the larger remodeled University Avenue variety store. Wilderness supply stores also opened at the Castro Valley Center in May 1973 and the South Main Center at Walnut Creek in June 1973. This initiative by the CCB failed to sustain sales, and the Wilderness Stores in Corte Madera and Walnut Creek were closed in September 1974, while the University Avenue store became a catalog order department and was moved back to the Shattuck Avenue hardware variety store in 1976. The CCB opened a Garden and Plant Shop at the El Cerrito Center on the old gas station site in April 1974 after strong support in a questionnaire undertaken by the local Center Council, but it was closed in May 1978 due to poor financial returns. Natural Foods products from 1980 were emphasized in special departments in all stores, with four specially remodeled for the purpose. There were problems at the CCB's service stations with gas shortages, uncertainty about continuing supply, higher unionized wage rates than most competitors and increased costs arising from mandatory pollution controls. The service stations at the Walnut Creek Geary Road Center and El Cerrito were closed in 1976, though the former was reopened in October 1977 as a combination service station and garage, but again closed in June 1978. The BD decided to close the money-losing University Avenue garage and service station in January 1978. Growing financial problems led the conversion of the Castro Valley Center in September 1977 to a food depot with reduced hours, sales direct from shipping crates and discounted prices, but continued losses led the BD to revert Castro Valley back to the same price levels as other CCB stores with longer hours in May 1978 (Fullerton, 1992, p. 95; Neptune, 1977, pp. 62–63).[12]

Members

As Table 7.2 indicates, while CCB membership grew dramatically between 1972 and 1980, there was a decline in 1974 due to 11,600 inactive members being removed from the membership rolls (BHS, 1995, p. 67). There had been caution in interpreting this data overall. Yasukochi (1992, p. 27), the CCB controller, later estimated that 30,000 of the 102,500 members in 1980 "had moved away or were totally inactive." By October 1976, the percentage of membership in Berkeley had fallen to 25.6 percent, but contributed 39 percent of the patronage, 30.4 percent of share capital and 35.1 percent of the investment in share certificates. While Oakland had 19.8 percent of the members, its contribution to CCB finances was relatively lower with 17.5, 15.1 and 12.7 percent. Other high areas of membership concentration were Walnut Creek (14.2 percent) and Marin County (9.5 percent). While a member ballot to increase the minimum shareholding from $5 to $10 was defeated in January 1978, the joining fee was increased from $1 to $2. The poor finances resulted in members receiving patronage refunds only in 1973–1975 and 1980,

Table 7.2 Number of Members from 1972 to 1980 and Member Per Capita Equity, Interest on Capital and Patronage Refund (BHS, 1995, pp. 52, 56, 67; Neptune, 1977, p. 191, 1982, p. 21)

Year	*No. of Members*	*Member Per Capita Equity $*	*Interest %*	*Patronage Refund %*
1972	66,000	54	0	0
1973	71,900	50	2.16	0.4
1974	71,000	57	4.0	1.0
1975	80,500	55	2.9	0.44
1976	86,000	52	0	0
1977	92,200	45	0	0
1978	96,200	35	0	0
1979	98,700	33	0	0
1980	102,500	38	1.13	0.04

but these ranged from a low of 0.04 percent in 1980 to a maximum of 1 percent in 1974. Payments on share interest only matched the 4 percent of the early 1960s in 1974, with members receiving no payments on five occasions. Member per capita investment overall continued its downward trend, with older members with higher investments being replaced by younger ones who bought one $5 share. The purchase of the Mayfair Stores was a major contributing factor for the decline of patronage refunds and payments on interest between 1974 and 1975. The CCB did reach out to people with disabilities to increase access to its stores in September 1976 by establishing a working committee with the CIL to examine the issue. There were new approaches to communication, such as membership hotline to the CCB head office introduced in 1972, where members could leave suggestions or complaints on an automated telephone answering machine. The CCB continued to use membership surveys to obtain opinions on CCB operations and membership motivation, with a November 1977 survey finding that co-operative principles/values followed by lower prices were the main reasons for joining and being a member, with the main difference between the CCB and non-cooperative stores being the provision of consumer and nutritional information. Membership apathy, however, remained an issue, with the BD election participation falling from 22 percent in 1974 to only 13 percent in 1978 (BHS, 1995, pp. 52, 56; Schildgen, 1992, p. 42).[13]

The financial problems facing the CCB led to a decline in the funding and status of its education activities. Enda Haynes, CCB director and President, criticized the Education Department for failure to provide proper costings for its activities and costs of practices such as the employment of part-time home economists rather than a smaller number of full-time home economists. The moderate-dominated BD dismissed Rothenberg in one meeting in September 1974, with accusations of factional bias toward the Progressives and poor performance, and then reversed its decision at its next meeting with a reprimand. Rothenberg eventually resigned in August 1977, being replaced in November 1977 by Lee Awner in the retitled position of Member and Community Relations Director. Awner, a CCB education assistant, was an activist for the extension of the CCB into Marin County and the first woman to be appointed dean at Camp Sierra in 1974. Levitt in 1978 dismissed all the education assistants in the stores and five of the eight home economists to cut costs. The education assistants played an important role explaining the co-operative difference and values at an education booth in each Center. Two education assistants were rehired in May 1979 as "member service coordinators" at the central CCB office to develop self-service member information desks at each Center. There was a greater emphasis on advertising, initially on radio, but this shifted back to the *CN* in 1979 with member coupons for specials (Awner, 1979, p. 22; Rauber, 1992, p. 14; Schildgen, 1992, p. 43; Illustration 7.1).[14]

Home economists found their ability to comment on significant issues and products being increasingly restricted with the factionalized BD and the deteriorating financial position. The support for home economists declined. Home economist Helen Black was criticized in June 1979 by

Illustration 7.1 CCB Education Staff, 1975. Courtesy of Berkeley Historical Society.

Alfred Haldeen, Natural Foods Center Council Chair, for misleading CCB members over her concerns about the nutritional value of trace mineral supplements, and there were ongoing tensions with some members at the Natural Foods Center over water fluoridation.[15] Home economists found that they had to go through more levels of approval to make clear statements on products. According to Black (1996, p. 64), "commenting by home economists was virtually over by the end of 1979."

Despite these debates over the role of co-operative and consumer education, the CCB continued to be a center for consumer activism with the CPIC, which became the Consumer Protection Committee (CPC) in March 1970, still playing significant role in raising consumer awareness.[16] During September 1972, the CPC, with the assistance of CCB pharmacy staff such as Aldoph Kamil, launched a campaign to educate consumers about the benefits of plain aspirin relative to expensive painkillers to help members save money. Home economist Helen Black gained national attention in 1972, when she challenged the idea that the oat-based cereal granola was good for you by highlighting that her granola sample contained five times the number of calories as standard cereals such as Cheerios. The CCB responded to inflationary pressures in April 1973 and September 1974 by rolling back beef prices, which attracted favorable media coverage, and taking successful antitrust action against Safeway and Foster Farms in July 1975 over a monopoly, which forced the CCB to pay higher wholesale prices for chicken compared to Safeway. Home economists and volunteers also prepared a cereal information bulletin, *Cereal Breakfast of Champions*, in 1974, which reduced the purchase of high sugar cereals by CCB shoppers by 48 percent within eighteen months. By May 1978, 33,000 copies were sold to people outside the CCB and many more were given away, with the CCB in 1980 rearranging the cereal shelves and marking them green, yellow or red to indicate what cereals the home economists recommended. In 1975, the CCB responded to calls by environmentalists for a tuna boycott as porpoises were being killed when certain types of tuna were netted. It placed shelf cards urging shoppers to avoid light tuna meat and introduced them to alternatives such as albacore and bonito, with sales of the alternatives increasing dramatically and tuna sales slumping. In June 1976, the CCB remodeled all produce departments to have large wooden bins that contained produce such as cabbage, peaches, oranges and broccoli that would otherwise be discarded as they did meet usual market standards and at lower prices. It began marketing in 1979 "Natural Park" CO-OP-labelled canned food, which contained no added sugar, no added salt, preservatives or artificial colors. The BD ceased purchasing aerosol spray containers using fluorocarbons in September 1975, with a ban of sale by 30 December, even though there were no replacement products available, with the justification that environmental hazards outweighed the inconvenience to customers and the loss of sales.

Environmental concerns led to the sponsorship of energy and water conservation clinics in April 1977 and the provision of refunds for reused paper bags in 1979, with Save-A-Tree reusable canvas bags being sold in stores in May 1979. The CCB also continued to produce food books with the *Co-op 35th Anniversary Menu Book* in 1973, which contained complete gourmet menus donated by CCB members with accompanying music and wines, and the *Berkeley Co-op Food Book* in 1980 edited by home economist Helen Black, which consolidated the food preparation, health and safety information published in previous home economists' handouts, store special exhibits, point-of-purchase cards posted on store shelves and *CN* columns. The CCB continued action against products because of labor relations and social concerns such as the shelf-labeling in April 1977 of all Florida Orange products, which was promoted by singer Anita Bryant, a leading antigay activist (BHS, 1996a, p. 77; Black 1980; CCB, 1972; Fullerton, 1992, p. 95; Neptune, 1977, p. 102).[17]

Following from the White House Conference on Food, Nutrition and Health in 1969 and lobbying by Ralph Nader, the FCA and others, the US Food and Drug Administration (USFDA) decided to act on the Conference recommendation concerning a plan for testing and evaluating a listing on labels of the amount of essential nutrients in food. The USFDA in 1971 chose the NC as one of five groups to nationally test nutrition information on food labels. This arose from concerns by the FCA that the testing by non-cooperative stores, such as Jewell and Kroger, were financed and funded by the food industry and would undermine the credibility of the tests with the consumers. Former CCB home economist, Mary Nelson, was placed on special assignment to NC and worked in the CCB offices to develop the nutrient labeling. The CCB, unlike the other food stores, could obtain directly the views of consumers through its membership. Based on these tests, the USFDA adopted new and better standards for nutritional labeling, including many CCB consumer suggestions obtained by survey and interviews (Fullerton, 1992, p. 95; Illustration 7.2).[18]

The CCB continued to lobby for legislative reforms. California required retailers to sell milk at a specified price that increased costs for consumers in an inflationary period. Roy Alper, cochair of the CPC, gave testimony in September 1973 to a public hearing conducted by the Californian Department of Agriculture, calling for the elimination of state price controls on milk and its replacement by a system that ensured adequate supply, reasonable prices and adequate profits without monopoly. Against the background of rising milk prices in November 1973, 12,000 CCB members signed a petition to relevant Californian authorities protesting the rises. Linda Akulian, cochair of CPC and CCB Director, presented further evidence to a state inquiry in February 1974, with CCB members and shoppers being transported to Sacramento to hear the testimony. There was another petition presented with 9,660

Illustration 7.2 Nutrition Labels, 1972. Courtesy of Berkeley Historical Society.

signatures protesting the price rises and a survey of CCB and PAC members, which further highlighted opposition to the price increases, presented to support the CCB opposition to milk prices. Bryant in May 1974 told two Californian Assembly Committee hearings in San Francisco that the CCB could cut milk prices by 5 percent and still make a reasonable margin. There were also several meetings between CCB members and dairy farmers to hear their perspective. Rival chain stores such as Lucky in January 1975 and Safeway in February 1975 joined the call for the repeal of milk pricing laws. The CCB reduced the price of milk below the minimum statutory price in February 1976 and the California Director of Food and Agriculture persuaded a judge to issue a temporary restraining order, which was upheld despite a CCB challenge, with CCB paying a civil penalty that was reduced from $19,000 to $500. The CCB reluctantly complied, but launched a petition campaign against the milk price minimum to new Democratic Governor Jerry Brown, which attracted the signatures of over 55,000 CCB shoppers in support, and directly lobbied government officials. Its actions contributed to the government suspending the policy of minimum milk prices in January 1977 and the ending of the policy in January 1978 (Fullerton, 1992, p. 95).[19]

The Center Councils continued to be the focus of activists who wished to break the factional control of the CCB and revive grassroots democracy. The Center Councils' influence was weakened by the CCB's factional politics with BD's distrust of their motives being exacerbated if the Center Council was controlled by an opposing faction, as occurred with the Progressives at the SACC. Jerry Kresy, who was founder of the Marin Ecology Center and from Port Reyes Station in Marin County and later Castro Valley, and others began agitating for the legal recognition of Center Councils by their inclusion in the CCB bylaws. Kresy later also worked for both the CCB and AC. The Center Council Chairperson's Committee (CCCC), formerly the Center Council Chairman's Committee, spearheaded a campaign that led the BD in October 1972 to allow a ballot to change the bylaws, which was defeated in January 1973. Despite this, the CCCC voted in March 1973 to continue their campaign and persuaded President Duga to establish a joint committee to review the bylaws. An amended proposal, which had unanimous BD support, was passed by general ballot in January 1974. Despite Kresy's hopes, the BD, whatever faction was in control, would not increase the Center Councils' power (BHS, 1984, p. 23; Kresy, 1980, pp. 4–6; Neptune, 1982, p. 9). The CCC, which was renamed the Center Co-ordination Committee from March 1975, tried to raise its profile by launching its own newsletter, *Swamp Monster Speaks*, in July 1979. By December 1980, however, Carroll Melbin, the Interim Chair of the Committee,[20] claimed that "little authority and recognition" had been given the Center Councils, and that the Center Councils could relieve the BD of time-consuming activities by performing many "non-business and non-management activities."[21]

Employees and Community

The CCB again avoided strikes during this period, such as the 1973 butchers strike, the four-month Teamsters' warehouse strike that began in August 1978 and a supermarket clerks strike in 1980, which disrupted its competitors such as Safeway and Lucky bringing new shoppers into its stores and increasing sales. Its operations, however, were disrupted by a strike of more than a month by Office and Professional Employees Union (OPEU) at the CCFCU in February 1975 over the CCFCU's unwillingness to negotiate a contract, with management claiming that the CCFCU could not meet the union claims and survive. One long-standing benefit of being a CCB member was access to CCFCU finance, which provided cheaper loans and was more sympathetic to minorities such as African Americans than established financial sources. The CCFCU offices in the CCB Centers were picketed by striking employees and CCFCU was a convenient provider of food stamps for eligible CCB shoppers, which meant lost sales for the CCB. CCB president Lundin tried to persuade both the CCFCU BD and the strikers to reopen negotiations, with CCFCU directors claiming that CCB pressure in the last round of labor negotiations had led to a too generous contract that weakened the CCFCU financially. The strikers eventually returned to work under the old contract on 31 March 1975 pending a new contract. The strike led to CCFCU member dissatisfaction, with the heavy withdrawal of deposits and the closing of accounts. The CFCCU, which reviewed its operations with five new BD members and a new manager, negotiated a new contract with the union which commenced on 1 November 1975. The OPEU did file grievances against the CCB in 1978 over the education department retrenchments and made an "unfair labor practice" charge with the National Labor Relations Board against the CCB for failing to negotiate about the dismissals of the education assistants, with the union able to have two education assistants later rehired (Berkeley Public Library, 2003, pp. 38–40; BHS, 1993, pp. 6–7; Neptune, 1977, p. 140; Tworek, 2008, pp. 39–44).[22]

While employment expanded to 749 employees in September 1975, the financial problems led to a workforce of 659 by June 1980, with major issues being affirmative action and worker morale. There was some progress in affirmative action for women, with two female assistant managers appointed to CCB Centers in 1972. Kathie Kelly, who was employed by CCB as a gas station attendant, became in 1972 an auto apprentice at the CCB University Avenue service station, which the CCB claimed was the first appointment of female auto apprentice in the Bay Area. By January 1979, 33 percent of women held senior and top management positions, with the ethnic breakdown for these positions being 67 percent white, 22 percent African American and 11 percent Asian, with no Hispanics filling these positions. The CCB attempted to address this by hiring more Hispanics at entry-level positions. Despite the program, there was little change based on gender between September 1975 and June 1980 with 63 percent and 65 percent of employees being male. There were some changes in the ethnic composition of the workforce with the number of whites falling from 51 percent to 45 percent, while African Americans grew from 23 percent to 28 percent, Asians were static at 19 percent and Hispanics were 8 percent. Women held none of the 13 of the Assistant Managers positions and only 2 of the 13 Center Managers in June 1980. Management in 1972, to encourage employee commitment to the CCB, ran an employee suggestion contest with letters of appreciation to all participants and gift certificates to winners ranging from $5 to $15. The top two winners suggested employee training programs for dealing with shoplifters. Employees received rewards for additional service such as during the butchers' strike of 1973 with a certificate for a free 14-pound frozen turkey. The CCB launched a new major orientation and training program for its employees in January 1978, which involved small groups of workers learning about co-operative history and

CCB policies and practices as well as being an open forum for employee feedback to management. Neptune in October 1980 introduced regular meetings of employees at all CCB Centers to improve worker morale and encourage belief in the co-operative "again." The BCEA continued to play an important role in organizing employee social events; but in June 1972, the BD acceded to a BCEA request to be relieved of an employee discount scheme for BCEA members, and in September 1972 accepted a BCEA proposal that the scheme be extended to all employees.[23]

There were growing frustrations with turnover of senior managers and the factionalized BD by lower level management and employees. BD members openly sided with employees and lower managers in their dispute with managers, while some lower managers and employees found it necessary to bypass the management structure by appealing to BD through sympathetic members on the local Center Councils. There were tensions between managers, the BD and the CCB employee grievance committee, which consisted of CCB members, over issues of employee discipline and recruitment. In September 1973, after the management unsuccessfully appealed to the BD to overturn a Grievance Committee decision to reinstate a dismissed employee, the BD threatened store managers with penalties unless they issued written warning notices to employees before dismissal. One noted case of management discontent occurred where the decision to appoint a qualified African American male candidate for Assistant Controller after a three-month search was overturned by BD pressure for affirmative action with the appointment of Sarah Jane Moore in May 1974. There were complaints about Moore's management style and several staff threatened to resign. Yasukochi, her supervisor, dismissed Moore, but her appeal for reinstatement was upheld by the Grievance Committee as she had not been issued with a warning letter despite sufficient time to do so and did not receive sufficient guidance on her duties by senior management. The BD upheld a management appeal against the Grievance Committee and Moore was dismissed. Moore later became infamous for an attempt to assassinate President Gerald Ford in San Francisco in 1975 (Balnave and Patmore, 2017, 14; Yasukochi 1992, p. 27).[24]

There was growing employee concern about the impact of financial cutbacks on working conditions and the "non-cooperative" attitude of management. Employees formed in March 1976 a group, Concerned Co-op Employees, which combined with a group of sympathetic members, Concerned Co-op Members, claiming the CCB's problems had arisen from the enhancement of management control at the expense of member control and employee rights and the emergence of a concern with "corporate image." They demanded a greater role in the selection of the general manager and employee representation on all governing bodies, including the CCB. While the employees in December 1976 did gain an Employee Advisory Council, which obtained a BD decision in

March 1977 to protect employees from management in their right to exercise free speech, it complained about being frustrated and ignored by the BD. A petition signed by over 200 CCB employees was presented to Levitt in October 1977 expressing concerns about the impact of financial cutbacks on employees (Curl, 2012, p. 201).[25]

Volunteer labor by members continued to be important for the CCB. The Walnut Creek South Main Center in August 1973 revived the idea of a hospitality table, where volunteers on a Saturday morning served coffee with samples from the CCB Natural Foods Center and provided information on the CCB. A prime mover in this initiative was Florence Greve, who had served in the South Main Center soon after it was taken over from Sids in 1963 and successfully agitated for the store to become a CCB Center. A similar service was provided by volunteer "hostesses" at the Walnut Creek Geary Road Center on Thursday, Friday and Saturday, with activist Celia Jaffe volunteering at the Center for over 14 years by August 1973. Volunteer members, who were also qualified workers, used materials provided by the CCB to construct an education and relaxation area in Park Boulevard Center in March 1975. Volunteer labor was important for collecting and coding data for member surveys. There were limits with a proposal for volunteers to provide child care at the Park Boulevard Center First Anniversary Celebrations in July 1975, which did not proceed further as it breached union agreements. There was also strong union resistance to union members being replaced by volunteers as education assistants in the wake of their dismissal in 1978.[26]

The CCB was caught up in the community campaign for the control of police and the concerns of Berkeley street people. Following the fatal shooting of an armed robber in the Telegraph Avenue Center in January 1971, a deputation from the Flatlands Neighborhood Committee to the BD demanded that the BD not call the police into any of its stores under any circumstances, with the Black Panthers being called in as an alternative, form a community task force to control the CCB, give the money stolen by the deceased robber to his family or the Black Panthers and endorse the campaign for the community control of police. After a long and heated debate, the CCB rejected these demands and decided to review the situation with a focus on reducing the cash in each store to reduce the motivation for the robbers.[27] During 1972, an organization known as the Street Peoples' Liberation Front threatened to have a campaign of shoplifting against the CCB unless it provided a free box of damaged but edible food for street people and panhandlers. CCB President Duga in an open letter in the *CN* in March 1972 replied by highlighting that the CCB donated such food to community groups such as Emergency Food Project, which provided free meals to the poor, and called shoplifting in CCB stores unlike Safeway or Lucky a "robbery of the people."[28]

The Center Councils remained an important CCB link with its local communities. The CCB gave them funds to donate to local community groups, which for the NOCC in 1975 included the Claremont High School musical show, the Longfellow School's camping project and the public television KQED auction. Student scholarships were provided through fundraising activities that included the sale of used paperbacks through the Stan Brown book exchange, named in honor of a deceased BD member who initiated the idea, handicraft fairs and flea markets. The Center Councils also hosted a range of events, including samplings of CO-OP labels, French cooking classes and free speech tables, with the UFW having a table at the Park Boulevard Center in July 1975. The Center meeting rooms provided venues for local community groups such as the Bay Area Photography Society in the Castro Valley Center in April 1974. The Centers assisted those in need in the local community. The Walnut Creek Geary Road Center in 1974 raised funds through the collection of returnable bottles to help the medical expenses of a local paperboy who had been the victim of a violent assault. The University Avenue and Walnut Creek South Main centers chartered buses to help senior citizens do their shopping.[29]

CCB and the Co-operative Movement

The CCB continued to depend on the AC as its principal wholesaler, which in turn relied heavily on the CCB for its sales. The CCB had looked to AC to reduce its costs, with the AC adjusting its Cost-Plus System as early as August 1976 to assist the CCB. As Table 7.3 indicates, AC sales increased during the 1970s, with a decline in 1980. While some long-standing members ceased to operate, such as the Fort Bragg Co-operative which closed its doors in May 1974, the AC benefited from a growing interest in co-operatives with membership doubling between

Table 7.3 AC Membership and Financial Performance 1972–1980 (Neptune, 1977, p. 190; Neptune, 1982, p. 21)

Year	*No. of Members*	*Turnover*	*Net Savings*
1972	10	24,143,000	56,000[a]
1973	10	32,053,500	60,000[a]
1974	9	38,013,500	75,000[a]
1975	10	42,162,900	90,000[a]
1976	14	44,611,100	96,000[a]
1977	18	45,206,400	120,000
1978	19	51,307,300	120,000
1979	20	55,405,000	120,000
1980	20	54,716,400	120,000

a Amount of Net Savings Determined by Cost-Plus Contracts

1974 and 1980. The AC faced the challenge of the wave of new US consumer co-operatives from the 1970s, outlined in Chapter 3. While many of these co-operatives and buying clubs only had a short existence, they were reluctant to deal with the established consumer co-operatives they saw as too large and not sharing their objectives. Some of stores were controlled by employees through collectives and established truck collectives to supply their goods independently of the AC. The Arcata Co-operative, which later changed its name to the North Coast Co-operative (NCC), began as food buying club in 1972 and incorporated in August 1973, became an AC member, but operated its own large truck to transfer goods from the Bay Area to Arcata in Northern California. There were efforts to bring the "new wave" and older co-operatives together with conferences to discuss issues of mutual concern, the first being in Palo Alto in 1975. Activists from these newer co-operatives brought renewed energy to co-operative institutions such as Camp Sierra. The AC continued to promote co-operative expansion through the Co-operative Development Committee, which had its origins during 1975, and raised funds to allow committee consultants to travel throughout California. The AC reformed a Development Department in 1980, with Fred Stapenhorst, the first department manager, having a background in the "new wave" Arcata Co-operative. Other new co-operatives that joined the AC included Davis and Grass Valley in 1976 and 1979, respectively. Californian co-operatives formed the California Co-operative Federation, which the CCB joined in 1980, to lobby legislators and promote co-operatives (Awner, 1979, p. 22; Neptune, 1977, pp. 66–67, 174; Neptune, 1982, pp. 2–3; North Coast Co-op, 2019).[30]

Following the election of Governor Jerry Brown in 1974, California provided a favorable climate for co-operative development and consumer activism. It established a Department of Consumer Affairs in 1976 and appointed a consumer co-operative specialist in the Department in 1977. The Department functions included developing technical manuals to assist co-operatives, develop training programs for the directors of consumer co-operatives and establish public policy in support of the co-operatives. Following a study by a food project coalition, the Department provided support for the supervision and organization of three co-operatives in low-income minority neighborhoods – East Oakland, South of Market in San Francisco and the Watts in Los Angeles. While capital was provided by the NCCB, these co-operatives attracted few members and insufficient member capital (Neptune, 1977, p. 129; Neptune, 1982, p. 2).

The AC encouraged the CCB to modernize its retailing practices by electronic scanning of products at the cash register and encouraged the CCB to move further into recycling. The AC through its relationship with Universal Co-operatives assigned Universal Product Code numbers to CO-OP products. The CCB began using 11 new electronic cash registers in June 1974 at Shattuck Avenue store, which weighed priced items and could calculate change automatically. The registers had a capability to add scanning equipment. These registers could automatically identify and provide correct change for food stamp purchases as well as distinguish between member and nonmember purchases for the purpose of calculating patronage refunds. They were also linked to an in-store minicomputer that transmitted data to a receiver in the CCB central office. The CCB began replacing old registers with the new ones at other stores, but management concerns about CCB finances delayed progress with all stores not having electronic registers until April 1980. The CO-OP-branded one-way soda bottles became returnable in 1972 to reduce packaging and conserve resources, but this increased handling costs for both the CCB and the AC (Neptune, 1977, pp. 100, 102).[31]

The AC had labor relations issues in its warehouse that impacted on the CCB. As early as January 1971, 20 of the 25 employees at the warehouse brought their grievances directly to the CCB BD. These grievances included racial discrimination, harassment by supervisors and the unjust dismissal of one employee. The workers circulated leaflets about the dispute, which included a call for a boycott of the CCB, and the BD requesting the AC to urgently settle the dispute to the "workers' immediate satisfaction" and establishing a joint inquiry with the workers to examine their grievances. The AC subsequently settled these grievances, with assistance from the CCB joint committee, by reinstating the dismissed employee and transferring a supervisor. Grievances flared up again in September 1974, when drivers, members of Teamsters Union Local 315, at the AC warehouse struck over contract negotiations and picketed the warehouse for two weeks. The CCB, which had member complaints, shortages of CO-OP goods and shut its offices at the AC warehouse, was not covered by the union contract and warned Teamster members that any picket of CCB stores was neither sanctioned nor legal (Neptune, 1977, p. 113).[32]

The CCB supported other co-operatives. It provided management services and a $10,000 loan to the Consumers Co-operative of the Monterey Bay (CCMB), previously a buying club, allowing CCMB to take over the NCS Monterey store in August 1976. The CCMB faced mounting losses with the store, which eventually closed in November 1979. The CCB terminated the arrangement with the NCS at Salinas in September 1976. It provided finance that helped the ACCI finally purchase in 1976 its current property on the corner of Shattuck Avenue and Lincoln Street in North Berkeley, which it had been renting since 1963. The Housing Sub-Committee of the CCB Planning and Development Committee, established in October 1975, elected a five-person board in February 1978, incorporating as the University Avenue Housing Inc., which aimed to establish a housing co-operative and bought CCB property in August

1980 surrounding the University Avenue Center for $590,000, providing the CCB with a much needed cash inflow. The establishment of a co-operative bank was a long-standing CCB goal. The Finance Committee in March 1967 set up a subcommittee to look at the development of the Bank. Home economist Betsy Wood, representing the CCB, attended a meeting with President Carter in the Cabinet Room of the White House in June 1977 with other consumer activists such as Ralph Nader when the NCCB legislation was in the balance. Wood and Nader spoke in its favor and gained President Carter's support. Wood also lobbied then Republican Senator Hayakawa, who spoke in support of co-operatives and the legislation on the US Senate floor (BHS, 1995, p. 55, 1996a, pp. vii, 30–32, Neptune, 1977, p. 65; Illustration 7.3).[33]

The CCB's links with the international co-operative movement continued. A delegation of approximately 60 from the Zenkoran, Japan's major co-operative purchasing federation and wholesaler of agriculture machinery and supplies, visited the CCB in February 1972 with a primary interest in learning about the CO-OP label. There were similar delegations from co-operatives in West Germany and the USSR. The CCB continued to support overseas co-operative aid, with the BD in June 1974 supporting the CARE drought relief fund to assist West Africa through publicity and providing facilities to collect individual subscriptions. During 1980–1981, the CCB provided facilities for two trainee managers from Danish co-operatives.[34]

White House Meeting with President Jimmy Carter, 1978. (l. to r., left side of table): Mark Green, Esther Peterson, President Jimmy Carter, Betsy Wood, Glenn Nishimura, Ralph Nader. (l. to r., right side of table): Ellen Haas, Kathleen O'Reilly, Rhoda Karpatkin. (not easy to see or out of picture): Sandra Willett, Lola Redford, Alfreda Riley, Jim Boyle, Mercedes Kelly.

Illustration 7.3 White House Meeting, 1978. Courtesy of Berkeley Historical Society.

Conclusion

The CCB's financial performance deteriorated following the departure of Mannila. High levels of management turnover and factional politics on the BD delayed and disrupted managerial decision-making. Employee morale and member participation further deteriorated. Efforts to increase participation through the Center Councils, which played an important role in channeling discontent and community outreach, had little effect as the BD was reluctant to decentralize power. Employee unrest led to the establishment of the Employee Advisory Council, which workers viewed as ineffective, and there were union tensions over Education Department dismissals. The continued expansion of the CCB, particularly into Oakland, despite concerns about assisting low-income areas and increasing economies of scale, was to create further financial burdens for the CCB. While there were problems with obtaining finance from traditional banking sources and a steep decline in membership investment, the CCB found lines of finance available from MSI and the NCCB. The good relationship with organized labor helped the CCB avoid strikes and gain customers and additional sales from its competitors when they faced labor unrest. The CCB also began to introduce economies to avoid financial disaster with the leaseback on its first store in Walnut Creek, the early closure of one of the new Oakland stores and the shutting of gas stations. These economies also weakened the "co-op difference" with its major rivals. The traditional financial advantages of consumer co-operative membership, dividends on purchases and interest on share capital, were reduced and even disappeared in some years. CCB services were either eliminated in the case of the Kiddie Korrals or minimized regarding co-operative education. While a distinguishing feature of the CCB compared to its rivals remained its consumer activism and concern with social issues, this would not be enough to save it in the 1980s.

Notes

1 *CN*, 17 August 1977, p. 1.
2 Interview with Bob Schildgen by author, CCB employee and director, Berkeley, 18 June 2013.
3 BD, 23 April 1973, Carton 8, Folder 60, 26 October 1976, Carton 10, Folder 72, BANC MSS 90/140 c, CCB Records, UCB BL; *CN*, 29 December 1975, p. 2, 13 October 1976, p. 1, 3 November 1976, p. 1, 15 December 1976, p. 1, 5 January 1977, p. 1, 28 December 1977, 20 February 1978, pp. 1, 12, 6 March 1978, p. 7, 2 October 1977, p. 3, 1 January 1979, p. 5, 15 January 1979, p. 1, 2 April 1979, pp. 1, 10, 15 October 1979, p. 6, 12 May 1980, p. 14, 25 August 1980, p. 1.
4 BD, Listening Meeting 8 November 1976, Carton 10 File 72. BANC MSS 90/140 c. CCB Records, UCB BL; *CN*, 1 July 1974, p. 3, 12 February 1979, p. 1, 2 July 1979, p. 2, 7 January 1980, p. 3, 4 February 1980, p. 2; Interview

of Bob Arnold by James Mass, 18 April 1987. Transcripts. BHS; Letter Curt Aller to Olva Nurmela, 9 July 1981, Carton 1 File 13. BANC MSS 94/220. RNLP, UCB BL; *Oakland Tribune*, 10 January 1973, p. 44.

5 BD, Special 12 January 1976, Carton 10 File 72, Central Council Coordinating Committee, 5 January 1976, Carton 13 File 12, BANC MSS 90/140 c. CCB Records, UCB BL; *CN*, 20 December 1971, p. 1, 31. July 1972, p. 1, 4 December 1972, p. 1, 1 January 1973, front cover (fc), 18 February 1974, p. 2, 5 August 1974, p. 1, 12 August 1974, p. 1, 12 January 1976, p. 1, 19 January 1976, p. 1, 1 March 1976, p. 1, 29 September 1976, p. 1, 6 October 1976, p. 1, 24 January 1977, p. 1; Interview of Bob Arnold by James Mass, 18 April 1987. Transcripts. BHS; *San Francisco Chronicle*, 5 August 1972, p. 9.

6 *CN*, 4 May 1977, fc, 31 August 1977, p. 1, 20 February 1978, p. 1, 28 August 1978, p. 1, 11 September 1978, p. 2, 21 July 1980, p. 1; Interview of Bob Arnold by James Mass, 18 April 1987. Transcripts. BHS; Memo from Bob Neptune to Center Managers, 2 October 1978, Carton 19 File 25. BANC MSS 90/140 c. CCB Records, UCB BL.

7 *CN*, 8 May 1967, p. 3, 2 October 1967, p. 2, 23 October 1967, p. 1, 30 October 1967, p. 1, 30 March 1970, p. 1, 6 April 1970, p. 1, 15 June 1970, p. 1, 11 January 1971, p. 1, 31 May 1971, p. 7, 30 August 1971, p. 10, 13 March 1972, p. 1, 3 July 1972, p. 1, 2 October 1972, p. 1, 13 August 1973, p. 5, 24 September 1973, p. 4, 1 October 1973, pp. 1, 10, 5 November 1973, p. 1, 18 March 1974, fc.

8 Acorn Shopping Center Feasibility Analysis, 30 October 1980, Carton 49, Folder 7, BANC MSS 86/178c. HNC, UCB BL; BD, 24 February 1975, Carton 9 File 61. BANC MSS 90/140 c. CCB Records, UCB BL; *CN*, 8 April 1974, p. 1, 17 June 1974, p. 11, 15 July 1974, p. 1, 29 July 1974, p. 1, 6 January 1975, p. 7, 7 April 1975, p. 1, 12 June 1978, p. 1, 19 June 1978, pp. 1, 3, 17 July 1978, p. 1; Interview of Michael Fullerton, CCB employee and director, by author, Berkeley, 19 February 2013; Interview of Bruce Miller, CCB activist, by author, Berkeley, 26 February 2013; Interview with Bob Schildgen, by author, Berkeley, 18 June 2013.

9 BD, 11 January 1965, Carton 4, Folder 35, Future Plans Committee Meeting, 4 January 1962, Carton 3, Folder 28, BANC MSS 90/140 c. CCB Records, UCB BL; *CN*, 30 November 1964, p. 2.

10 BD Special Meeting, 8 July 1974, Carton 9, Folder 63. CCB Records, BANC MSS 90/140 c. UCB BL; *CN*, 4 November 1974, p. 3, 9 June 1975, p. 1, 21 July 1975, p. 2, 20 August 1976, p. 1, 7 August 1978, p. 1.

11 BD Executive Sessions, 16 September 1975, 29 September 1975, Special Meeting, 23 October 1975, 24 November 1975, Carton 9 File 61, BANC MSS 90/140 c. CCB Records, UCB BL; *CN*, 20 October 1975, p. 2, 1 December 1975, p. 1, 2 August 1976, p. 1.

12 *CN*, 27 August 1973, p. 11, 2 September 1974, p. 1, 14 September 1977, fc, p. 1, 18 January 1978, pp. 1, 6 March 1978, p. 1, 29 May 1978, p. 4, 12 June 1978, p. 1

13 Co-op Member Survey, November 1977, p. 12, Carton 31, Folder 3, George Yasukochi, 'Co-op Financing Revisited', unpublished typescript, 11 October 1977. Carton 28, Folder 1, BANC MSS 90/140 c. CCB Records, UCB BL; *CN*, 9 April 1973, p. 11, 4 June 1973, p. 8, 11 February 1974, p. 1, 17 June 1974, p. 1, 4 October 1976, p. 1, 18 May 1977, p. 1, 6 February 1978, p. 7.

14 BD, Executive Session 23 September 1974, 11 October 1974. Carton 9 File 61, Memo Edna Haynes to Education Committee, 19 April 1976, BANC MSS 90/140 c. CCB Records, UCB BL; *CN*, 10 August 1977, p. 1, 9

November 1977, p. 1, 13 March 1978, p. 2, 28 August 1978, p. 1, 28 May 1979, p. 5, 31 December 1979, p. 6; Interview of Bob Arnold by James Mass, 18 April 1987. Transcripts. BHS.

15 Management Report to BD, 28 April 1980, Carton 48, Folder 37, BANC MSS 86/178c. HNC, UCB BL; *CN*, 11 June 1979, p. 2.

16 BD, 23 March 1970, Carton 6, Folder 49, BANC MSS 90/140 c. CCB Records, UCB BL; CN, 11 January 1971, p. 4.

17 CN, 8 September 1972, p. 3, 30 September 1974, fc, p. 1, 18 November 1974, p. 3, 7 July 1975, p. 1, 20, 14 July 1975, p. 1, September 1976, p. 1, 30 March 1977, p. 1, 22 May 1978, p. 4, 4 May 1977, p. 1, 21 May 1979, p. 3, 21 May 1984, p. 11; *NYT*, 20 August 1972, p. 25.

18 *CN*, 20 September 1971, p. 1, 8 May 1972, p. 8, 18 September 1972, pp. 1, 5, 29 January 1973, p. 3.

19 *CN*, 10 September 1973, p. 1, 5 November 1973, fc, p. 1, 7 January 1974, p. 3, 25 February 1974, p. 1, 11 March 1974, p. 1, 18 March 1974, p. 1, 10 June 1974, p. 1, 25 June 1974, p. 1, 1 July 1974, p. 4, 17 February 1975, p. 10, 23 February 1976, p. 1, 1 March 1976, fc, 22 March 1976, fc, 7 June 1976, p. 1, 13 September 1976, p. 1, 5 January 1977, p. 1, 7 September 1977, p. 1; 21 May 1984, p. 11.

20 *CN*, 3 January 1972, p. 12, 13 November 1972, p. 1, 23 January 1973, p. 11, 12 February 1973, p. 1, 26 March 1973, p. 2, 3 September 1973, p. 5, 31 December 1973, p. 2, 7 January 1974, p. 11, 17 March 1975, p. 3, 28 October 1977, p. 1; *Swamp Monster Speaks*, July 1979, Carton 13, Folder 15, BANC MSS 90/140 c, CCB Records, UCB BL.

21 *CN*, 29 December 1980, p. 10.

22 *CN*, 10 September 1973, p. 1, 15 December 1973, fc, 18 November 1974, p. 10, 10 February 1975, p. 3, 3 March 1975, p. 1, 31 March 1975, fc, 10 November 1975, p. 1, 14 August 1978, p. 1, 2 April 1979, p. 1; Letters, Clark Finkbiner to Ned Fine, 17 November 1978, 8 December 1978, Nancy Gaschott to Pat Scott, 30 April 1979, Bob March files, Box 2. BHS.

23 BD, 26 June 1972, Carton 8, Folder 58, 26 September 1972, Carton 8, Folder 59, Management Report to BD, 30 September 1980, Carton 31, Folder 12, Memo Pat Scott to Personnel Committee and Bob Neptune, 17 June 1980, Carton 30, Folder 10, BANC MSS 90/140 c, CCB Records, UCB BL; CN, 5 June 1972, p. 5, 17 July 1972, p. 2, 8 January 1973, p. 3, 31 December 1973, p. 1, 18 January 1978, p. 1, 1 January 1979, p. 4, 4 February 1980, p. 1.

24 BD Special Meeting, 24 September 1973. Personnel Committee, 10 October 1971, Carton 8, Folder 61, BD, 29 October 1973, BD Executive Session, 26 August 1974, BD, 23 September 1974, Carton 9, Folder 63, BANC MSS 90/140 c. CCB Records, UCB BL; CN, 27 May 1974, p. 4, 27 October 1975, p. 3.

25 BD, 26 October 1977, Carton 10 File 74, BANC MSS 90/140 c. CCB Records, UCB BL; *CN*, 13 October 1976, pp. 2–3, 12 January 1977, p. 1, 23 March 1977, p. 1, 11 May 1977, p. 3.

26 *CN*, 13 August 1973, p. 11, 20 August 1973, p. 11, 17 March 1975, p. 1, 31 March 1975, p. 4, 28 July 1975, p. 11, 18 May 1977, p. 1, 1 January 1979, p. 9; Memo Neptune to Members of the Education Committee, 4 October 1978, Carton 11, Folder 9, BANC MSS 90/140 c. CCB Records, UCB BL.

27 BD, 25 January 1970. BANC MSS 90/140 c, Carton 7, Folder 51. CCB Records, UCB BL; *CN*, 1 February 1971, p. 1

28 *CN*, 6 March 1972, p. 2.

29 *CN*, 8 April 1974, p. 7, 22 July 1974, p. 15, 28 April 1975, p. 11, 23 June 1975, p. 3, 21 July 1975, p. 10, 27 April 1977, p. 2.

30 *CN*, 27 May 1974, p. 5, 29 December 1976, p. 2, 29 December 1980, p. 6.
31 BD Special Meeting, 6 January 1975, Carton 9 File 61, BANC MSS 90/140 c. CCB Records, UCB BL; *CN*, 1 July 1974, p. 1, 10 December 1979, p. 4.
32 BD, 25 January 1970, Carton 7, Folder 5, BANC MSS 90/140 c. CCB Records, UCB BL; *CN*, 1 February 1971, p. 1, 8 February 1971, p. 1, 16 September 1974, p. 1, 23 September 1974, fc, 6 January 1975, p. 1.
33 BD, 28 October 1975, Carton 9, Folder 61, Management Report to BD, 27 June 1977 to 5 July 1977, Carton 11, Folder 7, BANC MSS 90/140 c. CCB Records, UCB BL; *CN*, 8 May 1967, p. 3, 22 March 1976, p. 1, 20 September 1976, p. 1, 1 January 1979, p. 1, 17 December 1979, p. 15, 25 August 1980, p. 1; *NYT*, 26 January 1978, p. D9.
34 Management Report to BD, 30 September 1980, Carton 33, Folder 13, BANC MSS 90/140 c, CCB Records, UCB BL; *CN*, 28 February 1972, p. 1, 24 April 1972, p. 1, 3 July 1972, pp. 1, 3, 24 June 1974, p. 1, July 1974, p. 3, 14 August 1976, pp. 1, 3.

References

Awner, L., 1979, "Confessions of a Camp Dean," In Thompson, D., and Awner, M., eds., *A Rainbow on the Mountain. Cooperators Celebrate forty years of Camp Sierra*, Richmond, CA, AC, pp. 22–23.

BAHA and D. Thompson, 2019, "Kawneer Manufacturing Co.," available at http://berkeleyheritage.com/berkeley_landmarks/kawneer.html (accessed 28 January 2018).

Balnave, N. and Patmore, G. (2017), "The Labour Movement and Co-operatives," *Labour History*, 112, pp. 7–24.

Bay Area Census, 2019, available at www.bayareacensus.ca.gov (accessed 5 November 2019).

BHS, 1983, *Appendix. Consumers Co-operative of Berkeley Oral History Collection*, Berkeley, CA, BHS.

BHS, 1984, *Margaret Shaughnessy Gordon. Past President of the Consumers Co-operative of Berkeley, Research Economist, and Community Leader*, Berkeley, CA, BHS.

BHS, 1987, *Laurie Leonard Lehtin. A Finnish leader's Perspective on the Co-operative Movement*, Berkeley, CA, BHS.

BHS, 1993, *Matt Crawford: Reflections on the Cooperative Center Federal Credit Union of Berkeley, and the Consumers Co-operative of Berkeley*, Berkeley, CA, BHS.

BHS, 1995, *A Conversation with George Yasukochi: Controller of the Consumers Co-operative of Berkeley, 1956–1982*, Berkeley, CA, BHS.

BHS, 1996a, *A Conversation with Betsy Wood: A Home Economist's Perspective on the Berkeley Co-op*, Berkeley, CA, BHS.

BHS, 1996b, *A Conversation with Robert Neptune – Pioneer Manager of the Consumers Co-operative of Berkeley, and Long-Term Manager at Associated Co-operatives*, Berkeley, CA, BHS.

Berkeley Public Library, 2003, *The Struggle Continues. Interview with Maudelle Shirek*, Berkeley, CA, Berkeley Public Library.

Black, H., ed., 1980, *The Berkeley Co-op Food Book*, Palo Alto, CA, Bull Publishing.

Black, H., 1996, "Dear Hearing Clerk," In BHS (ed.), *A Conversation with Betsy Wood: A Home Economist's Perspective on the Berkeley Co-op*, Berkeley, CA, BHS, pp. 62–65.

Brand, W., 1982, "Can the Co-op Be Saved?" *Express. The East Bay's Free Weekly*, 22 January, pp. 1, 5–6.

CCB, 1972, *Co-op 35th Anniversary Menu Book*, Berkeley, CA, CCB.

Curl, J., 2012, *For All the People: Uncovering the Hidden History of Co-operation, Co-operative Movements, and Communalism in America*, 2nd ed., Oakland, CA, PM Press.

Fullerton, M., ed., 1992, *What Happened to the Berkeley Co-op? A Collection of Opinions, Centre for Co-operatives*, Davis, CA, Center for Co-operatives, University of California.

Gordon, M., 1992, "The Rise and Fall of CCB," In Fullerton, M., ed., *What Happened to the Berkeley Co-op? A Collection of Opinions*, Davis CA, Center for Co-operatives, University of California, pp. 57–64.

Hopkins, D.R., 1978, "Development of Black Political Organization in Berkeley since 1960," in Nathan, H. and Scott, S, eds., *Experiment and Change in Berkeley. Essays on City Politics 1950–1975*, Berkeley, CA, Institute of Government Studies, UCB, pp. 105–135.

Johnson, W.J.S., 1978, "Berkeley: Twelve Years as the Nation in Microcosm, 1962–1974," in Nathan, H., and Scott, S., eds., *Experiment and Change in Berkeley. Essays on City Politics 1950–1975*, Berkeley, CA, Institute of Government Studies, UCB, pp. 179–230.

Kresy, G., 1980, 'The Berkeley Co-op – An Economic and Political History 1964–1980 as Seen By One Individual,' Unpublished Typescript, Carton 49, Folder 13. BANC MSS 86/178 c, HNC, UCB BL.

Landis, J. and Cervero, R., 1999, Middle Age Spread and Urban Development, Access, Spring at www.accessmagazine.org/spring-1999/middle-age-sprawl-bart-urban-development/ (accessed 28 January 2019).

Neptune, R., 1977, *California's Uncommon Markets. The Story of Consumers Co-operatives 1935–1976*, 2nd ed., Richmond, CA, AC.

Neptune, R., 1982, *Update 1982. California's Uncommon Markets*, Richmond, CA, AC.

North Coast Co-op, 2019, Our Story at www.northcoast.coop/about_us/our_story/ (accessed 29 January 2019).

Rauber, P., 1992, "Decline and Fall of the Berkeley Co-op," In Fullerton, M., ed., *What Happened to the Berkeley Co-op? A Collection of Opinions*, Davis, CA, Center for Co-operatives, University of California, pp. 11–17.

Rubenzahl, J., 1978, "Berkeley Politics, 1968–1974: A Left Perspective," in Nathan, H., and Scott, S., eds., *Experiment and Change in Berkeley. Essays on City Politics 1950–1975*, Berkeley, CA, Institute of Government Studies, UCB, pp. 317–361.

Schildgen, R., 1992, "Failure from Neglect of Co-op Principles," In Fullerton, M., ed., *What Happened to the Berkeley Co-op? A Collection of Opinions*, Davis CA, Center for Co-operatives, University of California, pp. 39–49.

Schuermann, J., 2018, "World-Renown Fantasy Studios Slated for September Closure," *The Daily Californian*, 1 August, available at www.dailycal.org/2018/08/01/world-renowned-fantasy-studios-slated-september-closure/ (accessed 28 January 2019).

Tworek, C.J., 2008, *Background for an Exhibit. The Creation and Development of the Co-operative Center Federal Credit Union*, MA History Project Proposal, California State University East Bay.

UCB Office of the Vice Chancellor of Finance, 2019, "Our Berkeley. Enrolment History Since 1869," available at https://pages.github.berkeley.edu/OPA/our-berkeley/enroll-history.html (accessed 14 April 2019).

Yasukochi, G., 1992, "The Berkeley Co-op – Anatomy of a Noble Experiment," In Fullerton, M., ed., *What happened to the Berkeley Co-op? A Collection of Opinions*, Davis CA, Center for Co-operatives, University of California, pp. 23–32.

Weinstein, D., 2008, *It Came from Berkeley. How Berkeley Changed the World*, Layton UT, Gibbs Smith.

Wollenberg, C., 2008, *Berkeley. A City in History*, Berkeley, CA, University of California Press.

8 Chaos and Collapse

1981–1993

This chapter explores the final years of the CCB, whose finances deteriorated even further in the 1980s. From 1981, the CCB began shutting stores to save costs and withdrawing back to Berkeley. In 1988, the CCB closed the last three Berkeley stores. It filed for bankruptcy in January 1989 and was dissolved in May 1993. While there were tensions between the CCB and organized labor, the CCB turned to its employees to help save the organization with employee representation on the BD and a hybrid co-operative. The relationship with the AC collapsed, with disastrous consequences for both. Despite these problems, the co-operative remained innovative, with its involvement in the Bay Area Community Memory Project (CMP), an early form of a platform co-operative, which is an alternative to the shared economy phenomena such as Uber.

Berkeley

Berkeley, unlike Oakland and San Francisco, continued to decline in population during the 1980s, with its population slightly falling from 103,328 in 1980 to 102,724 in 1990. The decline in the white and African American populations in Berkeley slowed, falling to 62.3 percent and 18.8 percent, respectively. Ethnic groups that increased were Asian and Pacific Islander, from 10 percent to 14.8 percent, and Hispanic from 5.0 percent to 7.8 percent. By contrast, Oakland's population grew, with similar declines in the white and African American being outweighed by the growth of Hispanic and Asian populations. Rising housing costs forced poor and working-class African Americans to leave Berkeley, while African American families that had bought their Berkeley homes after the Second World War were willing to move as they aged and found potential middle-class White and Asian buyers willing to buy their homes. Berkeley also attracted 'yuppies', a term popularized by Berkeley writer Alice Kahn, to describe young, college educated, urban professionals. They were drawn by the 'university town' appeal of Berkeley, with its multicultural atmosphere and lower living costs relative to San Francisco. Other areas of the Bay Area continued to benefit from suburbanization, with Walnut Creek growing to 60,569 and Marin County to 230,096 by 1990. Walnut Creek and Marin County had white populations of 90.8 percent and 88.9 percent by 1990. There was a major expansion of retail services in Walnut Creek with a Town Centre development being approved in 1984, which included a Macy's Department Store, an upscale Nordstrom Department Store and assorted retail stores (Bay Area Census, 2019; Rovanpera, 2009, p. 126; Weinsten, 2008, p. 186; Wollenberg, 2008, pp. 160–161, 165).

Berkeley, like the rest of the US, continued to see deindustrialization in West Berkeley and the growing inequality in the loss of well-paying union jobs with technological change and globalization of the US economy. The unionized Colgate-Palmolive Factory closed in 1982 with the loss of 400 jobs. These jobs were replaced by employment in the biotech, computer software and service sector, which were nonunion and required higher levels of training and education. A prosperous new retailing center, Fourth Street, developed in West Berkeley during the 1980s. This contrasted to downtown Berkeley, which faced challenges from malls such as Richmond's Hilltop Plaza and lost long-standing retail businesses such as Hinks Department Store. UCB, meanwhile, continued to be a significant contributor to the local economy, with student numbers fluctuating between 29,313 in 1982 and 32,046 in 1987 (Fourth Street Berkeley, 2019; UCB Office of the Vice Chancellor of Finance, 2019; Wollenberg, 2008, pp. 158–163, 169).

On the BCC, the traditional conflict between the moderates and the progressives continued. The progressive BCA changed the BCC elections from April to November, which coincided with state and national elections and increased student participation. This favored the Progressives in 1984, when BCA Mayor Gus Newport and his Progressive allies captured eight of the nine seats on the BCC. Moderates challenged this surge of support for the Progressives in 1986 by changing the City Charter from citywide elections to district or ward elections. While this restored the balance of power on the BCC, it reduced African American representation on the BCC. The BCA Mayor Loni Hancock, with a narrow Leftist majority, retained power from 1986 to 1994. Rent control remained a major issue of BCC politics, with the debate being centered on the right to shelter versus the right to property, with landlords withdrawing properties from the market and legally challenging the rent control policies, which were some of the toughest in the US (Wollenberg, 2008, pp. 152–154). The BCC also continued to support progressive issues, such as in February 1986 calling for the boycott of Chilean produce and wine following representations from the Chilean refugee community about the military dictatorship in Chile.[1]

Managing the Co-operative

As Table 8.1 indicates, the CCB's finances deteriorated in the 1980s with the $5 share having a book value of $2.46 by September 1982 and falling even further to 65 cents in September 1983, with a revival to $1.49 by

Table 8.1 CCB Assets, Volume, Financial Performance 1981–1987 (Neptune, 1997, p. 20; Patmore, 2017, p. 523)

	Assets	*Volume*	*Net Savings (Loss)*
1981	14,397,500	82,068,700	(1,103,100)
1982	13,254,000	73,211,000	(865,198)
1983	11,946,600	71,459,174	(1,130,690)
1984	8,597,000	57,775,600	(81,359)
1985	8,938,800	52,281,200	131,800
1986	7,249,000	52,746,300	(1,251,200)
1987	5,446,700	39,853,100	(1,807,200)

September 1985, but falling again dramatically to 4.5 cents by January 1987. By December 1980, out of 12 food stores, only the 4 Berkeley and the San Francisco stores were both growing and delivering financial returns that would justify patronage refunds. Grevious initiated the appointment of new staff to the CCB central administration, which increased overhead costs and eroded Neptune's surplus. The CCB began shutting stores to save costs, with the Macarthur-Broadway store and El Cerrito bakery closing in August 1981, the South Main (Walnut Creek) store closing in November 1981 and the Castro Valley store closing in January 1982, with the sale of the latter two leases generating capital gains of $277,600. The CCB did keep the profitable Castro Valley Wilderness Shop open, but it began making losses when it moved location following the closure of the Castro Valley Center and was eventually closed in April 1984. The need for cash arising from continued operating losses led to the closure in January 1984 of the Marin and North Oakland stores, despite a new merchandising program at North Oakland that featured greater variety and lower prices in the produce and meat departments, and the Diablo Valley (formerly the Walnut Creek Geary Road store and renamed in May 1983) store in February 1984. The El Cerrito store was originally meant to close in February 1984, but remained opened until April 1984 due to management consideration of a membership proposal to prevent closure. While the stores at Marin and El Cerrito were owned and the increased cash from the sale of these assets helped reduce losses in 1983–1984 and a surplus in 1984–1985, it was not enough to prevent further financial deterioration. Some funds were used to upgrade the remaining stores, with a new 'Uncommon Fare' Delicatessen being opened in the Shattuck Avenue store to help shoppers make restaurant-quality meals at home. The Natural Foods Store was consolidated into the University Avenue Store in April 1986 after its lease expired and the San Francisco Northpoint store ended operations in September 1986 after losses and disagreements with the landlord, who wanted the CCB to leave despite a lease until 1991 and undermined efforts to promote the store in a mall that was losing tenants (BHS, 1996a, p. xii; Fullerton, 1992, p. 96; Gordon, 1992, p. 64; Neptune, 1982, p. 6; Neptune, 1997, pp. 1–4; Rauber, 1992, p. 12).[2]

The BD announced in May 1988 that it was selling the final three stores, and by June 1988 the CCB was on a Cash Only Delivery (COD) with all its suppliers, with many items disappearing from the shelves. During the negotiations for the sale of its stores, the CCB closed the University Avenue Store on 3 September 1988 and closed the two remaining stores, Shattuck Avenue and Telegraph Avenue, on 1 October 1988. One view in 1988 was that CCB could rebuild as an organization advocating nutrition and consumer activism through the continued publication of the popular *CN*, but the BD were reluctant to act until the financial matters were settled and there was membership support through either a plebiscite or general meeting (Baird, 1992, pp. 69–70; BHS, 1996a, p. xii; Fullerton, 1992, p. 96; Gordon, 1992, p. 64; Neptune, 1997, p. 4).[3]

In January 1989, the CCB filed for bankruptcy and over the next three years the CCB BD sold off the remaining assets. The final payments were made to creditors in 1992, including CCB certificate of interest holders, who received 97.5 percent of their claims plus 7 percent annual interest, with a write-off members' shares of $4.4 million. Members could take an income tax loss deduction on their shares. The CCB was discharged from bankruptcy on 26 February 1993 and the Superior Court approved the dissolution of the CCB on 6 May 1993 (BHS, 1996a, p. xii; Neptune, 1997, pp. 4–5).

Factional politics remained a feature of CCB governance. Moderate Curtis Aller retained the presidency in 1981 and was succeeded by fellow Moderate Margaret Gordon in 1982. Gordon ran in the 1983 BD elections, but only secured an alternate board position, and was replaced by Fred Guy, the Food Services Manager for USCA with four years' experience on the BD. The Progressives were again the dominant faction after 1982. Rival factions eroded confidence in the CCB by highlighting their opponent's role in placing the CCB at the point of bankruptcy during elections. Concerns about the impact of factional politics on CCB management led the CCB Education Committee in October 1981 to call for the voluntary dissolution of the factions, claiming that there was no significant difference between the factions and preferring independent candidates only. There was some reconciliation of the factions during the final years of the CCB, with Progressives and Moderates supporting a Unity Election Slate in 1985 BD elections, where there were only four candidates for four vacant seats with Bruce Miller, who was a UCB administrator, replacing the retiring Guy as President in 1985. There was, however, a Progressive ticket in the 1986 elections, with Miller and Margo Robinson winning two seats for the Progressives and independent former *CN* editor Robert Schildgen winning the remaining seat. Miller was again President from 1986 to 1988, with Bruce Black, a CCB member since 1943 and Helen Black's husband, becoming President in 1989 after the declaration of bankruptcy. The BD continued to take stands on broader issues, with a unanimous decision to support a nuclear weapons' freeze initiative that was on the Californian ballot in November 1982, which was successful, and ban Chilean produce in May 1984 due to concerns over "serious human rights violations" in Chile. The BD in May 1985 also decided to donate $100 in groceries to UCB students and staff protesting UC investment in firms doing business with Apartheid South Africa (BHS, 1984, pp. 19–20, 24–25; Black, 1992a, pp. 71–73; Fullerton, 1992, p. 96; Gordon, 1992, pp. 57, 62; Neptune, 1982, p. 23, 1997, p. 15; Rauber, 1992, p. 14).[4]

There was continued management turnover and conflict. Grevious, unable to stem the losses, was terminated in March 1982. Neptune, who was still the AC General Manager, then returned for six months until Roy Bryant, a former General Manager, was rehired and returned as General Manager and CEO on 1 October 1982. Bryant left the Greenbelt Co-operative in 1980 after turning its finances around and had returned to California serving as Associate Pastor and Chairman of Financial Planning at Calvary Community Church in San Jose. He was also unable to stem the CCB losses and was replaced by Lynn MacDonald, the first and only female General Manager, in October 1983, initially as Acting General Manager. MacDonald had co-operative experience as manager of the NCC in Arcata, head of the AC Development Department from October 1981 and served simultaneously as CCB Education Director, paid by the AC, from September 1982. MacDonald, however, was unable to turn around the CCB, with a CCB Strategic Options Task Force (SOTF), which was supported by the Concerned Employees Coordinating Group to restore the CCB's "economic balance" and consisted of management, member and employee representatives, recommending a sharp cut in overhead costs in July 1986. MacDonald announced in June 1986 that she was resigning her position on 1 October 1986, and was replaced by a management team with Allan Gallant as CEO and Jeffrey Voltz as General Manager. Gallant, who left the day-to-day operations to Voltz and would occasionally inspect CCB operations, managed a group of stores in Alaska, where Voltz was his regional supervisor. Neither Gallant nor Voltz were CCB employees but had a one-year contract to provide management services, with Voltz later becoming a CCB employee in September 1987. Gallant and Voltz were replaced in October 1988, after the CCB closed its stores, by Terry Baird, who was AC General Manager from January 1987, on a part-time basis. Both Baird and his successor Karl Kruger oversaw the liquidation of assets and payment of creditors. The CCB also lost its long-serving Controller, George Yasukochi, who retired in August 1982, but would later return in October 1988 to provide advice during the windup of the CCB. The loss of managers such as Grevious and Bryant undermined the confidence of CCB members in the organization, as the management refused to provide reasons for their departure due to legal issues relating to their employment contracts (Baird, 1992, pp. 65, 69–70; BHS, 1984, p. 25, 1995, p. 68, 1996a, p. xiii, 1996b, p. 19; Cooper and Mohn, 1992, p. 205; Gordon, 1992, p. 63; MacDonald, 1992, p. 51; Neptune, 1982, p. 5, 1997, pp. 2–4).[5]

External financing became even more difficult after 1980. The NCCB provided a second loan to the CCB of $300,400 in November 1981. It insisted that the CCB and the AC be reviewed by a management consultant. Touche Ross & Co., the chosen firm, described the CCB's financial position in 1982 as "extremely precarious" and facing insolvency within three years unless projected losses of $800,000 per year were reversed. The report saw the financial problems as arising from top-level mismanagement, declining sales, uncompetitive pricing and inadequate employee training. The relationship deteriorated as the NCCB required the CCB to obtain its approval before selling a store and to pay down the loan if it closed stores reducing CCB savings arising from the closure. The CCB accused the NCCB in July 1984 of taking "harsh action" against it and other Californian consumer co-operatives. The CCB later became reliant on credit finance from Certified Grocers or Cergro, a retailer co-operative based in Los Angeles that took over CCB wholesaling after a dispute between the AC and the CCB in 1985, as the NCCB refused two requests for bridging loans from the CCB, agreeing eventually to provide only $300,000 due on 31 March 1988. The MSI rejected a CCB approach in March 1987 for $300,000, as its credit situation did not meet MSI loan underwriting standards. Gallant negotiated in May 1987 a $1,000,000 loan from Cergro secured by a mortgage on CCB property, with CCB director Margaret Gordon voting for the loan but doubting whether the CCB would ever have sufficient cash flow to repay the loan. The loan was conditional on the CCB showing a significant financial improvement by 31 December 1987 and selling or leasing its remaining stores if it failed to do so. Cergro's decision to call in its loan ultimately contributed to the CCB decision to sell its remaining stores in May 1988 (BHS, 1984, p. 24; Gordon, 1992, p. 64; Neptune, 1997, p. 4; Rauber, 1992, p. 16).[6]

The CCB continued to look for ways to attract customers and successfully compete against its rivals, such as an extensive radio and television advertising campaign in October 1984, but was constrained by limited capital. The major chain stores, however, adopted many of the innovations of the Berkeley Co-operative, such as unit pricing. Safeway and Andronico's provided a wide variety of food types, including natural foods, ethnic foods and gourmet foods. Berkeley 'yuppies' sustained the 'Gourmet Ghetto' in North Berkeley and several nonunion independent retailers, such as the Berkeley Bowl and Monterey Market, which specialized in high-quality produce at competitive prices and attracted the growing patronage of CCB members. In the 1980s, there was little effort by the Reagan administration to restrain anticompetitive practices in retailing, with the CCB having an estimated market share for the East Bay by February 1982 of 28 percent compared to 28 percent for Safeway and 12 percent for Lucky, its main chain store rivals. The CCB by November 1984, according to one market survey, was being undercut by its main rivals, with a complete market basket of traditional brands being $106 compared to $99 at Safeway and $94 at Lucky (Black, 1992b, p. 34; Gordon, 1992, p. 64; MacDonald, 1992, pp. 52–53; Patmore, 2017, pp. 523–524).[7]

The CCB opened a new venture during this period despite its financial difficulties. At the initiative of General Manager MacDonald, with a management view that the project was low risk, the BD in September 1984 by five votes to four decided to lease space and opened Savories, for a projected cost of $600,000, on the premises of its former Marin Center, which had been sold to developers because of persistent losses in April 1984. The CCB, despite the closing of its supermarket in January 1984, tried to keep its profitable Natural Foods Store in the Center open, but was forced to close it in August 1984 due to declining patronage. The developers invited the CCB to reopen a food store, but the CCB decision was conditional on the sale of its El Cerrito center on satisfactory terms and BD approval of the final contract, which occurred in December 1984 by five votes to four. The store was a high-end quality service market with a focus on natural foods and luxury items at premium prices. There was an expensive glassed-in meat and fish counter and an extensive produce department. One feature of the proposal that swayed some directors was the installation of sophisticated equipment for testing produce for pesticide/contaminant and washing it, which would appeal to affluent and health conscious Marin residents and be extended to other CCB stores to gain a quality advantage over the lower priced chain stores, but was never installed as it could not be financed. Local CCB members did not feel committed to the new store, which opened in August 1985, as they were not involved in its planning and were critical that the new facility was not being called a co-operative. The store was a financial disaster for the CCB, with sales around $60,000 a week rather than the $100,000 needed to break even and estimated losses of more than $2,000,000, despite management's expectations of high financial returns in an affluent area to support other CCB stores. One of the demands for any further finance by the NCCB in early 1987 was that Savories be closed, which occurred in April 1987 (Gordon, 1992, p. 62; Neptune, 1997, pp. 2, 13–14; Rauber, 1992, p. 15; Schildgen, 1992, pp. 47–48; Yasukochi, 1992, p. 31).[8]

Members

As Table 8.2 indicates, CCB membership peaked in 1984 and never recovered. The long-standing registration fee of $2 for new members was

Table 8.2 CCB Membership 1981–1987 (Neptune, 1997, p. 20; Patmore, 2017, p. 523)

1981	106,800
1982	106,411
1983	114,456
1984	116,232
1985	83,112
1986	84,784
1987	87,076

raised to $5 in August 1982 to cover the increasing costs of processing new members, but new members were still only required to purchase one $5 share, which had declining real value. From May 1984, new members were required to pay the $5 fee plus purchase four $5 shares to join. When the remaining stores were put up for sale in May 1988, it was estimated that there were only 36,000 active members who spent a minimum of $100 a year at the CCB stores, which was the equivalent of two shopping cartloads. The closure of stores in areas outside Berkeley led to those members shifting their allegiances to more convenient local stores despite incentives such as special coupons, special food events and food certificates to get them to shop at nearby CCB stores. There was member criticism of product quality, prices, erratic check cashing policies, the failure to pay patronage refunds and share interest unfriendly staff, the lack of new products and no Kiddie Korrals, the reintroduction of which was rejected by the BD in August 1985 and March 1987 on the grounds of insurance costs and inability to break even. Members who wished to leave were constrained by freezes on the redemption of shares and the early redemption of certificates of interest due to financial problems. The CCB attempted to compensate for the loss of patronage refunds by offering special member coupons with discounts and in October 1982 by introducing monthly member appreciation days, usually on Tuesdays that had slow sales, when members received a 5 percent discount on their purchases. The idea was extended with additional Senior Appreciation Days for members over 62 years of age (BHS, 1984, p. 26; Patmore, 2017, p. 524).[9]

Membership apathy remained a problem with 10 percent of members voting in the 1982 BD elections for only six candidates. The Center Councils went into decline, with many disappearing as stores were sold and complaints by Center Councils, such as El Cerrito, about the lack of input in the decisions to close stores and TACC about the lack of consultation concerning a long-standing request for a delicatessen. There were tensions with TACC in July 1981, over the independent action on boycotted products, and SACC, which passed a resolution in November 1982 refusing to recognize the authority of the BD and its committees to set policies on Center Council newsletters. The 1982 Touche

Ross report, after consultation with the Center Councils, criticized the BD for ignoring a "valuable resource." There were local initiatives by Center Councils and CCB members to reintroduce and maintain the popular aspects of the CCB. At the Walnut Creek Geary Road Store in October 1982 there was the short-lived reintroduction of Kiddie Korral service on a limited basis with fees to finance attendants and financial support from the Center Council. Even with closure, some Center Councils continued to explore the idea of buying clubs to sustain co-operative activity. The CCB committees were also less effective with the TACC withdrawing its committee representatives in November 1982, claiming that the BD ignored the committees' work and recommendations. By 1986, membership interest in serving on committees had declined, with committees generally not functioning and little BD interest in reviving them. The BD functioned largely without committee input and ad hoc committees were formed for specific tasks (Black, 1992a, pp. 72–73; Schildgen, 1992, p. 41).[10]

There were efforts to increase membership participation. There was an unsuccessful proposal in 1981 where the Center Councils would be the basis for electing a Delegate Assembly, which would elect the BD. This would replace the direct election of the BD, which opposed the proposal because less people participated in the Center Council elections than BD elections, greater bureaucracy and members lost their right to directly elect the BD. The supporters of the Delegate Assembly believed it would weaken the factional control of BD and increase the importance of the Center Councils and democratic control of the CCB. The BD did allow members a vote, but on advisory basis to the BD, for the first time to boycott a product in the January/February 1986 BD elections with a favorable majority of 1,867 to 1,518 votes against stocking Coors beer. This followed a BD decision in November 1985 not to advertise Coors beer or place it in promotional sales to protest the company's labor practices, and the BD decided in March 1986 to accept the member's ballot boycotting Coors beer after the present stocks were exhausted (Black, 1992a, pp. 72–73; Rauber, 1992, p. 14).[11]

There were further cuts to education budget, despite the benefits for CCB members. Education staff and the Education Committee complained about the lack of respect and priority by CCB employees and management toward educational displays, hospitality tables and bulletin boards. The Committee criticized the BD in May 1981 for "out-Safewaying" its competitor Safeway by focusing on discounts rather than a co-operative education program.[12] Tensions persisted between supporters of natural foods and home economists over issues such as the benefits of aloe vera in November 1981. While CCB members questioned home economist Mary Gullberg's expertise on natural foods, Gullberg noted that the home economists' relationship with CCB "has been unique in that we have been allowed to state our position on products no matter what effects this may have on sales."[13] The Center Council Coordinating Committee condemned a decision by the BD in September 1982 to transfer the control of the CCB education activities to an Education Director paid by the AC with a new CCB Director of Marketing and Services, to whom the CCB home economists and CCB directors were responsible, but reporting to the Education Director. They viewed the Director of Marketing and Services as a diversion of funds away from education that undermined "the vital education function of the co-operative" and contradicted the "Rochdale commitment to education."[14] Lynn MacDonald, the future CCB General Manager, was the new Education Director, and Lisa Van Dusen, who had worked as management consultant providing marketing and general management services to community businesses, became the new Director of Marketing and Services until her resignation in December 1984. Nancy Snow, the CCB Education Director appointed in July 1984, resigned to allow the CCB to create a new part-time position of Consumer Information Director in October 1986, but the Education Director was recreated with the support of Gallant by the BD in December 1986, with Snow reappointed as the Member and Community Relations Director, whose duties included supervision of the *CN* and the Consumer Information Director.[15]

By May 1984, there was only one half-time home economist Helen Black with Gullberg's retirement. A UC Davis survey in 1983 found that CCB shoppers purchased more bulk foods, whole grains and whole wheat breads than shoppers at other nearby stores. They were also less likely to buy less fatty or salty foods, such as beef, pork, franks and cold cuts. Black retired in March 1986 without a replacement. A new Consumer Information Director, Elaine Moquette, was to cover the home economist's duties, but Moquette was trained in nutrition science rather than home economics. The CCB consumer information program accordingly became focused on nutrition, with Moquette introducing a "Best Choices" program in September 1987 with shelf cards that identified products low in sodium, sugar and/or fat. Black later linked the emphasis on nutrition, at the expense of cost and product information, to the influence of 'yuppies' with their interest in gourmet foods and the growth of dietary supplements (BHS, 1996a, p. 77; Black, 1992b, p. 34).[16]

The CCB showed an interest in internet-based platforms such as the Bay Area CMP in the mid-1980s, which Snow, the CCB Education Director, saw as "a natural progression of Co-op's consumer education and information programs"[17] and a "community bulletin board."[18] The CCB provided services for members that allowed them to exchange both goods and services since 1952. In April 1966, the University Avenue, Shattuck Avenue and Telegraph Avenue Centers reintroduced, for example, a Members Exchange Service, whereby members could fill out cards outlining a range of services, including babysitting, tutoring, painting or electrical work. Members, who were independent contractors, could use the service. The cards were placed in metal file boxes and managed by staff.[19] As Weinstein (2008, p. 124) noted, the bulletin boards "helped people find cheap apartments, rides to Los Angeles, and wood burning stoves."

The first computer terminal or "bulletin board," as a part of the CMP, was installed in the Telegraph Avenue Center in August 1984. The main terminal was based in West Berkeley and anyone could walk up and post a bulletin at the Telegraph Avenue Center and two other locations. Initially the service was free, but the TACC had the discretion to install a coin deposit box to fund it. The service was sponsored by Village Design, a nonprofit organization based in Berkeley, and began in 1972 with one terminal in Leopold's Records in Berkeley, where users could read other users messages in that one location – with messages covering subjects from ads for taxi services to finding the best bagels in Berkeley. The CMP was extended to the CCB Shattuck Avenue Center in February 1986, which became the fourth terminal in the network (Tierney, 2013, p. 146).[20]

The CCB continued as a center for consumer activism. One long-standing CCB consumer action against Nestlé ended in 1984. The CBB placed shelf cards in its stores in 1978 alerting members to both sides of the debate about Nestlé's aggressive marketing of baby formula in developing countries, which resulted in infants' death because poor people lacked clean water, refrigeration and sterilization facilities to make the formula safe. The BD in April 1983 voted to join INFACT, which promoted the boycott. Approximately 10,000 CCB members signed petitions that led to Nestlé complying with World Health Organization marketing code on infant formula in 1984. The CCB in 1981 had a display entitled "The Junk Food Hall of Shame," which featured a range of products from disposable spice grinders to sugary breakfast foods, some of which were sold by the CCB. It joined TURN in 1981, a utility monitoring group, which reduced the increase in the utility PG&E gas and electricity prices. While Safeway and Lucky opposed on cost grounds the unsuccessful Proposition 11 in November 1982, which encouraged recycling by imposing 5 cents return fee on beverage containers, the CCB joined groups such as the Californian PTA, the Sierra Club, the Farm Bureau, RCIA and the League of Women Voters to support it. The BD in June 1985 publicly opposed the irradiation of food until its safety could be conclusively proved, with calls for the labeling of irradiated foods and supported a letter writing campaign to the USFDA highlighting its concerns. The CCB in 1986 won a Nutrition Pace-Setter award from the Center for Science in the Public Interest for its innovations in nutrition information and consumer protection (BHS, 1996a, pp. 78–79; Fullerton, 1992, p. 96).[21]

As the financial position deteriorated, management criticized the CCB's controversial products policy. The management in December

1983 argued that boycotts had a deleterious effect on sales and a revised policy allowing Center Councils the right to determine the boycott policy for individual stores "unworkable." Voltz in August 1987 claimed that the CCB could not afford to stop selling nonunion grapes and Departmental Heads at Shattuck Avenue in April 1988 stated they could not "live" with the policy due to merchandising requirements.[22]

Employees and the Community

The deteriorating financial position of the CCB led to the termination of employee benefits. The BD in 1981 ended the long-standing Deferred Savings Program, which allowed employees a share in the annual net savings that accumulated and be paid when CCB employees resigned or retired. This amounted to more than $400,000 since the Program was introduced in 1956. The CCB justified the termination of the Program because employee benefits had improved since the Program was established and the deterioration of the CCB's financial performance made the Program less meaningful. In compensation, 432 employees with more than four years' service received $686,000, with 31 employees receiving more than $5,000 each. The BD in June 1987 withdrew from a pension plan for nonunion management personnel, which was cosponsored by AC and PAC, which it was estimated would free at least $200,000 for the CCB.[23]

Management was also concerned with CCB wages costs as finances deteriorated. While the good relations with the labor unions gave the CCB a competitive advantage in avoiding strikes, it paid relatively good rates to its employees. Between 1981 and 1985, it was estimated that the wage gap between the CCB and industry average had risen from 1 to 5 percent of sales. One implication of the wage gap was that as stores closed, the financial gains were undermined by seniority provisions in union contracts that did not guarantee the retention of the best employees and ensured that relative labor costs remained high as senior rather than junior staff were retained. By September 1982, approximately 50 employees had been retrenched with the store closures, many of whom were junior apprentice retail clerks. The 1982 Touche Ross report called for a renegotiation of union contracts to reduce labor costs. During the 1984 store closures, approximately 125 junior employees were dismissed. The CCB's labor costs were a major concern for NCCB in providing finance to the CCB. By May 1988, there were only 240 CCB employees (Neptune, 1997, p. 15; Rauber, 1992, p. 16; Schildgen, 1992, p. 46; Weinstein, 2008, p. 125).[24]

As the CCB's financial position deteriorated there was some hardening of the CCB position toward labor unions. The Personnel Committee in November 1981 protested a BD decision to require Center Managers to resign from labor unions or face demotion if they wished to retain union membership, with three taking demotion rather than resigning. While the Personnel Committee noted that it was a long-standing CCB policy for Center Managers to be union members, President Aller responded that management had the support of labor unions and chastised the Committee for not consulting him. While Aller argued that managers were permitted to retain union membership because of a more generous union pension scheme, the union scheme was now on par with the management pension scheme. Margaret Gordon supported Aller by arguing that center managers being union members blurred the line between management and labor and that many employee grievances had not been resolved accordingly. Gordon also argued that the CCB's policy was an "anomaly" in the retail industry. There was still resistance by some CCB directors to obtaining concessions from the unions for the contracts, even after MacDonald in 1986 provided wages data to the BD highlighting that this is a necessary alternative to declaring bankruptcy. Despite the concerns about union labor costs, the BD continued to follow the traditional policy of supporting organized labor, with the BD decision in December 1985 not to stock or sell CO-OP-labelled goods, which were supplied and packed by union-busting companies, after it was found that CO-OP bacon was packed by Armour, a company boycotted by the AFL-CIO for its anti-union activities.[25]

One idea that was explored to save the CCB was employee representation on the BD. There were calls for greater employee control of the CCB by members as early as 1971 to combat employee alienation but rejected by the BD arguing it was illegal under CCB bylaws. Following the recommendation of a special committee to examine CCB rules, the BD decided in October 1982 to establish a special committee to examine the issue of worker representation on the BD. The special committee, which supported the idea of employee representation, included CCB directors, managers and employees, with external expertise provided by Professor George Strauss, Associate Director, IIR, UCB and a judge as chair. Simultaneously a petition drafted by employees at the Berkeley and Shattuck Avenue Centers, frustrated at the lack of input during a period of financial crisis despite the Employee Advisory Council, with more than 500 member signatures was presented to the BD calling for bylaws amendments to provide for BD employee representation. This passed the threshold of 250 names required for an amendment to be placed on the ballot at the next BD elections, which would allow non-salaried workers to have two of the nine seats on the BD, the practice of the NCC in Arcata. Supporters argued that workers could see management mistakes and bring forward member and customer grievances directly to the BD. There was opposition to this proposal by Moderates such as Helen Nelson, who criticized the proposal for supporting an undemocratic process of guaranteeing workers the directors' seats on the BD even though they gained less votes than the consumer directors, creating a conflict of interest in labor negotiations and undermining the authority of management in dealing with staff, noting that the NCC was not organized. Employees had their interests served by organized labor. Nelson also drew upon the Webb notion of 'consumer sovereignty' by arguing the consumers ran consumer co-operatives and worker co-operatives "were a different animal." While 63.5 percent and 56 percent of members voting in 1983 and 1984 ballots, respectively, supported the representation of workers on the BD, it was insufficient to meet the two-thirds of votes required to change the CCB bylaws. CCB management looked at quality circles and an Employee Advisory Council as a means of increasing employee participation, organizing with unions a Labor Management Council, to oversee these initiatives and ensure that the iniatives did not infringe collective bargaining arrangements. The CCB introduced a 24-hour employee hotline in 1984 where employees could make complaints and suggestions. At the University Avenue store in 1985 additional hours were budgeted for to allow teams of workers to meet with their managers during alternative weeks to discuss problems and suggest improvements. Management, however, was reluctant to hold employee meetings, which increased employee anxiety over job security, with productivity declining and customers complaining about employee attitudes and service (Balnave and Patmore, 2017, p. 11; Fullerton, 1992, p. 96).[26]

By 1986, however, there was no established training program for employees or system of regular work evaluations. The SOTF identified employee morale as a major CCB problem, with a study committee formed by the BD in August 1986 of members and employees to develop a program to stimulate employee interest and suggestions. Employees held further meetings in 1986 calling for more regular sessions with the management, with Voltz introducing monthly center staff meetings in May 1987, and resuscitating the idea of direct representation of employee members on the BD. Employees circulated a petition for an amendment to CCB rules in the December 1986/January 1987 CCB elections, which was signed by 298 CCB members and received BD endorsement in November 1986 subject to conditions relating to conflicts of interest. Employees formed Co-op Employees United to promote greater employee input into CCB and change the CCB rules. While opposition based on 'consumer sovereignty' continued, the amendment passed with 77 percent of members in favor. It was not until March 1987 that the first employee member director, Frank DeBerry, filling an alternate director vacancy, joined the BD. Two of the four directors, Adolf Kamil and Marcia Edelen, elected in 1988, with the highest number of votes, were employees (Balnave and Patmore, 2017, p. 11; Black, 1992a, pp. 71–72; Schildgen, 1993, p. 1).[27]

More radical proposals for employee involvement in the CCB called for converting it to an Employee Stock Option Plan (ESOP), whereby employees would use part of their wages to purchase CCB shares and help recapitalize the CCB and a worker-consumer hybrid co-operative. Gallant and Voltz advocated an ESOP, which they believed was a better model for the future of the CCB than the conventional consumer co-operative, citing the successful ESOP operating at the Alaska Commercial Company where they had both worked. Following discussions concerning the restructuring of the CCB, the BD decided in July 1987 to proceed with the hybrid model, which would involve increased worker financial investment through payroll deductions and greater participation in management and the BD. The CCB began negotiations with the United Food and Commercial Workers Union (UFCWU), which had risen from a merger of the former RCIA and the Amalgamated Meat Cutters and Butcher Workmen of North America. The BCC provided support for the negotiations, viewing the survival of the CCB as important for the local economy, with funding, staff assistance and Berkeley Mayor Loni Hancock mediating. A transition committee with the union, CCB and BCC representation put together a general structure. There would be a new operating entity, the Consumer Employee Co-operative (CEC), with the CCB continuing to own the real estate and leasing the stores to the new entity. The UFCWU insisted on an employee majority on the CEC BD and a change in management. The BD unanimously supported the agreement with the UFCWU on 3 December 1987. There was an overwhelmingly favorable vote of CCB members in January 1988 by 2,058 to 106. Cergro agreed to extend its finance by 90 days from 1 April 1988, if at least 85 percent of employees supported the hybrid co-operative, with a near unanimous vote by UFCWU CCB members of support for the hybrid on 15 April 1988 and employees initially investing 15 percent of their wages in the CCB on a mandatory basis. There was a delay, however, with the hybrid, due to the BD and the UFWCA disagreeing over the extent of employee control, with the union wanting employee dominance and the BD wanting joint control by consumers and employees. The BD finally agreed to accept the union proposal and endorsed a Memorandum of Understanding with the UFWCA, which provided for a CEC BD consisting of three employee directors, three consumer directors and three independent directors, with one coming from the unions, one nominated by the CCB on behalf of the consumers and one elected by employees and their unions. While the final CEC Board favored employee interests, the BD supported the UFCWA proposal to obtain employee investment. Cergo ignored the overwhelming employee support for the hybrid. It had already stopped supplying goods on credit in April 1988, leading to stock shortages, and on 5 May 1988 refused to supply any further additional funds or credit, claiming that the length of time to negotiate the deal with the unions was "fatal," forcing a financial crisis for the CCB. While the NCCB was willing to extend its loan of $30,000 until 1 July 1988, it was to be the last extension. The UFCWU withdrew its support for the hybrid, claiming that the lack of interim finance breached their agreement with the CCB and stopped the wage deductions financing the hybrid. The BD moved to sell or lease its remaining stores and declare the hybrid arrangement terminated on 17 May 1988 (Black, 1992a, pp. 74–75; Neptune, 1997, p. 4; Rauber, 1992, p. 16; Schildgen, 1993, p. 1).[28]

With the CCB moving to sell its stores, many long-term members and employees tried to retain the CCB through further discussions around the hybrid model. The New Co-op Organizing Group (NCOG), initiated by the SACC, organized members and raised funds to keep the three Berkeley stores operating, with priority being given to the profitable Shattuck Avenue store, even if it meant selling or leasing the other two Berkeley stores. Robert March, a former CCB and AC employee, who had personally donated substantial funds to the CCB in 1986 to ensure its survival, became the NCOG chair. The NCOG initially put a proposal to only purchase the Shattuck Avenue for $4,100,000 plus inventory, but this was rejected by the BD. NCOG put together a deal to purchase all three stores for approximately $750,000 with the CCB having a 10 percent interest in the new operating company. They would sell the Telegraph Avenue store to a retail operator and reorganize the other two stores into consumer-worker co-operatives. Gallant condemned the proposal as "woefully inadequate." The NCOG further increased its offer to $8,200,000 and 25 percent stake in the new business. The proposed BD would consist of two CCB representatives, two consumer representatives, three employee representatives, a union representative and one external business expert. The financial consultant who helped NCOG develop its revised plan warned that it would barely cover the CCB's liabilities and that a second store might have to be sold to meet further financial obligations. Members voted, however, at the unanimous urging of the BD, to support in August 1988 by 4,584 to 3,139 votes an alternative $9,000,000 offer from Berkeley Food Source, which was owned by Living Foods, a natural food store chain that provided a loan of $550,000 to CCB during the sale negotiations to keep the CCB stores stocked. Ultimately Living Foods could not find the funds to support their offer, while the supporters of NCOG, to keep the co-operative idea alive, formed a Pacific Co-operative buying club, which held its first meeting in October 1989 and was still operating in 1993 (Neptune, 1997, p. 4; Rauber, 1992, p. 16; Schildgen, 1993, pp. 2–3).[29]

With the negotiations were proceeding concerning employee ownership, the relationship with the UFCWA deteriorated. The CCB moved away from collective bargaining and engaged in direct negotiations with employees. The UFCWU threatened to file an unfair labor practice suit against the CCB when management circulated a questionnaire to its employees in October 1987 asking for their opinions on a 10 percent wage reduction without consulting the union.[30]

The CCB continued to use volunteer labor, maintaining the volunteers' skill bank to draw upon volunteer labor for member recruitment, educational programs, election management, assistance with bulk mail-outs and maintaining bulletin boards. They also entered contracts with volunteers as with employees and held award ceremonies which recognized outstanding volunteers. The NOCC relied on volunteers to shop for and deliver from the store groceries to people unable to shop due to health difficulties, but faced the challenge of finding sufficient volunteers to maintain it. The availability of eager and competent volunteers declined due to broader social changes such as the growing number of women entering the workforce. By July 1986, the SOTF noted that volunteer activity was at an "all time low" and the BD set up a committee in August 1986 to review its role in the CCB (Balnave and Patmore, 2017, pp. 13–14; Black, 1992b, p. 34).[31]

The CCB continued to develop links with local community groups and engage in community issues. It established a Speakers Bureau in 1981 to help raise community awareness of the co-operative philosophy and CCB services. The CCB encouraged schools, churches, environmental groups, labor organizations and community groups to invite speakers from the Bureau. Speakers included Margaret Gordon and Robert Schildgen, *CN* editor. In 1983, the CCB supported the Berkeley Food Project, which was part of the Alameda County Coalition, which collected and distributed surplus food to 80,000 low-income people. The BD in April 1984 voted to oppose a Californian Bill that would take away the rights of Californian cities such as Berkeley to enact effective rent and eviction controls and lobbied members of the Californian legislature to stop the Bill. One of the last decisions of the TACC was to donate $50 to the Berkeley Black Repertory Group in August 1988.[32]

CCB and the Co-operative Movement

The AC saw changes in senior management. Neptune, the long-standing AC manager retired in 1983 and was succeeded by Warner Isaac, who had started as a buyer and rose to chief AC merchandiser. After Isaac left AC, he was succeeded in April 1985 by John Corbett, who was on loan from his position as manager of retail and warehouse operations at the NCC, and Lawrence Johnson, appointed in November 1985 with no experience in managing co-operatives. By August 1982, the AC had 21 members and sales of approximately $51,000,000. Due to financial constraints, the AC transferred its Development Department to BAND in March 1985 to ensure the continuation of educational activities, with BAND being given responsibility to manage Camp Sierra in April 1986 (BHS, 1996b, pp. 13–14, 42; Neptune, 1997, p. 3; Rauber, 1992, p. 15).[33]

The AC continued to encourage the CCB and the PAC to integrate the buying and distribution functions between the warehouse and the retail stores with use of price scanning EDP, but there was

CCB discontent with AC overheads. The CCB BD decided in December 1979 to install electronic price scanning in at least one center by late 1980, but unlike its competitors continued individual price markings on products after scanning was introduced despite potential cost savings. The BD supported the retention of price marking on each item because it allowed customers to easily compare each item and assisted those customers, particularly the elderly, who could not read shelf tags. While the El Cerrito Center was chosen for the trial of price scanning, there were delays with ensuring that the computer system did not have any "bugs" and concerns about disrupting trade during busy seasons. It was not until October 1981 that price scanning began at El Cerrito. While there were 16 stores participating in this integrated warehouse system in 1982, financial problems by July 1987 prevented the CCB extending price scanning to its surviving stores increasing queue times compared to its major competitors. The AC also opened a second warehouse at San Leandro in 1981 to expand its nonfood inventories and provide better services to members, and in 1982 acquired the San Francisco Common Warehouse, which specialized in natural and bulk foods and became an AC subsidiary, the Twin Pines Distributing Company. While the AC moved to achieve economies, the CCB complained in April 1983 that high AC produce handling charges cost up to $500,000 per year and transferred their produce business to non-cooperative Richmond Produce, which reduced prices and increased freshness with six rather than five deliveries each week and next day deliveries as opposed to a two-day delay with AC. The AC closed its Produce Department due to the loss of the substantial CCB business. The CCB continued to press the AC to review its wholesale prices on other goods (Neptune, 1982, p. 2).[34]

The relationship of the CCB with AC eventually collapsed, which had negative implications for the development of the Californian consumer co-operative movement. The CCB accounted for 75 percent of AC purchases in 1979–1980. As the CCB closed stores, shifted suppliers and reduced operations, the AC began to lose revenue and by December 1985 had a debt of over $1,000,000. AC employees considered wage concessions if necessary and corresponded with the CCB BD asking to be consulted in any CCB decisions that affected them. An audit in January 1985 found that AC lost money in 1984 because its accountant undercharged its customers $386,662 for their groceries, placing unexpected cost pressures on the CCB as the AC tried to recoup its losses. The CCB switched from AC to Cergro in August 1985 to supply some grocery lines at a lower cost than the AC, with MacDonald later claiming the AC had an overhead charge of 11.5 percent compared to Cergro's 5.5 percent. The BD in November 1985 also expressed concern about the continuation of quality control by AC following the dismissal of the AC home economist Betsy Wood (MacDonald, 1992, pp. 52–53; Neptune, 1997, pp. 1–3; Rauber, 1992, p. 15).[35]

The lack of cash flow, with the CCB falling behind in its AC payments, led Johnson on Christmas Eve 1985 to request COD on all orders by the CCB from 26 December, which left CCB shelves empty for several weeks in the middle of a crucial holiday season. The CCB obtained further supplies from the wholesaler Cergro, which was willing to provide limited credit to the CCB to obtain the large CCB order. The CCB dropped AC CO-OP-labelled goods, with some temporary exceptions such as eggs and frozen foods, and replaced them with the Cergro house brand, which alienated many CCB shoppers who were accustomed to CO-OP labels, quality and prices, with CCB management stating there was no difference, despite the CCB's long-standing claims of the superiority of CO-OP goods. CCB management was also willing to switch from the AC because their long-standing concerns about their wholesale prices. This accelerated the decline in sales volumes at the CCB's remaining stores and heightened the CCB cash crisis, with the SACC in March 1986 offering to pay for a mediator to end the conflict with the AC. The relationship between the AC and CCB deteriorated to the level that the AC manager constructed a wall between them at their shared facilities in Richmond and locked the doors with the CCB moving its head office to the University Avenue Center in June 1986. The AC also forced the CCB to remove the CO-OP symbol from the CN with a threat of legal action. The CCB, which had $1.3 million invested in AC, proposed to use this as a deposit for its goods, but AC obtained a legal ruling that this was equity in April 1986 and could not be used as a deposit for transactions. The judge ruled that a lien be placed on the CCB's Hardware Variety store to pay the AC $1.16 million that was owed by the CCB. The CCB agreed to sell the store and close it in August 1986 to settle its debts to the AC with a payment of $690,000. The CCB also ended its membership of the AC by giving up its AC shares. The loss of the CCB ended the integrated merchandising and distribution system between the AC and its members. The AC closed its warehouse operations, entering into a contract with Sierra Natural Foods, a warehouse in San Francisco from March 1986, as an alternative source for CO-OP products to reduce costs, but these arrangements provided a limited range of goods at higher prices compared to the previous supply. The AC liquidated its remaining inventories and drastically reducing staff. Johnson left AC to become the manager of PAC in January 1987. While the CCB did attempt to reconcile with the AC, successfully re-affiliating in February 1987, on the condition that the CCB accept an amendment to AC rules that each affiliated co-operative have only one vote and restock more CO-OP labels, the AC was no longer the CCB's principal wholesaler. Meanwhile many small co-operatives that depended on AC services went out of business (Gordon, 1992, pp. 62–63; Neptune, 1997, pp. 3–4, 13; Rauber, 1992, pp. 15–16; Schildgen, 1992, p. 48).[36]

The CCB continued to support the broader co-operative movement. The CCB forwarded a petition to CLUSA signed by 9,600 individuals in April 1981 protesting against funding cuts to the NCCB. Following the demutualization of the Twin Pines Federal Savings and Loan, which had deteriorating finances, in March 1983, the BD called upon its members to transfer their funds to the CCFCU after the new owner of Twin Pines terminated most employees who were union members, thereby removing Twin Pines from labor representation and allowing it to pay less than the labor contract. The CCB promoted local worker co-operatives through the *CN* publicizing the first Collectives Fair at the Berkeley Veterans Memorial Building in October 1983. The Fair highlighted the products and services of worker-owned businesses such as Heartwood, a woodworking collective. The CCB was a major sponsor the Co-op Harvest Fair in October 1985 to promote co-operatives through workshops and booths in Martin Luther King Jr. Park in downtown Berkeley representing Bay Area co-operatives and collectives as well as local Berkeley businesses. There was also food, juggling, music and a range of social activities, including a Cajun dinner dance and a Pet Parade, with all funds raised to go to the BAND Co-operative Education Fund, which was established in 1982 and later became the Consumer Education Fund, to develop co-operative education programs for schools and the public in the Bay Area. Unfortunately, due to lower level of sponsorships, the lateness of the decision to put on the Fair, higher costs than expected and organizational difficulties, the Fair made a loss. While the CCB encouraged members to form co-operatives and buying groups in areas where it had shut stores, the BD rejected in March 1985 a proposal for $20,000 for a fund to assist these new co-operatives, attracting criticism from their promoters. During the CCB bankruptcy, the CCB transferred its preferred stock in the NCCB with a nominal value of $124,100, but not negotiable on the open market, to the Twin Pines Co-op Foundation, formerly BAND and the nonprofit arm of AC, which promoted co-operatives (BHS, 1996a, p. xiii).[37]

The CCB continued to have international links during its final years. It continued its relationship with the Japanese co-operative movement with regular visits by Japanese co-operators. It hosted a visit by 220 JCCU delegates in June 1982, who were returning from a UN Conference on Nuclear Disarmament in New York. They were divided into five buses to visit facilities at CCB and PAC. The successful Nadakobe Co-operative in Kobe sponsored a visit by two CCB employees and retired home economist Helen Black in February 1987 to observe its practices. The close relationship between the CCB and the JCCU led the JCCU to offer financial assistance to the CCB during late 1987. The CCB considered negotiating with the JCCU in April 1988 to establish a joint venture whereby the JCCU would provide $5.5 million, which would match the CCB's net worth.[38]

Conclusion

From 1981, the CCB was unable to regain a solid financial base in a period of changing demographics and fierce competition not only from Safeway, but from specialist natural food and produce stores, which targeted the growing demand for better quality food in Berkeley. Its financial constraints weakened its ability to promote its stores and implement new retail technology such as price scanning. The CCB lost many of its co-operative features such as purchase rebates and share interest, with shares no longer reflecting their real value. Special features such as the Kiddie Korrals were not reinstated and the CCB closed many of its stores and retreated to its Berkeley base. The focus on education weakened to save costs and the CCB lost its home economists. The opening of Savories in an area where the CCB had closed its store and withdrawn accelerated the financial decline. As the CCB declined in turnover, the AC which heavily relied on the CCB for orders also declined, with the CCB criticizing the AC for it costs. The eventual clash between the CCB and the AC in December 1985 not only had serious consequences for both organizations, but for the Californian consumer co-operative movement as well. The CCB also faced difficulties with raising finance with sympathetic lenders such as the NCCB and MSI losing confidence in the CCB. It faced continued problems with factional politics and turnover of senior management, which undermined general confidence in the CCB and further eroded employee morale.

The CCB turned to its employees despite job losses and low morale. While the CCB remained sympathetic to the labor movement, there were growing tensions with the unions over labor costs, with CCB management requiring managers to resign union membership and complaints over management bypassing the UFWCA to directly communicate with its employees. While there was resistance on the grounds of consumer sovereignty to involving workers on the BD and the proposed hybrid co-operative, most CCB members saw this as a way of saving the CCB. The UFWCA negotiated an employee-controlled hybrid, but the withdrawal of credit by the CCB's lenders led it to withdraw from the agreement.

Although the CCB faced major financial problems, it continued its links to the local community and the broader co-operative movement as well as consumer activism and innovation. It took stands on a range of consumer issues, including the irradiation of food and bottle recycling. The CCB was also a pioneer in platform co-operatives with the CMP. Its international links, particularly with the Japanese, remained strong, with the JCCU being considered a possible lifeline to save the CCB.

Notes

1 CN, 7 April 1986, p. 1.

2 CCB, 1984–1985 AR, p. 2. BHS; *CN*, 15 December 1980, p. 1, 7 December 1980, p. 1, 28 December 1981, p. 1, 1 March 1982, p. 1, 27 December 1982,

p. iv, 3 January 1983, p. 1, 18 July 1983, p. 1, 6 February 1984, p. 1, 16 April 1984, p. 16, 18 March 1985, p. 1, 16 December 1985, p. 1, 17 February 1986, p. 10, 17 March 1986, p. 3, 25 August 1986, p. 1, 28 January 1987, p. 3; *The Centerline*. 6/83, p. 1, Box 1, File 8. BANC MSS 94/220. RNLP, UCB BL.

3 *CN*, 31 August 1988, p. 1; *NYT*, 6 June 1988, p. A14.

4 *CN*, 26 October 1981, p. 4, 20 September 1982, p. 1, 7 March 1983, p. 1, 11 June 1984, p. 1, 17 December 1984, p. 2, 18 February 1985, p. 3, 25 February 1985, p. 11, 13 May 1985, p. 3, 3 March 1986, p. 3, 17 March 1986, p. 1, 18 February 1987, p. 3, 16 March 1988, p. 3; Interview of Bruce Miller, CCB activist, by author, Berkeley, 26 February 2013.

5 BD, 1 October 1987, Box 25, File 35, Memo Allan Gallant to All Co-op Family, 3 September 1987, Box 31 File 7, Memo Concerned Employees Coordinating Group to BD, 7 May 1986, Box 17, File 20, SOTF Report, typescript, 1 July 1986, p. 3, Box 30, File 41. BANC MSS 90/140 c. CCB Records, UCB BL; CN, 13 September 1982, p. 1, 4 October 1982, p. 3, 24 October 1983, p. 1, 5 December 1983, p. 2, 28 July 1986, pp. 1, 4, 9, 29 September 1986, pp. 1, 3, 8 December 1986, p. 13, 2 November 1988, pp. 1, 5; Interview of Bob Schildgen, employee and director, by author, Berkeley, 19 February 2013; *San Francisco Chronicle*, 25 April 1988, p. C1.

6 *Berkeley Gazette*, 24.01.1983, p. 5; *CN*, 28 December 1981, p. 6, 31 May 1982, p. 3, 22 December 1986, p. 3, 4 March 1987, p. 1, 13 May 1987, p. 3, 20 May 1987, p. 1, 3 June 1987, p. 1, 29 July 1987, p. 9; Letter BD to T. Condit, 5 July 1984. Box 17, File 23, Letter Loren Haugland to Allan Gallant, 4 March 1987, Box 32, File 21. BANC MSS 90/140 c. CCB Records, UCB BL; Touche Ross & Co., 'Report and Recommendations,' Unpublished typescript, 16 July 1982, Carton 49 Folder 5. BANC MSS 86/178c, HNC, UCB BL.

7 *Bay Area Consumers' Checkbook*, April 1985, p. 52; Interview of Michael Fullerton, CCB employee and director, by author, Berkeley, 19 February 2013; Management Analysis Center, 'Annotated Presentation,' 25 February 1982. Unpublished typescript. Box 11, File 31, BANC MSS 90/140 c. CCB Records, UCB BL; *NYT*, 23 February 1985, pp. 29, 40.

8 CCB, 'Proposal for the Development of the Market Place,' August 1984, Unpublished typescript. Box 14, File 32, BANC MSS 90/140 c. CCB Records, UCB BL.

CN, 16.07.1984, p. 1, 17 December 1984, p. 3, 4 March 1987, p. 1, 18 March 1987, p. 1; Interview of Michael Fullerton by author, Berkeley, 19 February 2013; Interview of Bruce Miller, 26 February 2013.

9 CN, 20 July 1981, p. 1, 10 August 1981, p. 1, 14 December 1981, p. 3, 3 May 1982, p. 1, 18 October 1982, p. 5, 7 February 1983, p. 3, 13 February 1984, p. 2, 16 April 1984, p. 16, 12 August 1985, p. 11, 25 November 1985, p. 1, 25 March 1987, p. 3; *NYT*, 6 June 1988, p. A14

10 BD, 29 November 1982. Box 17, File 23. BANC MSS 90/140 c. CCB Records, UCB BL; *CN*, 5 July 1982, p. 5, 27 September 1982, p. 1, 1 November 1982, p. 16, 16 January 1984, p. 14, 6 February 1984, p. 3; Letter Curt Aller to Olva Nurmela, 9 July 1981, Carton 1 File 13, TACC, 2 November 1982, Carton 1 File 2. BANC MSS 94/220. RNLP, UCB BL.

11 *CN*, 11 May 1981, p. 1, 1 June 1981, p. 1, 13 May 1985, p. 3, 18 November 1985, p. 3, 3 March 1986, p. 3, 17 March 1986, p. 11, 2 September 1987, p. 10.

12 Education Committee Recommendations, 8 January 1981, 5 May 1981. Box 11, File 12. Memo from Nancy Snow, 22 December 1986. Box 16, File 42. BANC MSS 90/140 c. CCB Records, UCB BL.

13 *CN*, 9 November 1981, p. 2.

14 *CN*, 18 October 1982, p. 10.

15 *CN*, 20 December 1982, p. 14, 7 January 1985, p. 2., 13 October 1986, pp. 1, 5, 22 December 1986, p. 9, 21 January 1987, p. 12; Memo Nancy Snow to Lynn MacDonald, 'December 1984 Report.' Box 16, File 17, BANC MSS 90/140 c. CCB Records, UCB BL.

16 *CN*, 16 April 1984, p. 3, 11 June 1984, p. 2, 3 February 1986, p. 1, 13 October 1986, p. 11; CCB, News Release, 8 September 1987. Box 17, File 24. BANC MSS 90/140 c. CCB Records, UCB BL.

17 *CN*, 10 September 1984, p. 10.

18 Memo Nancy Snow to Lynn MacDonald, 29 October 1984. Box 16, File 17. BANC MSS 90/140 c. CCB Records, UCB BL.

19 *CN*, 18 April 1966, p. 2, 9 April 1973, p. 11.

20 *CN*, 13 August 1984, p. 16, 22 July 1985, p. 16, 3 March 1986, p. 1; Memo from Nancy Snow to Lynn MacDonald, 27 July 1984. Box 16, File 37. BANC MSS 90/140 c. CCB Records, UCB BL.

21 *CN*, 31 July 1978, p. 1, 16 February 1981, pp. 1, 14, 16 November 1981, p. 1, 5 April 1982, p. 3, 11 October 1982, p. 1, 2 May 1983, p. 1, 23 May 1983, p. 1, 17 June 1985, pp. 3–4.

22 Memo Department Heads at Shattuck Avenue to Members of Merchandising/Consumer Protection Committee, 27 April 1988, Box 20, File 23, Merchandising/Consumer Protection Committee, 13 August 1987, Box 20, File 21, BANC MSS 90/140 c. CCB Records, UCB BL; Management Report to BD, 28 November 1983, Carton 1 File 13. BANC MSS 94/220. RNLP, UCB BL.

23 *CN*, 23 February 1981, p. 1, 25 March 1987, p. 1, 13 January 1988, p. 12.

24 *CN*, 28 June 1982, p. 11, 13 September 1982, p. 2, 31 December 1984, p. 1, 4 March 1987, p. 1; *Oakland Tribune*, 20 May 1988, p. A1.

25 CN, 21 December 1981, p. 3; Interview of Bob Schildgen, 19 February 2013; Memo Curt Aller to Personnel Committee, 10 November 1981, Personnel Committee Meeting, 20.10.1981, Personnel Committee Special Meeting, 20 November 1981, Box 32, File 3, BANC MSS 90/140 c. CCB Records, UCB BL.

26 *Berkeley Gazette*, 24 January 1983, p. 5; BD, 23 August 1971, *Employee Bulletin*, 24 July 1984, Box 30, File 40, Letter R. Schneider to BD, 17 August 1971, Carton 7 Folder 54, BD, Listening Meeting 8 November 1976, Carton 10 File 72; *CN*, 13 September 1971, p. 7, 1 November 1982, pp. 3–4, 8 November 1982, p. 10, 20 December 1982, pp. 12–13, 10 January 1983, pp. 3, 10, 21 February 1983, p. 1, 14 March 1983, p. 1, 22 August 1983, pp. 3–4, 3 October 1983, p. 11, 28 November 1983, p. 3, 20 February 1984, p. 1, 8 April 1985, pp. 1, 9, 25.

27 *CN*, 25 August 1986, p. 4, 27 October 1986, p. 12, 17 November 1986, p. 3, 15 December 1986, pp. 5–6, 11 February 1987, p. 1, 18 February 1987, p. 2, 15 April 1987, p. 3, 3 February 1988, pp. 1, 4; Memo Jeff Voltz to All Employees, 6 May 1987, Box 32, File 6, SOTF Report, typescript, 1 July 1986, p. 6, Box 30, File 41. BANC MSS 90/140 c. CCB Records, UCB BL.

28 *CN*, 28 July 1986, p. 11, 29 September 1986, pp. 1, 3, 25 March 1987, p. 4, 3 June 1987, p. 1, 29 July 1987, p. 9, 18 November 1987, p. 1, 16, 16 December 1987, pp. 1, 13. 9 March 1988, p. 3, 16 March 1988, p. 3, 20 April 1988, p. 1, 11 May 1988, pp. 1, 4, 18 May 1988, pp. 1, 11, 25 May 1988, p. 1, 29 June 1988, p. 8; Interview of Bruce Miller, 26 February 2013; Letter William Christy to BD, 5 May 1988, Box 29, File 33. BANC MSS 90/140 c. CCB Records, UCB BL; *San Francisco Chronicle*, 25 April 1988, p. C8.

29 Pacific Co-operative Minutes, 3 October 1989, Box 1, Bob March files, BHS; *CN*, 1 July 1987, p. 9, 1 June 1988, pp. 11–12, 15 June 1988, p. 3, 22 June 1988, p. 2, 13 July 1988, p. 1, 27 July 1988, p. 1, 3 August 1988, p. 5, 10 August 1988, pp. 1, 5, 17 August 1988, p. 2, 14 September 1988, p. 1; *San Francisco Chronicle*, 11 November 1988, p. C3.

30 Letter Stephen Rodriguez to Bruce Miller, 28 October 1987, Carton 36, File 6. BANC MSS 90/140 c. CCB Records, UCB BL.
31 BD, 7 August 1986, SOTF Report, typescript, 1 July 1986, p. 9, Box 30, File 41. BANC MSS 90/140 c. CCB Records, UCB BL; *CN*, 20 December 1982, p. 2, 30 May 1983, p. 13.
32 *CN*, 16 February 1981, p. 1, 22 August 1983, p. 4, 25 June 1984, p. 1; TACC, 15 August 1988, Box 29, File 17. BANC MSS 90/140 c. CCB Records, UCB BL.
33 BAND Foundation, AR 1990, Box 29, File 12. BANC MSS 90/140 c. CCB Records, UCB BL; *CN*, 19 January 1981, p. 3, 6 May 1985, p. 10, 4 November 1985, p. 10; Memo Terry Baird to AC members, 7 April 1986. Carton 48 Folder 5. BANC MSS 86/178c, HNC, UCB BL.
34 *CN*, 14 April 1980, p. 1, 13 October 1980, p. 12, 19 October 1981, pp. 1, 5, 15 March 1982, p. 4, 4 July 1983, p. 3, 8 August 1983, p. 3, 22 August 1983, p. 4; Letter Chair Finance Management and Planning Committee to Jeff Voltz, 13 July 1987, Box 31, File 4. BANC MSS 90/140 c. CCB Records, UCB BL.
35 AC, 6 June 1985, Box 23, File 22, Report AC General Manager to AC BD, 21 March 1985, Box 23, File 24. BANC MSS 90/140 c. CCB Records, UCB BL. CCB, 1984–5 AR, p. 1. BHS; *CN*, 9 March 1981, p. 1, 13 May 1985, p. 3, 18 November 1985, p. 3.
36 *Employee Bulletin*, 20 March 1986, Box 30, File 40, Letter Lynn MacDonald to Lawrence Johnson, 2 January 1986, Box 29, File 19, SACC, 11 March 1986, Box 20, File 25. BANC MSS 90/140 c. CCB Records, UCB BL; *CN*, 13 January 1986, p. 3, 3 February 1986, p. 3, 10 February 1986, p. 8, 17 February 1986, p. 2, 3 March 1986, p. 5, 21 April 1986, p. 3, 5 May 1986, p. 1, 30 June 1986, p. 4, 14 July 1986, pp. 1, 3, 15 September 1986, p. 12, 28 January 1987, p. 3, 4 February 1987, p. 1, 18 February 1987, pp. 2, 9, 23 March 1988, p. 11.
37 *Buyline*, April 1983, p. 1, Box 1, File 8. BANC MSS 94/220. RNLP, UCB BL; *CN*, 20 April 1981, p. 4, 30 May 1983, p. 2, 3 October 1983, p. 1, 18 March 1985, p. 3, 7 October 1985, p. 1, 14 October 1985 Harvest Festival Supplement, p. 2, 24 March 1986, p. 1; BD, 29 November 1982, Co-operative Education Fund Committee, Report to CCB BD, 25 November 1983. Box 17, File 23. Memo Nancy Snow to Lynn MacDonald, 3 July 1986, Box 17, File 8. BANC MSS 90/140 c. CCB Records, UCB BL.
38 BD Executive Sessions, 3 November 1987, Box 29, File 35, 11 April 1988, Box 29, File 33, 16 June 1988, Box 36, File 27, Memo from Vangie Elkins and George Yasukochi, 18 May 1982, Box 36, File 20, Memo from Margo Robinson, 11 April 1988, Box 29, File 32. BANC MSS 90/140 c. CCB Records, UCB BL; *CN*, 08 March 1982, pp. 3–4, 24 May 1982, p. 8, 21 June 1982, pp. 1, 9, 11 February 1987, p. 5.

References

Baird, T. (1992), "Governance Factors as a Key Element in the Decline of CCB – A Personal Perspective," In Fullerton, M., ed., *What Happened to the Berkeley Co-op? A Collection of Opinions*, Davis CA, Center for Co-operatives, University of California, pp. 65–70.

Balnave, N. and Patmore, G. (2017), "The Labour Movement and Co-operatives," *Labour History*, 112, pp. 7–24.

Bay Area Census, 2019, available at www.bayareacensus.ca.gov (accessed 14 April 2019).

BHS, 1984, *Margaret Shaughnessy Gordon. Past President of the Consumers Co-operative of Berkeley, Research Economist, and Community Leader*, Berkeley, CA, BHS.

BHS, 1995, *A Conversation with George Yasukochi: Controller of the Consumers Co-operative of Berkeley, 1956–1982*, Berkeley, CA, BHS.

BHS, 1996a, *A Conversation with Betsy Wood: A Home Economist's Perspective on the Berkeley Co-op*, Berkeley, CA, BHS.

BHS, 1996b, *A Conversation with Robert Neptune – Pioneer Manager of the Consumers Co-operative of Berkeley, and Long-Term Manager at Associated Co-operatives*, Berkeley, CA, BHS.

Black, B., 1992a, "The Final Years," In Fullerton, M., ed., *What Happened to the Berkeley Co-op? A Collection of Opinions*, Davis CA, Center for Co-operatives, University of California, pp. 71–75.

Black, H., 1992b, "A Home Economist's Point of View," In Fullerton, M., ed., *What Happened to the Berkeley Co-op? A Collection of Opinions*, Davis CA, Center for Co-operatives, University of California, pp. 33–37.

Cooper, D.H. and Mohn, P.O., 1992, *The Greenbelt Co-operative: Success and Decline*, Davis, California, Centre for Co-operatives, University of California, Davis.

Fourth Street Berkeley, 2019, "Fourth Street Shops, Berkeley California," available at www.fourthstreet.com/history (accessed 14 April 2019).

Fullerton, M. (ed.), 1992, *What Happened to the Berkeley Co-op? A Collection of Opinions, Centre for Co-operatives*, Davis, Center for Co-operatives, University of California.

Gordon, M., 1992, "The Rise and Fall of CCB," In Fullerton, M., ed., *What Happened to the Berkeley Co-op? A Collection of Opinions*, Davis, CA, Center for Co-operatives, University of California, pp. 57–64.

MacDonald, L., 1992, "An Unsuitable Job for a Co-operative," In Fullerton, M., ed., *What Happened to the Berkeley Co-op? A Collection of Opinions*, Davis, CA, Center for Co-operatives, University of California, pp. 51–56.

Neptune, R., 1982, *Update 1982. California's Uncommon Markets*, Richmond, CA, AC.

Neptune, R., 1997, *Epilog. California's Uncommon Markets. 1983–1988*, Berkeley, CA, BHS.

Patmore, G., 2017, "Fighting Monopoly and Enhancing Democracy: A Historical Overview of US Consumer Co-operatives," In Hilson, M., Neunsinger, S., and Patmore, G., eds., *A Global History of Consumer Co-operation since 1850: Movements and Businesses*, Leiden, Brill, pp. 507–526.

Rauber, P., 1992, "Decline and Fall of the Berkeley Co-op," In Fullerton, M., ed., *What Happened to the Berkeley Co-op? A Collection of Opinions*, Davis, Center for Co-operatives, University of California, pp. 11–17.

Rovanpera, B., 2009, *Walnut Creek. An Illustrated History*, Walnut Creek, CA, Walnut Creek Historical Society.

Schildgen, R., 1992, "Failure from Neglect of Co-op Principles," In Fullerton, M., ed., *What Happened to the Berkeley Co-op? A Collection of Opinions*, Davis, CA, Center for Co-operatives, University of California, pp. 39–49.

Schildgen, R., 1993, "Epilogue 1987–1993," Unpublished Typescript, Berkeley, BHS.

Tierney, T., 2013, *The Public Space of Social Media: Connected Cultures of the Network Society*, New York, Routledge.

UCB Office of the Vice Chancellor of Finance, 2019, "Our Berkeley. Enrolment History Since 1869," available at https://pages.github.berkeley.edu/OPA/our-berkeley/enroll-history.html (accessed 14 April 2019).

Yasukochi, G., 1992, "The Berkeley Co-op – Anatomy of a Noble Experiment," In Fullerton, M., ed., *What happened to the Berkeley Co-op? A Collection of Opinions*, Davis, CA, Center for Co-operatives, University of California, pp. 23–32.

Weinstein, D., 2008, *It came from Berkeley. How Berkeley Changed the World*, Layton, UT, Gibbs Smith.

Wollenberg, C., 2008, *Berkeley. A City in History*, Berkeley, University of California Press.

9 Conclusion

This book is not about the failure of the co-operative business model, with its emphasis upon member democracy and ownership, but about the failure of a specific iconic US consumer co-operative. The CCB was part of an international co-operative movement, whose origins lay in mid-eighteenth-century UK against the background of the turmoil of the industrial revolution. While the Rochdale model spread internationally, there were variations in practice, with some co-operative movements aligning themselves with political parties and the US movement in the 1930s emphasizing its 'political neutrality' to defeat a Communist takeover. The UK movement developed the notion of 'consumer sovereignty', where the interests of consumers outweighed those of workers in the consumer co-operatives as the movement grew employing large numbers of workers in stores, factories and farms. Workers were expected to resolve their grievances through joining labor unions.

While the CCB and many other traditional US consumer co-operatives failed to survive by the 1990s, the movement remained strong internationally and consumer co-operatives in countries such as Italy and Japan thrived, with the UK movement recovering from a major slump. Even in the US, there were 'new wave' consumer co-operatives eventually forming the NCGA in 1999. There are current examples of large-scale successful consumer co-operatives that operate in North America such as the Calgary Co-operative and REI. While critics of the co-operative business model may claim that the CCB is an example of the failure of that business model, the extent and persistence of co-operatives challenges that contention.

The CCB also survived for over 50 years, which is longer than many IOBs. While there is no equivalent data for the US, Australian data (Co-operatives Research Group, 2019) suggests that co-operatives generally and consumer co-operatives specifically have a life span of 25 and 21 years, respectively, from formation to cancellation of registration, which highlights the CCB's longevity. While some of the other Berkeley co-operatives also did not survive such as Books Unlimited, which became bankrupt,[1] others such as ACCI and the CCFCU continue to thrive. Failure did not arise from an inevitable co-operative 'life cycle', but from strategic management decisions and its specific social, economic and political context.

The CCB's early years faced several challenges, but the CCB expanded after the end of the Second World War with steady growth and good financial results. The CCB was built on a period of unrest associated with Great Depression and the co-operative alternatives provided by Upton Sinclair's EPIC. Immigration and religion strengthened these foundations with the presence of a sizable Finnish community in Berkeley, highlighted by the absorption of the Finnish BCU in 1947, and the influence of Kagawa. There were wartime labor and goods shortages. These wartime years also involved a failed experiment with branches in Berkeley, senior management turnover and concerns about membership participation, issues that were to again surface later when the CCB was much larger. The economic prosperity of the postwar boom in the Bay Area helped the CCB. During these early years, however, there were organizational issues that were to have implications for later years. There was increasing oversight over management, which diminished their authority with the Personnel Committee acting as a grievance committee for employees, and over governance to the extent of an establishment of a 'committee of committees'. Membership apathy was also an issue with the idea of a Parliament being introduced in 1958 to encourage participation.

The CCB, however, eventually failed, paralleling many IOBs. There were major decisions to expand and re-expand beyond Berkeley that undermined the financial health of the CCB and weakened the advantages of the co-operative model. The 1962 purchase of Sids stores, which overturned the previous cautious approach of the BD, and the 1974 purchase of Mayfair Stores were motivated by a desire to increase economies of scale to compete with rivals such as Safeway and extend the co-operative philosophy. The 1974 purchase also was driven by concerns about providing retail services to low-income areas of Oakland that were being deserted by non-cooperative supermarket chains. As the CWG experiments in England and efforts such as the San Francisco Neighborhood Co-operative in the Bay Area, there are issues with consumer co-operatives operating in low-income areas with capital raising and providing quality food at low prices. While there were areas, such as Walnut Creek, Marin County and San Francisco, where grassroots campaigns led to the establishment of CCB stores, the chain stores acquired by the CCB covered areas that did not have strong local co-operative support and even competed with a CCB existing store in Walnut Creek. The Savories venture in Marin County in 1984, which was an area that the CCB had abandoned, accelerated the demise of the CCB, with a technology to ensure pesticide-free food that could not be financed.

The growth beyond Berkeley created two major problems. The CCB covered an increasingly diverse range of communities in terms of income, ethnicity, political outlook and sympathy toward the co-operative ideal, which weakened the ability of the CCB to attract members in new areas and increased sources of division within the co-operative. Competing interest groups within the CCB increased organizational heterogeneity and exacerbated conflict in a democratic governance model, assisting the decline of the CCB (Cook, 1995, p. 1157). The expansion and growth of the CCB also raised issues in terms of member participation and voice in the CCB that were exacerbated by factional divisions within the CCB.

The CCB's factional divisions relates to its political environment. Berkeley reflected the deep divisions of US Society in the 1960s. Political unrest encouraged a distrust of authority which flowed into the management of the CCB. The relationship between the managers and the BD deteriorated even further with the departure of Mannila. There was a turnover of managers, which undermined staff morale and member confidence, with members through several CCB committees intervening in specific management decisions such as hiring and firing. The maintenance of trust between management and member activists is an essential feature of the survival of consumer co-operatives. The formation of entrenched factions along political lines from the 1960s led to shifts in policy and a further weakening of confidence in the CCB, as each faction criticized the others' management policies. The rise of factions also chilled membership participation as faction activists placed their interests, which were concerned that alternative sources of member voice could provide their opponents with alternative forums to raise their viewpoints, over a broader organizational interest of membership engagement. Experiments such as the Parliament, the CCB Congress and the Center Councils where never fully accepted by the BD, despite later recognition by the 1982 Touche Ross Report that Center Councils could play an important role in turning around the CCB. When the CCB did engage in broader political issues, irrespective of the merits, there was a flight of capital with older conservative members, withdrawing or running down their capital, being replaced by younger radical members such as students with lower levels of capital investment.

The relationship between the CCB and its employees remained problematic. The idea of 'consumer sovereignty' remained dominant until the 1980s with employees being able to join the CCB, but not allowed to participate in key areas of governance such as the BD due to perceived conflicts of interest. As Wetzel and Gallagher noted (1987), the CCB became indistinguishable to IOBs, in that it subjected its employees to a managerial hierarchy and labor management professionalism, with employees encouraged, as outlined in the 'consumer sovereignty' principle, to join unions to protect their wages and conditions. Despite pioneering policies regarding employment discrimination at the end of the Second World War arising from the treatment of workers of Japanese descent, the CCB was challenged over its treatment of African American and women workers by the late 1960s. The sympathetic policy toward organized labor had advantages in the avoidance of the large-scale industrial disputes of its competitors, but led to higher labor costs and reduced flexibility in downsizing as higher paid senior staff was retained at the expense of lower paid junior staff. Tensions did appear with organized labor over the issues of volunteer labor and as the CCB faced serious financial problems, over management membership of unions, retrenchment and the avoidance of collective bargaining. The deterioration of finances led to a rejection of the 'consumer sovereignty' principle during the 1980s with employees on the BD and the failed worker-consumer hybrid co-operative initiative.

The deterioration of the CCB's finances undermined many general advantages of the co-operative business model and specific benefits for CCB members. The introduction of discount pricing, which was viewed as crucial to the survival of the CCB in a competitive market and necessary to stop losses in some of the former Sid stores, ended the CCB's appeal of a relatively high price quality outlet to an affluent clientele and traditional Rochdale member financial incentives, such as the patronage refund or dividend and interest on share capital. The further deterioration of CCB finances ended its extensive co-operative and consumer education programs along with specific CCB services such as the Kiddie Korral. Rivals such as Safeway adopted successful CCB initiatives and competitors such as the Berkeley Bowl and Monterey Market, which specialized in high-quality produce at competitive prices, attracted the growing CCB member patronage. The closed flagship CCB store in Shattuck Avenue was eventually taken over by Andronico's Community Markets and then Safeway (Illustration 9.1).

Illustration 9.1 The Former CCB Store in Shattuck Avenue, Berkeley, a Safeway Store in September 2019. Courtesy of Helen Warner, photographer.

The CCB's failure also reflects the weakness of the broader Californian co-operative movement. Despite the initial optimism and an upsurge of interest in the 1970s, the Californian movement did not grow to become a key player in the Californian supermarket sector, and the AC, which encouraged the CCB to expand, became increasingly reliant on the CCB. The AC could not match the growing economies of scale for transport and logistics of rivals such as Safeway. Its cost structure became a burden for the CCB, leading to the breakdown in relations in December 1985, which neither recovered from. The CCB did engage an alternative supplier, but it was too late. While the establishment of the NCCB provided a hope for financial support, the CCB's growing financial liabilities, even with the closure of its stores and sale of assets, was too great a risk for the NCCB, despite its foundations in the co-operative sector.

While the CCB faced major problems, it developed a strong co-operative culture, with an emphasis on co-operative education and social interaction. There were social activities such as picnics in Tilden Regional Park and Camp Sierra and its own publication, the *CN*. The CCB also engaged in its local communities through sponsorship of local sporting and social activities. It also provided spaces for community debates about political issues. A 1977 survey found that co-operative principles/values were a major reason for joining and staying for a member of the CCB. The legacy of the CCB's culture can be seen almost three decades later in former members and employees, who can remember their membership number without prompting and become emotional when they remember its closure. The development of a co-operative culture, however, was not enough in the long term to prevent its final collapse and alienate a growing number of inactive members, both in terms of participation and buying behavior.

The eventual failure of the CCB should not overshadow its innovative activities in areas ranging from consumer protection to early platform co-operatives. These initiatives attracted widespread interest, including the *New York Times*, consumer advocate Ralph Nader and overseas co-operatives. Its home economists, with their concerns about merchandise quality and nutrition, and the CPIC were a focus for consumer activism. During the 1950s, early CCB concerns included chemical additives in food and subliminal advertising. While it did not enter the area of organic food until 1970, it did encourage the establishment an organic food co-operative in 1958, which was claimed to be the first in the Bay Area. There were other significant initiatives for the Bay Area and beyond, including Kiddie Korrals, low-cost cookbooks, which emphasized price and nutrition, unit pricing, bans on the sale of hazardous pesticides, recycling and nutritional labels. The CBB engaged in early models of collective/community ownership of the early internet through its involvement in the CMP, a precursor to the current interest in platform co-operatives, which is an alternative business model for an industry dominated by IOBs such as Google and Facebook.

Note

1 *CN*, 18 October 1982, p. 9, 28 March 1983, p. 3, 4 April 1983, pp. 3, 14.

References

Cook, M.L., 1995, "The Future of US Agricultural Co-operatives: A Neo-Institutional Approach," *American Journal of Agricultural Economics*, 77 (5), pp. 1153–1159.

Co-operatives Research Group, 2019, "The University of Sydney Business School, 2019, Co-operatives in Australia: Growth, Decline and Revival," available at https://sydney.edu.au/content/dam/corporate/documents/business-school/research/research-groups/co-operatives-in-australia-growth-decline-revival-2017-19_october19.pdf (accessed November 5 2019).

Wetzel, K.W. and Gallagher, D.G., 1987, "A Conceptual Analysis of Labour Relations in Cooperatives," *Economic and Industrial Democracy*, 8 (4), pp. 517–540.

Index

Abbott, Park 95
Acorn Project (West Oakland) 176–178
activism 43, 66, 71–72, 79, 81, 83, 85, 92, 97, 99, 105, 108, 113, 118, 131, 137–138, 153–154, 157, 172, 182–184, 186, 189, 191, 193–194, 203, 210, 220, 228, 230
Adelaide Co-operative, Australia 50
adulterated food, avoiding 3, 12, 20, 26, 28, 32, 65
advertising 8, 11, 46, 68, 85, 88, 127, 148, 153, 158, 182, 205, 208; subliminal 118, 230
AFL-CIO (US) 70, 212
Africa 36; agricultural co-operatives 39; and CARE 193; and CLUSA 162; consumer co-operatives 39; and the ICA 50; *see also specific countries*
African Americans 153; Berkeley 77, 79–81, 98, 106, 108–109, 137, 139–141, 159, 163, 171–172, 200–201; co-operatives 65, 69, 161–162; credit unions 186; employment 123–4, 157, 176, 187–188; *see also* Black Panther Party
agricultural co-operatives 1, 4, 16, 18–19; Australia 19; Denmark 37; and the ICA 50; Italy 16; Palestine 15; South Africa 39; US 19, 95; USSR 42
agricultural economics 18
Ahonen, Tauno 109, 116
Akulian, Linda 175, 184
Alameda, California 83–84, 177
Alameda County, California 78, 81, 140, 149
Alameda County Central Labor Council 154–55
Alameda County Coalition 216
Alameda Unit (PCS) 84, 87
Alaska Commercial Company 214
Albany, California 81, 94, 106, 111
alcohol 57, 78, 125, 184, 201, 208
Alfalfa House, Sydney, Australia 50
Algeria 39
All-American Co-operative Commission 63
All-Berkeley Coalition 172
Allendale Unit (PCS) 84
Allende, Salvador President (Chile) 176
Aller, Curtis 175–176, 203, 212
Alper, Roy 184
Amalgamated Meat Cutters and Butcher Workmen of North America 214
American Federation of Labor (AFL) 62–63, 66, 70
American Federation of Teachers 70
Andronico's 205, 229
Anglo American Co-operative Company 59
Anti-Communism 107–108
Antigonish movement 16, 44, 65
Apartheid 204
apprenticeships 124, 187, 211
April Coalition Slate (Berkeley) 141
Arab co-operatives 15
Arcata (California) 191, 204, 212
Argentina: consumer co-operatives 39, 44, 49; co-operative legislation 44; credit unions 44; and the ICA 40, 45; rural co-operatives 44; wholesaling 44
Armour and Company (US) 5, 212
Arnold, Robert (Bob) 141–143
Arts and Crafts Co-operative Inc. (ACCI), Berkeley 112, 128–129, 192, 226

Ascher, Gertrude 118
Ashworth, Samuel 29
Asia 36, 46; consumer co-operatives 36, 48; and CLUSA 162; and the ICA 50; *see also specific countries*
Asian Americans: Berkeley 79, 200; employment 157, 187; *see also* Japanese Americans
Associated Co-operatives (AC) 96, 99, 110, 116, 118, 123–129, 131, 155, 160–162, 165, 176, 179, 186, 190–191, 200, 204–205, 209, 211, 215–220, 230; Development Department (ACDC) 161–162
Associated Co-operatives of Northern California (ACNC) 87–88, 95–96, 98–99
Associated Co-operatives of Southern California (ACSC) 95
Associated Co-operator (California) 126–127
AT&T (US) 176
Australia: agricultural co-operatives 19; consumer co-operatives 5–6, 13–18, 39, 44, 50, 226; co-operatives 226; and the CWS 33; dairy co-operatives 5; food co-operatives 51; and the ICA 40; women's guilds 45
Australian Association of Co-operatives 11
Austria: consumer co-operatives 42–43; and the CWS 33; and the ICA 43
Awner, Lee 182

bacon industry 33, 212
Bailey, Larry 157
Baird, Terry 204
bakeries, co-operative 4, 26, 44, 63, 110, 145, 202; *see also* flour and bread societies
Ballew, Robert 112, 115
banking: Belgium 42; France 42; Great Britain 35; Japan 42; US 129; *see also* National Consumer Co-operative Bank (NCCB)
bankruptcy 42, 44, 49, 63, 69, 147, 200, 203–204, 212, 219, 226
Barankin, Edward 143
Battilani, Patrizia 11
Bay Area Co-operative 162
Bay Area Neighborhood Development Foundation (BAND) 162, 216, 219
Bay Area Photography Society 190
Bay Area Rapid Transit (BART) 106, 140, 159, 171
Belgium: banking 42; consumer co-operatives 38, 43, 51; organization along religious/political lines 3–4
Bemis, Edward 60
Berkeley, CA: before 1947 76–82; 1947–1961 105–109; 1962–1971 137–141; 1972–1980 171–173; 1981–1993 200–201; *see also individual organizations*; North Berkeley; police; South Berkeley; West Berkeley
Berkeley, George 78
Berkeley Architectural Heritage Association (BAHA) 173
Berkeley Barb 139
Berkeley Better Citizenship League 94
Berkeley Black Repertory Group 216
Berkeley Bowl 205, 229
Berkeley Caucus 108
Berkeley Chamber of Commerce 94, 125, 160
Berkeley Citizens' Action (BCA) 172, 201
Berkeley City Council (BCC) 108–109, 125, 140–141, 144, 172, 174, 201, 214
Berkeley Co-operative *see* Consumers Co-operative of Berkeley
Berkeley Co-operative Employees' Association (BCEA) 123, 188
Berkeley Co-operative Union (BCU) 21, 76, 86, 88–89, 91–92, 95, 99, 115, 227
Berkeley Democratic Club (BDC) 108, 172
Berkeley Food Project 216
Berkeley Free Clinic 143
Berkeley Gazette 108
Berkeley Historical Society (BHS) 173
Berkeley Medical Aid Committee 141
Berkeley Neighborhood Food Conspiracy 147
Berkeley Newspaper Co-operative 163
Berkeley Rose Garden 79–80
Berkeley School Board 109, 140, 144
Berkeley Unit (PCS) 84–86
Berkeley Veterans Memorial Building 219
Berkeley Women for Peace (BWP) 140–1, 159

Bernard, A.J 172
Best, Charles 83
Birchall, Johnston 1–2
Black, Bruce 203–204
Black, Helen 182–184, 204, 209, 219
Black Caucus (Berkeley) 172–173
Black Employees of the Consumer Co-operative (CCB) 157
black markets 94
Black Panther Party 106, 139, 159, 173, 189
Blatchley, Cornelius 56
Blue Ball Club (Blidworth, Great Britain) 26
Blue Fairyland (Elmwood) 139
Blue Lake Producers Co-operative (Oregon) 95
Board of Directors (CCB, BD) 84, 87–94, 99, 109–112, 116, 119–123, 125, 127, 131, 141–145, 147, 149, 151–158, 160, 162–164, 171, 174–183, 186, 188–190, 192–194, 200, 203–204, 206–217, 219–220, 227–229
board members 69, 140, 143
bogus co-operatives 63, 129
Bohemianism 79, 98
Bonanza (US television series) 153
bonuses 34, 60, 111
Books Unlimited 97, 128, 130, 149, 226
bookselling 128, 139; *see also individual bookstores*
Bowen, E.R. 64, 66–67, 69
boycotts 5, 10, 13, 32, 34, 41, 69, 122, 124, 137, 154–156, 157, 159, 165, 174, 183, 192, 201, 207–208, 210–212
brands, co-operative 6, 23, 48, 65, 69–70, 89, 94–95, 97, 121, 127, 149, 161, 178–179, 183, 190–193, 206, 212, 218
Bratt, Nancy 146
bread 3, 11, 28, 42, 44, 175; additives 154; as focus 26
bread societies 26; *see also* bakeries; flour and bread societies
Brighton Co-operative Society (Great Britain) 27–28, 58
Brisbane Co-operative Society (Australia) 39
Brown, Jerry California Governor 185, 191
Brown, Pat California Governor 131
Brown, Stan 115, 190
Brotherhood Economics (Toyohiko Kagawa, 1934) 16
Bryan, William 28, 58
Bryant, Anita 184
Bryant, Roy 175–179, 185, 204
building societies: Great Britain 35
Burcham, George 83
Burcham, Margaret 83
business services, provision 35
butter 5, 33, 47, 128; *see also* dairy co-operatives
'buy local' campaigns 17
buying clubs 6, 58, 83, 147, 191–2, 215; *see also* Pacific Co-operative
buying groups 48, 83, 219

Calgary Co-operative (Canada) 226
California Co-operative Federation 191
California Co-operative League 126
California Director of Food and Agriculture 185
California Farmer Labor Consumer Committee to Combat Inflation 94
California Hardware Retail Association 128
California Medical Association 97
California State Board of Pharmacy 112
Californian Army National Guard 137–139, 144
Californian Consumer Association 131
Californian Co-operative Finance Corporation 128
Californian Co-operative Wholesale (CACW) 94–96
Californian Democratic Council 108
Californian Department of Agriculture 184
Californian Department of Consumer Affairs 191
Californian Department of Corporations 174
Californian Department of Industrial Relations 131
Camp Ashby (Berkeley) 80
Camp Sierra 97–98, 123, 129, 156, 182, 191, 216, 230
Campbell, Alexander 31
Campus Committee for New Politics (Berkeley) 159
Canada: Antigonish movement 16, 44, 65; consumer co-operatives 13,

38–39, 49–51, 71; co-operatives 12, 16; and the CWS 33
capital: access to 3, 7–8, 20, 49, 62, 128, 162, 191, 205, 227; accumulation 10, 27, 29, 41, 58; Australia 6; capital withdrawals 9, 69, 122, 151; consumer co-operatives 1, 6, 9–11, 20, 42, 49; Finland 41; from philanthropy 27; Great Britain 27–29, 31–33, 35, 42; and the ICA 45; Italy 11; MOBs 1; Rochdale consumer co-operative model 2; US 57, 61–62, 71, 85–86, 90, 110, 112–113, 119, 122, 126, 144, 146–147, 149, 156, 158, 164–165, 180, 228
Caribbean: and the Antigonish movement 16
Carnation Milk 124
Carter, Jimmy President 71–72, 193
cash trading principle 2–3, 31, 58–59, 85, 91, 96, 150, 165, 179
Castro Valley (California) 147–149, 153, 158–159, 164, 174, 180, 186, 190, 202
Catholic Church: Antigonish movement 16, 44; Berkeley 77; co-operative division 59; promotion of co-operatives 16, 38, 83
Cegro *see* Certified Grocers
Center Council Chairperson's Committee (Berkeley, CCCC) 186
Center Councils (CCB) 118, 151–153, 156, 159–160, 164–165, 175, 178–180, 183, 186, 188, 190, 194, 207–209, 211, 216, 228; *see also individual Center Council organizations*
Center for Independent Living (Berkeley, CIL) 172, 181
Center for Science in the Public Interest (US) 210
Central Co-operative (Modesto, California) 126
Central Co-operative Wholesale (Wisconsin, CCW) 64
Central Industry Co-operative Bank (Japan) 43
Central Intelligence Agency (CIA) 182–183
Central Pacific Railroad (US, CPRR) 77–78
Central Union of Co-operative Societies of Japan 40
centralization 12, 17, 33, 46–47, 63, 86, 88
Centrosoyus (All Russian Union of Consumer Societies) 41
Certified Grocers (Cegro, US) 205, 214, 217–218
Ceylon 33
chain stores 21, 25, 32, 42–43, 46–47, 49–50, 68, 70, 83, 85, 88, 137, 147, 171, 176, 179, 185, 205–206, 227
Challenge Cream and Butter Association 128
Chamber of Commerce of the United States 66
charities 1, 3, 19
Chartist movement (Great Britain) 26, 28, 30
Chatham Docks 26
Chavez, Cesar 69, 155
Chez Panisse (Berkeley) 172
Chicago School of Economics 18
children's activities 97, 110, 119, 151, 189; *see also* Kiddie Korral
Children's Community Center Co-operative Nursery (Berkeley) 124
Chile: military dictatorship 176, 201, 204
Chinese Americans: Berkeley 77
Christian Socialist 7
Christianity: co-operative expansion 16, 37, 43–44, 65, 76, 83; *see also* Catholic Church; Methodism; Quakers; Protestant Church; religion
civil rights 71, 124, 131, 138, 140, 155, 157
Claremont (California) 78, 190
Coady, Moses 44
coalmining 13, 34, 50, 60, 62
Cobden, Alfred 39
cocoa 34
Codornices Village (Berkeley) 81, 106
Cody's bookshop (Berkeley) 139
coffee 33, 91–92, 95, 117, 189
Cold War 46–47, 50, 105
Cohelan, Jeffrey 108, 141
Coles, Jessie 143
Colgate-Palmolive 79, 122, 154, 201
collectivism 12
College of California 77
Collins, Larry 94
colonialism 35–36, 39
Commercial Services Systems 157

Committee for a San Francisco Co-operative 178
Common Warehouse (San Francisco) 217
Communism 18, 40, 47, 64, 68, 72, 105, 107–108, 142, 153, 226
community, significance of 1, 16–17, 20
Community Memory Project (CMP) 200, 209–210, 220, 231
commuting to work 78, 98
company stores 16, 38, 51, 59
company unions 63
competition: between co-operatives 5, 7, 126–127; chain and 'dime' stores 42, 47, 49–50, 68, 70, 85, 148; impact on dividends 9, 47; from non-co-operative businesses 3–4, 9–14, 17, 20, 32–34, 37–38, 42, 44, 46–47, 49–51, 58, 61, 66, 68, 70, 72, 83, 85, 90–91, 94, 99, 115, 124, 127, 148–149, 157, 160, 164, 176, 180, 186, 194, 205, 208, 211, 217, 220, 227–229
compulsory co-operative membership 42
computer technology 9, 145, 161, 201, 210, 217; *see also* Community Memory Project; Electronic Data Processing; internet; price scanning
Concerned Co-op Employees (CCB) 188
Concerned Co-op Members (CCB) 188
Concerned Employees Coordinating Group (CCB) 204
Conference on World Disarmament and Economic Development (UCB, 1956) 125
Congregationalist 77
Congress (CCB) 119, 121, 151–152, 156, 228
Congress of Center Councils (Berkeley - CCC) 152
Congress of Industrial Organizations (CIO) 70, 124
Congress of Racial Equality (CORE) 124, 157
conservative co-operatives 38
consumer activism 105, 118, 131, 137, 153–154, 171, 183, 191, 193–194, 203, 210, 220, 230
Consumer and Information Protection Committee (Berkeley, CIPC) 118, 154
consumer communes 42
Consumer Co-operatives Managers' Association (US) 69
Consumer Employee Co-operative (Berkeley, CCE) 214
consumer co-operatives: Africa 39; Asia 36, 48; collapse of 9, 11, 17, 28, 45, 50, 57–60, 63–64, 70–72, 82, 230; definition 4–5; as distribution centers for rationed food 40–41, 43, 67; formation of 2, 6–7, 14–18; overview 2–20; pre-industrial co-operatives 26–28; *see also* credit to members; employees of co-operatives; *individual co-operatives and countries*; Rochdale consumer co-operative model; wholesale consumer co-operatives
Consumer Education Fund (BAND) 219
Consumer Federation of America (CFA) 154
Consumer Protection Committee (Berkeley, CPC) 183–184
consumer sovereignty 13, 20, 34, 51, 213, 220, 226, 228–229
Consumer Trade Association (US) 176
Consumers Advisory Board 65
Consumers Co-op Stations (Oakland) 97
Consumers Co-operative Association (CCA) 65, 67, 95
Consumers Co-operative of Berkeley (CCB): community relations 94, 124–125, 158–160, 189–190, 192, 214, 216; conclusions 226–231; employees 93, 122–124, 154, 156–158, 186–189, 211, 216; formation 86–87; origins 82–86; management 87–91, 109–115, 141–150, 173–180, 202–206, 209–210, 215; membership 91–93, 115–122, 150–154, 179–186, 206–209, 215; relationship with co-operative movement 96–98, 128–131, 161–164, 191–193, 219; relationship with labor unions 93–94, 122–125, 154–156, 186–187, 192, 214–215; relationship with wholesalers 94–96, 125–128, 160–161, 189–192, 216–218; *see also* Board of Directors; Center Councils; Congress; consumer activism;

individual centers; *individual center councils*; Parliament; volunteer labor
Consumers Co-operative of Monterey Bay (CCMB) 192
Consumers Group Legal Service (Berkeley) 150
Consumers League for Lower Prices (Berkeley) 159
Continental Breads (US) 175–176
cookbooks 118, 137, 153, 164, 230
Co-op Center Federal Credit Union (CCFCU) 88–89, 110, 112, 114, 116, 124, 129, 145, 186–187, 219, 226
Co-op Employees United (CCB) 213
Co-op Harvest Fair (Berkeley, 1985) 219
Co-op News (Berkeley, CN) 92, 93, 116, 118, 122, 124, 131, 144, 152–153, 155, 159, 163, 175–176, 182, 184, 189, 203, 216, 218–219, 230
Co-op News (MidWest) 141
Co-op Travel 112
Cooper, William 32
Cooperativa Obrera Limitada (CO, Argentina) 44
Co-operative Central Exchange (CCE) 61, 64
co-operative coal mines 34
Co-operative Commonwealth 38, 51
Co-operative Congresses 28, 31
Co-operative Consumer 62
co-operative education *see* education
Co-operative Enterprises (Ohio) 110, 128, 147
Co-operative Federation of America 69
Co-operative for American Remittances to Europe (subsequently the E stood for Everywhere, CARE) 67, 193
Co-operative Household Associations (Japan) 43
Co-operative Independent Commission (Great Britain) 14
Co-operative Insurance Society (Great Britain) 35
Co-operative League of the United States of America (CLUSA) 56, 62–64, 66–72, 82, 94–95, 116, 118, 128–129, 144, 147, 153, 162–163, 165, 219
Co-operative News (Great Britain) 35
Co-operative Party (Great Britain) 3, 16, 41, 163
Co-operative Service (League of Nations) 45
Co-operative Union (Great Britain, CU) 35, 51
Co-operative Union of America 60
Co-operative Union of Canada 38–39
Co-operative Union Store (San Francisco) 60
Co-operative Wholesale Association of Southern California 82
Co-operative Wholesale Society (Great Britain, CWS): banking and insurance 34–35; depots outside Britain 33; farming 34, 41; formation of 5, 32–33; growth 33; international trade relationships 33–34; labeling 5; labor unions 13; mergers 47; production of basic products 17, 34; in South Africa 39; tourism 34; and the US 59, 163
Co-operator, The 27, 29
Coors 208
Corbett, John 216
corruption 17–18, 48
Corte Madera (California) 146, 179–180; *see also* Marin County; Savories
Cost-Plus (AC) 126, 161, 190
cotton 26, 29
Council of Federated Organizations (Mississippi) 157
Council for Advancement of Secondary Education (US) 68
counterculture 15, 71, 139
Cramlington, Newcastle, Great Britain 32
Crawford, Matt 124
credit to members: Australia 13, 50; Canada 13; cash trading principle 2–3, 17; coalmining 13; early origins of co-operative movements 29, 31; Great Britain 13, 17; New Zealand 50; and tokens 11; US 59, 62–63; *see also* credit cards; hire purchase
credit cards 149–150, 165, 179
credit unions 10; Argentina 44; Canada 16; and CLUSA 69; Palestine 15; US 65, 69, 88–89, 97, 131, 162

Creedence Clearwater Revival (band) 172
Cross, Laurance 108
Crumpsall (Great Britain) 34
culture, co-operative 17, 35, 115, 230; *see also* ideology, co-operative
Cutter Laboratories (Berkeley) 107–108
Czechoslovakia: consumer co-operatives 42–43

dairy co-operatives 5; *see also* co-operative
dairy farmers 185
David Dale 26
Danish Americans: Berkeley 77
Davies, Margaret Llewellyn 7
Davis (California) 191, 209
Davis, Adelle 118
Davis, Charles 117–118
debating fora 35
DeBerry, Frank 213
decentralized structures 84, 160, 194
decline of consumer co-operatives, theories of 17–19
Deferred Savings Program (CCB) 123, 211
definition of a co-operative 1–4
Dellums, Ron 141
democratic principles 2, 19–20, 46, 175, 186, 226
Democrats (US) 70–72, 79, 82, 97, 108–109, 137, 139–142, 153, 172, 185
demographics 17, 29, 77–79, 81, 105–106, 108, 137, 159, 171, 173, 200, 220
demutualization 18, 219
Denmark: consumer co-operatives 37, 42–43, 193; and the CWS 33; and the ICA 40; wholesale co-operatives 37, 41
depots 33, 46, 83, 93, 180
deregulation 18, 46, 49
desegregation of schools (Berkeley) 140
discount pricing 4, 148, 150, 164, 229
distribution systems 218
distributive co-operatives 59–60, 63, 67
dividends (the 'divi') 2, 4, 7–11, 32, 34, 83, 85, 90–91, 116, 194; drops in 9; early origins of co-operative movements 28; postwar period 9, 47; principle of 2, 45; and recruitment of new members 9; Rochdale movement 4; tokens 11; worker co-operatives 2; *see also* patronage refunds
dockyard workers 26
Dos Palos Rochdale Co. (California) 59
Dorst, Ann 110, 120
Dow Chemical 156
Draper, Phil 172
Driver Superstore (Griffith, Australia) 18
Dryer, Stanley 162–163
dried fruit 34
Duga, Larry 175, 186, 189
Durant, Henry 77
Duttweiler, Gottleib 7

early origins of consumer co-operative movement 25–31
East Bay Committee against Fluoridation Committee Inc. 154
East Bay Food Dealers Association 125
East Bay Memorial Association 142
East Oakland 83, 176, 191
ecological issues 48
economic rationalism 46
economies of scale 11, 17, 20, 160, 177, 194, 227, 230
Economist, The 27
Edelen, Marcia 213
education (co-operative) 11, 35, 38, 60, 62–65, 68–9, 71, 84–85, 87, 92–93, 95–97, 105, 115, 117–118, 122–123, 126, 128, 131, 138, 143, 149, 152–154, 159, 161–162, 165, 176, 181–183, 187, 189, 194, 208–209, 216, 219–220, 229–230; principle of 3
education assistants (CCB) 118, 153, 182, 187, 189
Education Committee (CCB) 85, 92, 122, 153, 203, 208
Egypt: co-operatives 130
El Cerritto, California 111, 121, 145, 149, 151, 159, 161, 180, 202, 206–207, 217
El Cerritto-Richmond Housewives League for Lower Prices 159
El Hogar Obrero (Argentina, EHO) 39, 44, 49

electoral franchise 26
electricity co-operatives 65
electricity prices 154, 210
Electronic Data Processing (EDP) 116, 145, 160–161, 216; *see also* price scanning
Elmwood, CA 78, 139
Emergency Food Project 189
Employee Stock Ownership Plans (ESOP) 213–214
Employee Advisory Council (CCB) 188–189, 212
employees of co-operatives 1, 12–13, 20, 28, 69, 76, 81, 85, 88, 90, 93–94, 98, 115, 117, 120, 122–124, 127, 129, 131, 144, 147, 149, 154, 156–158, 160, 165, 175, 178, 186–189, 191–192, 200, 204–205, 208, 211–217, 219–220, 227–230
End Poverty in California Campaign (EPIC) 76, 82–83, 98, 227
enfranchisement 26
environmental movement 5, 20, 47, 49, 56, 71, 171, 183, 216
equality, values of 1, 40, 56–58, 86
Eroski (Spain) 5
Europe *see individual countries*
Exeter, Great Britain 27
exhibitions 151
expansion of co-operatives 7, 9–10, 21, 25, 31, 34–35, 39, 40–42, 45, 48–49, 51, 60, 66, 68–69, 72, 86, 88, 95–96, 105–107, 109–112, 114–115, 117–119, 121–22, 127–128, 131, 137, 141–142, 145, 147–149, 151, 164, 171, 176–179, 191, 194, 217, 227–228, 230

Facebook 231
factions (CCB) 110, 131, 137, 141–143, 149, 151–152, 158, 160, 164, 171, 174, 176, 182, 186, 188, 194, 203, 208, 220, 228
fair wages 13
Fair Housing Ordinance (Berkeley) 144
Fair Packaging and Labeling Act (US, 1966) 154
Fair Play Committee (Berkeley) 81
Fair Trade 47
fair trade legislation 115
Fantasy Records (West Berkeley) 172
Farm Bureau 210
farmer co-operatives *see* agricultural co-operatives
Farmer-Labor Conference 62
Farmers' Co-operative Company, Michigan 61
farming *see* agricultural co-operatives; Co-operative Wholesale Society (Great Britain)
Farris, Tom 143
Fascism 18, 40–41, 45
Federal Council of Churches (US) 83
feminism 118, 158
FBI 138, 172
Fed Up Co-op Wholesale (Canada) 49
Federal Home Loan Bank of San Francisco 129
Federación Argentina de Cooperativas de Consumo (Argentina) 44
federalist principle co-operatives 34
Federated Co-operatives Limited (Canada, FCL) 49
federations of co-operatives 7, 33, 37, 44, 50, 60, 65, 193
Finance Committee (CCB) 109, 113, 119, 193
financial co-operatives: Germany 37
Finland 36, 81, 116; consumer co-operatives 38, 41–42, 51; co-operatives 3, 130
Finnish Americans: Berkeley 81–82, 171, 227; co-operatives 15, 61–2, 64, 66, 72, 76, 82, 85–86, 91, 115–116, 121–22, 151, 164, 171; politics 61, 72, 82, 227; religion 82, 227
Finnish Brotherhood Hall (Berkeley) 82, 115, 120
First World War 10, 40–41, 43–44, 62–63
Fish, Bonnie 179
fishing co-operatives: and the ICA 50
fixed and limited interest on capital 2, 31
Flatlands Neighborhood Committee (Berkeley) 189
Florida Orange 184
flour and bread societies 26
fluoridation 154, 183
Flynn, Thomas 109
Fogerty, Robert 88, 92
Fonda, Jane 139
food additives 12, 154, 230
Food Control Committees (Great Britain) 41
food co-operatives 50–1, 230; *see also* agricultural co-operatives; consumer co-operatives

food prices 2, 4, 8, 11–13, 15–16, 25–26, 28–29, 32–33, 35, 41–44, 46, 48, 51, 61–62, 66, 68–69, 81, 83, 85, 88, 90–91, 94, 114–115, 121, 124, 126–128, 148–151, 153, 158–161, 164–166, 175, 178, 180–181, 183–5, 202, 205–207, 216–218, 227, 229–230
food riots 26
food stamps 149, 154, 186, 192
Ford, Gerald President 188
Fort Bragg Co-operative, California 82, 85–86, 94, 127, 190
Foster, Marcus 172
Foster Farms 183
fragmentation of the co-operative movement 47
France: 1968 student revolt 139; colonies 39; consumer co-operatives 37–38, 40, 42–43, 47, 50–1, 68, 71; Co-operative Bank 42; Co-operative legislation 38; education 38; food co-operatives 47, 51, 71; hybrid co-operatives 5; opposition to co-operatives 38; Rochdale model 37, 40; socialism 38, 51; wholesale consumer co-operatives 37
franchising 50, 127
Frank, Dana 63
Franklin, New York 57
Free Speech Movement (FSM) 138, 142, 172
Frentz, Anne 158
friendly societies 26, 30
Friendly Society legislation 28
Fukuda, Shigeru 129
Fuller, Earle 143
Fund for International Co-operative Development (FICD) 129, 162–163
fundamental principles co-operatives 2–4
Future Plans Committee (CCB) 110–111, 129, 178

Gallagher, D.G. 12, 228
Gallant, Allan 204–205, 209, 214–215
gas stations 86, 88, 97, 110, 112, 115, 124, 145, 180, 187, 194
gasoline 67, 81, 89–91, 95
gay rights 184
German Central Union 18
German Labor Front 43
Germany 36, 39; co-operatives 18, 130, 193; consumer co-operatives 31, 37, 40, 42–43, 46; co-operative legislation 38, 40; and the CWS 33; fascism and co-operatives 18, 43; financial co-operatives 37; and the ICA 18, 40, 45, 50; wholesale consumer co-operatives 37
Gibson, D.G. 108
Gide, Charles 38
globalization 201
Gold 'N Rich Dairy Corporation (Berkeley) 128, 147
Google 231
Gordon, Margaret 174, 203, 205, 212, 216
Gordon, Robert 109–110, 131, 156, 174
Gourmet Ghetto (North Berkeley) 172, 205
government funding 71, 77, 154, 162–3, 214, 219
government loans/subsidies 40, 106, 112
grain elevators 1, 59
Grange Movement 59
grapes 69, 137, 155, 211
Grass Valley (California) 191
Great Britain: building societies 35; colonies 39; consumer co-operatives 3, 7–9, 11, 13–14, 16, 31–35, 37–8, 40–43, 47–48, 51, 68, 130, 163, 226; co-operative banking 34–35; dominance of the ICA 40, 45; early origins of co-operative movements 15, 25–31, 51, 226; education 38; legislation 10; Ministry of Health 153; producer co-operatives 35; spread of co-operative ideas 15, 37–39, 119; wholesale consumer co-operatives 5, 32, 47, 51; *see also* Co-operative Wholesale Society (Great Britain); Rochdale consumer co-operative model; Scottish Co-operative Wholesale Society (Great Britain)
Great Depression 15, 25, 40–42, 44, 65, 82, 227
Greek Theatre (UCB) 79, 107
Greve, Florence 189
Grevious, Herbert 176, 202, 204
Greece: and the CWS 34
Greenbelt Co-operative (Maryland) 70, 72, 119, 176, 204
Greene, Lorne 153

GreenStar Co-operative (Ithaca, New York) 71
Griffith consumer co-operative (Australia) 17–18
Gullberg, Mary 118, 124, 154, 164, 208–209
Gurney, Peter 5
Guy, Fred 203

Hagelberg, Ed 110
Haldeen, Alfred 183
Han system 48
Hancock, Loni 201, 214
Hansalim Community Consumer Co-operative (South Korea) 49
hardware 89, 91, 109–110, 115, 120, 124, 128, 146, 179–180
Harlem River Consumer Co-operative (New York, HRRC) 70
Hayakawa, Margedant 141–143, 149
Hayakawa, Samuel US Senator 141, 193
Hayden, Tom 139
Hayward (California) 112
Haynes, Edna 175, 181
Headstart Food Co-operative (New York) 69
health co-operatives 97, 116; *see also* medical co-operatives
health insurance 97
Hearst, Patricia 172
Hearst, Phoebe 78
Heartwood Co-operative (Berkeley) 219
Hill, Lewis 108
Hillberg, Don 88, 91
Hilltop Plaza (Richmond, California) 201
Hinks Department Store (Berkeley) 201
hippies 139
hire purchase 63
Hispanic Americans 187, 200
Holmgren, Virginia 87
Holyoake, George 32, 37, 39, 58
Holyoake House (Manchester, Great Britain) 35–36
home delivery 48–49, 83, 88–90, 93, 110, 216
home economists 105, 118, 124, 131, 147, 153–154, 164, 181–184, 208–209, 217, 219–220, 230
homeless 139; *see also* panhandlers; street people
Hoover, J. Edgar 138
House Un-American Activities Committee (US) 138
housewives 48–49, 109, 118, 159
housing 82, 177; Berkeley 79–81, 106–107, 119, 138, 140, 144, 171, 173, 174, 192, 200; consumer co-operatives 4, 29
housing co-operatives 39, 79, 159, 192; and CLUSA 69; and the ICA 50; Palestine 15
housing finance 105–106
Huichin Indians (Berkeley) 76
Hull Anti-Mill 26
Hungary: consumer co-operatives 42
hybrid co-operatives 4, 19, 200, 214–215, 220, 229
Hyde Park Co-operative (Chicago) 141
hyperinflation 42, 49
hypermarkets 11

IBM 160
Iceland: co-operative wholesaling 41
ideological challenges 18, 20
ideology, co-operative 8, 12, 14, 17, 35; *see also* culture, co-operative
Illinois State Federation of Labor 70
immigration 15, 20, 35–36, 38–39, 59, 61, 64, 71, 77, 81–82
income, low *see* poverty alleviation, as goal
Independent Grocers' Association (US) 96
India 151; co-operatives 130; and the ICA 40, 45, 50; village co-operatives 16
Indians (North American) *see* Huichin Indians
Industrial and Provident Societies Act (Great Britain, IAPSA) of 1852 10, 32–33
industrial revolution 15, 25, 51, 226
Industrial Workers of the World (IWW) 82, 86
inflation 15, 41, 46, 48–49, 68, 70, 171, 183–184
insurance, co-operative/mutual 4; Great Britain 34–35, 51; US 59, 96, 127, 163
Institute of Industrial Relations (University of California, Berkeley, IIR) 156, 174, 212

International Co-operative Alliance (ICA): 1895 London Congress 40, 60; 1927 Stockholm Congress 45; 1937 Paris Congress 45; 1965 Switzerland Congress 164; and the Cold War 47, 50; and CLUSA 62; Co-operative Union of America 60; development fund 50; and fascist Germany 18, 45; formation of 25, 40, 51; governance 40, 45, 50–51; and the ILO 45; and fascist Italy 45; membership 45; Relief Fund 50; and the Rochdale principles 3, 19, 45, 179; and the USSR 45
International Co-operative Day 45
International Co-operative Women's Guild 45
International House (UCB) 79
International Labour Organization (ILO) 45, 51
International Longshore and Warehouse Union (US, ILWU) 122
internet: platform co-operatives 209, 230
investor-owned business (IOB) 1–2, 12, 18–19, 226–228, 231
Iraq: co-operatives 163
Ireland: building societies 35; and the CWS 33–34; early origins of co-operative movements 28; producer co-operatives 35
Irish Americans: Berkeley 77
irradiation of food 120, 210, 220
irrigation co-operatives: Palestine 15
Isaac, Warner 216
Italy 36; agricultural co-operatives 16; consumer co-operatives 11–12, 41, 48, 51, 226; co-operative legislation 15; fascism and co-operatives 41, 45; federations of co-operatives 37; financial co-operatives 15; and the ICA 40, 50; influence of Rochdale movement 32, 37; organization along religious/political lines 3–4
Ithaca Consumer Co-operative Society (New York, ICCS) 68, 70–71
Ithaca Real Food Co-operative (New York, IRFC) 70–71

J.C. Penny 162
Jacobs, James 77
Jaffe, Celia 189
jam 34
Japan 151; colonies 36; consumer co-operatives 39–40, 43–44, 48–49, 51, 164, 226; co-operative influence 16, 44, 65, 76, 83, 92, 129, 219; co-operative legislation 40, 48–49; co-operatives 40, 43, 193, 219; and the ICA 45
Japanese Americans: Berkeley 81, 93, 98, 151, 228; co-operatives 67, 95; US Second World War internment 67, 81, 93, 95
Japanese Consumers' Co-operative Union (JCCU) 129–130, 219–220
Jewell (US) 184
Jewish co-operatives in Palestine 15
JF Kennedy School (Oakland) 159
Johnson, Lawrence 216, 218
Johnson, Lyndon B. President 141
Johnson, Wallace 140
joint buying organizations 48; *see also* buying clubs and buying groups
Justo, Juan B. 39

Kagawa, Toyohiko 16, 43–44, 65, 76, 83, 92, 97–98, 129, 227
Kahn, Alice 200
Kallinen, Yrjö 116
Kamil, Adolph 112, 183, 213
Katei Kobe Co-operative (Japan) 43
Kaulback, John 58
Kaufman's Drapery Store (Berkeley) 125
Keen, George 38
Keeler, Charles 79
Kelly, Kathie 187
Kerr, Catherine 140
Kerr, Clark 85, 137–138, 140
Key System (California) 78
Keynesian economics 46
Khrushchev, Nikita 142
Kiddie Korral 110, 112, 118, 147–48, 156, 164, 174, 179, 194, 207–208, 220, 229–230
King, William 25–27, 29, 58
Knight, Galdieux and Smith 175, 177
Knights of Labor 59
Knights of St Crispin 59
Kobe Co-op (Japan) 43
Kooperativa förbundet (Sweden, KF) 10–12, 70, 164
Korby, Herman 85–86, 94
KPFA (Berkeley) 108, 143
KQED (San Francisco) 159, 190

Kresy, Jerry 186
Kroger (US) 184
Kruger, Karl 204

labeling standards 12, 137, 153–154, 184–5, 210, 230
Labor Bank (Belgium) 42
Labor Co-operative Co-ordination Committee (CCB) 154
labor exchanges 59
labor movement 12, 16, 20, 56, 65, 72, 220
labor notes 58
labor organizations 31, 59, 216; *see also* labor unions
labor relations 1, 12, 20, 122, 184, 192
labor unions 13; Great Britain 13, 28–29, 31; US 93, 99, 108, 122, 124, 131, 137, 154–157, 165, 194, 200, 211–213, 226, 228–229; *see also individual labor unions*
laboratory testing of products 85, 120, 184, 206
Labour Party (Great Britain) 3, 16
land purchases 27, 29, 41
Latin American Americans 157
Lawrence, Ernst 81
Lawrence Laboratory (Berkeley) 81
League of Nations 45
League of Women Voters 210
Leavitt, George 121
Lee, Homer 111
Lee. Robert 109, 115, 141, 144
legislation about co-operatives: Argentina 44; France 38, 40; Germany 38, 40, 43; Great Britain 28–29, 32; Italy 15; Japan 40; US 82, 211
Lehtin, Laurie 116
Leicester, Great Britain 34
Leo XII, Pope 16
Leopold's Records (Berkeley) 210
Lescke, Hans 143
Levering Act (California) 107
levies 3
Levitt, Leonard 176, 182, 189
Liberated Women of Berkeley 139
life cycle theory of co-operatives 18–20, 226
limited interest on capital principle 2, 31, 45
limited liability 10, 32
Lincoln, Murray 67, 118, 128, 147
Little, George 109, 121, 141–143
Litton, Val 163, 175
living standards 27, 31
Llewellyn Davies, Margaret 25
lobbying 4, 32, 35, 71, 85, 94, 118, 152, 154, 158, 184
local communities and the survival of co-operatives 16–17, 20
local food movements 50–51
localism 16–17
London, Great Britain 27–28, 31, 35; and the CWS 33; and the ICA 40, 51
London Co-operative Society 48
Los Angeles (California) 82, 94–96, 129, 153, 191, 205, 210
loyalty oath (UCB) 107, 124
Lucky 148, 157, 160, 171, 185–186, 189, 206, 210
Lundin, Jane 175, 186
Luton, Great Britain 34

Macleay Co-operative, New South Wales (NSW) Australia 5
MacDonald, Lynn 204, 206, 209, 212, 217
Macy's (US) 201
Madera (California) 125
Malaysia: co-operatives 130
Management Committee (CCB) 87, 110, 124, 152
management of co-operatives: Australia 17–18; consumer co-operatives 1, 4, 9–10, 12–14; co-operatives versus IOBs 19–20; corruption 17–18, 28; Great Britain 5, 14; growth 11; Italy 11, 41; Japan 48; management commitment 14; management training 14, 64, 69, 191; professionalization 165, 228; Rochdale model 2; US 61–62, 69, 72, 165, 228; *see also individual co-operatives*
Manawatu Co-operative (NZ) 50
Manzanar War Relocation Camp (California) 67
Manchester, Great Britain 28–30, 32–36
Manchester Co-operative Congresses/ Conferences 28, 32–33
Mannila, Eugene 21, 86, 90–91, 109–110, 115–116, 123, 125, 128,

131, 141, 143–144, 151, 153, 155, 164, 171, 175–176, 194, 228
Mannila, Sylvia 90
March, Robert (Bob) 87–89, 93, 98, 115, 123, 215
Marin County (California) 21, 112, 121, 131, 137, 141, 145–146, 148–150, 164, 171, 179–180, 182, 186, 200, 202, 206, 227; *see also* Corte Madera; Savories
Marin Buying Group 146
Marin Ecology Center 186
marketing 1, 11–12, 183, 209–210; *see also* advertising
marketing co-operatives 128
Martin Luther King Jnr. Park (Berkeley) 219
Marxism 38, 79
Maybeck, Bernard 79
Mayfair Stores 21, 171, 175–179, 181, 227
Mazzini, Giuseppe 37
McCarthy, Joseph Senator 107
McGovern, George Senator 172
medical co-operatives 69; *see also* health co-operatives
Melbin, Carroll E. 86, 186
Member Action Committee (CCB) 142
member-owned businesses (MOBs): definition 1
Membership Committees (CCB) 109–110, 115–118, 120, 128, 161
membership numbers 92, 116, 126, 145, 150, 152, 161, 181, 191, 207, 230
mergers 11, 21, 48–49, 70, 76, 91, 99, 115, 127–128, 162–163, 214
Methodism 29, 83, 97, 125
Mid-Eastern Co-operatives (US) 70
middle classes 37, 40, 57, 78, 106, 159, 172, 200
"middle way," co-operatives as 38, 65
Migros, Switzerland 7
milk 3–4, 11, 42, 93, 118, 120, 128, 184–185; *see also* co-operative; dairy co-operatives
Miller, Bruce 203
Miller, Maudelle 143
Miller, Merlin 97
mills 26–27, 29, 31, 57, 77
mining 13, 17, 34, 38–39, 50, 61, 70, 78
"missionaries," co-operative 32
Mitchell, John 33–34
Mitford, Jessica 142
Modesto (California) 126
Mohr, Lotte 89
Mondragon (Spain) 16
monopolies 61, 183–4
Monterey, California 76, 179, 192
Monterey Market (Berkeley) 205, 229
Moore, Sarah Jane 188
Moquette, Elaine 209
Mormons 83
Morrill Land College Act (US) 77
mutualism 15, 25
mutualization 6, 179
Mutual Service Insurance Companies of St. Paul (MSI) 112, 127, 145, 160, 163, 173, 194, 205, 220
mutuals 112, 163

Nada Co-operative (Japan) 43
Nadakobe Consumers Co-operative (Japan) 164, 219
Nader, Ralph 154, 184, 193, 230
Nash, George 88
Nashoba, Tennessee 57
National Consumer Co-operative Bank (NCCB) 71–72, 174, 191, 193–4, 205–206, 211, 214, 219–220, 230
National Co-operative Business Association (NCBA) 71
National Co-operative Grocers' Association (NCGA) 71, 226
National Co-operative Manifesto (US, 1919) 62
National Co-operative Wholesale Association (US) 62–63
National Co-operatives Inc. (US, NC) 56, 64–65, 67, 79, 95, 184
National Industrial Recovery Act (NIRA) 83
National Labor Relations Board 187
National Negro Congress 124
National Refinery Company (US) 67
National Tax Equality Association (NTEA) 68, 70, 72, 128
National Union and Distributive and Allied Workers (Great Britain) 13
Nationwide Insurance Group (US) 67
natural foods (CCB) 147, 179–180, 183, 189, 202, 205–206, 208, 220
Nazis 43

Neighborhood Co-operative (San Francisco) 161–162, 164, 178, 227
neighborhood groups (CCB) 92, 117
Nelson, Arvid 91, 111
Nelson, Helen 131, 174, 212–213
Nelson, Mary 184
neoliberalism 46
Neptune, Robert (Bob) 83–84, 87–88, 90, 93–95, 99, 110, 126–127, 160–161, 176, 179, 188, 204, 216
Nestlé 210
Netherlands: co-operatives 43
New Australia (Paraguay) 15
New Co-op Organizing Group (Berkeley, NCOG) 215
New Day Co-operative (Oakland, California) 82
New Deal 65, 79, 108
New Economic Policy (USSR, 1923) 42
New England Association of Mechanics (US) 58
New England Protective Union (US) 58
New Harmony community (Indiana) 15, 57–58
New Lanark mills (Great Britain) 27
New Left 139
New Pioneer Food Co-operative (Iowa) 71
New South Wales (NSW, Australia) 5, 39, 44–45
New South Wales Co-operative Wholesale Society (NSWCWS, Australia) 39, 45, 50
New York Community Training Institute 69
New York Times 230
New York Tribune 58
New Zealand (NZ) 15, 44; co-operatives 163; consumer co-operatives 39, 44–45, 50, 68; co-operative wholesaling 45
Newcastle and Suburban Co-operative (Australia) 50
Newport, Gus 201
newspapers 11–12, 39, 60, 67, 141, 148
Newton Huey P. 139
Nichols, Roy 109
Niven, John 179
Nixon, Richard President 69, 154
Nobel Prizes 81, 120
Nominating Committee (CCB) 87, 123, 142
non-co-operative subsidiaries 61, 217
Nordisk Andelsforbund (NAF) 41, 164
NORCO (Australia) 102
Nordstrom (US) 201
North Berkeley 76, 78, 140, 172, 192, 205
North Coast Co-operative (NCC, Arcata, California) 191, 204, 212–213, 216
North Oakland 152, 177–178, 190, 202, 216
North Oakland Center Council (NOCC) 178, 190, 216
Northern California Co-operative Council (NCCC) 96
Northern California Supermarkets (NCS) 179, 192
Northern Californian Co-operator 114
Northern States Co-operative Women's Guild (US) 66
Norway: co-operative wholesaling 41
nuclear issues 120, 159, 204
Nuriootpa Co-operative, Barossa Valley of South Australia (SA) 6
Nut Hill (Berkeley) 79
nutrition 12, 105, 118, 153–4, 184–185, 203, 209–210, 230

Oakland, California 21, 61, 77–78, 82–84, 87, 95, 97–98, 105, 111, 121, 137, 139, 149, 159, 171–172, 176–180, 194, 200, 227; *see also* East Oakland; North Oakland; West Oakland
Oakland Symphony Orchestra 159
Oakland Unit (PCS) 84, 87, 97–98
Office and Professional Employees Union (US, OPEU) 186–187
Ohio Farm Bureau Co-operatives 118
Oldham Co-operative Supply Company (Great Britain) 26
oil 46, 67
Olson, Culbert Governor 97
One Flew Over the Cuckoo's Nest (film) 172
one member one vote 2, 19, 30, 85
open membership principle 2, 45
Oppenheimer, Robert 79, 81, 107
opposition to co-operatives 5, 38, 41–42, 51, 72; *see also* National Tax Equality Association
Orbison, Great Britain 27
organic co-operatives 47, 49

organic food 12, 20, 47, 49–50, 71, 129, 137, 147–148, 230
Organic Foods Co-op (OFC, Berkeley) 129, 147–148
overseas development aid, co-operatives 130, 164, 193; *see also* Co-operative for American Remittances to Europe
Overton L. Joseph 69
Owen, Robert 15, 25, 27–32, 56–58
Owen, Robert Dale 57–8

Pacific Coast Co-operative Union (Oakland) 61
Pacific Co-operative (Berkeley) 215
Pacific Co-operative League (PCL) 61, 63–64, 82
Pacific Co-operative Services (PCS) 83–87, 90, 93–94, 96–97
Pacific Gas and Electricity (PG&E) 154, 210
Pacific League Co-operative Stores (PLCS) 63
Pacific Islander American 200
Paddock co-operative society, West Yorkshire, Great Britain 28
Padi, Paul 116
Palestine: co-operatives 15; and the ICA 45
Palo Alto Co-operative (California, PAC) 95–96, 113, 125–129, 153, 159–160, 162–163, 179, 185, 211, 216, 218–219
panhandlers 189
Paraguay 15
parastatal co-operatives 46
Parliament (CCB) 119–121, 123, 125, 131, 164, 227–228
Parti Ouvrier (Belgium, France, PO) 38
patronage refunds 83, 91, 111–114, 116, 125, 127, 142, 150, 173, 180–181, 192, 202, 207, 229; *see also* dividends
Patrons of Husbandry 59
Peddie, James 163
People's Park (Berkeley) 137–139
Peralta, Domingo 77
Peralta, Don Luis 76–77
Personnel Committee (CCB) 123, 131, 156, 211–212, 227
PG&E *see* Pacific Gas and Electricity
pharmacy services 68, 112, 145–146, 183
Philadelphia Industrial Co-operative Society 60
philanthropy 64
Phillips, Thomas 60
Pine Knotts (Camp Sierra) 97
platform co-operatives 200, 220, 230–231; *see also* Community Memory Project
Plymouth Co-operative Society (Great Britain) 13
Poland: consumer co-operatives 42–43
police (Berkeley) 138–139, 172–173, 189
political neutrality, principle of 3–4, 21, 38, 41, 50, 64, 69, 72, 91, 120, 125, 142–144, 153, 163, 226
Port Chicago Vigil Group 159
Port Huntley Co-operative 98
postage systems 32
postwar reconstruction 67
Potter, Beatrice *see* Webb, Beatrice
poverty alleviation, as goal 1–2, 7–8, 16, 69, 147, 149, 161–163, 176, 178, 189, 191, 194, 216, 227
Presbyterian 108
prices *see* food prices, electricity prices
price scanning 46, 216–217, 220
privatization 18, 46; *see also* demutualization
producer co-operatives: and the CWS 34, 51; Great Britain 35; *see also* worker co-operatives
profit 1, 3, 9, 15, 17, 28, 34, 65, 91, 96, 164, 184, 202, 206, 215; *see also* surplus
profiteering 16, 41, 43, 62, 94
Proffitt, Russell (Rusty) 97
Promoters of Active Co-operatism (Berkeley, PACT) 174
proportional representation 41
Protestant Church: expansion of co-operatives 16
protests 56, 81, 107, 120, 125, 137–139, 144, 157–160, 174, 178, 184–185, 204, 208, 219
publishing 60, 97; *see also individual publications*

Quakers 56, 139
quality circles 213
quality standards 2, 4, 8, 13, 19, 25–26, 29, 34, 48, 51, 65–66, 85,

87, 90, 93, 105, 118, 121, 161, 202, 205–207, 217–218, 220, 227, 229–230

race 80, 86, 93, 106, 120, 138, 140, 158–159, 163, 192
Racine Consumers' Co-operative (Wisconsin) 66
railway workers 62
railways expansion 35, 59, 77
Rainbow Flag 45
Rational Sick and Burial Society (Great Britain) 30
rationing 41, 43, 64, 67, 81, 89–91, 95, 105
Rautenberg, Irv 152
reading rooms 17, 35
Reagan, Ronald: as Governor of California 131, 137–139, 144; as President 71, 159, 206
recessions 46, 63
recreational activities 17, 123, 140; *see also* social programs
recycling 12, 154–155, 184, 190–191, 210, 220, 230
Red Family commune (Elmwood) 139
refineries 67
regional associations 64, 66, 71
REI (US) 226
religion: discrimination 158; division of co-operative movement 3–4; early origins of co-operative movements 27, 56; and the expansion of co-operation 15–16, 96, 227; principle of religious neutrality 3, 91; Rochdale pioneers 29; *see also* Catholic Church; Christianity; Congregationalists; Methodism; Mormons; Presbyterian; Protestant Church; Quakers
Reidenbach, Nan 153
Republicans (US) 70, 72, 79, 82, 98, 108, 131, 139–141, 193
Rerum Novarum (Poe Leo XIII) 16
Reserve Officers' Training Corps (UC) 138
Retail Clerks International Association (US, RCIA) 93–94, 122, 210, 214
retail consumer co-operatives: after Second World War 50; labour movement support 16; overview 4–5; *see also individual countries and co-operatives*
Retail, Wholesale and Chain Store Food Employees Union (US) 69
Rhodes Scholar 175
Richmond, California 111, 121–122, 137, 159–161, 201, 218
Richmond Festival of the Arts 159
Richmond Produce 217
Right Relationship League (US, RLL) 61
riots 26
Ripponden Co-operative, Great Britain 31
risk 11, 20, 33, 89, 96, 178, 206, 230
Roberts, Ed 172
Robertson, Nicole 16
Robinson, Margo 203
Rochdale consumer co-operative model: Argentina 44; Australia 39, 44, 50; Canada 38–39; colonialism 36, 39; establishment of (1844) 25–26, 29–31; export of 37, 226; France 37, 40; Great Britain 7, 28, 32–33; Japan 39–40; NZ 39, 44, 50; principles of co-operatives 2–4, 12, 17, 19, 21, 32, 63–64, 85, 91, 121, 144, 150, 163–165, 209, 229; rural areas 16; US 21, 58–61, 63–66, 71, 81, 85, 91, 119, 121, 124, 144, 150, 163–165, 209, 229
Rochdale Friendly Co-operative Society (Great Britain) 29, 31
Rochdale Institute (US) 64, 81
Rochdale Pioneers 2, 29, 32, 37, 60, 65, 119
Rochdale Society of Equitable Pioneers (Great Britain) 29, 32
Rochdale Wholesale Company (San Francisco) 61
Roman Catholic Church *see* Catholic Church
Roosevelt, Franklin Delano President 65–67, 70, 81, 83, 108
Rothenberg, Don 153, 175–176, 181–182
Royal Arsenal Co-operative (Great Britain) 14
Rumford William Byron 108, 140, 144
rural areas 3, 11, 14, 16–17, 44, 47, 50, 58–59, 65, 68, 71, 125, 172
Rural Co-operative Development Grants program (US) 71

Rural Electricity Administration (US) 65
Russia: consumer co-operatives 37–38, 41; wholesale co-operatives 37; *see also* USSR
Russian Civil War 42
Russian Revolution 41

Sacramento (California) 96, 107, 152, 184
Sacramento Co-operative 96
Safeway 94, 99, 109, 148–149, 160, 162–163, 171, 176, 183, 185–186, 189, 205–206, 208, 210, 220, 227, 229–230
Salinas, California 179, 192
San Francisco, California 21, 60–61, 76, 78–79, 81, 83, 95, 98, 105–106, 111–112, 121–122, 126, 129, 137–138, 140–141, 151, 159, 161, 164, 171, 175, 178–179, 185, 188, 191, 200, 202, 217–218, 227
San Francisco Common Warehouse 217
San Francisco earthquake (1906) 78, 81
San Francisco General Strike (1934) 79
San Francisco Giants 151
San Gabriel Co-operative (California) 129
San Jose (California) 127, 204
San Jose Co-operative 127
Santa Monica Co-operative (California) 129
Santa Rosa (California) 162
Satake, Robert 145
saving and loan associations 129; *see also* Twin Pines Federal Savings and Loans
savings, co-operative 2, 9, 11, 27, 32, 40, 62, 85, 89, 123, 128, 145, 150, 161, 205, 211
Savio, Mario 138
Savo Island (Berkeley) 80
Savories (CCB) 206, 220, 227; *see also* Corte Madera; Marin County
Schildgen, Robert (Bob) 203, 216
Schweitzer, Albert 120
Sealy Mattress Company 172
Sekerak, Emil 118, 121, 128–129, 153, 160, 165, 174
Seldman, Joel 156
Scotland: consumer co-operatives 33; flour and bread societies 26; early origins of co-operative movements 26–27; spread of co-operative ideas 27, 31; wholesaling 33
Scott, Vernon 68
Scottish Co-operative Wholesale Society (Great Britain, SCWS) 5, 33, 35, 47
Searle, Bobby 106, 139
Seattle Consumers Co-operative Association 62
Second World War 5–6, 15, 25, 41, 43, 45–46, 50, 56, 67, 70–72, 76, 80–81, 86, 89, 97–98, 105, 137, 200, 227–228
self-help, values of 8
Self-Help by the People (Holyoake) 39, 58
self-help co-operatives 82, 94
self-responsibility, values of 7
self-service retail 9, 47, 50, 67; *see also* supermarkets
self-sufficient communities 27
Serbia: consumer co-operatives 43
Shadid, Michael 97, 116
shares 4, 7, 9–10, 12, 18–19, 27–28, 32–33, 42, 58, 60, 63, 66, 69, 85, 112–114, 122, 147, 150, 165, 174, 180–181, 194, 201, 203, 207, 21, 213, 218, 220, 229; disposal of net assets without profit to members 3; IOBs 1; limitations on size of shareholdings 2, 10; MOBs 1; one member one vote 2, 19; outside investors 3; *see also* dividends (the 'divi'); patronage refunds
Shattuck, Francis Kitteridge 77
Shattuck Avenue Center (CCB) 112–113, 121, 146, 151–153, 172–173, 179, 192, 202–203, 209–212, 215, 229
Shattuck Avenue Center Council (SACC) 152, 156, 186, 207, 215, 218
Sheer, Robert 141
Sheerness Economical Society (Great Britain) 26
shipping: blockade 41; CWS 34
Shirek, Maudelle 152
Sierra Club 210
Sierra Natural Foods (San Francisco) 218
silk 57
Sinclair, Upton 76, 82, 85, 108, 227
Slate (UCB) 138

slavery 57
Smallwood, Catherine 87
Smith, Francis 78
Smithies, James 29
Snow, Nancy 209
soap 33–34
social development 15
social issues 194
social justice 56
social programs 11, 16, 38, 85, 92, 117–118, 123, 151, 158, 188, 219, 230
social unrest, and the growth of co-operatives 15, 20, 38
social work 8
socialism: Belgium 38, 51; Berkeley 79, 85, 98; Christian Socialism 7; co-operatives 38, 41; Finland 41, 51; France 38, 51; Germany 40; and the ICA 40; Italy 41; and Rochdale model 37; "third way," co-operatives as 38, 65; Great Britain 7, 31; US 61, 65
Society for Promoting Communities (New York) 56
Solloway, Barry 145, 175, 177
Sonne, Hans Christian 37
Soujanen, Waino 109
South Africa: agricultural co-operatives 39; Apartheid 204; consumer co-operatives 39; and the CWS 39
South America: and CLUSA 162; *see also individual countries*
South Berkeley 80, 139–140
South Korea: and the Antigonish movement 16; consumer co-operatives 48–49
South Shore Co-operative (Chicago) 141
Southern California Co-operative League 96
Southern Pacific Railroad 78
Spain: Berkeley 76; California 76; hybrid co-operatives 5; Mexico 76; Mondragon 16; and the Rochdale movement 32
Spanish Civil War 79
Sproul Hall Plaza (UCB) 138–139
Sproul, Robert 81, 107
Sri Lanka *see* Ceylon
SS Pioneer 34
SS Plover 34
Stalin, Joseph 18, 43, 142
Stapenhorst, Fred 191
state concessions 38
State Fair Employment Practices Commission (California) 158
state role 15
state takeovers 18, 43
steamship transportation 34
Stevenson, Adlai II Governor 108
stores, co-operative 7; Great Britain 7, 28, 32–33, 131; Japan 39–40; Rochdale 39, 59–60; US 58–61, 63, 67, 119; *see also* retail consumer co-operatives and *individual co-operatives*
Strategic Options Task Force (CCB, SOTF) 204, 213, 216
Strauss, George 156, 212
street people 189
Street People's Liberation Front (Berkeley) 189
strikebreakers 79
strikes 2–4, 12–14, 29, 61, 69–70, 79, 94, 122, 154–155, 165, 176, 186–187, 194, 211
students 78–81, 106–107, 117, 121, 137–140, 156, 159, 172–173, 201, 204, 228
Students for a Democratic Society (SDS) 139, 159
study circles 16
substitute ingredients, avoiding 3
suburbanization 105–108, 111, 137, 171, 200
sugar 29, 33, 85, 115
sugar, content in foods 183, 203, 210
supermarkets 5, 9, 11, 46–47, 50, 67–68, 72, 110, 112, 124, 145, 147, 157, 159, 176–177, 186, 206, 227, 230; *see also* self-service retail
supply chain management 46
surplus 1–2, 4, 10, 12, 15, 27–28, 30, 34–35, 41, 57, 64, 86, 148, 174, 176, 202
survival of co-operatives 4–5, 7, 11–12, 16, 19, 47, 50, 62, 85, 125, 129, 186, 214–215, 226, 228–229
Swamp Monster Speaks (CCB) 186
Sweden: consumer co-operatives 48, 119; co-operatives 163; and the CWS 33; as the "the middle way" 65; wholesale co-operatives 10, 12, 41, 70, 164

Switzerland: consumer co-operatives 7, 37, 42; and the ICA 164
Sweeny, Wilmot 109
Symbionese Liberation Army 172

takeovers 48, 82, 137, 147, 162, 165, 176, 178, 205, 226
Tanganyika: co-operatives 163–4
Tanzania: and ICA 50–51
tariffs 29
taxation 15, 32, 38, 41, 42, 48, 62, 68, 70, 72, 94, 96, 107, 150, 203
Taxi Unlimited (Berkeley) 163
tea 9, 28, 33
tea parties 17
Teamsters Union 122, 186, 192
technology 9, 25, 201, 220, 227; *see also* Community Memory Project, Electronic Data Processing, price scanning
Telegraph Avenue Center (CCB) 148, 153, 164, 174, 177, 189, 203, 209–210, 212, 215
Telegraph Avenue Center Council (CCB, TACC) 153, 157, 174, 207–208, 210, 216
telephones 35, 124, 161, 181
Temperance 29
"third way" or "middle way," co-operatives as 38, 65
Thedin, Nils 164
Thompson, Ray 157, 164
Tilden Regional Park (Berkeley) 79, 117, 230
Time Store, Cincinnati 58
Tinny, Jack 107
Toad Lane store, Rochdale 29–30
token systems 11
Tolman, Edward 107
Tompkins, Jimmy 44
Toniolo, Giuseppe 16
totalitarianism 25, 40, 42, 45
Touche Ross & Co. 205, 207–208, 211, 228
tourism 34, 112, 149
Toward an Active Student Community (TASC) 138
trade links, development of 33–34, 51, 59, 69–70
trade unions *see* labor unions
transformational co-operatives 5, 19
Treuhaft, Robert 141–143, 160, 162–163
truck system 25
Truman, Harry President 70, 72
Twin Pines Co-op Foundation 219
Twin Pines Distributing Company 217
Twin Pines seal 62; *see also* Circle Pines seal
Twin Pines Federal Savings and Loan Association (Berkeley) 129, 219
types of co-operatives 4–5

Uber 200
Ukraine: consumer co-operatives 38
United Nations (UN) 51, 115, 117, 124, 151, 163–164
UN Conference on Nuclear Disarmament (1982) 219
UN Food Conference (1943) 67
unemployment 17, 27, 29, 41, 64, 68, 79, 82
UNICEF 164
Union Co-operative Association No. 1 of Philadelphia 60
Union of Soviet Socialist Republics (USSR) 68, 107; agricultural co-operatives 42; consumer co-operatives 18, 41–43; co-operatives 41–42, 46–47, 193; financial co-operatives 42; and the ICA 45; *see also* Russia
union shops 27, 66, 69, 125
unit pricing 153, 205, 230
United Co-operative Society of Maynard (Massachusetts) 67
United Co-operatives (US) 70, 135
United Farm Workers (UFW, US) 69, 137, 155, 190
United Food and Commercial Workers Union (US, UFCWU) 214–215
United Grocers (US) 96, 122, 128
United Kaleva Lodge of Brothers and Sisters No. 21 (Berkeley) 82, 86
United Kingdom (UK) *see* Great Britain
United Mine Workers (US) 62
Unity Election Slate (CCB) 203
Universal Co-operatives Inc. 70, 191
University Avenue Center (CCB) 85–88, 90–91, 110–113, 116, 121–122, 124, 129–130, 140, 145, 147, 157, 159, 171, 174, 179, 190, 193, 202–203, 209, 212–213, 218
University Avenue Housing Inc. 192–3

University Avenue Merchants Association (Berkeley) 125
University of California (UC) 77–79, 81, 107, 137–138, 144, 204; *see also* University of California, Berkeley
University of California, Berkeley (UCB) 77–79, 81, 83, 85, 98, 106–107, 109, 121, 124–125, 137–139, 156, 159, 172–174, 201, 203–204, 212; *see also* Institute of Industrial Relations
University of California, Davis 209
University of Chicago 60, 156
University Students' Co-operative Association (Berkeley, USCA) 79, 85, 124, 163, 203
US (United States) 29, 35–36, 42; agricultural co-operatives 19; banking 129; community co-operatives 56–58; consumer co-operatives 13–15, 38, 51, 56–72; co-operatives 164; and the CWS 33–34; credit unions 65, 69, 88–89, 97, 131, 162; and the ICA 40; New Deal 65, 79, 108; utopian communities 15; wholesale consumer co-operatives 58–65, 67, 70, 72, 76, 83, 87, 93–96, 99, 122, 125–128, 160–162, 190–191, 205, 216–218; worker co-operatives 4, 219; *see also individual co-operatives*
US Civil War 58
US Federal Health Service 83
US Food and Drug Administration (USFDA) 184, 210
utopian communities 15

Valley Forge, Pennsylvania 57
values of a co-operative 48, 181–182, 230
Van Dusen, Lisa 209
vertical integration 26, 34
Vietnam War 56, 71, 131, 138, 140–142, 144, 156, 172
village co-operatives 16
Village Design (Berkeley) 210
villages of mutual co-operation 27
voice 14, 41, 125, 165, 228
Voltz, Jeffrey 204, 211, 213–214
voluntary membership principle 42–43
volunteer labor 6, 14, 66, 83, 94, 118, 124, 183, 189, 216
Voorhis, Jerry 6–8, 116
Vorberg-Rugh, Rachael 2

wages 2, 12–16, 25, 27–29, 40, 57, 64, 66, 72, 81, 86, 93, 109, 122, 180, 211–215, 217, 228
Wales: early origins of co-operative movements 28
Walker, Cora 69
Walker, Doris 107
Wallace, Sid 147
Walnut Creek, California 21, 105–106, 111–112, 114–115, 118, 121, 125, 131, 137, 147–151, 154, 159, 164, 171, 174, 180, 189–190, 194, 200–202, 208, 227
Walnut Creek Civic Center 159
war profiteering 41
Warbasse, Anges 62, 72
Warbasse, James 62, 64–65, 67
Warren, Joseph 58
waste minimization 61, 66
water 3, 77–78, 154, 183–184, 210
Waters, Alice 172
Weavers Union (Rochdale) 29
Webb (Potter), Beatrice 13, 34, 213
Webster, Tony 2
Weinberger, Casper 159
welfare state 46
West Africa 193
West Berkeley 77–78, 81, 98, 163, 172, 201, 210
West Oakland 176–177
Wetzel, K.W. 12, 228
wheat 35, 209
White, Clinton 143
White House Conference on Food, Nutrition and Health (1969) 154, 184
wholesale consumer co-operatives 10, 19, 25; Argentina 44; Australia 11, 50; Canada 49; Denmark 37, 41; farmer 67; Finland 41; Great Britain 5, 11, 31–35, 47, 51; France 37; Germany 37; Iceland 41; Japan 49, 193; and localism 17; Norway 41; NZ 45; overview 5; Russia 37; Sweden 10–11, 41, 70; US 58–65, 67, 70, 72, 76, 83, 87, 93–96, 99, 122, 125–128, 160–162, 190–191, 205, 216–218; *see also individual wholesale consumer co-operatives*
Widener, Warren 141
wilderness goods (CCB) 179–180, 202
Willey, Samuel 77

Wilson, Jackson Stitt 79, 85, 96–97
Wilson, John F. 2
Wilson, Roy 83
wine 125, 201
women 210; Berkeley 78, 80, 85, 87, 118, 139, 141–142, 157–8, 175, 182, 187, 204; and CLUSA 66; International Co-operative Women's Guild 45; as members in their own right 31; Northern Co-operative Women's Guild (US) 66; *see also* feminism; women's guilds; women's liberation
Women's Co-operative Guild (Great Britain, WCG) 7
women's guilds 7, 35, 45, 65–66, 72, 97; CCB 85, 92, 117
women's liberation 139
Wood, Betsy 118, 193, 217
Woolwich Docks 26
Woolworth 42
work credits 57; *see also* labor notes
worker co-operatives 213; Berkeley 4, 219; definition 2
worker morale 122, 187–188
worker participation 165
worker voice 14
worker welfare 14
working-class 7, 17, 26, 31, 37–38, 40, 43, 50, 77–79, 96, 159, 200
Workers' and Farmers' Co-operative Unity Alliance (WFCUA) 64
Workingmen's Protective Store 58
World Health Organization 210
World-Wide Co-op Partners 164
Wright, Frances 57–58

Yasukochi, George 81, 124, 144–5, 180, 188, 204
Yoshino, Suzako 43
Young Negroes Co-operative Leagues 65
Youth Group (CCB) 117
youth leagues 65
yuppies 200, 205, 209

Zaentz, Saul 172
Zane, S.G. 87
Zenkoran (Japan) 193
Zimbabwe: and the Antigonish movement 16